CHALLENGING THE FRONTIERS
OF AFRICAN INTEGRATION:
The Dynamics of Policies, Politics and
Transformation in the East African Community

Juma V. Mwapachu

E&D Vision Publishing
Dar es Salaam

E&D Vision Publishing Limited
P.O.Box 4460
Dar es Salaam
Email: info@edvisionpublishing.co.tz
Website: www.edvisionpublishing.co.tz

**Challenging the Frontiers
of African Integration:**
The Dynamics of Policies, Politics and
Transformation in the East African Community

First Edition
© Juma V. Mwapachu, 2012

International Edition
© Juma V. Mwapachu, 2014

ISBN 978 9987 521-81-4

Dedication

In everlasting memory of

Harith Volter (June, 1973 - October, 2011)

Tears, idle tears, I know not what they mean,
Tears from the depth of some divine despair
Rise in the heart, and gather to the eyes,
In looking on the happy Autumn-fields,
And thinking of the days that are no more.

Fresh as the first beam glittering on a sail,
That brings our friends up from the underworld,
Sad as the last which reddens over one
That sinks with all we love below the verge;
So sad, so fresh, the days that are no more.

Ah, sad and strange as in dark summer dawns
The earliest pipe of half-awakened birds
To dying ears, when unto dying eyes
The casement slowly grows a glimmering square;
So sad, so strange, the days that are no more.

Dear as remembered kisses after death,
And sweet as those by hopeless fancy feigned
On lips that are for others; deep as love,
Deep as first love, and wild with all regret;
O Death in Life, the days that are no more.

Alfred Lord Tennyson

Table of Contents

_____

Table of Cases

Democratic Party v. The Secretary General of the East African Community and The Attorney General of the Republic of Uganda, East African Court of Justice at Arusha, Reference No. 6 of 2011.

Hon. Sitenda Sebalu v. The Secretary General of the East African Community and Three Others, East African Court of Justice at Arusha, Reference No. 1 of 2010.

In the Matter between Mike Campbell (Pvt) Ltd. and 78 Others v. The Republic of Zimbabwe, In the Southern African Development Community (SADC) Tribunal, Windhoek, Namibia, SADC (T) Case No. 2/2007.

James Katabazi and 21 Others v. Secretary General of the East African Community and the Attorney General of the Republic of Uganda, East African Court of Justice at Arusha, Reference No. 1 of 2007.

Modern Holdings (EA) Limited v. Kenya Ports Authority, East African Court of Justice at Arusha, Reference No. 1 of 2008. This case is reported in East African Law *Society Law Digest 2005-2011*, p. 49.

Prof. Peter Anyang' Nyong'o and 10 Others v. Attorney General of Kenya and Others, Application No. 1 of 2006.

East African Law Society and 4 others V. the Attorney Generals of Kenya, Uganda and Tanzania and the Secretary General of the East African Community, Reference No. 3 of 2007.

Rewe-Zentral AG v. Bundesmonopolverwaltung für Branntwein (The Cassis de Dijon), ECJ Case Number 120/1978.

Flaminio Costa v. ENEL [1964] ECR 585 (6/64).

Glossary

a luta continua	the struggle continues.
ab initio	from the beginning.
Afrika Mashariki	East Africa.
Al Qaeda	"The Base" officially known as *Tandhim Qaidat al-Jihad* - a loose, a global militant Islamist organization operating terror network.
Al Shabab	"The Youth" or "The Boys", is the Somalia-based cell of the militant Islamist group al-Qaeda.
Alfajiri	Dawn or daybreak.
Bologna Process	European Initiative to standardise higher education. This process was initiated in a meeting in Bologna in Italy and hence the name.
Bongo Flava	Youth Music in Tanzania.
Chef de Cabinet	Head of the Office of the Secretary-General.
de facto	In Fact.
de jure	by right; by lawful title; by law; as a matter of law; where the title is clear.
Hip Hop	Youth music by the youth in Kenya.
Ibid	(*ib.* or *Ibidem*) just the same; in the same place; from the same source; in the same case.
Jumuiya	Community
Kilimo Kwanza	Agriculture First (Giving priority to Agriculture).
Kituo Cha Katiba	Centre for Constitutional Development.
Kuonekana	To be seen.
Luga Flow	Uganda youth blend of modern music.
Mabati	corrugated iron sheets.
Majimbo	regions or provinces in the context of devolution of powers.
Majimboism	Regionalism (Provisionalism).
Migingo	a small island on Lake Victoria whose ownership is contested between Kenya and Uganda.
modus vivendi	Signifying an agreement between those whose opinions differ, such that they agree to disagree.
Nyota Njema	Good Star.
Pambazuka	Dawn, get light, be daytime.
Problematique	Problematic (French).
Taarab	Coastal music played in the whole East African Coast.
Taarap	Modern Taarab being rapped by the youth.
Twaweza	We can.
Uhuru	Independence (can also mean freedom).
Ujamaa	Socialism.
Uongozi	Leadership.
Uwezo	Capacity (capability).
vis a vis	in relation to; compared with.

Abbreviations and Acronyms

ACABQ	Advisory Committee on Administrative and Budgetary Questions
ACEG	African Centre for Economic Growth
ADB	African Development Bank
AEC	African Economic Community
AfDB	African Development Group
AFRICOM	Africa Command (US)
AGOA	African Growth and Opportunity Act
ALAT	Association of Local Authorities of Tanzania
ALGAK	Association of local Government Authorities of Kenya
AMREF	African Medical and Research Foundation
APRM	African Peer Review Mechanism
ARTA	African Regional Trade Agreements
ASEAN	Association of South-Eastern Asian Countries
AU	African Union
BMZ	*Bundesministerium Für Wirtschaftliche Zusammenarbeit* (German Federal Ministry for Economic Development Cooperation)
BRICs	Brazil, Russia, India and China
CAADP	Comprehensive African Agricultural Development Programme
CARICOM	Caribbean Economic Community
CASSOA	Civil Aviation Safety and Security Oversight Agency
CBC	Commonwealth Business Council
CCM	*Chama Cha Mapinduzi*
CEO	Chief Executive Officer
CET	Common External Tariff
CIA	Central Intelligence Agency (US)
CIAA	Common Investment Area Framework Agreement
COMESA	Common Market for Eastern and Southern Africa
DBSA	Development Bank of Southern Africa
DFID	Department for International Development (UK)
DPMF	Development Policy Management Forum
DRC	Democratic Republic of Congo
EA	East Africa
EABC	East African Business Council
EAC	East African Community
EACB	East African Currency Board
EACHRC	East African Community Health Research Commission
EACJ	East African Court of Justice
EACM	East African Community Common Market
EACSO	East African Common Services Organization

EACSOF	East African Civil Society Organization Forum
EACU	East African Community Customs Union
EADB	East African Development Bank
EALA	East African Legislative Assembly
EALGA	East African Local Governments Association
EAMRC	East African Medical Research Council
EASSy	Eastern African Submarine Cable System
EC	European Commission
ECA	United Nations Economic Commission for Africa
ECOWAS	Economic Commission of West African States
EDF	European Development Fund
EMU	European Monetary Union
EPA	Economic Partnership Agreement
EPZs	Export Processing Zones
ESARF	Economic and Social Research Foundation
EU	European Union
FAA	Federal Aviation Agency (US)
FDI	Foreign Direct Investment
FM	Frequency Modulation
FTAs	Free Trade Areas
G77	Group of Seventy Seven Developing Countries
GATT	General Agreement on Trade and Tariffs
GDP	Gross Domestic Product
GMO	Genetically Modified Organisms
GSP	Generalised Scheme of Preferences
GTZ	German Technical Cooperation Agency
HESTC	East African Education Systems and Training Curricula
HIV/AIDS	Human Immune Deficiency Virus/Acquired Immunodeficiency Syndrome
IBM	International Business Machines
ICAO	International Civil Aviation Organisation
ICSID	International Centre for Settlement of Investment Disputes
ICT	Information and Communications Technology
IDs	Identity Cards
IGAD	Intergovernmental Authority on Development
ILO	International Labour Organisation
IMF	International Monetary Fund
IOM	International Organization for Migration
IPA	Investment Promotion Agencies
IPO	Initial Public Offering
IPPF	International Planned Parenthood Federation
ISO	International Organization for Standardization
IT	Information Technology

IUCEA	Inter-University Council of East Africa
JICA	Japan International Cooperation Agency
KA	Kenya Airways (Sometimes KQ)
KANU	Kenya African National Union
KCB	Kenya Commercial Bank
KCK	*Kituo Cha Katib*a (Centre for Constitutional Development)
KENGEN	Kenya Electricity Generation Company
LPA	Lagos Plan of Action
LVBC	Lake Victoria Basin Commission
LVEMP	Lake Victoria Environmental Management Project
LVFO	Lake Victoria Fisheries Organisation
M&A	Mergers and Acquisitions
MCA	Millennium Challenge Account
MDGs	Millennium Development Goals
MFN	Most Favoured Nation
MIGA	Multilateral Investment Guarantee Agency
MIP	Minimum Integration Programme
MIT	Massachusetts Institute of Technology
MOU	Memorandum of Understanding
NAFTA	North Atlantic Free Trade Area
NEPAD	New Economic Partnership for Development
NRM	National Resistance Movement
NSSF	National Social Security Fund
NTBs	Non-Tariff Barriers
NTMs	Non-Tariff Measures
NUR	National University of Rwanda
OAU	Organisation of African Unity
ODA	Official Development Assistance
ODM	Orange Democratic Movement
OECD	Organisation for Economic Cooperation and Development
OSBPs	One Stop Border Posts
PACM	Pan African Common Market
PPF	Parastatal Pensions Fund
PPPs	Public Private Partnerships
PRSP	Poverty Reduction Strategy and Programme
REACH	Regional East African Community Health
RECs	Regional Economic Communities
REDET	Research and Education for Democracy in Tanzania
RIEPA	Rwanda Investment and Export Promotion Agency
ROM	Results-Oriented Management
SACU	Southern Africa Customs Union
SADC	Southern African Development Community

SAPs	Structural Adjustment Programmes
SCT	Single Customs Territory
SG	Secretary General
SID	Society for International Development
SIDA	Swedish International Development Agency
SIDA/SAREC	SIDA - Department for Research Cooperation
SMART	Self-Monitoring, Analysis and Reporting Technology
SPS	Sanitary and Phyto-Sanitary Standards
SRH&R	Sexual and Reproductive Health and Rights
SSA	Sub-Saharan Africa
TANESCO	Tanzania Electricity Supply Company
TIC	Tanzania Investment Centre
TIFA	Trade and Investment Framework Agreement
TMEA	Trade Mark East Africa
TPDF	Tanzania Peoples Defence Force
TRIPS	Trade-Related Aspects of Intellectual Property Rights
UIA	Uganda Investment Authority
UK	United Kingdom
ULGA	Uganda Local Governments Association
UNAIDS	United Nations Programme on HIV and AIDS
UNCTAD	United Nations Conference on Trade and Development
UNECA	UN Economic Commission for Africa
UNEP	United Nations Environment Programme
UNESCO	United Nations Education, Social and Cultural Organisation
UNFPA	United Nations' Population Fund
UNHCR	United Nations High Commissioner for Refugees
UNIDO	United Nations Industrial Development Organisation
US $	United States Dollar
US	United States
USAID	United States Agency for International Development
USD	United States Dollar
VAT	Value Added Tax
WTO	World Trade Organisation

About the Author

Ambassador Juma V. Mwapachu is a Tanzanian national. Until recently, he served as Secretary General of the East African Community. His long career has seen him serve in various capacities in his home country spanning both public and private sectors. A lawyer by training, Ambassador Mwapachu is currently President of the Society for International Development (SID), a global non-governmental organisation engaged in promoting development ideas and practices focused on building a more equitable, just and sustainable world. He is also Chair of the Governing Council of the University of Dodoma, a new and fast growing Tanzanian public university. He is author and co-editor of several books and academic publications. He holds two honorary doctorates in literature and political sciences from the University of Dar-es-Salaam and the National University of Rwanda, respectively. In December, 2011, President Mwai Kibaki of Kenya conferred on Ambassador Mwapachu the Moran of the Order of the Golden Heart (MGH). He lives in Dar-es-Salaam, Tanzania.

Foreword

As the 21st Century is unfolding Africans are confronted with two major challenges. One is globalisation, its challenges, opportunities and possibilities; fears and threats as it impacts on the African economies, polities and societies. Globalisation is not subject to discretion or rejection. It is, however, an important object for discussions and deliberations on the best strategies and means by which Africans could effectively and timely respond to the challenges and opportunities.

Global economic integration is unavoidable. A new International Political Economy Order [IPEO] based on the 'market forces' and the private sector initiatives has emerged, with new centres of socio-economic and political powers competing for global recognition. Moreover, they are all looking to Africa for resources, markets and new spheres of influences. To be active and credible actors in the global economy Africans have to be competitive.

Continental economic and economic integration is the other major challenge confronting Africans. Appropriate policies have to be formulated, appropriate capacities created; the mobilisation and organisation of the human and material resources which; in turn, would require informed and committed leadership and the popular support of the people. As Africa has also undergone tremendous ideological shifts, from public sector dominated economic development to private sector led economic growth and development; from 'big government' to 'good political governance' popular participation in the policy formulation is critical. And this, inevitably, entails politics as the processes are likely to affect the interests of the people in the civil society as well as in the private sector.

As the frontiers of globalisation and continental integration are emerging-or incrementally identified-and the appropriate responses are explored, discussed and debated; in a world that is continuously changing, informed and inspired by the information and communication technologies, the entire process is bound to be dynamic.

At the regional East African subordinate system-the East African Community (EAC)-there are also major challenges of economic and political integration confronting the member states and their respective citizens. Conversion of the EAC into a Political Federation is the ultimate Vision of the regional political leaders. The movement for economic integration of the region-known as the 'Closer Union'-predates Independence, engineered by the colonial powers for their own respective Imperial interests and objectives.

The quest, or the *Vision,* for a closer political union - an East African Federation also predates Independence. But the *Vision* was conceived and promoted by Africans themselves in support of the promotion and consolidation of their economic and political independence. It was the late Julius Kambarage Nyerere, the then political leader of Tanganyika, who not only proposed the federal *Vision* in 1961 but was also prepared to delay the achievement of Independence in support of an East African Federation.

Since Independence in the early 1960s various attempts have been made in order to achieve the two objectives. Policies have been formulated and attempts made to implement them with various degrees of successes and failures. In the course of the 1961-2012 decades tremendous socio-economic and political changes have taken place in the region, including attempted but failed military coups; as well as one that succeeded in removing an elected leader and substantially undermined the promotion and consolidation of the fledgling EAC.

The region has also undergone major ideological paradigm shifts. The private sector has assumed the priority leadership in economic growth and development; multi-party politics has replaced the one-party state; and the aspirations for good political governance have been enhanced and continuously-albeit precariously-consolidated.

In a democracy, policies are the products of deliberation and discussions. Formulation of good-appropriate-policies are, however, the products of popular participation in a free and fair space in which the state and non-state actors, those in the civil society and the private sector, the press and the media can contribute. Hence, as it encompasses various societal interests, policy formulation is an inter-active process. And this inevitably entails politics which is itself a dynamic process, as those whose interests are involved, or affected-either in terms of aspirations or expectations, protection or promotion, preservation or consolidation-are bound to be actively involved.

Although the 'phasing out' of the socialist model of development continues, and the 'Ujamaa' and the 'Common Mans' aspirations have been replaced by the 'market-forces' and the 'entrepreneurship' of the individual, thus creating a new regional Political Economic Order; nonetheless, new interests have emerged, old fears, prejudices and anxieties reinforced. There are those who are worried about the acquisition of land or natural resources or the flooding of their markets with goods, labour or capital by their neighbours. And then there is the phenomenon of the new global actors interested in the regional natural resources. Hence, new frontiers are emerging, creating new challenges, demanding the formulation of the appropriate policies, entailing discussions and deliberations, on various issues, all related to the promotion and consolidation of the EAC, now enhanced by the inclusion of Rwanda and Burundi.

Economic integration is an on-going struggle sustained by those leaders in the public and private sectors who are committed to the creation of an enlarged economic community; promotion and consolidation of the domestic markets; as well as moderating the globalisation impacts on their respective countries. The East African Federal 'Vision' is also an on-going aspiration. It is sustained by those who are very keen to forge and deepen an East African identity, based on cultural and traditional values, inspired by the historical anti-colonial struggles and reinforced by the aspirations and determination to sustain their economic and political independence.

The economic integration and conversion of the EAC would require the formulation of the appropriate policies, informed by experience and insights gained in the course of the decades. Policies that are inspired by the visions of those who dedicated their lives, like Julius Nyerere, to the promotion of an East African community in which the people, irrespective of their race, ethnicity, faith or status in society pursue their respective interests, creating wealth and employment, and in the process promote the welfare of all the people.

All these are the basic issues of good governance. People have to be appropriately informed so they can participate in the deepening of the integration, and thus enhance their ownership of the EAC; and dedicated leaders-and leadership-whose vision of the welfare of their own respective states intricately coincides with those of the EAC.

Unlike the 20th Century in which African colonies were managed, influenced and controlled by the colonial powers-obviously for their own imperial interests-globalisation in the 21st Century poses multiple challenges to an independent Africa. Above all, the opportunities and possibilities to create Africans' own visions of the African economies and societies, polities and communities, identities and personalities based on African perspectives, informed by knowledge and experience and inspired by insights and visions.

Until the early 1960s, the East African region was under the control of the colonial powers that managed to exploit the economic resources of the region; and controlled its political development according to their imperial aspirations. As earlier noted, the East African region has undergone tremendous socio-economic and political transformation. East Africans are now well-informed of their colonial past and are enriched by the experience achieved in the management of their affairs since Independence.

Dr. Juma Mwapachu, the author of this book, has the unique experience of having witnessed the last phases of the colonial rule in the region, the ensuing period of Independence-as well as participating in the nation-building, democratisation and the development of his own native country, Tanzania. And for five years between 2006 and 2011, Dr. Mwapachu was the Secretary General of the EAC. He is thus not only versed with the regional scene in all its economic, political and cultural dimensions; he is also, eminently an 'insider' and well acquainted with the workings of the EAC, its challenges and frontiers, as well as the dynamics and politics of policy formulation and implementation, successes and failures.

Examining the salient and sensitive issues related to the EAC integration, touching on the critical actors in the state and non-state sectors, civil society and the private sector, the press and media, Dr. Mwapachu has empowered us with the information and knowledge to play our parts in the promotion of the regional identity and the consolidation of the EAC.

Dr. Mwapachu is a very reflective and thoughtful person. The core sources of the book are his speeches and writings, based on research, experience and observations of the on-goings within the EAC; and inspired by the philosophy and the power of ideas and their contribution in the promotion of better understanding of the dynamics of change and transformation.

As it grapples with the challenges of globalisation, the politics and dynamics of integration; as well as the implications of the domestic socio-economic and political transformations on the ultimate objectives of regional economic integration and the political federation, the book is *the* major source of materials for those interested in such issues.

Professor Ahmed Mohiddin,

Former Head of Political Science Department at Makerere University and the University of Nairobi;

Mombasa, Kenya.

July, 2012.

Preface

In his book, *The Next Global Stage-Challenges and Opportunities in Our Borderless World,*[1] the Japanese globalist, Kenichi Ohmae writes:

> ... ideas do not emerge perfectly formed. They are awkward amalgams of experience, insight, hopes, and inspiration. They arrive on stage blinking under the bright lights, hesitant, unsure as to the audience's likely reaction. They evolve and develop, alert to changing reactions and circumstances.[2]

This book, whose core is my speeches and writings over the past six years, is inspired by this philosophy of the power of ideas and how they can contribute to a clearer understanding of the dynamics of change and transformation in a particular setting and programme. Evidently, my ideas have to be viewed and judged within a time specific context always mindful that some of these ideas have a lofty purpose in terms of where the East African region should move to economically.

In April 2006, I was appointed by the Heads of State of the East African Community (EAC) to lead the EAC as Secretary General for a period of five years.[3] At the first occasion after my appointment, this is what I said at the Summit of the Heads of State in November, 2006:

> As the EAC progresses, the task to endear the EAC to the people of East Africa and ensure that the EAC pervades the people's hearts and minds, becomes ever more urgent and imperative. The EAC is seized of this challenge. Dynamic efforts, including the strengthening of the EAC publicity and marketing outfits and function, as well as re-branding the EAC are in the offing in order to better promote its identity and image around the goals of unity, progress and prosperity.

One of the central features of this book is how the EAC is working to realize an East African identity; an identity made possible by a traditional cultural bond that is more often taken for granted rather than seen as the most critical challenge to be tackled under an environment often charged by growing national identities and nationalisms.

During the period between August 2006 and April 2011, I was able to reflect on a number of challenges facing the EAC as it sought to realize deeper integration cutting across several fields. At the heart of my speeches and

---

[1] See OHMAE, Kenichi, *The Next Global Stage-Challenges and Opportunities in Our Borderless World,* Upper Saddle River, New Jersey: Wharton School Publishing, 2005.

[2] Ibid. at p. xvii.

[3] I was the third Secretary General after Mr. Francis Muthaura (Kenya) 1996-2001; and Mr. Amanya Mushega (Uganda) 2001-2006.

writings is the sense that regional integration is not so much a managerial issue, though important as I explain in the book with respect to the challenges of decision-making, as it is a social-political project. In other words, the functioning of regional integration is more rooted in the state of the national mindset of the participating partners. It is around this mindset issue that the main and almost enduring challenge, of how best to forge an acceptable model of integration and at what pace, crucially lies. It is a challenge that calls forth the optimum application of capabilities and political will of the leadership and of the broad citizenry to influence new thinking and attitudes about the economic benefits integration could bring to nations over time.

It is important to recognize, however, that this mindset challenge is preponderantly driven by zero sum politics. In his book, *Preparing for the Twenty-First Century,* Professor Paul Kennedy[4] poses a dilemma that has serious contextual ramifications to the obtaining integration challenges that the EAC faces. He quizzes:

> whether global forces for change are not moving us beyond our traditional guidelines into a remarkable new set of circumstances-one in which human and social organizations may be unequal to the challenges posed by overpopulation, environmental damage, and technology-driven revolutions and where the issue of winners and losers may to some degree become irrelevant.[5]

In this vein, making sense of national interests and their centrifugal forces that often constrain and undermine the pace and intensity of integration, even within the context of respecting and adhering to the core principles of integration such as subsidiarity, constitutes the most critical challenge of leadership in an integration project. In this book, an attempt is made to outline some of these challenges and how they could be addressed through the acceptance of some form of supranationality in the governance of the integration process.

In my view, political leadership stands out as the most critical factor in driving the ethos and thrust of integration. Needless to underscore, such leadership was vividly displayed by the late Mwalimu Julius Nyerere in the early 1960s to mid 1970s as he consistently led the East African integration and political federation agenda.[6]

---

[4] KENNEDY, Paul M., *Preparing for the Twenty-First Century,* New York: Vintage Books, 1994.

[5] Ibid., at p. 15.

[6] This is clear from his early writings. See for instance NYERERE, Julius K., "Desire for a Federation of East Africa," in NYERERE, Julius K., *Freedom and Unity*, Nairobi and Dar es Salaam: Oxford University Press, 1966, p. 295-297; NYERERE, Julius K., "Problems of

Evidently, in a complex world where the dynamics of global social and economic transformation and the challenges linked thereto are becoming more uncertain and unpredictable, the need for bold and entrepreneurial leadership, that is imbued with a world view, takes centre stage particularly in the pursuit of bold and lofty goals like deep regional integration. In his seminal book, *The New Harvest-Agricultural Innovation in Africa*, Harvard Professor Calestous Juma[7] places serious attention, in this regard, on the role of inspirational leadership in forging new ideas, innovations, change, economic growth and regional cooperation in Africa.[8]

In many respects, this book is a testament of East Africa's fast changing circumstances. The region's political, social and economic landscape has undergone a sea change; democracy has taken root; the demographic explosion is devastating, not simply in terms of the high population growth, averaging 2.9% in 2010 (with Uganda's population growth being at a high 3.3%) but more worryingly, in relation to the implications of the youth bulge with around 64% of East Africans in 2011 being under the age of 30 and 44% under the age of 15. In Kenya, it is estimated that 78% of the population is less than 34 years. The challenges this youth bulge poses in terms of access to education, health and jobs will prove to be the region's main economic headache. Whilst the national economies have taken wings with the market becoming the principal driver and achieving high economic growths averaging 6% between 2009 and 2011, the highest in Africa[9] they have not translated into inclusive development. On the contrary, challenges of poverty and entrenching income inequalities are becoming ever more pervasive.

A recent book of the Society for International Development (East Africa) titled *East African Integration: Dynamics of Equity in Trade, Education and*

East African Co-operation," in NYERERE, Julius K., *Freedom and Socialism*, Oxford University Press, 1968, pp. 60-70; and NYERERE, Julius K., "The Dilemma of the Pan Africanist," in NYERERE, Julius K., *Freedom and Socialism*, Nairobi and Dar es Salaam: Oxford University Press, 1968, pp. 207-217; NYERERE, Julius K., "East African Co-operation is Alive," in NYERERE, Julius K., *Freedom and Development*, Nairobi and Dar es Salaam: Oxford University Press, 1973, pp. 240-242; NYERERE, Julius K., "East Africa Needs the East African Community," in NYERERE, Julius K., *Freedom, Non-Alignment and South-South Cooperation: A Selection from Speeches 1974 – 1999*, Dar es Salaam: Oxford University Press (T) Ltd, 2011, p. 28; and NYERERE, Julius K., "An Obituary of the East African Community," in NYERERE, Julius K., *Freedom, Non-Alignment and South-South Cooperation: A Selection from Speeches 1974 – 1999*, Dar es Salaam: Oxford University Press (T) Ltd, 2011.

[7] See JUMA, Calestous, *The New Harvest: Agricultural Innovation in Africa*, New York: Oxford University Press, 2011.

[8] Ibid., at pp. 19, 22; and 213-214.

[9] See AFRICAN DEVELOPMENT BANK, *African Economic Outlook, 2011*, Tunis: African Development Bank, 2012.

Media,[10] shows that there is an East African-wide serious case of inequality in the primary school education sector but it is more heightened in Kenya. Tanzania's Household Budget Surveys have also consistently in the past few years pointed out an almost similar picture from the broad perspective of an entrenching and expanding wealth divide in the country. In sum, there is a North–South wealth divide emerging in East African societies that is largely driven by the effects of neo-liberal economic policies being implemented. These inequalities, which are also gender and region-based, will increasingly be accentuated by climate change as it wreaks havoc on agriculture upon which about 70% of the region's population depends on for sustainable livelihoods.

Paradoxical as it may seem, it is these challenges that catapult zero sum game policy thrusts at national levels in relation to the integration agenda. National politics are elevated above regional perspectives as political leaders seek to win the hearts and minds of their national electorates by appearing to confront the challenges with all available national resources. In this context, the need and urgency to strike a delicate balance between a thrust of development that is national focused and the pursuit of a development paradigm that views economic regionalism as the strategic imperative in attacking the scourges of pervasive poverty and creating the right conditions that spur wealth creation could not be more pertinent. Such balance can best be struck where regional integration agenda is mainstreamed in national development plans. However, such system lacks in the EAC region. Indeed, even the development visions of the five partner states have different life spans and varying thrusts and priorities. In contrast, the Southern African Development Community (SADC) has made serious attempt at mainstreaming regional integration plans in the development plans of its member states.[11]

This book views EAC regional integration as an important strategic vehicle for making poverty history in the region. However, it also recognizes that regional integration involves a complex set of policy issues rooted in national politics and whose interplay determines both success and setbacks over agreed regional objectives. Thus, how such policy issues are defined, clarified and given appropriate and timely political attention is what crucially determines both the direction, pace and robustness of the integration project.

---

[10] SOCIETY FOR INTERNATIONAL DEVELOPMENT (EA), *East African Integration: Dynamics of Equity in Trade, Education and Media*, Nairobi: Society for International Development (SID), 2011.

[11] See ECA-UEM Forum on Mainstreaming Regional Integration in National Development Plans, Maputo, Mozambique, 28th - 29th May, 2009. On SADC generally see SOUTHERN AFRICAN DEVELOPMENT COMMUNITY, "Major Achievements and Challenges," Volume 9 No. 1 *SADC Today*, April 2006.

A recent publication of the World Bank titled, *East African Community-Reshaping the Geography of East Africa: From Regional to Global Integration*[12] has made a huge contribution in analyzing the challenges and prospects of the EAC. The study evidently provides important data and statistics about the EAC and how the regional body can foster deeper integration as well as bolster the region's integration into global markets. In criticism, I have to state that the report lacks originality; it restates much of what the EAC Secretariat has written over the last few years on how deeper integration could be realized in the EAC region and what constitutes the main roadblocks in moving integration forward. In this sense, the World Bank study, with respect, lacks the deeper insights of what underlies and drives a political project like regional integration; what are the inner workings and challenges of day to day politics and decision making in an inter-governmental organization.

In contrast, this book has the advantage of being written by a former insider; a person who was deeply involved in the complex web of political machinations often driven by opposing national interests in the integration process. Such advantage underlies the unique approach taken in this book in the examination of the salient and sensitive policy and political issues that have underpinned EAC integration. Some of these issues have conventionally had a direct impact on the character of regional integration. These mainly cover trade, economic and decision making issues. On the other hand, there are other issues which, ostensibly, merely support integration, but which are yet of overbearing importance in making integration succeed and produce tangible benefits. They include the role of different stakeholders like the civil society, the media and business actors. The role of education in the integration process is also of critical importance.

The World Bank Report referred above, on the other hand, narrowly focuses on how economic geography of the EAC could be exploited to maximize integration benefits. The study falls short in addressing the fundamental and problematic issues which underlie the success of an integration project. Let me ramify. As a people-centred project, the EAC, for example, and this is a critical point, has to create a regional identity of East Africanness; an identity that could be the mobiliser and galvanizer of an ethos of collective understanding and appreciation of the pursuit of shared regional goals. This is why the role of civil society and the media is of special importance because, when well exploited, it can foster the realization of such regional identity. However, the challenge is always how to best structure and

---

[12] INTERNATIONAL BANK FOR RECONSTRUCTION AND DEVELOPMENT, *East African Community-Reshaping the Geography of East Africa: From Regional to Global Integration* Washington, DC: IBRD, 2012. This Report was release in Kampala, Uganda in February, 2012.

constitute a civil society on a regional scale and one with capacity to fulfil an exacting mission.

In turn, there is the challenge of how to get the media to be effectively disposed to champion the cause of integration amongst its largely competing commercial demands. The book examines such roles and tensions including outlining how civil society organizations such as *Kituo cha Katiba* and the East African Law Society have, for example, attempted to take leadership in promoting a regional perspective on issues such as political and human rights and the respect for constitutionalism that is in conformity with the fundamental principles of the Treaty establishing the EAC. In this vein, *Kituo cha Katiba* based in Kampala, Uganda, has produced a report titled, *Federation Within Federation: The Tanzania Union Experience and the East African Integration Process*[13] based on a fact-finding Mission to Zanzibar. The Report lays bare the challenges facing Zanzibar in determining how it may fit within the proposed East African Political Federation in the context of the framework of the Tanzania Union.[14]

---

[13] See JJUUKO, Frederick W. and Godfrey Muriuki (eds.), *Federation Within Federation: The Tanzania Union Experience and the East African Integration Process: A Report of the Kituo Cha Katiba Fact-finding Mission to Tanzania*, Kampala: Fountain Publishers, 2010.

[14] In fact Kituo cha Katiba has conducted fact-finding missions in all five member countries of the East African Community at different times depending on burning issues of the time in specific countries. See for instance the following: *Towards Political Liberalization in Uganda: A Report of the Uganda Fact Finding Mission*, Compiled and edited by Prof. Haroub Othman & Maria Nassali, Kampala: Fountain, 2002; *Constitutionalism and Political Stability in Zanzibar: The Search for a New Vision*, (*Utawala wa Katiba na Sheria, Utulivu wa Siasa Zanzibar: Muafaka na Utafutwaji wa Mwelekeo Mpya*), *A report of the Fact Finding Mission organised under the auspices of Kituo Cha Katiba*, Compiled and edited by Joseph Oloka-Onyango and Maria Nassali. Dar es Salaam: Friedrich Ebert Stiftung, 2003; *Constitutional Review Process in Kenya: Report of a Fact-Finding Mission*, Compiled and edited by Edward F. Ssempebwa & Chris Maina Peter, Dar-es-Salaam: E & D Limited, 2003; KITUO CHA KATIBA, *The East African Community – A Report of the Fact-Finding Mission to Review Progress of the East African Community*, Kampala: Kituo cha Katiba, 2005; *Searching for Sense and Humanity: Civil Society and the Struggle for a Better Rwanda: A Report of the Fact-finding Mission to Rwanda, organised under the auspices of Kituo Cha Katiba*, Edited by Chris Maina Peter and Edith Kibalama. Kampala:Fountain Publishers, 2006; *Moving the Kenya Constitution Review Process Forward: A Report of a Fact-Finding Mission to Kenya* by Saida Yahya-Othman & Joseph Sinde Warioba. Kampala, Fountain 2007; KITUO CHA KATIBA, *The Tanzania Union and the East African Integration Process: Lessons and Challenges – A Report of the Kituo cha Katiba Fact-Finding Mission to Tanzania*, Kampala: Kituo Cha Katiba, 2009; *Civil Society and Good Governance in Burundi: Promoting Inclusiveness and People Participation in the East African Community: A Report of the Fact-finding Mission to Burundi organized under the auspices of Kituo Cha Katiba*, Edited by Aliro Omara and Tulia Ackson. Kampala: Fountain, 2010; and *Federation Within Federation: The Tanzania Union Experience and the East African Integration Process. A Report of the Kituo Cha Katiba Fact-Finding Mission to Tanzania* (*Shirikisho Ndani ya Shirikisho: Uzoefu wa Muungano wa Tanzania na Mchakato wa Kuiunganisha Afrika Mashariki*), Edited by Frederick Jjuuko and Godfrey Muriuki. Kampala: Fountain, 2010.

The Society for International Development (SID), East Africa Region, has equally, through its Annual State of East Africa Reports and the Regional Scenarios projects, played an important role in galvanizing an East African identity and how it could constitute a strategic driver for promoting a shared vision of a politically federated East Africa. Its *State of East Africa Report, 2012* examines issues revolving around deepening integration in the context of intensifying challenges in a broad range of areas: population, urbanization, migration, resource use and vulnerabilities, human development, infrastructure, economic performance, politics and governance.[15]

The role of business and the private sector as whole is equally critical in the realization of the core EAC objectives especially in the areas of trade, industrialization and investments. How the EAC engages the business sector and promotes the adoption of right policies and measures that lower the costs of doing business, enhance investments, creates a large regional market and jobs at national levels, stand out as critical factors of EAC's success. It would be noted that recent World Bank Doing Business Reports have consistently painted a highly variable and largely poor picture of business enabling environments in the five EAC partner states. It is clear, that as a region, greater success in promoting investments and realizing higher intra-regional trade can best be realized if there is greater sharing of best practices that best foster and support doing business. Taking the cue from Rwanda's successes in reforming its doing business environment should be one of the ways in which the whole EAC region can begin a process of improvement in this area.

A number of shared challenges also continue to confront business in the region and they demand collective efforts on the part of the EAC partner states in addressing them. These challenges include the removal of Non-Tariff Barriers, improvement of infrastructure connectivity, including promoting energy power pools, integrating financial markets to leverage funding sources for business and infrastructure development, addressing piracy and imported counterfeits. Over all, the quest to realize a bigger internal EAC market hinges significantly on promoting manufacturing-based industrialization on a regional scale by bolstering agribusiness value chains[16] and regional business champions. Currently, low agricultural food production and agricultural productivity generally, high costs of transport logistics, power deficits and counterfeits militate against the realization of high levels of industrialization and growth of intra-EAC trade.

---

[15] See SOCIETY FOR INTERNATIONAL DEVELOPMENT, *State of East Africa Report 2012: Deepening Integration, Intensifying Challenges*, Nairobi: SID, 2012.

[16] See YUMKELLA, Kandeh K.; Patrick M. Kormawa; Torben M. Roepstorff; and Anthony M. Hawkins (eds.), *Agribusiness for Africa's Prosperity*, Vienna: UNIDO, 2011.

Moreover, realizing what is described as mobilization for a resource revolution globally[17] also crucially depends on countering huge wastages. It is estimated that between 20-30% of the world's food (which works out at about 10 million tons of food) is wasted somewhere along the value chain. Dobb's study shows that more than 60% of the food opportunity lies in reducing perishable waste through cold storage systems and better transport systems.[18] Of course much of the waste takes place in poor countries like Africa.

In the area of education, both basic and tertiary, the region's competitiveness and capacity to create a more robust regional market crucially hinge on how the education sector can be transformed into world class. There are observable serious shortcomings in the current quality of both basic and university education. The book sets out some of these challenges and proposes interventions that could help in addressing them within countries and regionally.

The book is structured in fifteen parts with a total of forty nine chapters. The book has a good balance of the author's speeches, technical papers submitted at various conferences during the currency of my Secretary Generalship of the EAC and new material written specifically for the book. I believe that the best way to capture the dynamic character of regional integration which, by its very nature, is not episodic but rather evolutionary in its process, is to use material such as speeches and technical papers, where they exist, to show how, at each moment in the critical phases of integration, an organisation such as the EAC confronted different challenges in the formulation of policies and strategies and in forging the realization of integration programmes.

Part one of the book has three chapters on African integration preceded by a prologue which provides the current state of play in Africa's integration. These chapters examine the overall challenges facing African integration and how the African unity project has fared so far. It is also a useful overview and context for benchmarking the EAC's challenges and achievements. Part two opens up a broad discussion about the EAC: the institutional evolution since its establishment in year 2000. Part three outlines in some detail the EAC's processes and stages of integration.

Part four critically examines the roles of EAC's Organs and Institutions. Part five deals with the challenges of building an effective organization from a very broad perspective. Relatedly, part six dwells on how national politics determine the whole pace and depth of integration. In part seven, I reflect on EAC's milestones: where EAC has come from, where it is today and what

---

[17] See DOBBS, Richard; Jeremy Oppenheim; and Fraser Thompson, "Mobilizing for a Resource Revolution," *McKinsey Quarterly*, January, 2012.
[18] Ibid.

lies ahead of it. Part eight outlines how the EAC has been able to respond to the challenges of becoming market driven by charting out close relations with business in the region. Part nine examines the role of the media in opening up a deeper understanding of the role of the EAC and how the citizens of East Africa can feel and imbibe ownership of the integration project.

Part ten examines the role of education in the integration project and outlines the challenges in harmonizing educational systems with a view to supporting the integration processes. Part eleven briefly discusses the process of integrating Rwanda and Burundi into the EAC. In part twelve there is a long examination of the challenges facing EAC integration in the context of how local communities could be better integrated in the mainstream of the integration agenda. The role of local governments and governance is given important attention in this regard. Part twelve addresses how defence cooperation constitutes a key pillar in EAC's integration and the need to foster such cooperation within the quest of realizing the political federation. In part thirteen, there is a brief coverage of the background to the COMESA-EAC-SADC Tripartite and the underlying objectives of this unique form of collaboration by African regional economic communities within the broad goal of getting Africa to realize a continental economic community pursuant to the Abuja Treaty of 1991.

Part fourteen outlines some of EAC's collaborations with foreign countries and international agencies within the organisation's efforts to realize a well integrated regional project. The concluding part fifteen of the book consists of my farewell address, as I completed my five year term as EAC Secretary General.

It is my hope that this book will help readers obtain an objective picture of the EAC's story; its successes, challenges and prospects. The book has attempted to capture important dynamics and their interplay in the construction of what is truly the most bold and unique regional integration project in Africa. Hopefully, the book will also overall provoke a wider debate and dialogue about the state and character of East African integration within the African and global contexts, leading to a more informed and purposeful discourse on regional integration in Africa.

I wish to thank all those who offered me the opportunity to serve East Africa; foremost being the EAC Heads of State; those who helped me to lead the Community, notably the various Ministers, Parliamentarians, Jurists, and functionaries, at all levels, from the EAC Partner States. Many colleagues in the EAC Secretariat contributed in several ways in inspiring me to write this book and, through a shared broad range of ideas and intellectual discussions and dialogues, they helped me to shape and sharpen its contents.

I wish to thank most heartily Professor Chris Maina Peter of the School of Law, University of Dar es Salaam, who, for the second time around, agreed to edit a book I have written. As customary for such a distinguished Don, Chris has helped in the restructuring and sharpening the contents of the book, including undertaking massive editorial work and organizing the footnotes. Elieshi Lema of E & D Publishers was ever ready to help me out in ensuring that this book is of the highest quality and is published on time. I cannot thank her more.

Finally, towards the end of finalizing the draft of this book, my wife and I suffered a devastating set back in our lives in the untimely passing of Harith, our second born son, in whose memory this book is dedicated.

Juma V. Mwapachu
Dar es Salaam
Tanzania

July, 2012

PART 1

Challenges of African Integration

The true revolutionary in Africa has to do two things at one and same time. He has to keep his eyes and his attention on the road ahead, and use all the pragmatism of which he is capable so as to negotiate a passage. But at the same time he must keep the goal clearly in his sights, and let it govern his direction at all times. He must in other words, be a realist idealist! I should add that I do not myself believe this is a contradiction in terms"!

Julius K. Nyerere[19]

Prologue

In the following opening part of the book, I focus on the context of the EAC in the African integration framework. I believe that it is important to provide this perspective before delving deeper into the different facets of EAC integration and considering a whole host of challenges the EAC faces in realizing deeper integration. The broad challenges which face African integration, in particular the low levels of intra-African trade are examined from a broad sweep of analysis. The EAC is also examined within the context of the ambitions to realize the African Economic Community (AEC). Since chapter one was written back in 2008, it is important that the data that is covered therein is updated to give as correct a perspective of the current reality as possible. In this context, it should be pointed out first that Africa's population has now reached almost one billion people. Africa's nominal GDP has equally gone up and in 2010 reached US $ 1.7 trillion, which is 2.3% of global GDP.[20] Evidently, Africa has to deepen self reliance because

---

[19] NYERERE, Julius K., "A New Look at Conditions for Unity," Address to the National Assembly of the United Arab Republic, 9th April, 1967. See also KALLEY, Jacqueline A. *et al* (Compilers), *Southern Africa Political History: A Chronology of Key Political Events from Independence to Mid – 1997*, Westport, CT: Greenwood Publishing Group, Inc., 1999, p. 591.

[20] See AFRICAN DEVELOPMENT BANK, *African Economic Outlook 2010*, Tunis: AfDB, 2010.

bilateral aid from the main donor countries in 2009 was a paltry US $ 28 billion. Generally, with the global financial crisis, especially in the US and the Euro zone, Official Development Assistance (ODA) will decline as the developed world shifts in aid policy from "blood transfusion" to "blood creation". In other words, increasingly, investment will become the basis of international cooperation rather than traditional aid.

The challenge though is whether blood creation in the form of investment will in fact increase. The record is not encouraging. According to UNCTAD's World Investments Report, 2012, total foreign direct investment to Africa in 2011 was only US $ 42.7 billion or 3.1% of the global share. The East Africa Community's share in total FDI inflows to Africa was only 5.5 in 2011. Moreover, according to the African Development Bank,[21] between 2007 and 2009, 60% of investment from the Organisation for Economic Cooperation and Development (OECD) countries which was 83% of total global investment to Africa went to three African countries- South Africa, Egypt and Nigeria. China and India contributed only 3.0% of such FDI. Whilst intra-African investment is on the rise, it is, on the other hand, largely represented by South Africa's outward investments which in 2009 amounted to US $ 1.6 billion.

In his article, "Building an African Infrastructure" published in *Finance & Development Journal*, Professor Paul Collier points out that prospects in the advanced economies for investment is bleak whilst in the BRICs - Brazil, Russia, India, China and South Africa, the future is more uncertain.[22] In holding that Africa is not immune to global risks, he advises that Africa's growth is "likely to rest on the potential for further resource discoveries and for commercial cultivation of its vast, underused agricultural land." He sees the development of infrastructure as vital to harnessing the potential that exists in these two economic sectors. Collier has a point. In the EAC, for example, freight costs par kilometre according to the World Bank, are presently estimated to be 60-70% higher than in the United States and Europe, 30% higher than in Southern Africa. In fact, for the EAC landlocked countries, these costs are as high as 75% of the value of exports.[23] If Africa will unleash value chains as strategic production and distribution systems for

---

[21] See AFRICAN DEVELOPMENT BANK, *African Economic Outlook, 2011,* op. cit.

[22] See COLLIER, Paul, "Building an African Infrastructure," Volume 48 No. 4 *Finance & Development*, December, 2011; see also OECD: Development: Aid to developing countries falls because of global recession, Paris, 2012; www.oecd.org/document/3/0,3746,en_21571361_44315115_50058883_1-1_1,00.html. The report shows that major donors' aid to developing countries fell by 3% in 2011 because of global recession. Bilateral aid to SSA fell by 0.9% in real terms in 2011 compared to 2010.

[23] See WORLD BANK, *East African Community-Reshaping the Geography of East Africa: From Regional to Global Integration,* Washington, DC: International Bank for Reconstruction and Development (IBRD), 2012.

bolstering trade, then trade logistics and trade facilitation overall have to be made more cost effective and competitive.

In the context of the scarcity of investments, an area that could help boost economic growth in Africa is undoubtedly the promotion of intra-African trade. Unfortunately, this area has remained Africa's nightmare. Africa's share of its intra-African trade to total global trade was only 11% in 2010 compared to Europe's 72% and Asia's 52%. In 2009, Africa's total merchandise exports to the world amounted to US $ 212.3 billion but 50% of which were accounted for by South Africa and Nigeria alone. And what is particularly disconcerting is the fact that the share of Africa's export of manufactures to total exports is on the decline. According to the UNIDO's *Economic Development in Africa Report, 2011*,[24] the share of African manufacturing in GDP fell from 15.3% in 1990 to 10.5% in 2008. In Eastern Africa, the share of manufacturing in GDP fell from 13.4% in 1990 to 9.7% in 2008. These statistics clearly explain that manufacturing industry is in crisis and decisive policy actions are needed to regenerate this important sector particularly within the contest of addressing the critical youth unemployment challenge.

In sum, Africa is not making the kind of improvements needed to make regional and continental integration meaningful. Whilst Africa and indeed the rich world are celebrating Africa's consistent high economic performance in the past decade with average GDP growths of around 5.6%, these achievements have not translated themselves into inclusive development and improved quality of lives. On the contrary, there are huge challenges that continue to stare Africa in the face. Africa has to particularly get more serious about its potential vulnerabilities which relate to poor infrastructure, an unproductive agricultural sector, over reliance on oil and mining exports whose share in trade with the rest of the world in 2011 was about 66%, the youth bulge with some 200 million Africans out of a population of 1 billion in 2011 are aged between 15 and 24 years and the growing adverse effects of climate change.

These challenges demand an African-wide strategic response. It is questionable though whether the African Union (AU) reflects serious, committed and ambitious leadership to spearhead such a response. In 2009, the AU and the Regional Economic Communities (RECs) as part of the process of arriving at a Protocol to govern the relationship and co-ordination of programmes and activities between the two, proposed the adoption of a Minimum Integration Programme (MIP). At face value, MIP is not dysfunctional and could, indeed, form a good mechanism to promote closer collaboration and co-ordination between the AU and the RECs in getting

---

[24] See UNITED NATIONS INDUSTRIAL DEVELOPMENT ORGANIZATION, Economic Development in Africa Report 2011, Vienna: UNIDO, 2011.

African integration in a number of important areas moving. Unfortunately, the MIP is too much informed by AU's own continental integration yardsticks which have little bearing on what constitutes the MIPs of the RECs as determined by the member or partner states that constitute the separate RECs.

One could of course argue that this is one of the challenges that arise out of multiplicity of RECs in Africa and of the overlapping memberships that are manifested therein. However, I am of the view that the argument about multiplicity of RECs is overplayed. Surely, and in practical terms, there could not have been an alternative, in the absence of a continental economic community and some would even argue, of a United States of Africa but to have RECs as building blocks. Some of these RECs, like SADC, moreover, were not conceived purely on trade and economic grounds. They were driven by strong political reasons. Overlapping membership was inevitable. Even post the liberation and post apartheid in Southern Africa, the legacy of those political factors subsists.

It is significant to hold that for the AU to have agreed and accepted the inevitability of RECs as building blocks for the realization of the African Economic Community as envisioned under the 1991 Abuja Treaty in the first place is sufficient reason to be positive about the inevitability of multiplicity of memberships within RECs. Having said this, it is important to recognize though that some efforts have taken place within some RECs to address the membership multiplicity phenomenon. In October, 2008, COMESA, EAC and SADC decided through a resolution of their Heads of State to plan an ultimate merger of the three bodies with priority being given initially to the establishment of a grand free trade area followed by a customs union. There are positive developments that have taken place towards realizing these goals including joint efforts by the tripartite to develop infrastructure transport corridors that are crucial in opening up the large economic space for a well functioning large market to emerge. These ambitions are covered later in the book.

Whilst I take a general positive stance about multiplicity of memberships in RECs, objectivity also demands that some downsides of the phenomenon are equally analysed. In some instances, this phenomenon has had dysfunctional effects in promoting collective positions over important negotiations. For example, for sometime in 2006-2007, Tanzania was not prepared to negotiate the Economic Partnership Agreement (EPA) with the European Union (EU) as part of the EAC. It wanted to do so as part of SADC. Kenya equally was jostling between negotiating as part of EAC and as part of a group within COMESA.[25] To the EAC this situation was puzzling in the

---

[25] On the background to some of these RECs see MUTHARIKA, Bingu wa, *One Africa One Destiny: Towards Democracy, Good Governance and Development*, Harare: Sapes Books, 1995.

sense that the EAC is a customs union and to the extent that EPAs have significant trade-related issues which fall within the ambit of the World Trade Organization (WTO) and WTO Rules forbid a country to be part of two separate customs unions, both Kenya and Tanzania could not opt out of the EAC block in the EPA negotiations.

These issues took an even more volatile turn in SADC where some member countries who also belong to the Southern African Customs Union (SACU) decided to break ranks with South Africa on EPA negotiations. South Africa had threatened to take retaliatory measures against them. In a statement made by the South African Foreign Minister in 2011 to a meeting of South Africa's envoys, it is possible to get a sense of the seriousness of these issues: She said:

> The challenge facing the SADC is that of a possibly divided SADC, in the Economic Partnership Agreement negotiations, due to conflicting interests which have led some member states (Botswana, Lesotho, Mozambique and Swaziland signing the Interim EPA, in spite of concerns raised by Angola, Namibia and South Africa - the future of South Africa's economic development and that of the region is linked to the future of the Southern African Customs Union (SACU). In this regard, the EPA, in its current form is threatening the existence of the SACU.[26]

More recently, Tanzania also postponed its decision to sign an EAC Defence Co-operation Protocol that contains an article on the conclusion of a Mutual Defence Pact by the EAC Partner States because, ostensibly, it has such a commitment in a SADC Protocol. These issues should not, of course, be underrated in terms of their sensitivities. There are strong sentiments and passions about some of these memberships. For Tanzania, for example, its membership in SADC conjures the days when it was Chair of the Frontline States,[27] fighting the apartheid regime in South Africa and providing leadership for the liberation of many Southern African states.[28] Tanzania is

---

[26] www.aucharter.org.

[27] Frontline States members included Angola, Botswana, Lesotho, Mozambique, Tanzania, Zambia, Zimbabwe.

[28] On liberation struggle in Southern African generally See NYERERE, Julius K., *Crusade for Liberation*, New York: Oxford University Press, 1978; MSABAHA, Ibrahim and Timothy M. Shaw (eds.), *Confrontation and Liberation in Southern Africa: Directions After the Nkomati Accords*, Boulder, Colorado (USA): Westview Press Inc. and London (U.K.): Gower Publishing Company Ltd., 1987; SELLSTROM, Tor (ed.), *Liberation in Southern Africa: Regional and Swedish Voices*, Uppsala: Nordiska Afrikainstitutet, 2002; SOIRI, Lina and Pekka Peltola, *Finland and National Liberation in Southern Africa*, Uppsala: Nordiska Afrikainstitutet, 1999; ERIKSEN, Tore Linne (ed.), *Norway and National Liberation in Southern Africa*, Uppsala: Nordiska Afrikainstitutet, 2000; OTHMAN, Haroub (ed.), *Sites of Memory: Julius Nyerere and the Liberation of Southern Africa*,

also a major beneficiary of investments from South Africa and enjoys good trade relationship with that country.[29] It is therefore not an exception. You could also bring in Zambia and Zimbabwe into the equation; both members of COMESA and of SADC. It would thus seem that the problem of overlapping membership will only end when the AEC is born and that is where the AU must put all its energies in achieving. So far, its record is wanting. I examine some of AU's shortcomings and the overall challenge of African integration in chapters one to three.

Zanzibar: Zanzibar International Firm Festival, 2007; and SOUTHALL, Roger, "Troubled Visionary: Nyerere as a Former President," in SOUTHALL, Roger and Henning Melber (eds.) *Legacies of Power: Leadership Change and Former Presidents in African Politics*, Uppsala and Cape Town: The Nordic Africa Institute and HSRC Press, 2006, p. 233. See also HAUSSLER, Peter, *Leadership for Democratic Development in Tanzania: The Perspective of Mwalimu Julius K. Nyerere During the First Decade of Independence*, Dar es Salaam: Mwalimu Nyerere Foundation, 2009; HAVNEVIK, Kjell, "A Historical Framework for Analysing Current Tanzanian Transitions: The Post-Independence Model, Nyerere's Ideas and Some Interpretations," in HAVNEVIK, Kjell and Aida C. Isinika (eds.), *Tanzania in Transition: From Nyerere to Mkapa*, Dar es Salaam: Mkuki na Nyota Publishers, 2010, p. 19; and CHACHAGE, Chambi and Annar Cassam (eds.), *Africa's Liberation: The Legacy of Nyerere*, Oxford and Kampala: Pambazuka Press and Fountain Press, 2010.

[29] On South African investment in Tanzania see *inter alia*, SCHROEDER, Richard, "South African Capital in the Land of Ujamaa: Contested Terrain in Tanzania," Volume 12 No. 1 *African Sociological Review*, 2008, p. 20.

CHAPTER ONE

Africa's Future through Regional Integration[30]

Introduction

I am extremely honoured to be invited to address this distinguished 83rd Rotary District Conference. I was a Rotarian many years ago; indeed, with my friend Hatim Karimjee, we were Charter members of Dar es Salaam Bahari Rotary Club. Thus today offers a nostalgic occasion for me to renew my commitment to the lofty ideals of Rotarianism and to pay special tribute to the philanthropic and humanitarian work that Rotarians undertake around the world and in our region. Your mantras, *"Service above self"* and *"They profit most who serve best"* clearly go to the heart of the human spirit which often escapes us in this world of growing individualism and greed.

The topic that you have invited me to address you on today, *Africa's Future through Regional Cooperation and Integration* is topical. It resonates well with the challenges poor countries face in a fast evolving and what, paradoxically, is increasingly becoming an interdependent world economic and social system. With the surge of globalization in recent decades, the least developed countries have become more seized of its marginalizing impact. As a result, they have embarked on redefining their development paradigms at both domestic and regional fronts. Pooling of scarce resources and uniting all other efforts, political and economic, around a common continental and regional vision and mission, have also become the central ethos and thrusts in mastering globalization. Interestingly, such strategy of collective pursuit of more meaningful development through integration systems is not limited to developing countries. On the contrary, rich countries, for over fifty years now, have also undertaken similar measures.

Regional integration is thus the new paradigm that is defining and, indeed, influencing regional and global economic relations. It would seem that no country in the world, however economically powerful, will, today or in the future, prosper, let alone survive, while acting alone. Consider the recent sub-prime mortgage financial crisis that has severely hit some of the top global banks and shaking the global financial infrastructure to its feet. One has seen in this situation, how close and effective co-ordination and intervention by the US Federal Reserve Bank, the Bank of England and the European Central Bank have made the difference in the global capital markets.

---

[30] Keynote Address to the 83rd Rotary District Conference, Dar es Salaam, 14th May, 2008.

Therefore, it is not surprising to observe today the robust integrative movement in the European Union; a movement that is expanding, consolidating and locking in, under its system, the lesser developed countries of Eastern and Central Europe. Similarly, in Asia, we see the solidification of the Association of South-Eastern Asian Countries (ASEAN) and the increasingly aggressive economic drives of India and China to claim a place of pride among the world's top economic league. And, further afield, we note the same preoccupation with the evolution towards a "One Market" for the Americas, beyond North Atlantic Free Trade Area (NAFTA). In sum, one can conclude that that there is a broad consensus around the world that regional integration is of particular strategic relevance in promoting higher and sustainable economic growth and improving the quality of life of the people. Indeed, the future of the global economic order is seen with the prism of regional integration and global co-operation. In his recent path breaking book, *Common Wealth: Economics for a Crowded Planet*, Jeffrey Sachs,[31] notes, "old nation-state boundaries have become too small to provide many public goods required at a transnational scale." He posits further that other regions of the world, notably Africa, "will follow Europe's lead in forging a much stronger transnational organization."[32]

Question is: Will Africa indeed follow Europe's lead? Moreover, will Africa's future in terms of eradicating poverty and bolstering the quality of life of Africans be enhanced by and through integration? What are the key prerequisites that Europe probably had pursued to underpin the role of regional integration? To answer these questions appropriately, it is necessary, first of all, to examine briefly Africa's history of integration.

Genesis of Regional Integration in Africa

With its genesis in the Pan Africanist movement[33] of the late 40's and the 50's, the drive for African integration peaked with the establishment of the Organization of African Unity (OAU) in 1963.[34] Since then, African leaders

---

[31] See SACHS, Jeffrey, *Common Wealth: Economics for a Crowded Planet*, New York, The Penguin Press, 2008.

[32] Ibid., at p. 333.

[33] On the Pan Africanist movement *see inter alia*, GEISS, Imanuel, *The Pan-African Movement: A History of Pan-Africanism in America, Europe and Africa*, London and New York: Methuen and Africana Publishers, 1994; ABDUL RAHEEM, Tajudeen Abdul Raheem (ed.), *Pan Africanism: Politics, Economy and Social Change in the Twenty First Century*, London: Pluto Press, 1996; and WALTERS, Ronald W., *Pan Africanism in the African Diaspora: An Analysis of Modern Afrocentric Political Movements*, African American Life Series, Wayne State University Press, 1997.

[34] On the establishment of this continental body see *inter alia*, SOOD, R.P. (ed.), *Organisation of African Unity: A Select Bibliography*, New Delhi: Department of African Studies, University of Delhi, 1990 and NALDI, Gino J., The Organization of African Unity: an analysis of its role, London: Mansell, 1999.

have articulated an ambitious vision of an African integrated economy whose pinnacle was the ratification of the Abuja Treaty in 1994. That Treaty pronounced the quest for an African Economic Community (AEC).

The African integration vision has played out at two levels. First, at the level of the continental organization where there has been an unequivocal political tone; and, secondly, at sub regional levels, where, essentially, several economic sub-regional arrangements have emerged, eight of them officially recognized by the African Union (AU). These institutions have predominantly focused on intra-regional trade promotion through preferential arrangements; establishment of common currency areas and harmonization of macroeconomic policies to achieve convergence. In a few cases, their collective measures have extended to promoting regional public goods such as infrastructure, higher education and attacking trans-boundary diseases. The promotion of peace and security has also been a dominant feature though the experience in dealing with the Burundi[35] and especially the Darfur crisis,[36] have not been that heartening.

What is important to point out though is that many of these sub-regional economic arrangements have remained loosely structured in their roles with national economies continuing to operate largely autonomously and thus continuing to be subjected to greater manipulation and marginalization by the rich countries. Indeed, it is this weak and balkanized character of African

---

[35] On the ever occurring problems in Burundi see BOWEN, Michael, *Passing By: The United States and Genocide in Burundi*, 1972, New York: Carnegie Endowment for International Peace, 1973; LEMARCHAND, René, *Selective Genocide in Burundi*, London: Minority Rights Group, 1974; LEMARCHAND, René, *Burundi: Ethnic Conflict and Genocide*, New York: Woodrow Wilson Center and Cambridge University Press, 1996; NYANKANZI, Edward L., *Genocide: Rwanda and Burundi*, Schenkman Books, 1998; SCHERRER, Christian P., *Genocide and Crisis in Central Africa: Conflict Roots, Mass Violence, and Regional War*; Westport, CT: Praeger, 2002; and MELADY, Thomas, *Burundi: Tragic Years*, New York: Orbis Books, 1974.

[36] The issue of Darfur has been extensively addressed because of its seriousness. See BURR, J. Millard and Robert O. Collins (2006) *Darfur: The Long Road to Disaster*, Princeton N.J.: Markus Wiener, 2006; CHEADLE, Don and Prendergast, John, *Not on Our Watch:The Mission to End Genocide in Darfur and Beyond*, New York: Hyperion, 2007; DALY, M.W., *Darfur's Sorrow: A History of Destruction and Genocide*, Cambridge: Cambridge University Press, 2007; DE WAAL, Alex, *Famine that Kills: Darfur, Sudan*, New York: Oxford University Press, New York, 1989; DE WAAL, Alex (ed.), *War in Darfur and the Search for Peace*, Harvard University Press, 2007; FLINT, Julie and Alex de Waal, *Darfur: A Short History of a Long War*, London: Zed Books, London, 2006; GRZB, Amanda (ed.), *The World and Darfur: International Response to Crimes Against Humanity in Western Sudan*, McGill-Queen's University Press, 2009; MAMDANI, Mahmood, *Saviors and Survivors: Darfur, Politics, and the War on Terror*, New York: Pantheon, 2009; PRUNIER, Gérard, *Darfur: The Ambiguous Genocide*, New York: Cornell University Press, 2005; TOTTEN, Samuel and Markusen, Eric, *Genocide in Darfur: Investigating the Atrocities in the Sudan*, New York: Routledge, 2006; and CAMPBELL, David (2007) "Geopolitics and Visuality: Sighting the Darfur Conflict," Volume 26, *Political Geography*, 2007, pp. 357-382.

---

regional integration that was the dominant feature when most African countries were subjected to the wave of World Bank and International Monetary Fund (IMF) - driven economic reforms in the 1980's and the early 1990s. It was thus somewhat inevitable that the Structural Adjustment Programmes, popularly known as SAPs, met only with a mixed bag of success. The interventions worked for some time in some countries but not for all the countries most of the time. The net result, overall, was that the African continent continued to lag behind in the development race. In fact, the 1980s are often referred to as the "lost decade" for Africa and other poor countries!

It is the lacklustre experience with the SAPs that largely led to a broad rethink of the African development challenge. The idea of strengthening and deepening African regional integration thus picked a new momentum from the mid 1990s. African leaders became better seized of the reality that regional integration was an effective vehicle for addressing Africa's economic *problematique* and for accelerating Africa's integration into the world economy. In this vein, regional economic institutions were conceived to spearhead a new development philosophy beyond structural adjustment.

AU and Deepening Regional Integration in Africa

This new African spirit of renewal centred on regional integration was boldly encapsulated in the Constitutive Act of the African Union of July 2000.[37] And, following the establishment of the African Union in 2003 that replaced the erstwhile Organization of African Unity (OAU), African countries re-launched their long-standing vision of economic and political unity.[38] The African Union was conceived as a continental vehicle of intervention for fast-tracking the promotion of Africa's development and peace and security.[39] At the continental level, key priority was placed on establishing institutions that can underpin African identity and spearhead progress. The institutions include the Pan-African Parliament, the African Court of Justice, the African Investment Bank, African Monetary Fund and African Central Bank.[40] The latter three financial institutions are yet to be established. At the

---

[37] The Constitutive Act of the African Union of 11th July, 2000 is analysed and reproduced in YUSUF, Abdulqawi A. and Fatsah Ouguergouz (eds.), *The African Union: Legal and Institutional Framework – A Manual on the Pan-African Organization*, Leiden and Boston: Martinus Nijhoff Publishers, 2012 at p. 525.

[38] On the transition and its implications see NDAGIRE, Josephine, "The Ghost of the Organisation of African Unity (OAU) Haunts Africa," Volume 17 No. 1 East African Journal of Peace & Human Rights, 2011, p. 53.

[39] See MPANGALA, Gaudens P., "Democracy and Development Challenges in Africa: The African Union Perspective," Volume 5 No. 2 *Tanzania Journal of Development Studies*, 2004, p. 97.

sub-regional level, on the other hand, regional economic communities (RECs), among them SADC, EAC, COMESA and ECOWAS (Economic Commission of West African States) were either reborn or re-branded to catalyse a more dynamic realization of the African Renaissance.

As I address you today, this spirit and tempo of co-operation and integration in Africa is growing. The AU - fronted *New Partnership for Africa's Development* (NEPAD), established in 2001, for example, has placed Africa in greater focus on the world stage of global development partnership, providing a much needed instrument for advancing a people-centred sustainable development.[41] Though at an apparently slow pace, both the AU and NEPAD have so far initiated ambitious programmes to integrate Africa. They include programmes in areas such as peace and security, where there is a continental architecture as well as a protocol to govern it; governance, through the African Peer Review Mechanism, though as we all know, Africa continues to be bedevilled by cases such as the Zimbabwe one which undermine the very essence and efficacy of instruments such as the APRM and the *African Charter on Elections, Democracy and Governance* adopted by the African Union in January, 2007.[42]

Other programmes are in infrastructure, especially in the energy sector through the promotion of regional power pools; promotion of Spatial Development initiatives such as the Maputo Development Corridor in Southern Africa and the Central Development Corridor in East Africa; industrialization, agriculture, science and technology, especially Information and Communications Technology (ICT), and rural development.

In this similar context, we are also seeing today some reawakening and re-invigoration of African regional economic communities. These are implementing projects and programmes that have an overarching continental vision of a united, peaceful and prosperous Africa. However, objectivity

---

[40] All these institutions are provided for in the Constitutive Act of the African Union as follows: the Pan-African Parliament (Articles 5(1)(c) and 17); the African Court of Justice (Articles 5(1)(d) and 18; the African Investment Bank (Article 19(c); African Monetary Union (Article 19(b); and African Central Bank (Article 19(a). On the African Union see *inter alia*, MELBER, Henning, *The New African Initiative and the African Union: A Preliminary Assessment and Documentation*, Uppsala: Nordiska Afrikainstitutet, 2002.

[41] On NEPAD see ANYANG' NYONG'O, Peter *et al* (eds.) *New Partnership for Africa's Development – NEPAD: A New Path?* Nairobi: Heinrich Boll Foundation, 2002; MELBER, Henning *et al*, *The New Partnership for Africa's Development (NEPAD) – African Perspectives*, Uppsala: Nordiska Afrikainstitutet, 2002; and OJIENDA, Tom O., "Implementing the New Partnership for Africa's Development (NEPAD): Evaluating the Efficiency of the African Peer Review Mechanism" Volume 1 No. 2 *Moi University Law Journal*, 2007, p. 34.

[42] The Charter was adopted by the 8th Ordinary Session of the Assembly, held in Addis Ababa, Ethiopia on 30th January, 2007. It came into force on 15th February, 2012 upon receiving the required number of ratifications by the Member States of the Africa Union.

demands that we critically examine the track record of these economic communities as well as the African Union itself to determine to what extent and how Africa's future crucially depends on them.

Africa's Balance Sheet on Regional Integration

Regrettably, the story of African regional integration, to-date, is predominantly a sad one. In my view, it is simply not enough for Africa to be merely passionate about cooperation and integration and to romanticize African renaissance. To be meaningful and supported by the people, integration has to deliver concrete results that reflect real improvements in the quality of life of Africans. I believe that this could be the reason for your choice of the theme of my address, Africa's future through Regional Integration. It is important, therefore, that serious questions be asked: Is African integration so far making a difference to the African people? Why and to what extent should Africans pin their hopes on the future on regional integration? Are African nation-states themselves, anyway, showing adequate seriousness on and commitment to the integration agenda?

Not many keen observers of the African integration scene are upbeat about the experience and results of African integration so far. Martin Meredith, in an important narrative history book bout Africa over 50 years of independence, published in 2005 titled: *The Fate of Africa: from the Hopes of Freedom to the Heart of Despair*, observes that 50 years after Ghana's independence, Africa's prospects are, in reality, bleaker than ever before.[43] Even though average economic growth in Africa has picked up and stands at 5.8% in 2007, which is still below the 7.0% minimum required to effectively begin to reduce poverty and uplift living standards, Africa remains the poorest region in the world. Sub-Saharan Africa's average GDP per capita income at US $ 842 (in 2006) is one third lower than that of Asia and lower than its 1980 figure. In fact, Sub-Saharan Africa has failed to achieve a rise in income per capita for the past generation, which is 30 years.

Put differently, in 2004, Africa accounted for 30% of all people living on less than US $ 1 a day. According to the World Bank's *Economic Prospects Report, 2008*,[44] this figure is expected to rise to 46% by 2010. Moreover, Africa's total economic output in 2007 was only US $ 420 billion or 1.3 % the world GDP. Its share of world trade, on the other hand, at 1.6%, has

---

[43] See MEREDITH, Martin, *The Fate of Africa: from the Hopes of Freedom to the Heart of Despair,* New York: Public Affairs, 2005, pp. 13-14. See also MEREDITH, Martin, *The State of Africa: A History of Fifty Years of Independence*, London: Free Press, 2005.

[44] INTERNATIONAL BANK FOR RECONSTRUCTION AND DEVELOPMENT, *Global Economic Prospects 2008: Technology Diffusion in the Developing World*, Washington, DC, World Bank, 2008. According to the CIA Factbook, 2012, this figure in 2011 was 36.2%.

declined to half of what it was in the 1980s. On the investment front, its current share of global investment is less than 1%. In addition, and Jeffrey Sachs, in the book cited before, presents these facts powerfully. He notes, for example, that Sub-Saharan Africa's population has more than quadrupled from 180 million in 1950 to 820 million in 2007. And according to the International Labour Organisation (ILO), these demographics have serious implications on employment. Africa's labour force is expanding at an annual rate of 2.5%, way beyond the ability of African countries to cope.

Overall, such population explosion cannot be absorbed safely even with the support of the rich world. Even more worrying is the fact that large percentages of this population boom are moving into urban areas and cities raising serious challenges. As Professor Sachs laments, the rural population migrants are moving because of desperation and hunger in the countryside. The result will be urban slums, urbanization of hunger and violence and insecurity. As he puts it, "a rural crisis can thereby become an urban nightmare."[45]

This is the broad context that leads Meredith and several critics of the African development paradigm to cast doubt about Africa's capacity to integrate itself into the global economy, drummed up sentiments about Africa's re-birth and renaissance, notwithstanding! Meredith's conclusion is that the prospects of Africa escaping from precipitous decline crucially hinges on the support of the rich world; in other words, not so much on regional integration. But then here lies the rub. The recent record of development assistance from the OECD countries in support of the world poor is abysmal to say the least.

The rich world has not honoured the commitments made under the Monterrey Consensus of 2000 in any meaningful sense despite the euphoria that surrounded the UN Millennium Summit of 2000 that brought about the Millennium Development Goals (MDGs). At the same time, the G8 Summit that met in Gleneagles in July, 2005, which came in the wake of the Commission for Africa Report that was framed within the ambitious goals of the Millennium Development Goals, has also not lived to Africa's expectations. According to the OECD, development assistance to Sub-Saharan Africa, excluding debt relief, increased by only 10% in real terms in 2007 leading it to conclude that "it is clear that donors still face a real challenge to meet the Gleneagles G8 Summit projection to double aid to Africa by 2010."

It is true though that many least developed countries in Africa have had their total debts cancelled. That said, Africa needs new capital to address some of its fundamental constraints, largely supply side, to trigger and stimulate economic growth. Yet, whilst Foreign Direct Investment (FDI) to Africa

---

[45] See SACHS, Jeffrey, *Common Wealth: Economics for a Crowded Planet*, op. cit., p. 27.

reached US $ 36 billion in 2006, double the 2004 figure, Africa's share of global FDI declined from 3.1% in 2005 to 2.7% in 2006. In fact, FDI to the whole developing world was US $ 397 billion in 2006; Africa thus benefiting only to the extent of less than 10%. But it is also important to underscore that most of this investment anyway was mainly directed to a few African countries that are rich in extractive natural resources, largely oil and minerals. At another level, it is also significant to note that trade barriers in developed economies continue to cost poor nations more than US $ 100 billion annually, more than twice those economies give in aid. Farm subsidies alone in rich countries cost poor nations some US $ 50 billion a year in lost exports. In fact, this is one of the primary contexts that underlie the failure, so far, to reach an agreement under the Doha Trade and Development Round.

What this overall bleak picture of North-South relations establishes is that Africa, probably, has little choice but to increasingly look inwards if it is going to sustainably liberate itself economically. Such goal, however, is easier said than realized. It raises a fundamental point though, whether regional integration is a panacea in addressing Africa's huge development deficit as well as in determining its future. Consider the present state of Africa's own intra-investment flows. Presently, they stand at about 0.3% of total global inward investments. South Africa is the major contributor of this investment flow, at between 60 to 80%. This low level of intra-African investment flows has to be contrasted with capital flight from Sub-Saharan Africa (SSA). For 46 SSA countries, for which data exists, total capital flight between 1991 and 2004 amounted to US $ 184 billion averaging US $ 13 billion per annum.[46]

Clearly, if Africa will not have enough confidence to invest in itself, who else would? Question is: How can these capital flight funds be invested in Africa if they constitute stolen funds and monies obtained through corruption? Put differently, Africa must, first of all, seriously solve its high level corruption malaise if it is to be able to channel its resources into much needed investments that drive economic growth. But secondly, Africa can

---

[46] The data on this is provided by the African Development Bank Group. See www.afdb.org/news-and-events/article/africa-lost-some-700-billion-dollars-to-capital-flight-in-a-decade-9299/. See also ALI, Abdilahi and Bernard Walters, "On the Causes of Capital Flight from Sub-Saharan Africa," University of Manchester, March, 2011(http://www.csae.ox.ac.uk/conferences/2011-EDiA/papers/679-Ali.pdf); NDIKUMAN, Léonce and James K. Boyce, *New Estimates of Capital Flight from Sub-Saharan African Countries: Linkages with External Borrowing and Policy Options*, Department of Economics and Political Economy Research Institute, University of Massachusetts, Amherst (Political Economy Research Institute, Working Paper Series No. 166, April, 2008 (http://www.peri.umass.edu/fileadmin/pdf/working_papers/working_papers_151-200/WP166.pdf); and AJAYI, Simeon Ibinayo and Mohsin S. Khan (eds.), *External Debt and Capital Flight in Sub-Saharan Africa*, Washington, D.C.: International Monetary Fund, 2000.

only invest in itself if it also has adequate domestic savings to do so even when some of the savings filter out through capital flight. However, domestic savings in Africa, on average, are too low. Their average ratio today is about 60% of the Asian average.

But there is also the bigger picture which Professor Carol Lancaster mused about in a chapter in the book, *Africa in the World Politics: The African State System in Flux*.[47] She wondered how Africa could prosper without the emergence of a leading role of "regional hegemons with the will and the resources to promote economic cooperation and integration." Looking at Asia today, it is India and China that are providing Asia with a protective shield against the kind of financial market contagion it suffered in 1997. Their economic vibrancy is also bolstering regional trade. So yes, South Africa, as noted earlier, is trying its best to play such a role.[48]

But where are the other hegemons in Africa? In search for an answer, it is important to provide a contrast with what is taking place in Asia. The financial markets in Asia are not just liberalized; they are also robust and are driven by effective macro-economic convergences of leading national players. These provide the fundamental drivers of the regional economy that we see consolidating in Asia. For example, intra-Asian trade in 2005 was 51.2% of Asia's total world trade. In contrast, for the same period, Africa's share was only 8.9%. In the European Union, on the other hand, it was 73.2%.

In other words, Africa is not even close to optimizing its vision of a common market. Of course, there are pockets of hope whose experience could probably help to bolster intra-regional trade. Take the case of the East African Community Customs Union. Since its establishment in January 2005, total intra-EAC trade has been growing rather slowly even considering that, between 2006 and 2007, some phenomenal growth of 41.3% has been achieved partly because of the accession of Rwanda and Burundi into the EAC. With the drive towards the establishment of an EAC Common Market by 2010 this growth could see higher trends especially as the economies diversify more deeply into value adding processing and manufacturing.

---

[47] See HARBESON, John Willis and Donald S. Rothchild (Eds.), *Africa in the World Politics: The African State System in Flux*, Boulder, Colorado and Oxford: Westview Press, 2000.

[48] See ERASMUS, Gerhard, "Regional Trade Arrangements: Developments and Implications for Southern African States," Volume 1 No. 1 *Namibia Law Journal*, 2009, p. 29. According to the African Economic Outlook, 2012 of the African Development Bank, intra-African trade in 2011 was 10%; EU-27 was 70%, intra-Asian was 52%, intra-North American was 48% and intra-South American was 26%.

Challenges Confronting African Regional Integration

In sum, whilst regional integration, in theory, enhances the prospects of accelerating growth because it partly tackles constraints emanating from small and fragmented markets, current intra-African trade data does not support such theory. Question is why? It is important to address this question dispassionately because its answers are what would crucially determine the success of regional integration. So what are the main challenges confronting regional integration in Africa today?

The first challenge is that most African economies are monocultural in nature. They produce almost the same primary commodities for export. There is thus very little to sell to each other. And this is because manufactures comprise a very insignificant share of exports. In fact, manufactures, in 2005, accounted for only 0.8% of Africa's share of global exports. The benchmark set by the UN Economic Commission for Africa (UNECA) for manufacturing exports as a share of GDP to manifest a threshold of an industrial take off is 25%. Given this state of depressingly low levels of African exports of manufactures, it is not surprising that Africa has failed to exploit fully the highly trade preferential African Growth and Opportunity Act (AGOA) and Generalised Scheme of Preferences (GSP) scheme. In fact, when you isolate exports of oil from Angola, Nigeria, Chad, Republic of Congo and Gabon, that range between US $ 6.13 billion for Nigeria, to US $ 2.23 billion for Angola to US $ 497 million for Congo, it is only South Africa that recorded exports of manufactures under the US schemes of US $ 467 million in 2007. For the same period, the rest of Africa reflects exports of anything between US $ 45 million and US $ 0 for Burundi. Tanzania's exports were US $ 162,000; Uganda 229,000; and Kenya US $ 34 million.

Secondly, Africa likes to pose the problem of poor infrastructure as a major constraint to bolstering trade within itself and with the rest of the world. In a sense this is correct because transport costs are too high and they erode competitiveness. Thus, reliable and robust infrastructure, especially energy, roads, railways, air transport, inland waterways transport, and ports and harbours, does indeed open up national economic spaces for economic activities to spring up and grow. Unlocking these supply side constraints promotes growth of domestic investment and attracts much needed foreign investment. Africa particularly needs regional axes of these key infrastructures urgently to make integration meaningful.

However, if there is one area that Africa could use regional integration to address its economic malaise, it is in the area of infrastructure development. A more collective approach is logical to address this challenge. And you would think that this is the direction being taken if you read, for example, the list of infrastructure priorities approved by the First Session of African

Ministers responsible for Transport and Communications that met in Algiers in April this year. But what comes out is a mere aggregation of the projects already being implemented at sub-regional and national levels. It is unfortunate, in this sense, that the African political leadership remains largely anchored in national infrastructure pre-occupations rather than seriously promoting the collective use of NEPAD and the Regional Economic Organizations to bolster infrastructure development that have strategic and beneficial cross-border spill-overs.

Resulting from this policy weakness, NEPAD finds itself increasingly ineffectual; much to the surprise of the OECD countries and even the African Development Bank Group that view it, given their support, as a strategic vehicle for promoting the regional axes, cutting across all the strategic infrastructures.

As a concrete example of integration policy weakness, let us examine the case of African air transport. In 1998, African Governments signed the Yamoussoukro Declaration to open up and liberalise African air space and transport. That Declaration took effect in 2000 as the Yamoussoukro Decision. Its primary aim was and remains to enhance continental air connectivity for promoting business and trade. Air fares were supposed to decline significantly driven by several entrants moving into the air transport industry and thus forging competition. However, the decision has seen disjointed implementation and frustrations largely because African governments remain protectors of their fledgling national flag carriers.

Thus, the ethos of regional integration continues to be sacrificed. This case raises fundamental issues about how African countries are positioned to deal with the complex negotiations of trade in services that lie at the heart of the global trade agenda. If Africa fails to come to grips with this agenda, within itself, as partly reflected in the failure to see through the Yamoussoukro Decision, how, surely, could it be better predisposed to tackle the same at the global level, either under the on-going Economic Partnership Agreements with the European Union, or under the broader Doha Round of Trade Talks? In contrast, however, the East African Community has established an institution, Civil Aviation Safety and Security Oversight Agency, not only to foster international safety and security standards in line with International Civil Aviation Organisation (ICAO) requirements but also to deepen liberalization of the East African regional air space and air transport pursuant to the Yamoussoukro Decision.

Yet another example one could cite to clarify the current weak results of regional integration is the African politicking that undermined the early take off of the Eastern African Submarine Cable System (EASSy) broad band telecommunications project. It is common knowledge that one of the reasons why Africa is excluded from the benefits of globalization is Africa's lack of state of the art and dynamic ICT infrastructure. It is high-bandwidth telecom systems that improve and enhance connectivity. They lower the huge costs of access to internet and thus the immense costs of business transactions. The EASSy project was conceived in December 2003 by several countries in Eastern and Southern Africa to address the serious deficit in the field of ICT network infrastructure. Thereafter, divisions and conflicts arose between interests of business and governments with damaging consequences on time effectiveness of project implementation. Thankfully, the project now appears to be taking off involving some 21 countries at a total cost of US $ 336 million. We have to keep our fingers crossed!

Yet there is the additional challenge, namely the broad accessibility of this broad band telecommunication facility. How does improved internet connectivity work in an environment of serious power deficit and unreliability, ranging all the way from South Africa to East Africa? And, in turn, it is questionable whether the current educational system, in many of the beneficiary countries, adequately empowers our young citizens to maximize the benefits that potentially accrue from improved ICT accessibility? It could thus be asked: how does regional integration bolster such empowerment? How far has science and technology education been taken up as an African regional integration issue?

The answer is that some start is being hatched particularly through the Nelson Mandela African Institute of Science and Technology. This institute will have four campuses in Sub-Saharan Africa, one each in the north, the west, east and south. The aim of the Institute is to foster economic growth and promotion of excellence in science and engineering and their applications in Sub-Saharan Africa. The first such campus, to be based in Nigeria, will open its doors to students in September this year. Much more needs to be done.

Thirdly, there is the fundamental challenge of serious absence of a liberal financial market mindset. The African financial market sector continues to suffer from a psychological inhibition by policy makers of capital account liberalization ostensibly because it drives capital flight. In this policy area, most of Africa remains prisoner to the IMF conventional wisdom. But then how can you have effective regional economic integration where you have closed capital markets in an environment of low levels of FDI, portfolio capital flows and domestic savings? In debunking the IMF conventional wisdom on this issue, MIT Professor Lester C. Thurow, in his book, *Creating Wealth*,[49] explains that, in spite of prohibiting free currency movement, China, for example, lost over US $ 60 billion in 1998 in currency

---

[49] See THUROW, Lester C., *Creating Wealth: The New Rules for Individuals, Companies and Countries in a Knowledge-Based Economy*, Boston and London: Nicholas Brealey Publishing, 1999 at p 30.

reserves. This is a year after the Asian financial crisis and China thought that it could completely shield itself from the contagion.

Thurow surmises, "exporters just didn't bring their earnings back to China." Put differently, you cannot, as a government, stop currency movements anyway. My view is that without a fundamental policy mindset shift in this area, Africa would not successfully exploit the benefits of regional integration to bolster meaningful change in development. Financial market liberalization crucially instils confidence in investors and bolsters a savings mindset in the people.

This policy mindset goes beyond mundane issues such as the recent disenfranchisement of Tanzanians from participating in the Kenya- based Safaricom IPO. It actually takes a more critical dimension when we focus, for example, on the current global food crisis, whose apparent causes range from climate change, technology deficits in the agricultural sector to the ethanol or bio-fuel issue. The question about how Africa would respond to this crisis goes to the heart of the poverty reduction agenda. A key question here is: Can and how does regional integration, by and in itself, help to address the food security question?

Undoubtedly, food security is defined in regional terms in Africa. Thus there is the Comprehensive Africa Agricultural Development Programme (CAADP) under the AU/NEPAD Initiative that is focused on accelerating growth, eliminate poverty and hunger among African countries. However, the focus of CAADP is predominantly on upgrading the physical and institutional infrastructure that supports Africa's agriculture. The programme is thus heavily dependent on national efforts to promote agriculture, notably the pursuit of a 6% average annual sector growth rate and the allocation of minimum 10% of national budget to the agriculture sector. As such, how can a regional initiative like CAADP succeed where national governments do not pursue agriculture-led growth strategies?

And here lies the challenge. Many African governments have so far given agriculture development lip service. This is why food insecurity remains precarious. There is very little that regional integration could do to eliminate such insecurity where nation state governments fail to adopt the right policies to promote agriculture development.

At the end of March and early April this year, the UN Economic Commission for Africa presented a seminal report to African Ministers of Finance and Economy that outlines the critical determinants for Africa to fair well in the 21st Century. Four determinants have been outlined: First, the acceleration of growth and employment. The report observes that the poor structural transformation of African economies is the main cause of lacklustre growth and jobs creation. The report in fact posits that current growth rates in Africa have failed to generate employment and significantly reduce poverty. In the context of current and continuing high food and energy prices, Africa will need to spur a more robust growth.

The second determinant is Africa's response to climate change. The ECA report postulates that there is adequate evidence to show that climate change will have serious adverse impact on the realization of the MDGs. African economies are particularly vulnerable to environmental changes, notably climate change. This is in part because of its geographical location in the warm tropics; but largely because Africa's key sectors like agriculture, fisheries, forestry and tourism are climate sensitive. Climate change is also affecting water levels, underground, on lakes and wet lands. But it is also giving rise to epidemics like malaria and diseases resulting from shortage of potable water and poor sanitation. Because of declining arable land and water sources, Africa may find itself facing new insecurities driven by conflicts over natural resources as people migrate in search of better habitat.

The third determinant is how to cope with emerging and intensifying social challenges. These fall under two areas: one, is how to address the legal empowerment of the poor. The ECA report argues that African governments will have to move beyond addressing poverty through economic and social policies to giving power to the people through legal means, for example, over ownership of land and other properties and assets. The argument falls in line with Hernando de Soto's thesis of the mystery of capital.[50] The unveiling of the mystery rests significantly on capitalizing the citizens by addressing the various encumbrances that throttle their enterprise. The second area is long-term financing of HIV and AIDS treatment. According to UNAIDS, more than 22.5 million people in Africa live with HIV; 1.7 million more were expected to be infected in 2007. The economic impact of the pandemic is calculated to be around 1.0 to 1.5 % of GDP growth in the medium term. In simple terms, African countries will experience reduced human capital and savings, leading, in turn, to lower investments and lower productivity.

The fourth and final challenge centres on consolidating and improving systems of governance and creating capable states. It is argued that the enabling factors for the private sector to play its expected role as the engine of development and for the civil society to flourish as a pillar of the democratic system and process, it is critical that good governance is accelerated and that the state is made to discharge its legitimate functions mindful of the rule of law, transparency of decisions and eradicating corruption. Of special importance is the performance of the state in the delivery of its core responsibility and services to the people. It is noted that

---

[50] DE SOTO, Hernando, *The Mystery of Capital: Why Capitalism Triumphs in the West and Fails Everywhere Else*, New York; Basic Books, 2000.

without a capable state, it would not be possible to effectively confront and overcome Africa's 21st Century challenges.

What puzzled me from the ECA report is the weak acknowledgement of or linkage with the role of African integration on the way forward in addressing the challenges the report so well outlines. Indeed, the report asserts, "the high level of commitment of African leaders to grow their economies and to improve the human condition of their people, coupled with firm support from Africa's development partners provide unique opportunity for bold action in the continent to address these challenges."

In fairness though, under sections where the report poses questions for discussion as part of the way forward, on all the four challenges, there is only one odd question under growth and employment that asks: How can regional and continental integration "contribute" to tackling the growth and employment challenge? Under climate change, the question is: "Is there a need to create new regional facilities for financing climate change interventions? How can the efficiency of existing facilities be improved"? The remaining two challenges have no African integration perspective in terms of roles. This position reinforces my point that African integration is yet to find a firm and overarching place and commitment in the search for effective solutions to Africa's social, political and economic challenges. At the heart of this shortcoming is the continuing mindset that champions national sovereignty and eschews integration because of a zero –sum mindset.

Zero Sum Game and Sovereignty Mindsets

Many of the challenges I have outlined which dampen the cause of regional integration flow, in my view, from predominantly the sovereignty issue which crucially informs the mindset of the majority of ordinary citizens and of the African state itself. As Yale Historian, Professor, Paul Kennedy aptly notes in his magisterial work, *Preparing for the Twenty First Century,*[51] the nation- state remains the primary locus of identity of most citizens. The people "still turn instinctively to their own governments in search of solutions". Thus the nation state remains, at its core, "the key unit in responding to global change" even at a time when the traditional instruments of the state are weakening in the light of the social and economic dynamics of the global economic order. Part of the reason for such negative mindset could be that regional integration is yet to show concrete benefits to the citizens *vis a vis* what they perceive to be substantial surrender of sovereignty, a rather moot issue.

---

[51] KENNEDY, Paul, *Preparing for the Twenty-First Century*, New York: Vintage Books, 1994.

But what is particularly disconcerting is that, in spite of most African countries pursuing open economy and export-oriented growth and development policies and strategies, which would, in theory, manifest a more positive outlook on and approach to regional integration, the nation-state- focused organizational paradigm still fuels a mercantilist view of regional trade as a zero-sum game. As a result, deeper integration is stifled. Indeed, one of the main reasons why regional economic communities have failed to realize greater effectiveness in propelling faster and deeper integration is precisely the lack of supranational decision making authority which partner states of RECs refuse to partly surrender or cede mainly because of this zero-sum game attitude.

Viewed more broadly, national policy choices in Africa remain the critical determinants of the extent to which regional economic integration unfolds. The ECA report earlier referred to has reinforced this position. Open regionalism remains largely an anathema. Part of the reason for the existence of such environment is that economic liberalization itself, which has catapulted the rapid and dramatic transformation of the national structure of production, has given rise to social dislocations at national levels. In turn, this has fuelled not only social resistance at the level of the ordinary people, but also to overly protectionist attitudes in the domestic business constituency.

Harvard Professor, Robert Reich, in an article, "The Nationalism We Need," published in the *American Prospect Magazine* in November 2002, contextually wrote:

> A healthy dose of positive nationalism can ease (these) sorts of anxieties by softening the burdens of economic change. When they feel especially connected to their compatriots, citizens who gain from change are more willing to support the kinds of strong safety nets, employment programs, and educational systems that help ease the burden on those who otherwise would fall far behind. And the generosity of the winners in turn allows the nation as a whole to better contend with the consequences of free trade, open capital markets, and more liberal immigration. But failure to choose positive nationalism almost surely promotes its negative twin because the losers are left vulnerable.

Nations now busily shredding their safety nets and slashing their social spending may believe they're moving toward free markets, and in a narrow economic sense, they are. But in the process, they risk breaking the bonds of positive nationalism and exposing their people to the very fears and uncertainties upon which negative nationalism feeds. The inadvertent consequence may be a backlash against not only free markets but also political freedom." Robert Reich could also have added, "backlash against regional integration."[52]

African regional integration mechanisms, even where they have achieved deep integration in the form of having Customs Unions and, in the specific case of the East African Community, even when moving towards the establishment of a Common Market and a Monetary Union, there are no development funds of the type that exist in the European Union set aside specifically to provide compensatory support for revenue losing members; for supporting infrastructure development in lesser endowed economies and for enhancing social cohesion. Such funds are important in dampening zero-sum attitudes because they create a hopeful win-win environment. This is one area that developed countries could step in and help. Unfortunately, the record of development assistance is horrid.

In this context, where there is a lukewarm disposition to regional integration, it could not come as a surprise that the case for African *political* integration should now emerge with such a force. The case clearly comes at a time when there is an entrenching fatigue and depression over the quick non-realization of an envisioned deep economic integration. In this context, a leading African intellectual mind, Professor Adebayo Adedeji, in a paper delivered to the African Development Forum in Addis Ababa in March 2002, argued that:

> the economism of regional cooperation (in Africa) is principally responsible for the low progress made during the past 40 years. By focusing virtually exclusively on economic cooperation and integration while making the heroic, ceteris paribus, assumption as far as political and social factors are concerned, has contributed significantly to the lack of progress in the actualization of the vision.[53]

However, in response, it could be argued that the grand debate about the formation of an African continental government is in fact obiter; a side issue. Indeed, the debate could even be begging the very question about the present unsatisfactory state of economic integration. Surely, if Africa is unenthusiastic about ceding part sovereignty on economic issues, how could it partly cede the more sensitive one, namely *political* sovereignty?

Related to this argument, is the often presented criticism about the multiplicity of African regional economic communities. It is argued that the balkanization manifested in the overlapping memberships of countries in

---

[52] Ibid.

[53] See the paper titled "History and Prospects for Regional Integration in Africa" presented at the Third Meeting of the African Development Forum Addis Ababa, Ethiopia, 5th March, 2002.

several RECs hampers regional integration. Even the European Union buys the idea, paradoxically when it is a guilty party, overtly or otherwise, in balkanizing Africa over the negotiations of the Economic Partnership Agreements. On this question of multiplicity of memberships, my view is that the arguments put forward, like those proposing the formation of a United States of Africa totally miss the point, namely that the African nation state remains the centre of development policy making and national social and economic direction. This is the reality and the future of Africa through regional integration must accept it. It is a condition that should be addressed objectively and not simply front loaded with political passions about Pan Africanism and the African Renaissance. It is a fallacy to attempt to build more robustly continental and even regional integration on the basis of weak economic foundations. Strong national economies are the critical building blocks of strong regional integration. Without it, you will continue to face zero-sum game attitudes that undermine regional integration.

Jeffrey Sachs deals with this issue of the imperativeness of strong national economies when he discusses in his book, *Common Wealth*,[54] the four hurdles that Africa must tackle if it is to become an emerging market economy. The hurdles are: First, achieving adequate domestic savings; second, creating a competitive export sector that earns foreign exchange required to pay for imported technology; third, achieving a financially strong government able to finance infrastructure (roads, power, hospitals etc); and fourth, ability to adapt international technologies to local ecological conditions and needs. Today, the ethos of regional integration in Africa is weak precisely because these hurdles are yet to be well addressed.

So yes, as the February 2008 Report of the Independent High Level Panel to the African Development Group,[55] co-chaired by former Mozambican President Joachim Chissano and former Canadian Prime Minister, Paul Martin and which included Nobel Laureate for economics, Professor Joseph Stiglitz, has observed, Africa, without regional integration, will remain disjointed. The report pointedly notes that underpinning integration are "capable states, offering good and accountable governance." And of course, capable states are those that pursue the right policies that bolster national economic growth, create jobs and sustain prudent governance.

In sum, we revert to the question: is there a promising future for Africa through regional integration? In my view, regional integration remains a key driver for the realization of a peaceful, stable and prosperous Africa. However, it is essential that African national economies, are, in the first place, transformed into more vibrant and robust economies to engender in

---

[54] See SACHS, Jeffrey, *Common Wealth: Economics for a Crowded Planet*, op. cit.,

[55] See AFRICAN DEVELOPMENT BANK, *High-level Panel Issues Report on Prospects for African Development Bank*, Tunis: ADB, 2008.

them the much needed confidence to venture out more aggressively at regional economic levels. I know that some critics will say that regionalism creates the conditions for bolstering national economic growth. The argument about larger markets, for instance, is a powerful one. But I do not share such a view though there are cases where, as in infrastructure development, regional integration can actually provide the critical mass for attracting funding and investments and thus constitute a critical factor in bolstering development at national levels. However, larger markets need right products to sell. And we have seen that the current record of intra-African trade is not as yet promising not simply for lack of good infrastructure but more importantly for low levels of industrialisation.

In fact, a respected Tanzanian economist, Delphin Rwegasira, has powerfully argued in a paper titled, "Key Issues in African Development in the 21st Century" delivered in October, 1998,[56] that the experience of ASEAN countries is that nation-states in that region have been able to attain high economic growth rates without a very formal institutional support for regional integration. In the past decade since Rwegasira's delivery of his paper, ASEAN countries have further reinforced this economic philosophy. Rwegasira's conclusion is that the political economy implication of the ASEAN experience is that governments at national levels have the strategic role to play in shaping pro-investment and pro-poor policies and in building the critical human and institutional capacities necessary to manage powerful development responses in the context of globalization.

I support this view. Take the case of food security as an example. Food capita in Sub-Saharan Africa has declined by 3% between 1990 and 2006. Compare this with Asia where there has been an increase of 30% in the same period. The comparable figure in Latin America is 20%. Now, at a time when global food prices have gone over the roof, what future can there be for a continent like Africa? Yet, there is no reason in the world why a rich and arable land- endowed country like Tanzania cannot transform its agriculture and make the country not only sufficient in food but a net exporter of food and cash-based agricultural crops as well. As Rwegasira points out, better policies to promote stronger agricultural growth not only lead to general economic improvements arising from trade but also create possibilities of diversification within agriculture. Tanzania has the best opportunity to attract investments for adding value to its agricultural commodity sector through agro-processing. But it must clearly clarify its policies in this sector.

My contention is that unless the zero-sum game mindset that rules at national levels in Africa is whittled away, *ab initio*, through the pursuit of

---

[56] See RWEGASIRA, Delphin G., "Key Issues in African Development in the 21st Century," a paper presented at the Public Forum on African Development in the 21st Century, United Nations University Headquarters, Tokyo, Japan on 16th October, 1998. The author was then Executive Director, African Economic Research Consortium based in Nairobi, Kenya.

development policies and strategies that effectively transform the national economies into more vibrant and robust ones, regional integration could face an uncertain future.

Conclusion

The overarching economic paradigm in Africa in the next few decades centres on deepening broad-based national economic growth that effectively addresses and reverses poverty levels and improves the living standards of the people. Policies that bolster savings and investments and generally enhance total factor productivity in sectors such as agriculture and manufacturing industry are very much national. Export-led growth would only thrive in an environment where these economic and structural transformations take effect. The potential that regional integration presents, on the other hand, in raising the rate of investment, especially FDI and portfolio investment flows at national levels, in creating larger markets that spur market growth and competition and thus efficiency and which catalyse critical knowledge sharing in key technology fields such as ICT, is clearly immense and should be exploited. Moreover, co-ordination and pooling of resources to develop infrastructures with cross border economic spill over as well as investment in developing and protecting shared natural resources such as the Lake Victoria and its basin would have positive impacts on economic growth of the cooperating countries and in addressing poverty.

However, for regional integration to enable a brighter future for Africa to emerge, it would have to be supported by a more positive policy mindset at national levels. In particular, regional institutions mandated to oversee and coordinate the development of regional programmes and projects will have to be given greater decision making powers than presently if regional integration is to become more effective and responsive to the challenges confronting Africa in the 21st Century. The most revered management guru, the late Peter F. Drucker, wrote in one of his best books, *The New Realities*[57] that "traditional politics differed over ends. The new realities largely impose the ends." The world of ideological differences, political and economic, is passé. In the new globalization era, global political and economic realities virtually impose the ends. These ends are normative; they have become largely shared core values. And we may shout and kick about them but to what result, even when, as Africans, we choose to be more inward looking in addressing the challenges we face.

In the next chapter, I turn to reviewing the context of the EAC integration process within the overall vision of the Abuja Treaty that set out the

---

[57] See DRUCKER, Peter F., 1989: *The New Realities: in Government and Politics, in Economy and Business, in Society and in World View*, New York: A Mandarin Paperback, 1989, at p. 105.

continental ambition of establishing the African Economic Community. As it will become evident, some regional economic communities like the EAC are far ahead in moving towards promoting the fundamentals for constructing an African-wide economic community. And maybe because of this kind of performance, I notice some disillusionment in many regional economic communities about the expected role and dynamism of the African Union. Of course, to describe the AU as irrelevant would be to go too far. However, the AU has to more clearly justify and legitimate itself beyond being an expensive huge bureaucracy that is disconnected from where real integration actions are taking place and tangible results realized in the overall objective of integrating the African economies.

CHAPTER TWO

African Economic Community and EAC Vision[58]

When I received the invitation to address you on this topic, my understanding was that the framers of the topic were focusing on the Abuja Treaty for the establishment of the African Economic Community (AEC). I hope I am right, for it is on this understanding that I am going to make my presentation.

In my presentation, I will briefly discuss the Abuja Treaty and its vision for the African Economic Community, without going deeper into the history of Africa's integration that led to this Treaty. My presentation would be too extensive were I to do so. I will then bring in the East African Community (EAC) into context; it being one of the Regional Economic Communities (RECs) supposed to play the role of building blocks towards the realization of the African Economic Community. I will do so by briefly tracing how the EAC has contributed to charting out the path towards the realization of the Abuja Treaty vision. While addressing the challenges faced on this front, I will also highlight some of the measures being taken to address the challenges.

Let me therefore start by acknowledging that the topic "Harmonization of EAC Vision: towards the actualization of the Abuja Treaty and the challenges faced" is of significant importance. This is particularly so given the fast evolving and what, paradoxically, is increasingly becoming an interdependent world economic and social system. I am making reference here to globalization and how poor countries are becoming more and more marginalized. Pooling of scarce resources and uniting all other efforts, political and economic, around a common continental and regional vision and mission, have inevitably become the central mantra and thrusts in mastering globalization. Interestingly, this strategy, of collective pursuit of more meaningful development through integration systems, is not limited to developing countries. On the contrary, rich countries, for over fifty years now, have also undertaken similar measures. Regional integration is thus the new paradigm that is defining and, indeed, influencing regional and global economic relations. Put differently, it is becoming ever clearer that no country in the world, however economically powerful, would, today or indeed in the future, prosper, let alone survive, while acting alone.

---

[58] Speech to the National Defence College, Karen, Nairobi, Kenya, 7th August, 2008.

EAC Treaty and the African Economic Community

With its genesis in the Pan Africanist movement of the late 40's and the 50's, the drive for African integration peaked with the establishment of the Organization of African Unity in 1963. Since then, African leaders have articulated an ambitious vision of an African integrated economy that translated into the quest for an African Economic Community. The Treaty for the establishment of the African Economic Community, which is popularly known as the Abuja Treaty, was signed on 3rd June, 1991 by the OAU Heads of State and Government. Its pinnacle was its ratification in 1994. It was a revised document of some sort, in that it succeeded the Lagos Plan of Action (LPA), adopted in 1980, which had aimed to establish a Pan-African Common Market by the year 2000.[59]

Vision for the African Economic Community

The Abuja Treaty envisaged the establishment of an AEC by the year 2025. It envisions an African Economic Community attained through promoting economic, social and cultural development as well as economic integration. To realize this, the Treaty earmarks, among others, trade liberalization and the establishment of customs unions. Its objective is the creation of a framework for promoting cooperation for development through mobilization of human and material resources in the 53 countries of Africa that are joined in the membership of the African Union.

Article 6 of the Abuja Treaty envisages attaining the AEC through six stages, lasting a period of 34 years from the date it was signed. Article 6(5) actually goes further to stipulate that the cumulative transitional period should not exceed 40 years from its date of entry into force. Effectively, this means from 1994, the year when the requisite number for its ratification was attained. What route does the Abuja Treaty propose?

Stages of the AEC integration

*   Stage 1: 1994-1999 (5 years): strengthening existing Regional Economic Communities (RECs) and creation of others where needed;

*   Stage 2: 1999- 2007 (8 years): stabilization of tariff and nontariff barriers; strengthening of sectoral integration (trade, agriculture,

---

[59] On this plan see ADEDEJI, Adebayo, "From Lagos Plan of Action to the New Partnership for African Development and from the Final Act of Lagos to the Constitutive Act: Wither Africa?" in IMUNDE, Lawford (eds.) *The Role of the Educated Class in Africa – Between African Renaissance and Globalisation Critique*, Loccum, Germany: Evangelischen Akademie Loccum, 2003, p. 97.

finance, transport, communication etc.) and coordination and harmonization of activities among the RECs;

- Stage 3: 2007-2017 (10 years): establishment of free-trade zones and customs unions at the REC levels;

- Stage 4: 2017-2019 (2 years): coordination and harmonization of tariff and non-tariff barriers among regional economic communities towards the establishment of a continent-wide customs union;

- Stage 5: 2019-2023 (4 years): establishment of an African common market (free movement of people, capital and services);

- Stage 6: 2023-2028 (5 years): integration of all sectors towards the creation of the AEC through consolidation of the African common market, the creation of an African Monetary Union and the establishment of a Pan-African Parliament.

What is Africa's Balance Sheet on Regional Integration?

Regrettably, the story of African regional integration, to-date, is predominantly a sad one. In my view, it is simply not enough for Africa to be merely passionate about cooperation and integration and to romanticize African renaissance. To be meaningful and supported by the people, integration has to deliver concrete results that reflect real improvements in the quality of life of Africans. It is important, therefore, that serious questions are asked about the state of African integration: Are African nation-states showing adequate seriousness on and commitment to the integration agenda? What strategies are being put in place to make integration deliver concrete results that reflect real improvements in the quality of life of Africans? How can progress in integration be benchmarked and its impact assessed more effectively? How far have the Regional Economic Communities reached in playing their role as building blocks for the African Economic Community?

How concretely can the gap between integration, as seen at level of the RECs, and integration as envisaged in the Abuja Treaty be bridged? These are some of the questions that should inform a more robust discourse among the African elite and civil society today. Clearly, some of these questions go beyond the subject before us here. Suffice to state that in the ensuing parts of this presentation, I will attempt a contribution to this discourse by contextualizing the specific experience of the East African Community.

The EAC Perspective

The EAC is the regional intergovernmental organization of the Republics of Kenya, Uganda, the United Republic of Tanzania, the Republic of Burundi and the Republic of Rwanda, the latter two having joined the Community in July, 2007. The Treaty for the establishment of the EAC was signed on 30th November, 1999, and entered into force on 7th July, 2000, following its ratification by the Partner States at the time.

The Vision of the EAC: The Treaty for the Establishment of the EAC sets out a bold vision for the eventual unification of the EAC Partner States: "a prosperous, competitive, secure, stable and politically united East Africa."

The Objectives of the EAC: The objectives of the EAC are guided by its mission, which is to widen and deepen economic, political, social and cultural integration in order to improve the quality of life of the people of East Africa through increased competitiveness, value added production, trade and investment for mutual benefit.

It is also important, in the context of the Abuja Treaty and the African Union Constitutive Act, to underline that, in its Preamble, the Treaty for the Establishment of the East African Community boldly embraces the objective to "maintain and enhance the economic stability, foster close and peaceful relations among African States and accelerate the successive stages in the realization of the proposed African Economic Community and Political Union."

The Stages of EAC Integration Process

Thus, much like the Abuja Treaty for the establishment of the African Economic Community, the Treaty establishing the East African Community also provides for stages of implementation of its regional integration agenda. The stages are:

- Customs Union as the entry point,
- Common Market;
- Monetary Union; and ultimately
- Political Federation of the East African States.

The EAC Integration and Spirit of Abuja Treaty

Before addressing the various EAC activities that fit the Abuja Treaty, it is vital to ask ourselves at least three questions:

The first question is: Was the Abuja Treaty the basis for the establishment of the EAC? As I have just mentioned, I do not intend to dig into the history behind the establishment of the EAC. Suffice to mention, however, that the EAC's history is much longer and predates the Abuja Treaty. This is considering that as far back as the 1920s, Kenya, Tanzania and Uganda united to form a free trade area, which by 1927 had mutated into a customs union, developing into the East African Community by the 1967 Treaty for East African Cooperation. Examples of the East African Railways, East African Airways, East African Posts and Telecommunications, East African Examinations Board, are known to you all. However, this first attempt at integration could not gain consolidation stage, leading to the collapse of the first East African Community in 1977.

There is also no evidence that directly links the revival of the EAC to the Abuja Treaty. It is therefore safer to say that the EAC's desire and justification for integration had apparently not died with the collapse of the first EAC and that this desire prompted the birth of the new EAC. However, if you really think there should be a link of the two, then one could conjecture that EAC's revival came at the time when the thirst and wave for economic integration was sweeping across the continent after the realization that individual state efforts were no longer adequate in addressing and mustering contemporary challenges of globalization.

The second question is: What safeguards does the EAC now have in place to avoid a tragic repeat of 1977?

The Treaty establishing the new EAC encapsulates the plug-ins that address the pit-falls that should be avoided. Thus Article 7 (a) of the Treaty provides that the Community shall be governed on the basis of the principles of "people-centeredness" and "market driven cooperation". This means that the overarching underpinning of EAC's objectives is ownership by the people, not by the political leadership which comes and goes.

The final question is: Why does the Abuja Treaty make explicit recognition of RECs as the building blocks of the AEC?

First of all, we have to clearly understand that economic integration mainly relates to integrating economic activities for purposes of promoting economic development. Yet regional integration involves a deeper meaning. It presumes the pooling of resources by participating states with the implied conceding of part of their "sovereignty" over economic matters to a supra-national entity. Underlying the regional integration model are goals to exploit geographic contiguity benefits as well as benefits arising from economic, socio-ethnic and cultural homogeneity. In this sense, regional integration takes into account a multiplicity of factors that support integration of countries. It importantly involves the establishment of institutional mechanisms that reflect a degree of shared sovereignty. It also demands addressing the concerns of multi-stakeholders: people who stand to benefit from it; those mostly affected by it, and those that consider themselves as likely to lose from it. In other words, it is a model that is broader than mere economic integration.

The framers of the Abuja Treaty hoped that once a cumulative consensus among actors at the national and regional levels had been reached through regional integration, it would become easier to explore and galvanize support for economic integration at the continental level. Therefore, yes, because RECs are closer to the grassroots and, moreover, because of their historical, ethno-cultural, economic and social homogeneities, they constitute the more realistic building blocks for the realization of the broader African Economic Community.

Secondly, one must consider the critical factors that underpin any integration. There are four key factors that are not necessarily symbiotic: first, the quest for power and influence; second, the quest to minimize threats that face the sovereignty of states; third, the anticipated costs and benefits of integration, and finally, the commitment attached to the relationship of states. Given the heterogeneous nature of these factors at the continental level in contrast to those at regional levels, it would seem plausible that forging practical alliances at the level of RECs is the more logical direction to take at the on-set of integration. In this vein, the Abuja Treaty realistically calls upon RECs to coordinate, harmonize and progressively integrate their activities in pursuit of the continental Economic Community.

It is in the context of this strategic role of RECs as building blocks for attaining the AEC, that a Protocol on Relations between the AEC and the RECs was concluded and signed in February 1998. That Protocol provides a framework within which the RECs, at the horizontal level, would work together on matters of harmonization and coordination in various areas. But the Protocol also spells out the vertical relationships between the RECs and the African Union in implementing the Abuja Treaty. This vertical relationship has now been given a shot in the arm through the conclusion of another Protocol early this year that spells out more effective mechanisms of co-ordination and reporting relationships between the AU Commission and the RECs.

Following the foregoing clarifications, allow me now to address the specific initiatives that the EAC is pursuing and implementing within the overall objectives of the Abuja Treaty.

EAC initiatives that fit AEC Objectives

A closer look at the Abuja Treaty brings out a State-centric approach to matters of integration and growth. In contrast, the EAC integration agenda is people-centred. In this regard, whilst Article 7(1) (a) of the EAC Treaty clearly stipulates that the Community shall be governed on the principle of people-centeredness and market-driven cooperation, the Abuja Treaty's preamble on the other hand calls on all concerned to be "mindful of the principles of international law governing relations between the States". This preamble raises the issue of sovereignty, or, put differently, the centrality of integration through decisions of the political leadership. It is because of such disconnect in the way in which decisions are taken at REC *vis a vis* AU level that we find some RECs are making faster headway in the integration process than as envisaged in the Abuja Treaty.

Indeed, an examination of EAC's institutional development and implementation of projects and programmes reveals that the Community is not only moving at a relatively much faster pace than other RECs but is also way ahead of Abuja Treaty's timelines for realization of integration measures. Let us examine a number of examples:

- **Regulatory frameworks in the EAC in support of the realization of the AEC**

A Customs Union was launched in January 2005 and its full operationalisation is expected in January 2010. The Abuja Treaty envisages the attaining of this stage at individual REC level (under Stage 3) by the year 2017. Therefore, judged on the basis of the Abuja Treaty timelines, the EAC is not only on track but is also far ahead.

Within a regional context, the EAC Partner States have put in place regulatory frameworks that support a regional long-term win-win situation in the development arena. For example, with the establishment of Investment Authorities and the enacting of related supportive laws, the EAC is witnessing vibrant greenfield investments and cross-border mergers and acquisitions. Examples include: Alam, Madhvani and Mukwano Groups of Uganda; Azam and Shellys Pharmaceuticals of Tanzania; East African Cables, East African Breweries, Bidco, Kenya Commercial Bank, Equity Ban, Sameer Group, Kenya Airways and Chandaria Group, all of Kenya.

The Common Market is another area in the EAC integration process that lays a firm foundation for the AEC. Negotiations were launched in January 2008 and are on-going, with a view to launching the EA Common Market by 2010. For the EAC border communities, given their history, the promotion of free movement of persons across the borders is tantamount to the sheer legal recognition of what is their everyday reality. This development is not to underestimate the fears that have been expressed in various fora and therefore the need for extensive negotiations on the common market's form and content. It is hoped that by the time the African Common Market is launched, during the period 2019-2023, going by the Abuja Treaty timelines, the EA Common Market would have been a grandfather.

With respect to the **Monetary Union,** it would be noted that there are fiscal and monetary policies that are being examined with a view to forging regional macro-economic convergences. Already achievements have been made in the areas of currency convertibility, liberalization of the capital account, and opening up of financial and capital markets. The EAC Governors of the Central Banks are on the march towards creating the necessary conditions for the establishment of a common currency in 2012. It can therefore be said that the foundation for the East African Monetary Union is way ahead of what the Abuja Treaty envisages since its plans for an African Monetary Union are set for the period 2023-2028.

There are also other integration measures being undertaken in various sectors aimed at identifying complementary policies with potential for promoting greater trade, including pinpointing those areas where there are opportunities to be exploited. Of particular importance is the ongoing development of the EAC Investment and Industrial Strategy, which should yield multiplier benefits.

- **Institutional Measures Supporting the Realization of the AEC**

The EAC has put in place institutional structures for ensuring effective and successful integration within the spirit of achieving the AEC. One can offer the following examples:

- Establishment of Ministries responsible for EAC Affairs in the Partner States. The Ministers are able to directly articulate the goal of integration both at the level of their national Parliaments and in the Cabinet meetings. They then have the opportunity to be a bridge between the Partner States and the EAC. Through this framework, the Ministries are expected to ensure that national policies related to regional development are cast in a regional perspective. This is a unique feature not replicated in any other REC in Africa. It's most important attribute is that through National Parliaments, the Ministers responsible for EAC Affairs are able to reach out to the broader national citizenry on EAC matters. Indeed, the people-centredness objective enshrined in the Treaty establishing the EAC is better assured through this process.

- Institutionalised consultations of Ministers responsible for Finance on matters relating to the EAC Customs Union and how the Union can be reinforced with the Annual Budgets read on the same day in all the EAC Partner States.

- Consultations amongst the Partner States' Governors of Central Banks on how to move towards the Monetary Union.

- Working with the East African Business Council, an apex body of business associations in East Africa in order to place the private and business sector at the heart of the integration agenda.

- Harmonization and coordination of policies and activities of Institutions like the Inter University Council for East Africa, Lake Victoria Basin Commission, Civil Aviation Safety and Security Oversight Agency, Lake Victoria Fisheries Organisation etc. Other areas include developing policies and programmes in science and technology, health, defence, peace and security, foreign policy, capital markets, social security, development of Kiswahili as the lingua franca, etc.

These measures are not an exhaustive inventory of what is being done. I am simply pointing out some of the more salient features of EAC's work that is linked to the objectives of the Abuja Treaty.

- **Structural Measures Supporting the Realization of the AEC**

In its integration agenda, the EAC is guided by the understanding that infrastructure projects should be embarked on jointly in the regional context in order to bolster production activities and lower production and transaction costs. Let me mention a few projects that fit into this framework: the EAC Power Master Plan, the EAC Railways Master Plan, and the EAC Roads Master Plan. The potential contribution of these programmes towards the realization of the AEC is evident.

- **Intra-Regional Co-ordinating Frameworks**

The EAC is also engaged in a tripartite mechanism with the COMESA and the SADC, which is now being elevated to the level of the Summit of Heads of State and Government of the countries in those RECs. This development is a manifestation that the EAC is not satisfied with balkanized integration but is prepared to embrace wider cooperation in development. It shows willingness to integrate beyond the confines of the EAC borders. It is above all a direction that fits in well the objectives of the AEC.

- **The AU Protocol on Relations with RECs**

The EAC is also implementing the AU Protocol on Relations with RECs, signed in Addis Ababa on 1st February, 2008, which provides for the mechanisms within which horizontal and vertical RECs-African Union matters related to continental integration can best be pursued. What I have just explained about the SADC-COMESA-EAC Task Force and Summit evidences our implementation of this Protocol.

Challenges in Realising the African Economic Community

The EAC prides itself for being the most successful REC in Africa. We are probably right because even the WTO and the European Union hold a similar view. However, the institution is also cognizant of a number of challenges that confront it in its goal of realizing a more vibrant and robust economic and politically united community and to respond to the objectives of the Abuja Treaty. I will now examine some of these challenges:

First of all, the Institutional Challenges

It is a fallacy for one to simply wish regional integration into existence. The need to address internal governance challenges lies at the core of whatever efforts deployed to promote the integration agenda, whether at the national, regional or continental levels. The regulatory provisions that have been developed and adopted in virtually all the countries are of no consequence if the implementation thereof is not vigorously pursued. At the EAC level, a framework on good governance that covers the three pillars: human rights, democracy and electoral practices, and anti-corruption, ethics and integrity is now being developed. It is based on the recognition that there is no integration process that will sustainably work, be it at the regional or continental level, if the tenets of good governance are not institutionally upheld, wholly embraced and indiscriminately practiced.

Second, the Financial Challenges

There are two sub-challenges involved. The first sub-challenge relates to Partner States' contributions towards funding the integration process. The primary purpose of any integration is to unite markets, human, natural and capital resources for development. This objective comes at a cost, the payment of which EAC Partner States have pledged to contribute annually. However, these contributions which are of an equal nature for all the Partner States are never adequate to meet the needs for realizing deeper integration. Moreover, it is evident that the smaller economies of Rwanda and Burundi are over burdened by the size of the contributions.

Second, is the challenge of over-reliance on foreign aid. Aid for Trade promotes growth when well applied. But there is negative aid that perpetuates dependence. Evidence abound from various Summits of Heads of State and Government and other high level fora that conditions are ripe for increased dialogue between development partners and African institutions in the pursuit of shared objectives and strategies. Yet this thrust also presents two challenges. One, the individual governments and RECs need to adjust their policy frameworks to promote trade oriented production. Two, adjusting such policies calls for deliberate pursuit of economic cooperation and integration programmes. In the EAC, a framework has been developed in the name of a Partnership Fund whereby funds from development partners are put in a common basket from where their use is centrally planned based on EAC's identified priorities. It is a framework that presents an example of how best development assistance can be channelled and managed to assure both harmonization and co-ordination of aid, pursuant to the 2005 Paris Declaration on Aid Effectiveness and a demand driven development programme.

Third: The Challenge of Inter-state Commitment to Regional Integration

It is observed that regional integration continues to suffer as a consequence of continuing zero sum game positions taken by the partner states. Regional interests are still subordinated to national interests. Because of the decision making structures that are based on consensus, the drive to integration is constantly undermined by national interests that sometime view deeper integration in the prism of a win-lose paradigm.

Another challenge, the fourth one, relates to the Principle of "Subsidiarity" especially as it relates to projects implementation. Essentially, subsidiarity vests the responsibility for execution of planned projects on the Partner States unless there are justifiable reasons that dictate otherwise. In this context, project implementation suffers because of varying systems applicable at national levels. A clear case was the implementation of the Arusha-Namanga-Athi River Road whose completion has had to suffer because Tanzania took longer to decide on the award of contract to the contractor.

Fifth: Challenges related to Policy and the Ideological Paradox

This challenge largely relates to changing mindsets in favour of integration. It is is a challenge centred on policy paradoxes. It is a matter that needs to be proactively addressed in order to prioritize and link research to policy making. In the words of President Paul Kagame expressed at the Commonwealth Business Forum in Kampala on 20th November, 2007, there is no meaningful integration unless a capability is built to transform institutions into effective agencies that conceive and execute policy with resolve. For example, there is a dominant view among senior bureaucrats in some Partner States that regards deeper EAC integration as being a threat to or an erosion of national economic interests. Such mindset has to change.

The task of changing mindsets is not, by any measure, a simple one, especially when linked to the broader population perception about integration. Popularizing the objectives of the EAC and the directives and decisions taken by the Presidents and other policy makers is not enough. What is more important and what indeed poses a huge challenge is how to cultivate and ingrain a sense of ownership of the EAC project by the people; articulating the integration movement along realistic and tangible targets.

Sixth: Diversification of the Economic Base to Focus on Regional Trade, Competitiveness and Value Addition

In virtually all the African countries, agriculture remains the major economic activity but with little value addition. Besides, production practices have not embraced appreciable agricultural modernization technologies to support higher production activities. The negative effects of global climate change and poor environmental management practices have all rendered the continent's agro-based practices vulnerable.

For the EAC economies, the shift from a monoculture economy to a broad-based diversified one that is driven by growing industrialisation is the strategic imperative if higher growth, jobs and incomes are to be bolstered. President Paul Kagame has challenged the EAC to pursue this line. For example, he has recently called for the development of tourism into dynamic clusters that generate wealth; utilizing ICT to create export-oriented service industries; exploiting the rich bio-diversity to create wealth without undermining environmental integrity; and optimizing the cultural industry where African artists can access the global multi-billion dollar music, films, arts and crafts as well as entertainment industries such as local dances. Knowledge, innovation, productivity, value addition and competitiveness based on science and technology are the driving forces for realizing such economic diversification. This is the sustainable and robust way to build a firm foundation for the realization of the Abuja Treaty's AEC.

The Seventh Challenge relates to Facilitating Acquisition of Credit for Trade

Relatively much has been achieved at national levels in terms of privatization, deregulation and addressing taxation bottlenecks that hamper trade. However, more needs to be done in the area of provision of credit for the commercial and agricultural sectors (including for the small-holder farmer) that are essential to foster integration activities. The ruling borrowing interest rates of Banks to support economic and trade activities remain rather high.

The **eighth challenge** is **Uneven Integration of African Economies and the Continued Dependence of the African Economies on Trading Partnerships with the Non-African States.**

This is a challenge that reinforces the need to develop, adopt and enforce development strategies that have a regional outlook, and thus becoming viable launching pads for continental integration. In order to realize the Abuja Treaty, there is need to give impetus to trade amongst economies with higher competitiveness in similar production activities. For example, even though the intra-EAC trade has been registering a steady growth since 2005, it still constitutes only 12% of its total trade with balance of its import and export trade being with countries that are not East African. This deficit calls for the adoption of industrial and agricultural development strategies whose design does not close doors to global export trade but which also promote production for the regional market. Moving quickly towards intensive agro-based processing would boost such intra-EAC trade.

There are other challenges of equal import that also confront the EAC. These include:

Regulatory Challenge

The challenge posed by high transaction costs amid a fragmented African market: East Africa does not lack the market for its goods, even if there were increased production. Rather, it is the transaction costs in local and trans-border exchanges that militate against robust trade. A multiplicity of unnecessary documentation (e.g. trade, customs, immigration, police, human, animal health, agricultural disease controls, etc.) curtails competitive delivery of goods and services to domestic markets.

Infrastructure Challenges

There are valid reasons why trade is biased in favour of outside partners. This is because of poor transportation infrastructure. Even where efforts have been made to invest in heavy infrastructure (roads, railways, ports and harbours, telecommunications etc), there is bias towards concentrating these projects along routes and networks connecting to the outside world rather than to directing investments to the countryside where agriculture produce is rotting and other resources like arable land are lying untapped. For trade to flourish, be it at national, regional or continental levels, and to promote realisation of the Abuja Treaty Vision, there is need to put in place a supportive, cost-effective and efficient transport infrastructure network that bolsters higher domestic production and lowers costs of logistics.

Security Challenges

Although the Abuja Treaty, for whatever reason, omitted issues related to peace and security, experience, overtime, has shown that trade and economic development are generally enhanced in an environment where peace and security prevail. Examples of Burundi and, lately, Kenya, have shown that insecurity has a damaging effect on the realization of the very goals that the Abuja Treaty espouses. Therefore, it is critical, in addressing the safeguards against non-realisation of the Abuja vision, that building the appropriate environment that supports peace and security is given high importance.

Exogenous Challenges

The integration process is taking place within a global context characterized by continued external marginalization of African countries through protectionist trading regimes and other factors. These regimes engender an unfavourable environment within which Africa's regional integration efforts operate. The impact is felt on all the African States, both individually and collectively. For example, the trade agreements being proposed in the form of Economic Partnership Agreements (EPAs) and the Doha Round of Talks could end up deflecting the focus of the African stakeholders from negotiating long term pro-integration deals. They are welcome but they do not address the resolution of the fundamentals that afflict the potentials of African economies.

Indeed, in some cases, they have also acted to undermine the quest for cohesive action by African states. Already, not all AU member states are talking the same language and embracing the same approach on EPA negotiations. The move by the EAC to initial the framework agreement on EPAs was not welcomed by some countries that prefer protracted or no negotiations. However, such negotiations demand comparable balance of impact amongst the negotiators; leave alone taking into consideration the risk of trade disruptions. Unfortunately, for the EAC and for Africa as a whole, there are not many choices on the shelves!

The collapse of the Doha Development Round talks in Geneva last week or so do also reflect a frightening fracture of South solidarity, of what Mwalimu Julius Nyerere described at the G77 Conference in Arusha in 1977, as the "trade union of the poor."[60] The South no longer represents the shared poverty it used to. With Brazil, India, China and South Africa rallying and galvanizing to protect their industrial sectors against competition from the developed world, their collective solidarity with a group of poor countries that rely on agriculture for their salvation is fast waning. This conflict of interests in the developing world is unhelpful in promoting South-South cooperation and using it as a building block for reinforcing regional integration.

The Secretariat's Lack of Executive Authority

Let me end my presentation by pointing out one more challenge that affects the EAC Secretariat in running the affairs of the Community. This is the lack of executive authority. With no tangible executive authority whereby every act of the Community is subjected to sovereign interests and concerns of the

---

[60] Some of the ideas around this theme are captured in THE SOUTH COMMISSION, *The Challenge to the South: The Report of the South Commission*, Oxford: Oxford University Press, 1990.

partner states, the movement towards the realization of a robust EAC integration not to speak of achieving the AEC goal is clearly slow tracked.

Conclusion

In conclusion, it has to be said plainly that effective African Economic integration remains miles away. However, the wind of political and economic liberalization sweeping the continent has diminished the role of governments in matters of economic management, while elevating the role of the private sector. Indeed, the role of the private sector and the civil society and their effective participation in mobilizing for ownership of the integration process has become central. More needs to be done.

Giving the devil its due, we should recognize that States have put in place the regulatory framework to support integration. However, there is still the challenge of ingraining a more pro-integration mindset amongst the national technocrats, on the one hand, and, on the other, the need to unpack the integration idea to engender broader ownership by the people. There is also need for countries and regions to get to know each other better and to cultivate confidence and mutual trust in pursuit of integration through the attainment of a variety of smaller but tangible and gradually incremental deliverables. We should also encourage those RECs that have attained higher levels of convergence criteria to forge ahead with fast-tracking arrangements with their peer RECs.

It is my hope that I have touched raw nerves in this presentation about Africa's future and how the EAC plays its part. Africans must hold themselves responsible for not changing their social and economic condition for the better. There is nobody else to blame. As Cassius says to Brutus in Shakespeare's Julius Caesar, "Men are sometimes masters of their fate: the fault, dear Brutus, is not in our stars, but in ourselves."[61]

---

[61] On this one of most famous Shakespeare Quotes see http://www.enotes.com/shakespeare-quotes/fault-dear-brutus-our-stars. See also HUMPHREYS, Arthur (ed.) Shakespeare, William, *Julius Caesar*, Oxford: Oxford University Press, 1999.

CHAPTER THREE

Enhancing Intra-African Trade[62]

The challenges of enhancing intra- African trade in goods and services are many with different manifestations. If we examine the current status of African trade overall, we are able to obtain a picture of these challenges. Based on data from the 2008 *African Economic Outlook Report*[63] of the African Development Bank, Africa's merchandise exports in 2007 totalled US $ 424.14 billion. However, only 9.5% of those exports represented intra-African trade. It is interesting to note though that 32.5% of intra -African trade comprised manufactured goods, 35.4% represented fuels and minerals and agricultural commodities took a share of a mere 17.1%. Whilst some regions in Africa, for example the East African Community (EAC) region, have been able to achieve higher intra regional trade, at 12% of total trade, the highest performance amongst the African Regional Economic Communities (RECs), intra African trade overall remains very low.

There has been significant literature as to why Africa suffers from this low level of intra -African trade. However, for purposes of this discussion, may I outline some of the key interventions that Africa needs to take in order to bolster higher continental trade.

Infrastructure Challenges and Interventions

The first area that I examine relates to what is described as trade related infrastructure. Trade related costs in Africa are 30% to 40% higher than in other developing regions. In 2008, the World Bank Development Research Group estimated that Sub-Saharan Africa could gain about US $ 20 billion annually from improvements in trade related infrastructure. And this is because it takes, on average, 48 days to simply get a container from the factory gate onto a ship. Reducing this length of time to 10 days is likely to increase exports by 10%. It is also important to recognize that also based on a recent study by the World Bank, only 25% of the trade related costs are attributable to poor physical infrastructure. 75% of the cost distortion is contributed by soft infrastructure deficits which centre on cumbersome customs procedures, bureaucracy and corruption. In this light, the key

---

[62] A Presentation at the Commonwealth Africa Investment Forum, Accra, Ghana, 9th February, 2010.

[63] AFRICAN DEVELOPMENT BANK, *African Economic Outlook Report,* Tunis: AfDB, 2008.

intervention to enhancing intra African trade is to address trade facilitation bottlenecks.

The establishment of One-Stop Border Posts would in this respect be one critical intervention. In November last year, the first One-stop Border Post in Africa was inaugurated at Chirundu at the border of Zambia and Zimbabwe. Chirundu handles an average of 268 trucks a day and it used to take 2-3 days for a truck to cross the border. Each truck costs US $ 140 in fixed costs and drivers time. This means that for 3 days the cost of each truck would be US $ 320. However, with the opening of the One-Stop Border post, each truck now takes 2 hours to cross and only 15 minutes in the case of pre-cleared traffic. The potential cost saving per annum is about US $ 486 million which can go towards improving the competitiveness of the export-import economies.

Through the World Bank's US $ 250 million support to the East African Trade and Transport Facilitation Project, a One-Stop Border Post is being established at Malaba at the border of Kenya and Uganda which will reduce border crossing times from 3 days to 3 hours. Similar One-Stop Border Posts are in the offing through funding from JICA at the Tanzania-Kenya border of Namanga and at the Tanzania-Rwanda border at Rusumo. At the same time, the World Bank is working with International Business Machines (IBM), Microsoft and the Global Express Association under a public-private partnership titled 'Aid for facilitation' to apply innovative IT solutions to streamline customs and other trade related border procedures.

There are other infrastructure challenges that need to be addressed in order to enhance intra African trade and these centre on the current poor state of the physical infrastructure especially roads, railways and ports as well as energy. How to upgrade and modernize these infrastructures constitutes the major agenda of regional integration in Africa. In particular, it is important to give greater focus to the improvement of the railway system if trade competitiveness is to be realized from lower costs of logistics. It is estimated that transport by road contributes to about 55% of logistics cost compared to rail which accounts for only 20%.

It is in this context that the World Bank and the African Development Bank are co-organizing with the EAC a Regional Railways Conference in mid March this year to address the challenges facing the East African railways system which is currently in a very poor shape.

The recently established COMESA-EAC-SADC Tripartite, whose major thrust is the establishment of a Grand Free Trade Area by 2012, has embraced the development of Transport Corridors as a key factor in unlocking the economic potentials of the broad region. In April last year, through an Aid for Trade Conference held in Lusaka Zambia, the tripartite was able to obtain pledges from the donor community amounting to US $ 1.2

billion and US $ 1.5 billion from the Development Bank of Southern Africa (DBSA). These funds will go towards upgrading and modernization of the North-South Corridor linking Dar es Salaam Port and the main Ports in Southern Africa embracing roads, railways, energy and civil aviation. A Tripartite Trust Account has been opened with DBSA, who will act as Fund Managers, and already the UK Department for International Development (DFID) has injected seed capital to the Trust Account to the tune of British Pounds 67 million.

Through the support of DFID and Japan International Cooperation Agency (JICA), progress is also being made to develop the Central Transport Corridor in Tanzania and the Northern Transport Corridor in Kenya, both linking Uganda, Rwanda, Burundi and the eastern Democratic Republic of Congo (DRC). A new Transport Corridor is also being opened up linking Lamu on the Indian Ocean coast, in Kenya, with Juba in Southern Sudan and Addis Ababa. Additionally, On 15th January this year, the African Development Bank signed a Loan Agreement with the Governments of Ethiopia and Kenya to finance the Mombasa-Nairobi-Addis Ababa Road Corridor project (phase II) which will cost US $ 125.6 million. The project will also include a One-Stop Border Post at Moyale, at the Kenya-Ethiopia border.

Critics of infrastructure development in Africa point out, however, that there is over reliance on donor funding and multilateral finance for infrastructure development in Africa. Two factors stand out in this context: one is Africa's fragmentation within the context of the existing REC blocs and, secondly, the reluctance of the private sector, global and African, to engage in Public-Private Partnerships (PPPs) in infrastructure development. The emergence of the COMESA-EAC-SADC tripartite is thus a welcome attempt at mitigating fragmentation and providing a more robust framework for mobilization of financial resources. As regards private sector participation, the challenge is for African governments to formulate clear rules regarding PPPs as well as coming up with innovative financial instruments for mobilizing regional savings. Such mobilization could be done through flotation of infrastructure bonds which are guaranteed by the Central Banks.

Another intervention that should quickly be taken up is the implementation of the Yamoussoukro Decision on liberalization of the African airline industry. Since its adoption in 1999, African governments have been lukewarm in enforcing the Yamoussoukro Decision. As a result, not only does Africa continue to be not easily accessible but the cost of air travel and cargo remain too high and thus thwarting contacts of business people and the growth of intra African trade.

Food Related Trade and Climate Change Impacts

As noted earlier, only 17% of intra African trade comprises food commodities. Trade in food could constitute a major component of intra African trade. However, with all its potential, arising from huge land resources, Africa is yet to grow adequate food for its own consumption and for export. Instead, Africa food and agricultural imports average US $ 20 billion per annum. These imports are largely from non African countries. Africa also receives US $ 2 billion in food aid annually. University of Oxford Professor Paul Collier in an article in the 2008 November/December issue of *Foreign Affairs* titled "The Politics of Hunger"[64] argues that for the first time in history, Africa has the potential to leverage its economic development through food exports in a world that will continue to face food shortages. He foresees food prices not decreasing in the light of growing population particularly in China and India and because of low growth in food production in the major food consuming countries.

Here then lies a huge potential for Africa to enhance, not only its intra African trade, but also trade with the rest of the world. To give an example, Tanzania has only 30 million hectares of land under cultivation but only 9.5% of it is under irrigation. To spur a green revolution, Tanzania would have to increase land under irrigation, not only for bolstering agricultural productivity, but also to mitigate the effects of climate change.

The other dimension of bolstering intra African trade through increased production of agricultural commodities is that the African industrial sector is highly agro-based, whether you look at the textile industry or the value-adding industries of edible oils, tea, coffee and fruit processing. However, Africa has to increasingly be more mindful of the impact of climate change if the vibrancy of its agricultural sector is to be scaled up to support the agro-based manufacturing industry. Failure to address and respond with right policies and measures, the adverse effects of climate change would clearly erode the potential of enhancing intra African trade. In East Africa, three years of continuous drought have not only wreaked havoc on food security, with pastoralists losing around 70% of their cattle, but have also given rise to serious shortages of agricultural commodities that support the manufacturing sector.

Trade In Services

Much of intra- African trade has been trade in goods. The main reason for this phenomenon is that under the framework of Free Trade Areas (FTA's) and Customs Unions, trade in services has been excluded. Yet many African

---

[64] COLLIER, Paul, "The Politics of Hunger: How Illusion and Greed Fan the Food Crisis," Volume 87, No. 6 *Foreign Affairs*, November-December, 2008.

economies are now seeing an increasing share in GDP being contributed by services, away from the hitherto dominance of agriculture. Kenya, for example, has, in recent years seen the share in GDP contributed by services reaching 65%. Even Tanzania and Uganda which have predominantly been agriculture-based economies have, in the last 3 years, seen huge growth in their service industries clocking about 45% of GDP. This trend is becoming predominant in several economies in Africa that are moving from less developed economies to medium developed economies. The challenge now is how to leverage the service sector to play a greater role in intra- African trade.

The East African Community is path breaking in this area with the adoption of the Common Market Protocol in November last year. This Common Market will be operationalised from 1st July this year and, with it, the free movement of services and capital will commence. This means that the regional market will open up to deeper integration through trade in services.

Regional Integration-Size Matters

One of the challenges in enhancing intra Africa trade is the overlapping memberships of African countries in Regional Economic Communities. I have alluded earlier to the economic dysfunctions of African's fragmentation. A move towards addressing such fragmentation and thus building a bigger capacity for enhancing intra Africa trade was the decision taken in October 2008 by the Heads of State of COMESA-EAC and SADC in Kampala, Uganda to establish a grand FTA. Once achieved as planned in 2012, the FTA is expected to deepen intra- African trade involving 26 countries with a combined population of 527 million people, almost half of African Continent, and a combined GDP of 624 billion.

Presently, the proposed FTA agreement has been completed and is undergoing review by the member states in readiness for its consideration at the planned summit of COMESA-EAC and SADC Head of State. This FTA initiative presents the most robust pathway towards the realization of the African Economic Community. Going by the experience of trade performance within the East African Community where, as a result of the establishment of the Customs Union in January 2005 which saw intra-regional trade going up by 37.6% between 2005 and 2008, the proposed Grand FTA should help to enhance trade within the broader COMESA-EAC-SADC economic space. Underlying such expectation is the fact that both COMESA and SADC are moving towards aligning their Common External Tariffs with that of the EAC.

Investments-Strategic Driver of Intra-African Trade

The principal logic of regional integration is that market size propels investment; in turn, growth in investment catalyses trade. The underlying thrust behind the COMESA-EAC-SADC tripartite is indeed that the potential of a huge market would, in itself, open up greater interest in investment flows to the region. One area of investment which we have already touched upon is infrastructure development which helps to unlock supply side constraints. But the other area is boosting of supplies themselves through investments in both the agricultural sector and in the other productive industries cutting across manufacturing, minerals, oil and gas and tourism. It is these investments, supported by robust trade facilitation, that are central to spurring intra- African trade.

In the East African region, we have seen in the past five years how the operations of the Customs Union bolstered a significant growth in cross-border investments in fields such as edible oils, retail trade, banking, industrial cables, electric transformers, fish processing, casements, airline, hotels and lodges, education establishments, dairy etc. In addition, cross-listing of company shares in stock exchanges in the region has propped up huge mobilization of non-debt capital that has gone into expansion of industrial capacities and n making available more robust portfolio funds for medium and long term credit including trade finance. Overall, however, intra- African investment represents only 13% of total inward foreign direct investment. This level is less than half that of the ASEAN region where intra regional FDI is around 30%. Evidently, intra- African investment is bound to grow as trade in services entrenches as an important component of regional integration in Africa.

This positive outlook of investment that induces greater intra- African trade is, however, dampened by the recent emergence of piracy and counterfeit imports throughout Africa. In the case of counterfeit goods, these have led, in some cases, to a process of de-industrialization with adverse consequences to exchequer revenues, jobs, intra- African trade and, above all, to the health of the people because of poor quality of counterfeited branded drugs. In the East African Community, this problem is now being tackled through the enactment of a special regional legislation that will criminalize trade in counterfeits and pirated products.

Peace and Stability- Strategic Factor

One of the contributing factors to the enhancement of intra- African trade is peace and stability. We have seen in recent years how the collapse of peace undermines trade and transportation. Suffice to give the example of the post-elections violence that took place in Kenya in early 2008 which brought about a halt to the movement of goods destined to the land-locked countries of Uganda, Rwanda, Burundi and eastern Democratic Republic of the Congo (DRC) from the Port of Mombasa. Generally, normal trade, particularly between Kenya and Tanzania and Kenya and Uganda, was brought to a standstill with huge losses in exchequer revenues as well as in jobs. Prices of industrial inputs and goods rose sharply. In Kampala, a litre of petrol rose from US $ 1 to US $ 5. Equally, the political stalemate in Zimbabwe undermined trade within the SADC region. It thus needs no emphasis to state that trade logistics are highly vulnerable to erosion of peace and stability.

Conclusion

We have seen that intra African trade in goods and services remains very low whilst the potential for growth is clearly high. Strengthening regional economic integration is an important recipe for increasing intra African trade and investment. It is through deeper regional integration that the structural deficits that afflict African economies and, in turn, which minimize the optimization of the potential for intra African trade can be effectively addressed. Regional integration has the potential to enhance the capacities in the productive and service sector, promote economic diversification and, generally, bolster competitiveness through utilization of economies of scale and scope and collective resources.

PART 2

EAC – Background and Establishment

In this part two, the EAC is examined in the context of its establishment, the nature and form of the Treaty that establishes it, the roles of different EAC Organs and Institutions and the challenges of organizational efficiency and effectiveness. However, I deem it appropriate to pose a few introductory remarks that I believe may set the stage for the ensuing chapters under this part of the book.

Setting the Stage

The East African Community (EAC) which comprises the countries of Burundi, Kenya, Tanzania, Uganda and Rwanda in 2010 had a total population of 139 million and a collective nominal GDP of US $ 79 billion, 40% of it contributed by Kenya. The average GDP per capita is US $ 500.[65] The EAC, without doubt, is the trail blazer in African regional integration's excellence today. US Secretary Hilary Clinton has described it as the "model" of African regional integration. The World Bank Report, *East African Community-Reshaping the Geography of East Africa: From Regional to Global Integration* describes the EAC as one of the most dynamic and advanced regional economic communities in Africa.[66] Indeed, in its April, 2011 Report, *Regional Economic Outlook: Sub-Saharan Africa – Recovery and New Risks,* the International Monetary Fund (IMF) has a chapter titled, "The East African Community – Taking Off?" wherein it states that the EAC member states "have been among the fastest growing in Sub-Saharan Africa and more broadly in the developing world "and singles out Rwanda, Tanzania and Uganda as being "among the fastest growing economies in the world during 2005-2009."[67]

---

[65] See SOCIETY FOR INTERNATIONAL DEVELOPMENT, *State of East Africa Report 2012: Deepening Integration, Intensifying Challenges,* op. cit.

[66] See WORLD BANK, *East African Community-Reshaping the Geography of East Africa: From Regional to Global Integration,* op cit.

[67] See Chapter Three of INTERNATIONAL MONETARY FUND, *Regional Economic Outlook: Sub-Saharan Africa – Recovery and New Risks,* Washington, D.C.: IMF, 2011.

As a Customs Union and a Common Market, the EAC boasts as having achieved the most advanced stage of trade and economic integration in Africa. The EAC is also moving ahead towards the establishment of Monetary Union and a draft protocol for its establishment is being finalized and would be ready for consideration by the EAC Summit of Heads of State in November, 2012. At the same time, progress has been achieved in laying down the basic framework for the realization of the East African Political Federation. At the EAC Summit of Heads of State that met in November, 2011 in Bujumbura, Burundi, a decision was reached that the EAC Secretariat develops a draft legal framework of the envisioned political federation.

As a regional inter-governmental organisation, the EAC has unique and most advanced institutional organs of regional governance in Africa. These are the East African Legislative Assembly (EALA),[68] a parliament with robust legislative, oversight and outreach roles and the East African Court of Justice (EACJ) which, in the past seven years in particular, has built up a credible regional jurisprudence over constitutional and human rights issues.[69] In the following chapters, a deeper examination is made of these two organs as well as the effectiveness of the EAC Secretariat.

Unlike most regional economic communities in Africa, where the thrust of their roles has manifestly centred on trade, infrastructure development and peace and security, the EAC, in contrast, has embraced a broader agenda of development. Thus institutions such as the Lake Victoria Basin Commission (LVBC), Lake Victoria Fisheries Organization (LVFO), the East African Development Bank (EADB), the Inter-University Council of East Africa (IUCEA) and the Civil Aviation Safety and Security Oversight Agency (CASSOA), which spearhead some of the critical facets of development-based integration, are unique in Africa's regional integration project.

Another unique feature of the EAC is the establishment of a specific Ministry in each Partner State responsible exclusively for EAC matters. These Ministries are headed by Cabinet Ministers who, in the case of Kenya, Uganda and Tanzania, which largely follow the Westminster model of government, are also Members of National Parliaments. All the Ministers responsible for EAC affairs, together with the Secretary General and the Counsel to the East African Community are ex-officio members of the EALA.

---

[68] On this legislative body see NANGALE, George, *The Politics of Partnership: A Reflection of Living Life in a Legislative Assembly and Other Organisations*, Dar es Salaam: Links Training Centre (LTC), 2006.

[69] On this Court see *inter alia*, OJIENDA, T.O., "The East African Court of Justice in the Re-established East African Community: Institutional Structure and Function in the Integration Process," Volume 11 No. 2 *East African Journal of Peace & Human Rights*, 2005, p. 220.

EAC's success story since its establishment in 2000 has evoked much interest around the world. There are some observers who contend, for example, that the EAC's achievements have been predicated on its small and thus manageable size and that the geographical proximity of its member countries that enjoy historical bonds through shared cultures and language has also contributed significantly to the institutions' speedy integration. Such observations of course obscure and miss the rude reality that the erstwhile EAC had collapsed in April 1977 at the highest level of integration not experienced anywhere else in the world including in the European Union.

Thus, one needs to examine rationally why the EAC can be considered to be the state of art in African integration today. The key aim is to clarify the factors that have contributed to the advanced level of integration that the EAC has realized. The other aim is to outline the challenges that have confronted and continue to afflict the EAC in deepening and widening integration and propelling the achievement of regional higher economic growth that translates into higher levels of living of the people. It should be noted that EAC per capita incomes remain very low explaining its endemic high levels of poverty. According to International Monetary Fund (IMF) data as at July, 2011, the average EAC nominal GDP per capita was only US $ 500. Burundi's was a mere US $ 181. Equally, the average EAC gross savings as a percentage of GDP at 14.6% are too low to drive an economic take off. Tanzania has the highest gross national savings to GDP in the EAC at 19.7%.

Overall, the EAC gross savings to GDP ratio is lower than the African average of 20.2% and even much lower than the going rates in the ASEAN countries where it is above 35% with countries like China and Singapore having rates as high as 54% and 46% respectively. Clearly, the EAC region will have to develop a higher savings habit if it is to create the domestic wherewithal to finance the development of sectors such as infrastructure which constitute the bedrock of an economic take off. To the credit of the region, however, there is great potential in the investment area since the level of investment as reflected in the average investment to GDP ratio of 20% is comparably quite high in relation to other regions in the developing world, with Tanzania enjoying the highest ratio in the region of near 28.9%. Kenya's rate is 22.6%.

There is also the broad question about how the EAC builds a sense of "Community." A Community implies, by definition, a Community of Peoples and not, narrowly, a Community of trade and economics. The EAC has so far engendered a Community that identifies itself more with the Customs Union and the Common Market. It is not as yet a 'Community' of East African people. And it could not be when the citizens of East Africa have still to move across borders with passports and visas. The EAC has to borrow a leaf from ECOWAS where, in a larger and more diverse geographical space, there is free movement of persons. Surely, this is one area that needs immediate attention in the EAC. In the following chapters under this part two of the book I take a close look at the role of EAC's Organs and Institutions, the process and stages of integration and the efficiency and effectiveness of the EAC as a whole in realizing the set out objectives.

CHAPTER FOUR

The Context of EAC's Establishment

It is evident that a clarified understanding of the EAC's successes and challenges demands a close analysis of the political and economic conditions and circumstances that obtained in the EAC region, especially in Kenya, Uganda and Tanzania at the time of EAC's establishment. This is particularly important because following the collapse of the erstwhile EAC in April 1977, bad blood had developed among the original EAC Partner States and, more especially, between Kenya and Tanzania. For several years after the break up, Tanzania labelled Kenya as a "man eat man" society and Kenya retorting that Tanzania was a "man eat nothing" society. Thus a long period of mistrust emerged undermining the strong and economic trade relationship that had existed between the EAC countries for half a century.

It is axiomatic that intra-regional integration is largely a function of dynamic economic activities driven by market forces. The re-establishment of the EAC can thus be seen within the context of economic liberalization policies especially those pursued by Tanzania and Uganda from the late 1980s. These policies triggered the adoption of outer-oriented strategies which encompassed openness to trade and investment. In the case of Tanzania, they involved massive privatisation of state enterprises, ushering in a new era of private enterprise as a strategic engine of development. With such policy transformations, business ties among manufacturing and trading enterprises in the East African region quickly developed, giving impetus to the re-birth of a spirit of regionalism. This was also the period when globalization was taking root in East Africa, with Kenya becoming the preferred location for multinational transnational business firms to set up production processes with a regional market in mind. Its impact was to create a favourable environment for trading activities to grow.

But there is also another dimension to EAC's re-birth at the time. The emergence of an avowed East Africanist in Uganda in Yoweri Museveni as President from 1986[70] helped to shape a powerful vision and agenda of East African integration. In Tanzania, on the other hand, the re-birth of multi-

---

[70] On Museveni see KANYOGONYA, Elizabeth and Kevin Shillington (eds.) *Yoweri Kaguta Museveni: Sowing the Mustard Seed – The Struggle for Freedom and Democracy in Uganda*, London: Macmillan Publishers Ltd, 1997; MUSEVENI, Janet Kataaha, *My Life's Journey*, Kampala: Fountain Publishers, 2011; and KOBUSINGYE, Olive, *The Correct Line? Uganda Under Museveni*, Milton Keynes, UK: AuthorHouse, 2010.

party politics from 1992 acted as a catalyst to more liberal thinking about the politics of regional integration, away from the mindset of the post 1977 period which viewed Kenya as a mere agent of imperialism and a country bent on exploiting its neighbours economically. This particular political context in the re-birth of the EAC is of significance in the sense that it goes to the heart of EAC's ambitions of a political federation. It also crucially informed the institutional and decision making framework the EAC should take in avoiding the pitfalls of the erstwhile EAC. I shall revert to this point in the next section of this introduction.

The Treaty Establishing the EAC - The Letter and Spirit

Underlying the ethos of the Treaty establishing the EAC, which was adopted in November, 1999, were the lessons learnt from the demised EAC. Much has been written about the principal causes for the break-up of the earlier EAC. I will thus not dwell on that subject. What is important to note for purposes of this introduction is how the 1999 Treaty was couched to avoid the mistakes that found root in the 1967 Treaty that established the demised EAC. There are a number of Treaty provisions that have done this. They are largely focused on removing the powers of the Heads of State in assuring the performance and sustainability of the organization and in making the Partner States key players in the EAC integration project. Of course, in doing so, a number of deficiencies have emerged particularly in relation to the structure and process of decision making leading to often unwarranted delays which frustrate the faster realization of deeper integration. In turn, however, some observers would hold that the success of the EAC has largely been enabled by the centrality of the Partner States in the EAC's decision making process.

Let us now examine some of the key provisions of the Treaty in trying to clarify the issues that specifically relate to avoidance of the pitfalls of the earlier EAC. These provisions can be classified as follows: first, those that deal with the establishment and principles of the Community which fall under Chapter two of the Treaty, second, those that define the functions and meetings of the Summit (Chapter Four) and the Council (Chapter Five); and lastly, the several provisions from Chapter 11 to 27 that deal with cooperation of the Partner States in various sectors of integration.

The Roles of the Summit and the Council of Ministers

As alluded to earlier, one of the root deficiencies of the demised EAC is the overconcentration of key decisions relating to EAC's integration in the EAC Authority of Heads of State, which is how called the Summit. At the height of Tanzania – Uganda friction and even military skirmishes following the accession to the Ugandan Presidency by Iddi Amin in 1971 in a military coup,[71] the EAC Authority often failed to meet. The result was that many crucial integration decisions could not be taken. This situation was heightened by the fact that in the erstwhile EAC, the Council of Ministers did not exist in the form as now enshrined in the Treaty. There were three Ministers (one from each of the old EAC Partner States) who were full time executives of the EAC each charged with a specific portfolio or responsibility. They did not have formal links with their national governments. In sum, their authority was purely of an administrative character. In fact, the Secretary General of the EAC then was the principal executive officer and the three Ministers were responsible to him.

To cure this deficiency, the 1999 EAC Treaty now provides a governance structure that assures an effective delineation of powers of the Summit and the Council of Ministers. Article 11(1) gives the Summit the function of "giving general directives and impetus as to the development and achievement of objectives of the Community." Emphasis should be placed on the words *"general directives"* as opposed to *"specific."* Of course, there are few specific functions vested in the Summit which include the appointments of the EAC Secretary General and Deputy Secretaries General. Indeed, all Protocols must be sanctioned by the Summit and all Bills must be assented to by the Summit before becoming law. Under Article 11(5), the Summit may "delegate the exercise of any its functions" to one of its members, to the Council or even to the Secretary General. This in-built flexibility in providing leadership for the EAC is a major legal coup to some of the decision making weaknesses that featured in the demised EAC.

In giving the Summit a lighter role, the framers of the Treaty were cognizant of the fact that it is the Council of Ministers that should shoulder greater responsibility in the day to day leadership of the EAC. Thus Article 14(1) stipulates that "the Council shall be the policy organ of the Community" and that it shall (Article 14(2)) "promote, monitor and keep under constant review implementation of the programme of the Community and ensure the proper functioning and development of the Community." The rest of Article 14 outlines in detail the Council's functions which range from making policy decisions, initiating and submitting Bills to the EALA, giving directions to the Partner States and other organs of the Community (other than the Summit, EALA and the EACJ), consider the EAC budget and table it before EALA for approval, make regulations and give opinions in accordance with the provisions of the Treaty.

---

[71] On Idi Amin see *inter alia*, SEFTEL, Adam (ed.), *Uganda: The Bloodstained Peal of Africa and its Struggle for Peace*, Kampala: Fountain Publishers, 2010; GWYN, David, *Idi Amin: Death-Light of Africa.* Boston: Little, Brown and Company, 1977; KYEMBA, Henry, *A State of Blood: The Inside Story of Idi Amin.* New York: Ace Books, 1977; MELADY, Thomas P., Margaret B. Melady, *Idi Amin Dada: Hitler in Africa.* Kansas City: Sheed Andrews and McMeel, 1977; and MARTIN, David, *General Amin*, London: Faber and Faber, 1974.

In both cases relating to the Summit and the Council of Ministers, the Treaty is succinct about their decisions being governed by consensus (Articles 12(3) and 15(4)). Interestingly, however, Article 15(4) did provide for flexibility on the consensus issue by conditioning it to a protocol on decision-making which was required to be concluded within a period of six months from the entry into force of the Treaty. That protocol could have set out, as in the European Union, a matrix of issues that would require different forms or modalities of decision-making – unanimity, consensus, qualified majority, etc. Unfortunately and again given the backdrop of the demised EAC and the remaining excess baggage in the Partner States regarding issues of differential stages of economic development of the Partner States, the concluded protocol retained a strict consensus requirement for all decisions made by the Council.

The requirement of consensus has logically meant that the quorum for EAC statutory meetings which involve all the Organs and Institutions of the EAC as established under Article 9 of the Treaty is representation by all the Partner States at the required competent levels. In other words, if the meeting involves Ministers, then it is Ministers who properly constitute a quorum and the same applies to Permanent Secretaries when they sit as a Co-ordination Committee. This quorum requirement has proved to be the pain in the decision-making process of the EAC. A deeper analysis of its dysfunctions will be undertaken in the section dealing with the challenges of efficiency and effectiveness of the EAC.

Principles of the Community

The Treaty provisions that relate to the establishment and principles of the Community are interesting in the sense that they clarify the underlying philosophies that underpin EAC integration. What is of particular relevance are Articles 6, 7 and 8 of the Treaty which outline the fundamental principles, operational principles and general undertaking as to implementation. In all the three Articles, the centrality of the Partner States features prominently. Thus in Article 6, it is stipulated that the fundamental principles that shall govern the achievement of the objectives of the Community (as set out under Article 5) by the Partner States shall include:

- mutual trust, political will and sovereign equality;

- peaceful co-existence and good neighbourliness;

- peaceful settlement of disputes;

- good governance including adherence to the principles of democracy, the rule of law, accountability, transparency, social justice, equal opportunities, gender equality, as well as the recognition, promotion and protection of human and people's rights in accordance with the provisions of the African Charter on Human and People's Rights, 1981;

- equitable distribution of benefits; and

- Co-operation for mutual benefit.

Article 7 stipulates that:

- the principles that shall govern the practical achievement of the objectives of the Community shall include:

- people-centred and market-driven co-operation;

- the provision by the Partner States of an adequate and appropriate enabling environment, such as conducive policies and basic infrastructure;

- the establishment of an export oriented economy for the Partner States in which there shall be free movement of goods, persons, labour services, capital, information and technology;

- the principle of subsidiarity with emphasis on multi-level participation and the involvement of wide range of stakeholders in the process of integration;

- the principle of variable geometry which allows for progress in co-operation among groups within the Community for wider integration schemes in various fields and at different speeds;

- the equitable distribution of benefits accruing or to be derived from the operations of the Community and measures to address economic imbalances that may arise from such operations;

- the principle of complementarity; and

- the principle of asymmetry.

- The Partner States undertake to abide by the principles of good governance, including adherence to the principles of democracy, the rule of law, social justice and the maintenance of universally accepted standards of human rights.

However, what should relate to Article 6 is then covered under Article 7(2) which states that "the Partner States *undertake* to abide by the principles of good governance including adherence to the principles of democracy, the rule of law, social justice and the maintenance of universally accepted standards of human rights." It is to be noted that the Partner States merely *"undertake"* and are not required by the Treaty to abide by the set out principles.

Challenges in Abiding to the Principles of the Community

What is interesting on this matter relating to issues of "undertaking" *vis a vis* to "abiding" is that the East African Court of Justice does not so far have jurisdiction over human rights. Article 27(2) of the Treaty states that "the Court shall have such other original, appellate, human rights and other jurisdiction as shall be determined by the Council at a suitable subsequent date." No such determination has taken place in the past twelve years of EAC's existence. The Court's jurisdiction remains limited to the interpretation and application of the Treaty. However, in *James Katabazi and 21 Others v. Secretary General of the East African Community and the Attorney General of the Republic of Uganda*[72] before the EACJ, the Court ruled that while it would not "assume jurisdiction to adjudicate on human rights disputes, it will not abdicate from exercising its jurisdiction of interpretation under Article 27(1) merely because the reference includes allegation of human rights violation."

This position has now opened a can of worms in the EAC region where cases of alleged violations of human rights are in the ascendancy. That ruling may also have left a large question about the relevance or efficacy of Article 27(2).

Implementation Roles and Cooperation among Partner States

With respect to Article 8 on general undertaking as to implementation, we again come across the stipulation that the Partner States shall undertake a whole host of activities. These include:

- Planning and directing policies and resources which stimulate the realization of EAC objectives;

- Co-ordinating economic policies to realize harmony;

- Work closely with the Secretary General on implementation of Treaty provisions; this requirement is also reinforced under Article 72(4) with respect to co-operating and assisting the Secretariat in the performance of its functions set out under Article 71.

The provisions of Article 8 cut across most areas of sectoral cooperation among the Partner States set out from Chapter 11 to 27. Except for four Articles on the Customs Union and the Common Market (Articles 75 to 78), the main responsibilities on the implementation of the sectoral areas for cooperation are vested on the Partner States. In this vein, the EAC, as a decision making body is often left at the mercy of the Partner States in terms of the pace and the depth of implementation of the different areas of

---

[72] East African Court of Justice at Arusha, Reference No. 1 of 2007.

cooperation. This challenge could of course be addressed through the legislative process since the Treaty clearly stipulates under Article 8(4) that the laws of the EAC "shall take precedence over similar national ones on matters pertaining to the implementation of this treaty." The conundrum, however, is how to secure consensus over a process of legislation that may be deemed to erode the discretion and authority of a Partner State in implementing any area of cooperation stipulated in the Treaty.

From a legal point of view, it would be interesting to determine, where the Treaty provides that the Partner States "shall" do such and such as reflected in several Chapters of the Treaty dealing with areas of cooperation, whether some form of censure or sanction could be invoked against a Partner State that fails to cooperate. What the Treaty provides, pursuant to Article 143, is merely the sanctions that are imposable by the Summit on a Partner State that defaults in meeting its financial and other obligations under the Treaty ("other obligations" remains a fuzzy term) and under Article 146(1) which provides that the Summit may suspend a Partner State from taking part in the activities of the Community if the State fails to observe and fulfil the fundamental principles and objectives of the Treaty including failure to meet financial commitments to the Community within a period of 18 months. Article 147(1) also allows the Summit to expel a Partner State for gross and persistent violation of the principles and objectives of the Treaty after giving such Partner State 12 month's written notice.

The most interesting feature in the Treaty is the exclusion of the role of consensus in the application of these articles relating to suspension and expulsion of a Partner State. A Partner State may, however, seek an advisory opinion of the EACJ pursuant to Article 36(1) regarding a question of law arising from the Treaty which affects her. This provision could be deemed to offer room of appeal by a Partner State against suspension or expulsion.

PART 3

Process and Stages of EAC Integration

Introduction

In this part I proceed to examine the various stages of integration as set out in the Treaty establishing the EAC and outline some of the processes involved and the challenges that surround the realization of the integration phases. There are two Treaty provisions that are relevant in defining the processes and stages of integration in the EAC. These are Articles 2(2) and 5(2). Article 2(2) provides that the Contracting Parties *shall* establish an East African Customs Union and a Common Market as transitional stages to, and integral parts of the Community. It is important to fully appreciate this article when examining the EAC's integration project. The article gives primary importance and priority to the establishment of the Customs Union and the Common Market before anything else. Put differently, the Treaty nips in the bud the often cited argument, following Kwame Nkrumah, that political integration should precede other forms of integration. This view could be contrasted with Mwalimu Julius Nyerere's approach that sought to delay the independence of the then Tanganyika had Kenya and Uganda been prepared to form an East African Federation upon their achieving independence as well.[73] A strong follower of Nkrumah's precept is President Yoweri Museveni of Uganda who, in the East African context, would rather see an East African Federation constituted first. In his view, a federation would constitute the catalyst and motive power of deeper trade and economic integration.

Article 5(2) of the Treaty, on the other hand, provides that:

> the Partner States undertake to establish among themselves and in accordance with the provisions of this Treaty (in specific reference to Article 2(2)), a Customs Union, a Common Market,

---

[73] On this contrast of views between these great African leaders see CHACHAGE, Chambi, African Unity: Feeling with Nkrumah, Thinking with Nyerere, Issue No. 427 *Pambazuka*, 2009.

*subsequently*_a Monetary Union and *ultimately* a Political
Federation ...

I have underlined the words *subsequently* and *ultimately* to underscore how
the Treaty itself provides the legal prioritization of the stages of integration
in the EAC. There are many observers in the EAC region and more
especially in Tanzania who consistently point out that what the Treaty spells
out should be strictly adhered to because there was a purpose behind the
prioritization in the stages of integration.

My view is different. The words "subsequently" and "ultimately"
encapsulated in Article 5(2) do not invoke the application of differential,
separate and exclusive policy strategies and actions for the implementation
of each phase of integration. One needs to examine closely Article 8(1) (b)
of the treaty which requires the EAC partner states to "plan and direct
policies and measures with a view to creating conditions favourable for the
development and achievement of the objectives of the Community." The
objectives of the Community are realizable through the defined stages of
integration viewed holistically and not in their balkanized fashion. Indeed,
some of the challenges facing the realization of the holistic objectives of the
EAC flow from such narrow interpretation of Article 5(2). This point will
further be amplified when I later examine the negotiations for the monetary
union under this part and, subsequently, the role of the East African Court of
Justice.

CHAPTER FIVE

Building the Customs Union

The East African Customs Union (EACU) is the only other such trading arrangement in Africa after the South African Customs Union (SACU) which was established in 1910. The East African Customs Union came into force in January 2005. Much has been written about it and I will thus avoid going into its background in terms of the difficult and complex three years negotiation process to establishing it which clearly reflected the fears and concerns that existed about the lack of economic asymmetry in the region. Suffice to state that the main challenges which remain in the EACU which I also separately examine under the chapter on Common Market are in four major areas which are integral to its Protocol and the Customs Management Act. These are:

- the workings of the Common External Tariff;
- the elimination of Non-tariff barriers;
- the elimination of internal tariffs;
- customs cooperation.

It may be pointed out though that The EACU has made significant progress in spite of the challenges that face it. This progress will be outlined at the end of this section.

Common External Tariff (CET)

Under the EACU, a minimum CET of 25% was imposed on goods imported into the Customs Territory. This has worked somewhat well in the past six years, offering a level playing field among the industrial manufacturing units in the EAC region. It has particularly enhanced predictability for exporters and investors. However, three main challenges remain. First, Uganda, as a landlocked country, had put up a huge list of sensitive products (of about 180 items of raw materials) from the outset of the EACU to be exempted from the CET application. The logic was that as a landlocked country that was building an industrial base, its costs of logistics were much higher than those for Kenya and Tanzania and thus it needed a breathing space of five years. This period has now been extended to eight years until June 2013. The paradox is that both Rwanda and Burundi which acceded to the EACU in July 2008 did not put up similar sensitive product lists. It is notable that all the other Partner States are now coming up with their own sensitivity lists and this features in the June 2012 Budget speeches. It augurs poorly for the future of the EAC Customs Union.

Whilst there has been a strict requirement imposed on Uganda in these past years that industrial products arising out of CET exempted raw materials would not be exported into the Customs Territory, abuses have actually occurred and Kenya paper convertors, for example, have specifically complained that paper products from Uganda which are prohibited to enter Kenya are being smuggled in and distorting trade. Tanzania has also complained that *"mabati"* (corrugated iron sheets) which are also prohibited from exportation from Uganda have found their way into the Tanzanian Lake Victoria Zone. An interesting feature is now emerging where MM Integrated Steel Mills of Tanzania has put up a US$ 30 million investment in Jinja, Uganda to manufacture corrugated iron sheets and various other construction steel products. However, given that this sub -sector is one of those that enjoys the CET exemption in Uganda, a specific Ugandan company will, in fact, be able to import the very products now manufactured in Uganda by MM Integrated Steel Mills and, given the tax exemption, would have a competitive advantage over a local value adding industry that has a larger tax contribution to the Ugandan exchequer and creates hundreds of jobs in the country. It is a recipe for destroying industrialisation in the EAC and cross-border investments in particular.

The second challenge relates to the frequent amendments made on the CET and the Customs Management Act by the Partner States thereby making the EACU rather unstable and later, unsustainable. Of course, all such changes are ostensibly well-coordinated and arrived at by consensus at what is called the Annual Pre-Budget Session of the EAC Ministers for Finance. Such sessions enable the Ministers for Finance to incorporate changes to CET and amendments of the Customs Management Act into their Annual Budget Speeches read on the same day in all the EAC countries. Such changes are then made part of the Finance Acts. However, frequent exemptions and remissions through the Finance Acts and the amendments of the EAC Customs Management Act distort the efficacy of the Customs Union; they erode revenue, destabilize the level playing field of the manufacturing sector and frustrate and undermine cross border and foreign investments.

The third challenge relates to low levels of intra-regional exports of agricultural products due to sanitary and phyto-sanitary rules obtaining in the Partner States and which are yet to be fully standardized. Work is going on to address this challenge but given the importance of exports of agricultural products across the EAC borders, and the large share of such trade in total intra-EAC trade, it could not be more important and urgent to address this problem. And seriously, how could this issue be problematic at all when the country Bureau of Standards work so closely together? My view is that national politics again is the obstacle. There is simply too much national protection and zero sum attitudes are at play. And it is not the poor people of East Africa who operate at the borders that suffer from these unnecessary encumbrances and resultantly, EAC integration suffers in the minds of key stakeholders. Let me cite an example. I visited the Tanzania-Uganda border at Mtukula in February 2008 to have a firsthand look at how border posts operated. I was shocked to see that peasants on the Ugandan side who had decided to cultivate sugar cane to sell to a sugar mill, Kagera Sugar Mills, on the Tanzanian side of the border, were being harassed and literally given a rough time for the reason that the crop protection authorities in the Tanzania border customs office had to take days to ensure that the cane from Uganda did not contain any diseases. Of course, by the time the officials in Tanzania had done their work with the cane loaded on Ugandan tractor trailers over two days, the cane had dried up and lost much of its value. The Ugandan cane had already been cleared by the Crop Protection Agency of Uganda. Clearly, something is wrong in promoting regional integration. Is it a matter of standardisation of phyto-sanitary standards and thus making a quick decision on mutual recognition of standards urgent and imperative or is it, and what I particularly fear, simply an issue of bureaucratic inertia and even corruption?

Elimination of Non-Tariff Barriers (NTBs)

NTBs remain a huge challenge and a bottleneck to the full realization of the objectives of the EACU. Free movement of goods is best realized when NTBs are eliminated. However, the EAC region is replete with NTBs which encompass long and cumbersome customs procedures at EAC ports and harbours and at border crossings; too many en-route weighbridges and police checkpoints; inadequate IT infrastructure at border customs posts; few border posts working hours (though Rwanda border posts are now open 24 hours); varying axle load requirements for transit vehicles crossing borders, etc. It is estimated that the costs arising from NTBs constitute, on average, about 40% of costs of trade logistics in the EAC region.

Such unnecessary costs raise the costs of doing business and thus erode the competitiveness of the EAC region. More specifically, one of the reasons why the EAC internal market remains small is because intra-regional trade is hampered by these high costs of trade logistics contributed by NTBs. When coupled with the prevailing poor physical infrastructure especially railways and inland waterways (Lake Victoria and Lake Tanganyika), the costs of trade logistics in the EAC region are one of the highest in the world. *The 2010 World Bank Logistics Performance Index*[74] covering 155 countries states that "East Africa's overall performance lagged behind all regions with an average score of 2.15 against SADC's 2.55 and low income countries' average of 2.42." In terms of individual EAC Partner States' index score,

---

[74] See INTERNATIONAL BANK FOR RECONSTRUCTION AND DEVELOPMENT, *The World Bank Logistics Performance Index 2010 and Transformational Logistics*, Washington, D.C.: IBRD, 2010.

Uganda is the highest performer at number 66 out of 155; Tanzania at 95, Kenya 99 and Rwanda 151. Burundi was not featured in the index. It is paradoxical that as a landlocked country, Uganda should perform better in logistics than Kenya and Tanzania.

One way to address NTBs is to cause the establishment at the EAC Secretariat of a Monitoring Unit with offices at all key border posts to follow up on how national institutions that manage border operations fulfil their tasks. Such an administrative structure could help to identify public officials who impede or hinder smooth movement of goods and services and bring them to account. This proposal will go a long way in assisting the current system of National NTB Monitoring Committees to work more effectively which is largely not the case presently.

Elimination of Internal Tariffs

By definition, elimination of internal tariffs refers to the entry of zero import duty on goods originating in the EAC customs territory. Value Added Taxes (VAT) and Excise Duties remain payable in the consuming or importing states in the region. In this regard, the EAC has succeeded to eliminate internal tariffs effective 1st January 2010 when the transitional period of five years for Kenyan goods attracting import duty on fluctuating basis from a level of 25% in 2005 to 0% ended in December, 2010.

The EAC region presently does not have a level playing field commensurate with a functioning Customs Union and Common Market largely because there lacks a harmonised tax regime. No doubt, Article 83(2) (e) of the EAC Treaty provides that the Partner States undertake to "harmonise their tax policies with a view to removing tax distortions in order to bring about a more efficient allocation of resources within the Community." However, the EAC countries depict wide variations in their tax regimes, ranging from VAT rates, Excise Duties and Income Tax. The variations cover the thresholds for one being registered for VAT, the VAT rates, types of goods subjected to excise duties and the rates thereof, and in determination of the tax base for income tax purposes due to differential definitions of income and expenses that are allowable and disallowable in computing tax.

Evidently, it is such domestic taxes that constitute the *"cash cows"* for the Exchequers in terms of Government revenue. They indeed define what national sovereignty is all about. As such, the question regarding harmonization of domestic taxes is a sensitive one. That said, in recent years, attempts have been made to forge some harmonization of domestic taxes. Tanzania, for example, lowered its VAT rate from 20% to 18% in the financial year 2009/2010 to bring it at par with Uganda and closer to Kenya's 16%. However, it is the continuing large varying rates in Excise Duties that are a huge area of sensitivity in the harmonization exercise. This is because consumption taxes, particularly those levied on alcohol and cigarettes, have a big impact on the revenue base of all the EAC Partner States.

It is important to underscore though that delays in harmonizing domestic taxes have serious implications in promoting a level playing field in the regional economy. Varying domestic taxes can be a source of uncompetitive behaviour amongst firms. Therefore, the EAC has to move quickly to establish a Development Fund that can respond to the challenges that would arise from the harmonization of domestic taxes as envisioned under Article 77 of the EAC Treaty. Article 77 provides for measures that need to be taken to address imbalances that arise from the application of the provisions for the establishment of the Customs Union and the Common Market.

Outside these issues, there is an emerging difficulty as to how to treat the roles of Export Processing Zones (EPZs) in a Customs Union. These EPZs are governed by national laws which are not harmonized and offer different and often competing incentives. Of course, EPZs are largely exports-focused and are not therefore supposed to distort the market in the Customs Union. However, most EPZs have a clause that allows them to offload up to 20% of their manufactured products onto the local market where they operate. How to stop such products whose raw materials are not governed by the CET from being "smuggled" into other Customs territory countries is what raises concerns. The EAC is presently discussing with EAC national governments to determine the right policies and measures that should be taken to ensure that EPZ products do not distort the customs territory market.

Customs Cooperation

In as much as the EACU enjoys a good legal framework through its Protocol and the Customs Management Act, 2004, the effective operations of the Customs Union crucially depend on how the disparate customs or revenue authorities cooperate. Whilst Article 75(3) of the Treaty invokes an authority on the EAC Council of Ministers to "establish and confer powers and authority upon such institutions as it may deem necessary to administer the Customs Union", no such institution has as yet been established. As such, customs cooperation has remained loose, largely driven by the whims of the leaders of customs authorities. Having said this, the EAC Secretariat through the Directorate of Customs has endeavoured to coordinate customs cooperation especially in areas relating to harmonization of customs documentation, removal of bureaucratic bottlenecks in the issuance of certificates of rules of origin, elimination of NTBs, improvement in systems of duty drawback claims, training of customs functionaries on the EACU legal and operations' regimes and generally promoting the large picture of the benefits of the EACU to the Partner States' economies.

The EAC is working with the national revenue authorities on the directive of the EAC Extraordinary Summit of Heads of State taken in April, 2011 on the establishment of a Single Customs Territory (SCT). It may be observed, however, that the 13th EAC Summit that met in Bujumbura at the end of November 2011 deliberated on proposals put before it on the SCT. The Summit called for more work to be done on the proposal. In this regard, a study was commissioned in December 2011 on how best the SCT could be realized. Adam Smith International of the UK and MA Consulting were appointed to undertake the study. The Consultants have finalized their report recommending the operation of a Single Customs Window which assures interconnectivity of all customs systems in the region. The IT system will facilitate a seamless flow of information between the revenue authorities as well as a payment system for management of revenue transfers between the partner states and legal provisions to be applied in enforcing such transfers and in dealing with accruing revenue debts.

Once established, the SCT should enable import taxes on goods entering the customs territory to be collected at the point of entry and not, as at present, at final destination. Such a move would help to inject greater efficiencies at the ports through quicker clearances of what are now deemed as transit containers, remove the necessity of cumbersome weighbridges on transit routes, and almost totally eradicate the illegal system of transit goods being off loaded in transit without import taxes having being paid and thus distorting the customs union market. The report further notes that the EAC Customs Union stands to benefit in several areas such as: reduction in internal border controls and application of Rules of Origin since it would not be essential to test locally manufactured goods for compliance with origin conferring criteria and there would be no need for strict customs bond controls. The report will be validated by all the partner states for ownership and endorsement prior to its being tabled before the EAC Summit at the end of April, 2012.

In my view, the decision to adopt the SCT is unfortunately hampered by fears about its effectiveness and transparency in the management of tax collection and early transference of revenue collected. Yet such fears are unrealistic; they are simply fuelled by unpreparedness on the part of some partner states to cede some sovereignty to a supra-national process. Old fears of the EAC that broke down in 1977 die hard and some of the causes for that break up had to do with transfers of import duties and taxes collected at points of entry.

An area of particular concern will be the proposal by the Consultants that the SCT be managed through a Regional Customs Authority under the EAC Secretariat. Such institution will be seen to be a superior body to the National Revenue Authorities and, given the bad past history of the erstwhile EAC, it will be fought against and may, indeed, undermine what is broadly an important proposal. The EAC Partner states are generally wary about the creation of supra-national institutions at the EAC Secretariat, including the upgrading of the Secretariat itself to a Commission with wider decision making powers. It is noted, for example, that the proposal to create the post of Director General for Trade Negotiations under the EAC Trade Negotiations Act has failed to see light of day because even though the law was assented by the EAC Heads of State, the partner states still want the law to be amended and one clause they seek to be removed is the one that creates the post of Director General. In their view, which I also endorse, the present Director General of Customs and Trade supported by an existing post of Director of Trade are adequate to manage trade negotiations.

Another important development in the area of customs cooperation is the emergence of the concept of One Stop Border Posts (OSBPs). It is generally agreed that effective customs cooperation, especially at border posts, is what drives better trade facilitation. The main plank of OSBPs is precisely to foster faster and smoother movement of goods and people across the borders. A number of such OSBPs are planned for establishment in all the key EAC border points. A legal framework governing such OSBPs has been finalized and EALA will consider the requisite Bill later in 2012. Evidently, the effectiveness of the OSBPs hinges significantly on the establishment of the Single Customs Territory because the necessity of transit stops at weighbridges and en-route police stops should significantly be minimized.

Another feature worthy of mention in the overall context of the EACU is the signing of the Double Taxation Avoidance Agreement in December, 2010. This Agreement will no doubt catalyse cross-border investments as well as foreign direct investment and thereby stimulating higher intra-EAC trade. Regrettably, there has been undue delay in the domestication of the agreement in the EAC partner states and thus frustrating its early operationalisation.

Benefits Arising from the Customs Union

In this section, we dwell only with benefits that have accrued from trade under the EACU. It is important to note, briefly though, that the EACU has engendered business confidence in the region contributing to significant cross-border investments in several goods and service-based economic sectors – pharmaceuticals, banking, insurance, cotton ginning, hotels and lodges, retail trade, cables, electric transformers, dairy products, agro-processing, brewing, fish processing etc.

Whilst the share of intra-EAC trade to total trade of the Partner States with the rest of the world in 2010 (US $ 37 billion) stood at only 21%, it is significant to observe that total intra-EAC trade has gone up from US $ 2.2 billion in 2005 to US $ 4.0 billion in 2010, a growth of 55%. This is the highest growth in intra-regional trade in Africa. Of special recognition is the significant growth of Ugandan and Tanzanian exports to Kenya. Between 2004 and 2010 Ugandan exports rose from US $ 476.10 million to US $ 701.83 million. Tanzanian exports, on the other hand, rose from US $ 95.5 million to US $ 276.0 million. However, in 2008 Tanzania exports to Kenya had reached US $ 408.19 million. The exports performances of Uganda and Tanzania in relation to Kenya to some extent dampen some of the enduring sentiments that the EACU merely supports the dominance of Kenya in the Ugandan and Tanzanian markets. Of course Kenya's exports to Tanzania grew from US $ 254.33 million in 2004 to US $ 553.59 million in 2010 whilst its exports to Uganda rose from US $ 486.70 million in 2004 to US $ 774.12 million in 2010.

It is noteworthy that in my book, *Confronting New Realities: Reflections on Tanzania's Radical Transformation,*[75] I argued that regional integration could never be a win-win relationship in terms of equal outcomes from the on-set of programmes such as the Customs Union. There is always a partial win, partial lose outcome as the trading partners acquire higher levels of industrialisation and competitiveness and as trade itself takes other forms such as improved marketing of food commodities. This thesis should inform an objective analysis of the character and performance of intra-EAC trade.

As noted earlier, enlarging the EAC internal market crucially depends on improving trade facilitation across borders as well as establishing legally recognized border markets where significant cross-border trade can take place. The EAC has started working on this latter objective, in collaboration with the UN Commission for Africa, with a focus on empowering border women trading entrepreneurs. This is an important development because informal trade across borders which is presently not well accounted for in trade statistics, though Uganda started doing so in 2010, is very high. According to the Uganda Bureau of Statistics and the Bank of Uganda, informal cross-border exports from Uganda, clearly to the EAC, South Sudan and the Democratic Republic of the Congo, the neighbouring countries Uganda shares borders with, fetched US $ 1.558 billion in 2009 compared to total merchandise exports to the whole world of US $ 1.567 billion. This data reveals the hidden potential of the EAC internal market which should be exploited by opening the borders widely and allowing smoother flow of trade.

---

[75] See MWAPACHU, Juma V., *Confronting New Realities: Reflections on Tanzania's Radical Transformation*, Dar es Salaam: E & D Limited, 2005.

CHAPTER SIX

Launching the Common Market[76]

1st July, 2010 marks the commencement of the operationalisation of the East African Community (EAC) Common Market. Following the completion of the ratification of the Protocol on the Common Market, the complex and long march towards transforming the EAC region into a Common or Single Market begins with resolve and fervour.

It is important to underline the words complex and long march. Unlike the operationalisation of the Customs Union which had a big bang start up with the Common External Tariff and zero rating of Customs duty in respect of intra-regional trade in goods (except for goods destined to Tanzania and Uganda from Kenya), taking effect from day one, the operationalisation of the Common Market is a process. Indeed, the process itself is complex in terms of what is required to be undertaken at the levels of the Partner States and, in certain respects, at the level of the EAC itself.

A New Milestone

In this context, it is important that the citizens of the East African Community Partner States and the economic players in the EAC region have a clear understanding of what the 1st of July holds and portends.

Yes, the date is a historic one and is deservedly celebratory. Achieving successful negotiations leading up to the adoption of the Common Market Protocol, its approval by EAC Heads of State and its ratification in record time is a milestone for the EAC. No other Regional Economic Community in Africa has achieved such milestone.

It is a milestone that epitomizes strong political will and firm commitment by all the EAC stakeholders in deepening and widening integration. Yet what we have achieved so far is only the basic legal framework that outlines what needs to be done and implemented for the Common Market to make meaning and have impact in transforming the lives of the East African Community citizens.

---

[76] Statement on the occasion of the commencement of the EAC Common Market on 1st July, 2010.

Hard Work Begins

Thus, 1st July, 2010 for the EAC Common Market, means entry of the critical phase when the Partner States, which, pursuant to the Treaty establishing the EAC are the principal implementers of EAC programmes, must begin to determine how the four freedoms encapsulated in the Common Market Protocol should resolutely be put into effect. It also marks the beginning of serious work at the EAC executive organ level, notably the Council of Ministers, in determining what regional-based interventions can and should be undertaken to speed up the process of getting the four freedoms to take force, mainly through a legislative process.

It is important to note though that the EAC region has, in the past decade, seen a number of policy and legal measures being effected at Partner States' level that are within the ambit of the Common Market Protocol. These measures will understandably make life easier in getting a fuller and quick implementation of the Common Market Protocol provisions. A number of examples can be adduced, particularly in the field of services, an area which, in other Economic Community regions, including the European Union, have posed serious challenges at the implementation level.

Some Common Market Freedom Already in Place

Examples in this regard span a wide range of services: banking and finance (including insurance and brokerage); distribution (retail in particular); transport and logistics; telecoms (notably mobile telephone); air transport; tourism (hotels and lodges, tour operators); education (primary, secondary and tertiary); retail business; energy; professional services (accounting and auditing, management consultancy and other knowledge services); ICT (plus broadband internet); media (print, radio and TV); and music. In other words, the EAC economies have seen significant cross-border services intensify, benefitting from bold economic liberation policies and measures effected in all the five EAC Partner States.

Immediate Challenges in the Services Sector

The entry of the Common Market Protocol will thus provide a fillip and impetus to an already thriving cross-border services industry. The impetus will largely lie in creating the empowering conditions at the level of the Partner States for the services sector to be scaled up and made more robust and buoyant. A few examples can be mentioned. First, the case of air transport which is yet to be fully liberalized within the framework of the Yamoussoukro Decision. The EAC region needs not only a "free skies" agreement but also deeper liberalization of air transport operations to bring down costs of passenger and cargo transportation which are currently too high.

Second, the securities market is yet to be "regionalized" and the capital account is yet to be sufficiently liberalized by Tanzania to enable Tanzanians participate outside the present framework of cross-listing of market shares at national level. Removal of restrictions on capital flows should serve as a catalyst for capital market development and the provision of long term and risk capital most needed to spur economic development. At the EAC level, there are definitive programmes on-going towards the promotion of a regional capital markets regime and institutions.

Third, the regulatory framework for cross-border television broadcasting is still stringent; it needs to be further liberalized to promote greater offerings by competing regional networks. Fourth, whilst there is significant cross-border tertiary education access, tuition fees, even in public universities, are yet to be harmonized in spite of decisions having been taken at the EAC level requiring charging of similar rates of fees.

Fourth, the cross-cutting challenge of work permits which underlie the effectiveness of the services sector needs to be frontally addressed. You cannot realize the full benefits of free movement of professionals under the services sector when labour market policies and laws stand in the way of such freedom. A starting point in leveraging this freedom could be to eliminate the requirement of work permits for citizens of EAC Partner States who have professional qualifications and who seek to set up their own business in fields such as law, medicine, engineering, accounting and auditing, architecture etc.

Making Free Movement of Labour Work

Turning to the aspect of free movement of labour, a key freedom in promoting human capacity in the EAC region for social and economic transformation, it is important that the EAC Partner States quickly work out the modalities for enabling such freedom to take effect. An initial word of appreciation to Rwanda and Kenya is deserved for leading the elimination of work permits, at a bilateral level, between them. In the case of Rwanda, the elimination of work permits is extended to all citizens of EAC Partner States. An important element in the process of elimination of work permits, wholly or partially, is the conclusion of the Mutual Recognition of Academic and Professional Qualifications.

The EAC, through its institution, the Inter-University Council of East Africa, has reached an advanced stage in setting up a mechanism through quality assurance that will form the basis for determining such mutual recognition. A related issue is mutual recognition of accreditation of higher education institutions which would remove the regulatory requirement of tertiary education institutions moving across borders applying for fresh accreditation. It should also be mentioned that the EAC is working towards the harmonization of social security benefits in order to support the free movement of labour. EAC Partner States are already at an advanced negotiating stage in this area.

Free Movement of Persons

It is notable that to most ordinary citizens of the EAC Partner States the 1st of July infers the free movement of persons in the region from that date. This is one issue that the Partner States will have to offer elaborate explanations. Suffice to state that citizens of the EAC region have enjoyed free movement across their borders for years.

The national passports and the East African passport travel documents are accepted and respected at border points without a visa requirement and six months' stay each time of entry is offered without hassle. This free movement will be further facilitated when all the five Partner States introduce Third Generation (Machine Readable) identity cards. Only Rwanda has such an ID in use. Kenya is about to introduce one in July this year. Tanzania and Uganda are in the process of introducing such IDs as well. Burundi will follow.

Conclusion

The EAC Common Market is finally here. It ushers in a higher level of integration beyond trade in goods which the Customs Union caters for, with positive impact on the economies of the Partner States as reflected by growing intra-regional trade in the past five years. The broad economic space which the services sector will unleash will trigger the expansion of economic activities and jobs in the region.

Cross-border capital movements will also spur the growth of industrialization driven by an expanding and more productive agricultural sector. East Africans have every right to be proud of the stage of integration the EAC has reached. But it is upon them to exploit all available opportunities to make the Common Market work for them and for the better livelihoods of all citizens of the EAC. We can do it; let us together make it happen. In the following chapter I critically examine the factors that crucially underpin the successful implementation of the common market.

CHAPTER SEVEN

Making the Common Market Work

Introduction

Regional economic integration is one of the notable features in the global political economy in the past half century. The erstwhile East African Community (EAC) established in 1967 and which collapsed in 1977 was the leading model of regional integration in the world. During its time, it comprised a common market and, at some point, within the framework of the East African Common Services Organization (EACSO), a predecessor institution of the EAC, it also boasted of a single currency managed by an East African Currency Board (EACB) up until 1966 which is close to five years after Tanganyika's (Tanzania Mainland) independence. The European Union (EU) may indeed have borrowed a leaf from the erstwhile EAC with respect to its Single Market and the Monetary Union.

Today, however, the EU constitutes the most ambitious form of economic integration in the world even when it now faces the worst testing time since the adoption of the 1957 Treaty of Rome which established it. Its ongoing sovereign debt crisis has resulted in the establishment of a one trillion euro Stability Fund, to be leveraged by other fund sources, for bailing out countries that find themselves in vulnerable public finance crises. The Fund may also help stabilize exposed banks as well as sustain the Monetary Union itself. Clearly though, the future viability of the Euro Zone is under question. What is of special interest is the existence of strong views that point to the fact that the sovereign debt crisis is not, in itself, the core problem; that the real problem lies in the lack of a robust political will in handling a crisis that is increasingly becoming contagious.[77]

Writing in the *New York Times* of 19th October, 2011 under the title "Euro, Meant to Unite Europe, seems to rend it" Stevie Erlanger elaborated:

> Leaders seem diminished; local politics trump solidarity. There is a new nationalism degrading the collective responsibility and shared sovereignty that defines the European Union. Euro-scepticism runs from far-right parties that simultaneously detest immigrants, globalism and Brussels to the governing parties of Europe's most successful countries.

---

[77] See MUNCHAU, Wolfgang, "Original Sin: the Seeds of the Euro Crisis are as Old as Euro Itself," *Foreign Policy*, 7th April, 2011.

I am raising this challenge of collective action with respect to the EU to merely set the stage for the ensuing discussion about what it would take to make the EAC Common Market work. The mindsets of member nation-states about the form and depth of integration is of pre-eminent importance. In fact, to place this challenge in a clearer perspective, it should be pointed out, that even in the context of the operationalisation of the EU Single Market established in 1992, there are still serious concerns in place that are largely centred on the attitudes of member states. These concerns were aptly encapsulated in a letter which the President of the European Commission (EC) wrote to Professor Mario Monti 'presently the Prime Minister of Italy, when appointing him to prepare a report on the state of the EU Single Market.

In that letter, dated 20th October, 2009, Jose Manuel Barroso observed, *inter alia*, as follows: First, that "there remains a strong temptation, particularly when times are hard, to roll back the Single Market and seek refuge in forms of economic nationalism." Second, that the "full potential of the Single Market has not yet been delivered. In many areas, the Single Market is far from being completely in place."

Mario Monti's report to the EC President titled, *A New Strategy for the Single Market - At the Service of Europe's Economy and Society* dated 9th May, 2010,[78] makes a profound statement, in the context of national sentiments about integration, to the effect that:

> the Single Market not only is not loved; it is seen by many Europeans - citizens as well as political leaders - with suspicion, fear, and sometimes open hostility.[79]

Professor Monti attributes this situation to two reinforcing factors which he describes as "integration fatigue that undermines the appetite for a single market" and "market fatigue" which is largely caused by the erosion in confidence on the role of the market itself.

Inasmuch as these lessons from the EU raise relevant questions which the EAC cannot escape from or, at least, should not underrate, it is nevertheless important to point out that the European model of integration may not altogether be appropriate or relevant for the EAC. As Peter Draper has cautioned, the European model may be useful as "an inspiration" but "given its unique geo-political foundations, complex governing institutions, elaborate coordination mechanisms, and levels of internal economic

---

[78] See MONTI, Mario, *A New Strategy for the Single Market – At the Service of Europe's Economy and Society: Report to the President of the European Commission José Manuel Barroso*, 9th May, 2010.

[79] Ibid., p. 12.

integration... it is very difficult to see how African political economy circumstances could replicate it."[80]

Apart from the EU, there are several regional economic integration arrangements around the world in the form of free trade areas, customs unions, monetary cooperation and common markets that could probably offer appropriate lessons for the EAC. In Africa alone, there are fourteen regional economic communities (RECs) though the African Union (AU) officially recognizes only eight which includes the EAC. These RECs are at different stages of integration. What is important to note is that economic integration in Africa in the past two decades is generally experiencing a process of widening and deepening but with different challenges. And whilst the multiplicity of membership of African states in different RECs, a generic facet, is viewed, in some quarters, as a setback to the quick realization of African-wide economic integration,[81] it is notable there are some serious efforts towards addressing the phenomenon. For example, the birth of the COMESA-EAC-SADC Tripartite in November 2008, heralded a positive trend at promoting a grand free trade area which embraces 26 countries with a population of 635 million people and a GDP of US $ 1 trillion.

The Tripartite aims at the future creation of a customs union and a possible merger of the three partnership RECs. The challenge for the EAC is mainly that it is leading from the front as a regional economic community and thus has little to learn from other experiences, neither from the Caribbean Economic Community (CARICOM) nor ASEAN.

The central purpose of this chapter is to assess the prospects of trade and economic integration in the EAC from the perspective of the Common Market. The underlying thrust is to determine what constitutes the driving forces for making the EAC Common Market work and outline the challenges that impact this process and how they could be mitigated and resolved. Comparisons and contrasts with the EU integration project with specific reference to its single market are made, drawing relevant lessons for making the EAC Common Market work.

---

[80] DRAPER, Peter, *Rethinking the (European) Foundations of Sub-Saharan African Regional Economic Integration: A Political Economy Essay*, Working Paper No. 293, Paris: OECD Development Centre, September, 2010, p. 22. For a different view which outlines financial contagion, fiscal consolidation and exchange rate effects from the euro zone debt crisis on developing countries, see: Mussa, Isabella, et al, The euro zone crisis and developing countries, Overseas Development Institute, London, May, 2012. www.odi.org.uk/resources/docs/7688.pdf.

[81] See GIBB, Richard, *Rationalisation or Redundancy? Making Eastern and Southern African's Regional Trade Units Relevant*, Brenthurst Discussion Paper No. 3, Johannesburg: Brenthurst Foundation, 2006, pp. 11-14.

EAC Integration prior to the Common Market

The rebirth of the EAC through the adoption of the Treaty establishing it in November 1999, is one of the ways in which the East African economies has sought to respond to the challenges of globalization. These economies came to realize and appreciate that it is largely through regional cooperation and integration that they could better seize, optimize and share available opportunities and resources and manage the risks associated with global interdependence and competition.[82]

It is well recorded, that Africa as a whole needs to build economies of scale to trigger supply-side dynamics that support the emergence of a strong and globally competitive African private sector. A key ingredient of such a strategic focus is the integration of markets on a regional scale; markets that aggregate demand and unlock not only unproductive economic spaces but also demographic dividends and, resultantly, spur both domestic and foreign direct investment.[83]

It is in this context that a key objective of the EAC as enshrined in Article 5 of the Treaty establishing it is stated to be the establishment of a Customs Union and a Common Market, other integration arrangements such as the Monetary Union and Political Federation being relegated for a subsequent period. In order to obtain a well-clarified picture of the EAC Common Market and how this advanced stage of economic integration can be made to work, it is essential, first of all, to examine how the EAC Customs Union, the entry point in EAC integration, has functioned. The rationale for this approach is that an important component of the Common Market is the free movement of goods whose critical building block is the Customs Union. Moreover, it is invariably expected that the Customs Union would create the key supporting conditions for making the Common Market work.

A Critical Review of the EAC Customs Union (EACU)

Established in January 2005, the EACU is the only other Customs Union in Africa after the Southern African Customs Union (SACU) whose members are South Africa, Namibia, Botswana, Lesotho and Swaziland. EACU achieved full customs duty free status in January 2010 when Kenyan exports of goods into the EAC territory became zero rated. As part of the objective to realize asymmetry in the region, pursuant to Article 7(i)(h) and 75(i)(a) of the EAC Treaty, the EACU had provided that Kenyan exports into the EAC

---

[82] See HILPOLD, Peter, "Regional Integration According to Article XXIV GATT: Between Law and Politics," Volume 7 *Max Planck Yearbook of United Nations Law*, 2003, p. 219 at pp. 220-221.

[83] FREEMANTLE, Simon, *Economics: BRIC and Africa*, Johannesburg: Standard Bank, 9th June, 2010, p. 5.

territory would attract customs duty on an annual fluctuating basis from the initial rate of 25% down to 0% over five years.

It is of note that the EACU has been quite successful in bolstering intra-regional trade even when there are a number of challenges that continue to afflict its enormous potential. Equally, the EACU has fostered increased intra-EAC cross border investments including foreign direct investment. A brief analysis of these successes is essential.

Growth in Intra-EAC Trade

According to the State of East Africa Report of the Society for International development, between 2005 and 2010, total intra-EAC trade grew from US $ 2.2 billion to US $ 4.1 billion, an increase of 53.7%. This is the highest percentage increase among the African Regional Economic Communities. The table below fleshes out the details of total intra-EAC trade by country with the other EAC partner states in the period indicated between 2004 and 2010. The data below is in US $ million.

Uganda

	2004	2010
Burundi	18.48 (*under Comesa*)	52.42
Kenya	476.10	701.83
Rwanda	25.32 (*under Comesa*)	156.73
Tanzania	27.93	94.14
Total EAC	547.54	1,005.13

Tanzania

	2004	2010
Burundi	13.40	0.6
Kenya	217.90	276.0
Uganda	63.39	17.9
Rwanda	7.84	1.4
Total EAC	302.53 (*Note Tanzania achieved 425.31 in 2008*)	295.9

Kenya

	2004	2010
Burundi	37.58 (*under Comesa*)	70.72
Uganda	486.70	774.12
Rwanda	78.57 (*under Comesa*)	138.40
Tanzania	254.33	553.59
Total EAC	857.17	1,536.82

Rwanda

	2004	2010
Burundi	2.06 (*under Comesa*)	5.44
Kenya	62.57	162.29
Tanzania	17.31	67.59
Uganda	61.82 (*under Comesa*)	159.66
Total EAC	**141.70**	**394.97**

Burundi

	2004	2010
Kenya	27.87 (*under Comesa*)	40.77
Uganda	11.75 (*under Comesa*)	31.54
Tanzania	15.06	28.35
Rwanda	5.0 (*under Comesa*)	4.57
Total EAC	**59.69**	**105.23**

However, whilst EAC total trade with the rest of the world in 2005 was US $ 17.5 billion, it rose to US $ 37 billion in 2010, a significant increase of 47.3%. What has happened is that the share of total intra-EAC trade *vis a vis* with the rest of the world has declined by 11% between 2005 and 2010 reflecting the level of challenge that exists in boosting intra-EAC trade. In contrast, in the EU, the share of intra-EU trade in world trade in 2010 was 72% whilst in the ASEAN it was 52%; for SADC it was 10%.[84] I

It would be noted that the decline in total intra-EAC trade to total trade is explained by the growing intensity of the integration of global markets and the growth in extra-EAC exports of primary commodities (coffee, tea, cut flowers, cashew) and natural resources such as minerals which do not constitute a major factor in intra-regional trade.

It is clear though, that whilst the EACU has made strides through the adoption of a Single Customs Management Act, similar rules of origin, a Common External Tariff (CET), which are good mechanisms for monitoring non-tariff barriers at each partner state level, and measures which have assisted in bolstering intra-EAC trade, the EACU, as noted before, still faces a number of challenges. These include the following:

First, the non-realization of a Single Customs Territory which would enable customs duties to be levied and collected at the point of entry of goods imported into the EAC customs territory. It is of regret that there is an enduring resistance on the part of some EAC partner states against the system of collection of customs duties at the point of entry of imported goods even when the benefits of the system in terms of efficiency and in curbing tax evasions, particularly involving transit goods, are enormous. The resistance seems to be founded on the apprehension about the smooth transferability of tax revenues collected on behalf of a partner state, an issue that is easily addressable through application of modern computer software systems that record each and every tax collected and also provide instantaneous transfer of data.

Second, the continuation of sensitivity lists of imports which are exempt from the CET undermines the efficacy and effectiveness of the EACU. Uganda has notoriously been the exploiter of the sensitivity lists regime in the name of being a landlocked country whose costs of trade logistics ostensibly undermine economic competitiveness. Paradoxically, Rwanda and Burundi did, not upon acceding to the EACU, demand similar kind of protection which Uganda has fought to sustain in the past seven years of the EACU. There is little doubt that the continuation of sensitivity lists undermines the level playing field in the Customs Union territory and distorts regional competitiveness as well.

---

[84] See ECONOMIC COMMISSION FOR AFRICA AND AFRICAN UNION, *Economic Report on Africa 2011: Governing Development in Africa – The Role of the State in Economic Transformation*, Addis Ababa, Ethiopia: United Nations Economic Commission for Africa, 2011.

Third, the massive entry of counterfeited and pirated products into the EACU territory undermines the viability of manufacturing firms. It would be an uphill task for the EAC region to promote robust industrialization in the face of the threat of counterfeits. According to the Kenyan Business Daily, Kenya loses Shs. 50 billion a year from illicit goods that enter the Kenyan Market. The Kenyan Exchequer also loses Shs. 19 billion in taxes a year from counterfeits. The EAC region as a whole loses over US $ 500 million annually in tax revenues from counterfeits.[85]

The EAC is at an advanced stage to enact a regional law, the *East African Community Anti-Counterfeit Bill, 2011* to counter and confront cross-border flows of counterfeited and pirated goods. The law follows a major study on the characteristics of counterfeits and piracy and how the various EAC partner states address the challenge. So far, these countries pursue varying approaches. However, from the study that was undertaken, it is clear that intellectual property law in the region generally remains weak.[86]

Fourth, the state of flux in putting in place effective Sanitary and Phyto-Sanitary Standards (SPS) which would spur cross-border trade in agricultural commodities, value added agricultural products, live animals and dairy products. Agriculture remains the dominant economic sector in the regional trade sector in the EAC and, clearly, the lack of well-harmonized SPS hampers the realization of optimal trade and integration. In October 2006, the United Nations Industrial Development Organization (UNIDO) concluded an agreement with the EAC and the original three partner states to provide trade capacity support in agro-industry products. The programme is titled, Trade Capacity Building in Agro-Industry Products for Establishment and Proof of Compliance with International Market Requirements. The purpose of the project is to enable the export institutions in the EAC partner states to develop capacity- related global SPS such as ISO 22000-2005.

With respect to the EAC, the UNIDO support is directed at the development and implementation of an EAC SPS Protocol in line with the requirements of Article 108 of the EAC Treaty and Article 38(i) and (ii) of the Protocol of the EAC Customs Union. Once ratified, the Protocol will provide the policy as well as the legal and regulatory framework for the management of food safety, animal and plant health among the EAC partner states. It is expected that the Protocol will help to boost intra-EAC trade by removing SPS-related non-tariff barriers (Jensen, 2010: 8-11). The EAC draft SPS Protocol was adopted by the Council of Ministers at its 20th meeting and at the end of October 2011 it was reviewed for legal input by the Sectoral Council for Legal and Constitutional Affairs. Unfortunately, that sectoral council took

---

[85] See *Business Daily*, Nairobi, 21st October, 2011.

[86] See NJAU, Adrian, *23rd EAC Council Meeting Concluded Partner States Agree on Key Issues*, Arusha: East African Community, September, 2009.

the view that more work needed to be undertaken with regard to policy issues calling upon the EAC Secretariat to revisit the draft Protocol.

In view of the importance of this Protocol in promoting trade of agro-based products, it is imperative that the EAC decision-making organs quickly bring the Protocol to finality because the optimal functioning of the Common Market hinges on SPS issues being effectively sorted out.

Fifth, the existence of numerous NTBs highly distorts the cost of doing business in the region. Notable are the high costs of trade logistics which erode the competitiveness of economic and business activities. A study by CPCS Transcom shows that to transport a 20 tonne container from Mombasa to Nairobi costs US $ 1,300 while a similar container from Mombasa to Kampala and Kigali costs US $ 3,400 and 6,500 respectively. A comparative cost for transporting a 20 tonne container from Mombasa to Japan is US $ 1,200.[87]

In a World Bank study, it was also concluded that "in the EAC, non-tariff measures, coupled with poor infrastructure, limited human skills capacity and considerable scope for corruption/fraudulent behaviour add to the difficulty and cost of trading goods."[88] The comprehensive report covers Non-Tariff Measures (NTMs) from various perspectives: cost of NTMs such as delays in transit time between Mombasa port and Malaba at the border of Kenya and Uganda, axle load limits (which have since been settled from September 2011), two weeks clearance at the port of Mombasa, too many police road blocks in the transit route, numerous weighbridges along the northern and central corridors, between Mombasa and Malaba/Busia and between Dar es Salaam and Rusumo on the Tanzania-Rwanda border; cumbersome customs and administrative cross-border processes; and other restrictive practices.

Interestingly though, whilst NTBs or NTMs constitute major impediments to intra-EAC trade, the World Bank report referred to above still notes that RECs in Africa:

---

[87] See www.trademarksa.org/news/nightmare-moving-cargo-mombasa. 3 October 2011: see also, Lowering Transport Costs in Eastern and Southern Africa, a Policy Position Paper, December, 2008, www.esabmonetwork.org/fileadmin/esabmo_uploads/Transport_Network_Policy_Position_Paper.pdf.

[88] See INTERNATIONAL BANK FOR RECONSTRUCTION AND DEVELOPMENT, *Non-Tariff Measures on Good Trade in the East African Community: Synthesis Report* (Report No. 45708-AFR), Washington, D.C.: The World Bank, October, 2008. See also JENSEN, Michael F. and John C. Keyser, *Non-Tariff Measures on Good Trade in the East African Community*, Washington, D.C.: The World Bank, 2008.

do not have an impressive record of dealing with contentious non-tariff measures ... the EAC has quickly achieved a lot that remains desirable in Sub Saharan Africa.[89]

In other words, the EAC is singled out to be a better performer in addressing the challenges posed by NTBs. Indeed, there are serious efforts being undertaken by the EAC to establish One Stop Border Posts (OSBPs) at key border points such as Malaba, Gatuna, Namanga and Rusumo in order to arrest bureaucratic bottlenecks which heighten costs of doing business.

The EAC is presently in the process of enacting, through the East African Legislative Assembly, an OSBP regional law which will put in place well-harmonised trade facilitating systems in the region. Equally, there are developments in the direction of adopting a single customs territory system, a point earlier referred to, though again sovereign issues seem to impede the adoption of the system sooner than later.

There are several other NTBs which the EAC has to grapple with. These include a dilapidated railway system; inefficient ports; a road system that is yet to be well interconnected on a regional scale; serious power shortages which are heightened by the lack of strategic cross-border power interconnections; a non-competitive air transport system that is yet to embrace a single and liberalised regional air space and high levels of corruption along the transit corridors.

All these NTB challenges when coupled with a persistent serious state of food insecurity arising from the adverse impacts of climate change and environmental degradation but also caused by the lack of adequate application of science and technology in agricultural production have together precipitated a grave economic situation in the region in recent years. The region has thus witnessed a foreign exchange crisis with local currencies in a freefall and the worst inflationary pressures experienced in decades. The Kenyan Shilling, for example, reached Shs. 104 to the US Dollar, down from the averages of Shs.80 to the Dollar in 2010.

The Ugandan and Tanzanian Shillings equally fell drastically in value in relation to the US dollar in 2011. Above all, the rates of inflation have shot up in all the EAC partner states except Rwanda, thereby distorting not only the cost of living, but also the cost of doing business. The Common Market would clearly suffer as a result of the weaknesses in the currencies of the partner states as well as from the inflationary pressures that have emerged.

---

[89] Ibid. at p. 49.

Cross-Border Investment Activity

The EAC region has witnessed significant growth in foreign direct investment between 2004 and 2009, rising from US $ 683 million to 1.7 billion. Equally, there has been sizable increase in cross-border investment flows reflected in buoyant mergers and acquisitions (M&A) as well as in greenfield investments. Data is lacking for actual values of such investments which is one of challenges facing the EAC statistical department to work upon with the support of the East African Business Council. However, there are notable examples of such cross-border investments, the flag bearer being Kenya's East African Breweries' acquisition in October 2010 of 51% shares in Tanzania's Serengeti Breweries at a cost of US $ 60.4 million. Other M&As include Kenya's Transcentury purchase of shares in Tanzania Cables and Tanelec; Kenya Airways acquisition of significant minority shares in Precision Air of Tanzania (which recently broadened its ownership through an IPO on the Dar es Salaam Stock Exchange); Kenya Nation Group acquisition of majority shares in Uganda's Monitor Newspaper Group and Tanzania's Mwananchi Communications; and Transcentury of Kenya acquiring majority shares in Tanzania Packers' Chai Bora.

At the level of greenfield investments, it is possible to see significant development from the confidence that is being manifested in greater reliance on the use of the regional risk capital market in contrast to the past when there has been overreliance on foreign direct investment to drive the development of the regional economy. There has been increasing acceptance of the reality that it is regional production, retail and service networks as well as champions that would foster regional competitiveness and sustained growth in intra-regional trade.

In this context, the EAC region celebrates cross-border greenfield investments of the likes of Azam of Tanzania whose investments in food processing now cover almost the whole EAC region. Serena Group of Kenya has also now invested in hotels and lodges in Uganda, Rwanda, Tanzania, and Burundi; BIDCO of Kenya has invested in a large palm oil agricultural plantation in Uganda and in edible oil production in Uganda and Tanzania; Sameer Group of Kenya has invested in the milk and dairy products in Uganda; Alam Group of Uganda has invested in steel rolling and mild steel production in Mombasa Kenya; Athi River Mining has invested in cement plants in Tanga and Dar es Salaam; Nakumatt, the leading Kenyan retailer has opened supermarkets in Uganda, Rwanda and in Moshi, Tanzania.

Moreover, Kenyan banks and insurance companies such as KCB, Equity, Jubilee and Heritage operate in most EAC partner states. In the field of air transport, Kenya's Fly540 has set up local companies in Tanzania, Uganda and Burundi. And finally, in the area of tertiary education, Uganda's Kampala International University has set up a university campus in Tanzania.

These are only a few examples of cross-border investments. Yet there are several other small industries that are part of the M&A and greenfield investments activity in the EAC region. Interestingly, these developments are taking place within the context of an uncertain regulatory regime governing cross-border mergers and acquisitions. For example, the M&A between East African Breweries and Serengeti Breweries was able to show that the East African Competition Act of 2006 could not be applied to guide the acquisition process. This is because the regional law is yet to be domesticated at national levels. Moreover, Uganda, Kenya and Rwanda are yet to even incorporate national competition laws.

It is clear that the delay in domesticating EAC laws and, in this regard, the competition law specifically, constitutes a serious challenge confronting the emergence of regional business champions. It is also notable that the EAC competition law itself is now out of date. When the law was drafted in 2005, the EAC had not considered the entry of a higher level of integration, namely the Common Market. As such, the competition law was drafted to fit a trade in goods regime and not trade in services as well as in capital. The law will thus have to be overhauled to respond to the new demands imposed by the entry of the Common Market. I will revert to this topic when I examine in greater detail what strategic factors will need to be considered in making the Common Market work.

The performance of the Customs Union as outlined above has important bearing on what awaits the Common Market. It is clear that the Customs Union has significantly shaped the conditions and the environment upon which the Common Market will operate particularly with respect to trade in goods. However, there are other important factors which would also impact the Common Market. These include: the high costs of trade logistics which arise from poor transport systems, public sector bureaucratic and corrupt behaviour and the uncertain legal and regulatory regime which impacts effective cross-border economic activity.

The Birth of the EAC Common Market

The EAC Common Market is a creature of Article 76 of the EAC Treaty. A Common Market has been defined as "a market in which every participant within the community in question is free to invest, produce, work, buy and sell, to supply or obtain services under conditions of competition which have not been artificially distorted."[90] The Treaty provides that the partner states shall allow free movement of labour, goods, services, capital, and the right of establishment. Moreover, Article 104 stipulates that the Partner States agree

---

[90] See KAPTEYN, P.J.G. and VerLoren van Themaat, P., *Introduction to the Law of the European Communities*, London: Graham & Trotman, 1998, p. 122.

to adopt measures to achieve the four freedoms and to ensure the enjoyment of the right of establishment and residence of their citizens within the EAC.

The Treaty recognizes that the establishment of the Common Market "shall be progressive." It is important to note that the EAC stages of integration which are outlined in Article 5 of the Treaty, namely the Customs Union, the Common Market, subsequently the Monetary Union, and ultimately the Political Federation are intended to underscore the need to "strengthen and regulate industrial, commercial, infrastructure, cultural, social, political and other relations of the Partner States." The ultimate goal in all these integration measures is for the EAC to realise accelerated, harmonious and balanced development and including sustained expansion of economic activities the benefits of which shall be equally shared.

It is these underlined collective needs and goals, which are often overlooked or given tacit consideration, that determine the pace and robustness of EAC integration. They encapsulate the shared goals that go to the heart and spirit of how EAC integration should be pursued and realised.

Notwithstanding the foregoing, it is clear, however, that in committing themselves to the establishment of the Common Market, the EAC Partner States were seized of the reality, in a fast globalising world, that it is through a Common Market that they can promote a large regional market in which they can realise greater division of labour through industrial rationalisation, consolidation and specialisation and reap the benefits of larger economies of scale. It is an accepted trade and economic theory that greater specialisation lowers costs, bolsters value-adding productivity and competitiveness. It also mitigates the inefficiencies in business firms in accessing essential services and diversity of skills.[91]

The central features of any Common Market are the free movement of labour, goods, services, capital and the right of establishment. Whilst Article 6 of the EAC Common Market Protocol provides that the free movement of goods between the Partner States shall be governed by Article 39 of the EAC Customs Union Protocol and other laws and Protocols set out in the Common Market Protocol, such as the *Protocol on Standardisation, Quality Assurance, Metrology and Testing and the Act of 2006* thereof, it remains paradoxical why the EAC Competition law of 2006 has not been mentioned in the Common Market Protocol. In my view, the EAC Competition law constitutes a critical law on the basis of which the free movement of capital and services is predicated upon.

---

[91] See HOEKMAN, Bernard and Aaditya Mattoo, *Services Trade and Growth* (Policy Research Working Paper 4461) Washington, D.C.: The World Bank Development Research Group, January, 2008, p. 21.

In the following sections of this chapter, I proceed to examine the strategic driving forces for making the Common Market work. Before I do so, it is important to set the stage by analysing what I see as the important conditions that have emerged prior to the establishment of the Common Market but which conditions have provided a supporting foundation for the Common Market to take off.

Conditions Supporting the Common Market's Take Off

Unlike in the European Union prior to the on-set of its Single Market in 1992, the EAC Partner States have, in the past decade and a half, witnessed a remarkable process of economic liberalisation, largely propelled by national governments but also partly by the business confidence engendered through the EACU. Thus, there has been significant opening up of the strategic services sectors (tourism, banking, insurance, telecoms, media, education, construction, retail, etc) to both foreign and regional economic players. This process of economic liberalisation has helped to shape and create the conditions which, with political will and commitment, should dampen and even arrest zero-sum concerns and fears among citizens of some Partner States (notably Tanzanians), that the Common Market will have negative impact on national economies.

In the realisation that liberalisation of services, trade and capital could leverage production and export of goods and services as well as infuse efficiency and competition in the economies of the EAC Partner States, the EAC region has accordingly witnessed robust policies and measures focused on enabling trade in services and capital to flow intra-regionally. Of particular significance has been the growth of capital markets and the move propelled by the East African Securities Exchanges Association, which is a membership organisation of the EAC National Stock Exchanges, with the EAC support, towards the establishment of a regional capital markets platform. This platform, which may take the shape of an East African Stock Exchange, will constitute a vehicle for the mobilisation of risk capital to fund both national and regional businesses and projects, including infrastructure development.

The development in the capital markets front has been reinforced by the full liberalisation of capital accounts by Kenya, Uganda and Rwanda, a process that has spurred cross-border capital flows so well manifested in the buoyancy of the regional stock market. Needless to underscore, there is also a growing trend in cross-listing of company shares in the stock exchanges of Nairobi, Kampala, Dar es Salaam and Kigali. Bujumbura is in the process of establishing one.

In this regard, the shares of the following Kenyan firms are cross-listed in Dar es Salaam Stock Exchange: Kenya Airways, East African Breweries,

Nation Media Group, KCB and Jubilee Holdings. In the Kampala Stock Exchange you also find the following Kenyan companies have shares cross-listed: Equity Bank, KCB, Jubilee Insurance, East African Breweries, Kenya Airways and Nation Media Group. Only KCB, of East African Companies is listed on the Kigali Stock Exchange. The overall picture that emanates from this stock market outlook is the preponderance and dominance of Kenyan companies.

Tanzania and Burundi are yet to full liberalise their capital accounts, a regrettable stance which could be viewed as a form of disenfranchisement of their citizens in participating in the broad ownership of fast developing regional assets such as Kenya Airways and East African Breweries. The Tanzania Central Bank made a pronouncement in October 2011 that the capital account will be fully liberalised for capital markets business within the EAC by 2015.

Kenya's dominance of the region's capital market activity is clear given the size of the Kenyan economy with 55 companies listed on the Nairobi Stock Exchange. Kenya's nominal GDP in June 2011 stood at US $ 33 billion; Tanzania's was US $ 23 billion; Uganda's was US $ 17 billion; Rwanda's was US $ 5.62 billion and Burundi's was US $ 1.5 billion. This economic size is also reflected in the huge differential in total market capitalisation among the four stock markets, as of September 2011:

Kenya	US $ 14.3 billion
Uganda	US $ 4.8 billion
Tanzania	US $ 3.7 billion
Rwanda	US $ 1.38 billion

The Growth of the Service Sector

The free movement of services which is also described as trade in services takes pre-eminence in the EAC Common Market largely because the services sector is becoming the lead contributor to GDP in the EAC Partner States. The table below shows the GDP composition by sector in the five EAC Partner States in 2010.[92]

---

[92] See CENTRAL INTELLIGENCE AGENCY, *The World Factbook 2011*, Washington, D.C.: CIA, 2011.

Tanzania			Kenya			Burundi		
	Agriculture	28.4%		Agriculture	22%		Agriculture	31.6%
	Industry	24.0%		Industry	16%		Industry	21.4%
	Service	47.6%		Service	62%		Service	47.0%
Uganda			Rwanda			European Union		
	Agriculture	23.6%		Agriculture	42.1%		Service	78%
	Industry	24.5%		Industry	14.3%			
	Service	51.9%		Service	43.6%			

Apart from Rwanda where agriculture is still an important contributor to national income, the situation in the three leading EAC economies (and strangely in Burundi as well), is a far cry from what obtained in the early 2000 when agriculture featured prominently in the share of GDP. However, the diminishing share of agriculture to GDP is worrisome at a time when food insecurity is becoming a serious challenge in the EAC. Moreover, EAC's industrialisation strategy is intimately connected to agribusiness which would falter if agricultural production declines. How the Common Market will play out in leveraging the growth of the services market is one of the key features of this chapter. In the following section, I examine some of the challenges which confront the Common Market and suggest measures that could help to make the market work optimally.

Making the Common Market Work

In the earlier part of this chapter, I have touched upon a number of challenges that continue to afflict the realisation of a fully fledged EAC Customs Union and, indeed, in making the EACU realise its full potential as a strategic legal and institutional vehicle for enhancing trading goods. Under the Common Market, trading in goods also features as a core objective, but from a different perspective that conjures deeper economic integration. It is important to have an appreciation of what free movement of goods under a Common Market regime involves because there is a marked difference between it and trade in goods as spelt out in the Customs Union framework. Under the Common Market, free movement of goods requires that the EAC

Partner States remove most restrictions with exception of restrictions that are justified on grounds of public health, environmental concerns and consumer protection. In other words, physical barriers, technical standards restrictions, and fiscal taxes are removed to a maximum extent.

In this regard, it could be noted, for example, that the adoption of the Double Taxation Avoidance Agreement in December 2010 by the EAC Partner States fits in well with the objective of making the Common Market work through the removal of the Double Taxation requirement.

In the EU, where there is free movement of goods under its Single Market, there is a law that harmonises the technical barriers to trade in goods which minimises some of the risks referred above. Currently, about half of trade in goods within the EU is governed by harmonised regulations with the other half falling under a non-harmonised regime and thus affected by national technical regulations. In the EAC, Article 6 of the Common Market Protocol makes reference to a number of Protocols and laws that have a bearing on free movement of goods. These Protocols and laws include aspects on standardisation and competition. However, it is crucially important that these Protocols and laws are revisited to bring them up to standard and conformity particularly with regard to their domestication and enforcement.

It is noted that several EAC Protocols are either yet to be ratified or domesticated in national laws. The same applies to a number of laws passed by the East African Legislative Assembly. In the EU, the EC is entrusted with a set of instruments to enforce the Single Market law. Moreover, the European Court of Justice exercises jurisdiction over the interpretation and application of the Single Market Act. However, given the sensitivity over the imposition of strict legal sanctions for violations of the Single Market Law, the EC is always cautious when exercising its supranational powers of enforcement, invariably electing to resolve violations through a process of consensus building.

Let me now turn to the other areas of free movement, namely that of labour, services, capital and people (which incorporates the right of establishment). However, two initial issues need to be raised which, in my view, constitute important underpinnings for making the Common Market work. These issues revolve around the questions of political and citizen will and commitment to the integration project, on the one hand, and the general performance of the national economies, on the other. For without the total support of the political elite and of the broad citizenry, along with well-functioning national economies, the Common Market would find it difficult to realise its broad objectives.

Political Will and Commitment to Integration

The question of political will in integration was well articulated back in August 1965 by the founding President of Tanzania, Mwalimu Julius Nyerere. In a speech to the visiting members of the Central Legislative Assembly comprising representatives of the then three East African Parliaments, Nyerere said:

> Ultimately, we are not in fact 'East African' leaders, but leaders of States in East Africa, and regional loyalty has sometimes to come second to our national responsibilities.[93]

This view finds powerful resonance in Professor Paul Kennedy's analysis of the weaknesses inherent in economic integration. Writing in his seminal book, 'Preparing for the Twenty First Century' he posits that "the locus of identity of most people is still the nation state. It is the nation state that is viewed to be the key unit in responding to global change."[94] He further argues that ordinary citizens instinctively turn to their own national governments, not to a supranational institution, in search of solutions for their social and economic livelihoods.[95]

Nyerere's and Kennedy's views underlie the fundamental question: what characteristics and what strengths are desirable for the EAC Partner States to pursue and realise deeper integration such as the Common Market? It is such questions that have catapulted the Nkrumahist thesis that regional and continental economic integration is best realised when a political kingdom is first established. A number of public intellectuals in East Africa, including political leaders like Uganda's President Yoweri Museveni, hold the view that acceptability, viability and sustainability of economic integration fundamentally rest on the establishment of the East African political federation. However, this view is rather simplistic in that it assumes that sensitive issues which currently affect the Common Market, such as land ownership, would necessarily be resolved under a political federation system. It would be recalled that even the Wako Report on Fast Tracking the EAC Political Federation had clearly spelt out that land ownership would not form part of the federal state in the realisation that its inclusion would spell the rejection of the political integration project.

In the light of the foregoing, the way forward in promoting the political will for deeper integration lies in transforming the EAC into a "people centred"

---

[93] See NYERERE, Julius K., "Problems of East African Cooperation," in NYERERE, Julius K., *Freedom and Socialism*, Nairobi and Dar es Salaam: Oxford University Press, 1968, at p. 63.

[94] KENNEDY, Paul, *Preparing for the Twenty-First Century*, New York: Vintage Books, 1994, p. 134.

[95] Ibid., p. 9.

community. This goal has been elusive, largely because of the heterogeneity and diversity of the civil society in East Africa making it difficult to galvanise a people-centred platform that can spearhead the broad citizenry support for deeper integration. In mid-2011, Trademark East Africa helped to forge an East African Civil Society Organization Forum (EACSOF) as an autonomous umbrella body of all East African Non-Governmental Organizations "to promote a platform and catalyse a critical mass of organised civil society to engage in need-driven, people-centred East African integration and cooperation process effectively and proactively for equitable and sustainable development." Trademark East Africa is funding EACSOF's capacity building including the salary of its Chief Executive.

It remains to be seen whether EACSOF will succeed to promote an East African ethos around the objective of winning the hearts and minds of ordinary East African citizens for deeper integration and upon whom political will so critically depends.

The Performance of National Economies

The second important underpinning in making the Common Market and the overall EAC integration agenda work relates to the performance of the national economies. Evidently, it is strong and self-sustaining national economies that provide the confidence for nation states to pursue deeper integration. This view finds support in Professor Mario Monti's thinking. In his report to the EC earlier referred to, Monti argues that "if the market and the social components do not find an appropriate reconciliation, something has to give in. Following the crisis,[96] with the declining appetite for the market and the increasing concern about inequalities, it is by no means clear that it would be the market - that is the Single Market, to prevail."[97]

In the speech earlier referred to the East African legislators, Nyerere equally noted that "Tanzania cannot be a large trading partner of anyone if she remains forever poor."[98] One could argue of course, that Nyerere's view begs the issue because regionalism could, in fact, improve Tanzania's economic condition. However, it would seem that Nyerere was actually speaking to the obtaining perceptions of many Tanzanians whose understanding at the time of the role of regional integration was low. Indeed, even presently, what seems to fuel the zero-sum attitudes in Tanzania with regard to deeper regional integration is the view that integration is a win-lose undertaking with Kenya ever becoming the dominant beneficiary.

---

[96] This is in reference to the 2007/2008 financial crisis.

[97] See MONTI, Mario, *A New Strategy for the Single Market - At the Service of Europe's Economy and Society: Report to the President of the European Commission José Manuel Barroso*, op. cit. at p. 26.

[98] See NYERERE, Julius K., "Problems of East African Cooperation," op. cit. at p. 65.

In this vein it is important that EAC Partner States foster rapid national economic growth which would have important ramifications in instilling higher confidence for embracing deeper integration. In this context, it is important to note that the Treaty establishing the EAC in fact recognises the centrality of strong national economies in the integration process. Article 79 calls on the Partner States to promote self-sustaining and balanced industrial growth, improve the competitiveness of the industrial sector and develop indigenous entrepreneurs. At the same time, Article 84(ii) calls upon the Partner States to improve their resource and production base in order to achieve balanced development within the EAC.

However, improved performance of national economies could also be made possible through regional measures. In this regard, Article 80 of the Treaty, for example, provides for the development of an East African Industrial Development Strategy. Indeed, the EAC Summit of Heads of State in November 2011 adopted such a strategy whose focus is on encouraging investments on a regional scale in priority sectors such as agro-processing, agro-chemicals, fertilisers, pharmaceuticals, petro-chemicals and natural gas products, iron ore and steel, minerals processing, bio-fuels, etc. The aim of the EAC industrialisation strategy is to transform the region into one that is climate-friendly, globally competitive and one that leverages standards of living of the people. It is envisaged that by 2030, the EAC countries should, overall, achieve a middle-income country status with an average GDP per capita of US $ 1,300 per annum. It is also planned that by that time the share of the manufacturing sector to GDP should be 25%, up from the current average of 9.7%. Job creation should also rise from the current regional level of 456,000 a year to 2.3 million a year.

Undoubtedly, the EAC industrialisation strategy is overly ambitious considering that according to *UNIDO's Partner for Prosperity Report 2010,* Africa accounted for only 1% of global manufacturing output in 2010 and that only 14% of Africa's exports were manufactures. In fact, Africa's manufacturing value added fell from 23% in 2000 to 20% in 2008. [99] Thus, whilst the promotion of industrialisation constitutes a strategic pillar for making the EAC Common Market work and for creating the new jobs that can respond to the challenge of the youth bulge whose potential negative impact on the region's peace and stability could be significant, the region cannot be oblivious of the enormity of the challenges facing the industrialisation process. This is evident from the region's overreliance on imports of consumer goods largely from China and India. Some of these consumer goods could easily be manufactured within the EAC region, either by indigenous East African firms or by foreign companies setting up manufacturing bases in the region.

---

[99] See UNITED NATIONS INDUSTRIAL DEVELOPMENT ORGANIZATION, *UNIDO-Partner for Prosperity Report 2010,* Vienna: UNIDO, 2010.

It is thus important that the EAC Industrialisation Strategy sets out the supporting legal and investment framework that can enable the mitigation of these challenges. In turn, the EAC needs to develop a regiment of powerful measures which not only provide incentives for the growth of the manufacturing industry capacity but also help to effectively counteract the process of de-industrialisation that is now triggered by illicit trade and the growing menace of counterfeits and pirated goods in the region.

An important area in addressing the performance of national economies centres on the role of governments in creating the appropriate conditions to spur investments, both domestic and foreign. It is such conditions or doing business environment that have a direct impact on the promotion of more balanced and harmonious development in the Partner States and on the basis of which there will be equitable sharing of accruing benefits. The Common Market will only work well when such conditions are well developed. The reason is simple. An economy that works below par cannot, for example, create new jobs and may raise strong sentiments against some of the Common Market objectives such as the free movement of labour. Job protectionism would then take command.[100]

Currently, and over the past three years, the *World Bank Doing Business Reports* have painted a poor picture of the doing business environment in the EAC with the exception for Rwanda. In the 2012 Report, the EAC as a region ranked 117th out of 183 economies ranked. In 2011, the EAC was ranked 116th. Rwanda itself is ranked 58th (up from 67th in 2010); Kenya is ranked 98th, Uganda 122nd; Tanzania 128th and Burundi 181st. The ranking is based on performance in key issues such as intellectual property rights, permits, licences, payment of taxes, registering property, regulation, corruption, rule of law, labour markets, access to land, ease of cross-border trade, power supply, etc.

In the same vein, the Reports of the World Economic Forum on competitiveness provide useful pointers on the role of governments in promoting the supporting conditions for improved national economic performance and regionalism. Much work still needs to be done to improve the competitiveness of the EAC Partner States. The World Economic Forum *Competitiveness Report for 2010-2011* ranks the EAC Partner States very low in the global competitiveness index comprising 142 countries:

---

[100] See for example, "Stringent Rules Hamper Business in the EAC," *The East African* (Nairobi), 29th August – 4th September, 2011, pp. 15 and 29.

Country	Rank
Rwanda	70th
Kenya	102nd
Tanzania	120th
Uganda	121st
Burundi	140th

What is particularly disconcerting about the rankings of the World Economic Forum Competitiveness Report 2012 is those areas that crucially matter in making the EAC Common Market work are generally distressingly low, with few exceptions in relation to Rwanda and somewhat for Kenya. These areas are in relation to the state of institutions, infrastructure, macro-economy, primary education, higher education and training, foods and market efficiency, labour market efficiency, financial market sophistication, technological readiness and market size. Clearly, for Tanzania and Uganda which are large players in the EAC Common Market, they will have to undertake radical reforms in the areas mentioned above if the Common Market is to work optimally and offer equitable benefits to them and to regional economic growth as a whole.

Free Movement of Labour: Challenges and Way Forward

Article 10 of the Common Market Protocol provides for the free movement of workers who are citizens of the EAC Partner States. By "free movement", it means, *inter alia*, entitlement to apply for and accept employment; move freely and stay within the territories of the Partner States for the purpose of employment in accordance with national laws, to enjoy freedom of association and collective bargaining as well as the rights and benefits of social security accorded to the workers of the host Partner State.

If there is one "freedom" that evokes a great deal of heat and concern in the EAC, and particularly in Tanzania, it is the one relating to labour or workers. Interestingly, even in the EU, this freedom has raised a great deal of tension. As Professor Monti observed in his report earlier referred to, "freedom of movement of workers is the most contested and at the same time the least used of the four freedoms. In fact, as at 2009, only 2.3% of Europeans lived in a Member state different from that of their nationality."[101]

In the EAC, the negotiations process relating to free movement of labour under the Common Market Protocol was both intense and conflictual. The

---

[101] See MONTI, Mario, *A New Strategy for the Single Market – At the Service of Europe's Economy and Society: Report to the President of the European Commission José Manuel Barroso*, op. cit., p. 56.

outcome, as reflected in the Regulations and Schedule for the Free Movement of Workers (Annex II of the Protocol), reflects the tortuous nature of the negotiations and the wide variance in the timeframes for opening up the national labour markets to free movement of workers and in the occupational categories available under the process. To cite an example, Kenya, Burundi, Rwanda and Uganda committed themselves to a comprehensive opening up of their labour markets to most categories of professional staff in the year 2010 when the Common Market Protocol came into force.

Tanzania, in contrast, committed itself to a gradual opening up of select professional occupations between 2010 (for a broad range of teachers, tutors and nurses) and 2015 (a broad range of engineers and life and health sciences). Paradoxically, Tanzania which is in dire need of professionals in the knowledge economy businesses and hospitality industry did not specify in the negotiated Schedule what its position was on the free movement of workers in these particular sectors. Put differently, Tanzania is the most intransigent of EAC Partner States in allowing free movement of workers.

Reflecting their openness to free movement of workers, Kenya and Rwanda have waived work permit fees to EAC citizens seeking employment in their countries. Such fees are still charged in the other EAC Partner States. In Tanzania and Uganda, for example, an EAC citizen has to pay US $ 1,000 and US $ 800 respectively to secure a two year work permit.

Some attempts are being made by the EAC to forge a harmonized response to the ideals of the Common Market Protocol on free movement of labour. In September 2011, the EAC Partner States met to identify areas that require harmonisation in immigration, employment and labour laws. Unfortunately, with respect to work permits, the meeting failed to make progress because of absence of labour experts.

Generally, the free movement of workers in the EAC faces two main challenges. The first challenge relates to the present lack of harmonised social security schemes. Even at national levels, there are differential members' benefits offered by different social security institutions. For example, in Tanzania, the National Social Security Fund (NSSF) offers benefits that are different from those offered by the Parastatal Pensions Fund (PPF) and yet the two institutions are the ones that compete in the same private sector employment regime. The bigger challenge, however, lies in the portability or transferability of members' benefits from one country to another which has the potential of impeding the incentive for cross-border movement of labour particularly where regional companies have to transfer their staff from one country to another.

The EAC is in the process of forging an acceptable system whereby members' social security benefits can be easily transferred across the EAC

Partner States. The EAC Secretariat, in this regard, is working closely with the Regional Social Security Association which brings together all the social security funds of the Partner States in promoting both harmonisation of benefits and their portability. Tanzania has taken a major lead in facilitating this process by establishing a national Social Security Regulatory Authority. Other EAC Partner States may replicate this framework.

There is another dimension relating to social security systems as a strategic factor in making the Common Market work. This has to do with the provision of social security on a regional scale. Whilst the role of secure, durable and effective social protection at national levels should be sustained and consolidated, it may be appropriate to consider an EAC legislative framework that allows social security institutions to provide occupational retirement and other provisions on a regional basis. Such a system would provide a solid catalyst for smoother cross-border movement of labour.

The second challenge facing the free movement of labour centres on the national recognition of academic and professional qualifications and certifications. Clearly, the absence of such a system is an impediment to the free movement of workers across the borders. The Inter-University Council for East Africa (IUCEA), an institution of the EAC, is at an advanced stage in proposing a system for mutual recognition of academic qualifications. This work would have been simpler has the institutions of higher learning been limited to public universities of the Partner States. But the work has become huge and complex because of the tremendous growth in private universities in the past decade.

Presently, the IUCEA has a membership of 86 public and private universities and colleges from the five EAC Partner States and undertaking the requisite rigorous quality assurance work and determination of mutual recognition of all the qualifications of all those universities is time consuming. Moreover, such an exercise may embrace a process of harmonisation of education systems and curricula of primary, secondary and tertiary education.

The EAC Council of Ministers responsible for Education met in July 2011 and reviewed a Regional Report on the Study of East African Education Systems and Training Curricula (HESTC) whose underlying thrust is the harmonisation of education and training systems. Undoubtedly, the task is huge and challenging and the Ministers, advisedly, decided to establish a High Level Task Force composed of experts from the Partner States well versed in education and training curriculum development, examinations and allied institutions to review the HESTC report. It was the firm view of the Ministers that focus should be given to quality assurance and accreditation issues rather than on curricula because harmonised curricula may stifle innovation and creativity as well as promotion of education competition in the region.

Related to the challenge of mutual recognition of qualifications is the broad question of regional integration of professional services in the EAC region. The World Bank recognises the centrality of professional services for development in East Africa. In an outstanding paper published in the World Bank's Economic Premise No. 2 of September 2010 titled *Reform and Regional Integration of Professional Services in East Africa,* Nora Dihel *et al*[102] observe that:

> national markets for professionals and professional services in East Africa remain underdeveloped, whereas regional markets are fragmented by restrictive policies and regulatory heterogeneity. An effective reform agenda will require policy action in four areas: education, regulation of professional services, trade policy, and labour mobility at both the national and international levels.[103]

The professional services covered include business skills and services (accounting, auditing and legal), engineering services (civil, mechanical and electronic) and backbone services (telecommunications, banking and transport).

The paper notes that there is substantive scope for trade in professional services in the EAC region given the present institutional weaknesses in generating capacities. According to Dihel's paper, four challenges confront this paucity in capacity. First, professional education is expensive in all the EAC countries contributing to inaffordability in acquiring professional qualifications. Second, a generally weak secondary education system limits the ability of students to pursue and attain professional qualifications. The low level mathematical skills underlies the paucity of students pursuing sciences, engineering and technology courses and the consequential acute shortage of engineering professional skills. Third, there are very few professional education institutions and those that exist are generally of poor quality. Fourth, links between academic institutions and industry are thin contributing to the production of "nominally qualified but effectively unemployable professionals."[104]

Overall, the paper by Nora Dihel et al attaches the underdevelopment of professional services to excessive domestic regulation of entry and operations of such services in all the EAC Partner States with the exception of Rwanda and, slightly, of Uganda. Since professional services go to the

---

[102] DIHEL, Nora *et al.*, *Reform and Regional Integration of Professional Services in East Africa: Time for Action* (Report No. 57672-AFR), Washington, D.C.: Poverty Reduction and Economic Management Unit 2 of the International Bank for Reconstruction and Development, October, 2010.

[103] Ibid., p. 1.

[104] Ibid., p. 3.

heart of most of the Common Market operations – labour, capital and services, it is imperative, in making the Common Market work, that the markets for professional services be urgently reformed. The reforms have to be holistic cutting across the regulatory framework in removing restrictive barriers to trade in professional services and promoting specialised academic and professional education especially at regional level. Allowing regional accreditation, rather than the current rigid national accreditation process, to enable private sector players to establish specialised regional educational institutions will go a long way in addressing the needs of dynamic professional services in the EAC region.

Free Movement of Services

Services and trade in services have a profound impact on growth and development in the EAC region. Services are crucial inputs into the production of goods and other services and, to that extent, have a close correlation to productivity and competitiveness. There is little doubt, based on recent economic data in the EAC region, provided in this paper, that providing greater availability and affordability of quality services will bolster economic growth, create jobs and reduce poverty. However, it is well recognised that liberalising services trade as envisaged under the EAC Common Market is more complex than liberalising trade on goods for which the EAC has already had some experience through the implementation of the Customs Union Protocol.

This complexity largely arises from the centrality of regulation of many services sectors in ensuring their efficient operation having in mind the potential for market failure. The challenge, as outlined in the World Bank Report titled, *Harnessing Regional Integration for Trade and Growth in Southern Africa*:[105]

> is one of integrating domestic services with regional and global markets, while providing a regulatory environment that delivers competitive service sectors and allows public policy objectives, such as universal access, to be met efficiently.[106]

The response to this challenge remains generally elusive in the EAC countries.

Earlier in this chapter, I outlined the challenges relating to professional services. However, there are additional challenges related to a broader scope of business services. Take the example of transport services. Whilst some

---

[105] See GILLSON, Ian, *et al., Harnessing Regional Integration for Trade and Growth in Southern Africa*, Washington, D.C.: International Bank for Reconstruction and Development, March, 2011.

[106] Ibid., p. 59.

form of liberalisation has taken place in allowing regional airlines such as Kenya's Fly540 to register outside Kenya and fly to national airports such as those in Tanzania, which, incidentally, has led to the collapse of hitherto exorbitant airfares, much to the benefit of customers, there is no good reason why some EAC airlines cannot operate at EAC national levels without registering as national companies.

Such deregulation and licensing liberalisation is what would boost services trade in the region and leverage competitiveness. Moving towards an East Africa-wide licensing system for regional services such as airlines, retail, energy and telecom services is the right way to proceed with unleashing the full potential of the Common Market. The services sector offers a unique opportunity for EAC Partner States to shift from protectionism and embrace effective regional integration.

An important to consider is that, generally, regional services trade is encumbered by a weak regional judicial system. Whilst the European Court of Justice has wide powers over the enforcement of the Single Market, the East African Court of Justice (EACJ), in contrast, has no defined jurisdiction over disputes that arise either from the working of the Customs Union or the Common Market. This is a serious weakness in making the Common Market work well. Article 27 of the EAC Treaty gives the EACJ initial jurisdiction over the interpretation and application of the Treaty. However, it boggles the mind as to what would restrict the EACJ from hearing disputes arising from the Customs Union and the Common Market when, pursuant to Article 151 of the EAC Treaty, all the EAC Protocols and Annexes "form an integral part of the Treaty."

Moreover, which agency within the EAC has authority to exercise oversight over the compliance and enforcement, for example, of the EAC Competition Law, 2006 which, though needing overhaul to fit the requirements of the Common Market, does not fall within the purview of the EACJ but of the municipal courts! Making the Common Market work will crucially hinge on immediate extension of the jurisdiction of the EACJ to handle all disputes that arise from the operationalisation of both the Customs Union and the Common Market Protocols.

There is also the broad question about the powers of the EAC Secretariat in administering the Customs Union and the Common Market. The EAC Secretariat is, to all intents and purposes, toothless in the oversight and enforcement process for these two important integration programmes unlike in the EU where the European Commission exercises considerable authority.

Free Movement of Capital

In an earlier part of this chapter, some examination was undertaken on the emergence of capital markets in the EAC region on cross-border flows of capital and cross listing of shares in the national stock exchanges. The general thrust is that free movement of capital is an essential condition for the effective functioning of the Common Market. It promotes better allocation of resources, facilitates cross-border trade, stimulates and enables the mobility of labour and creates the supportive conditions for businesses to mobilise risk capital. What remains to examine is the progress being made to integrate financial markets in the region. In February 2011, the EAC and the World Bank signed a grant agreement worth US $ 16 million to support a project that would transform the EAC financial services sector. The nine year project is intended to build a single financial services market for the EAC region, the grant being to support the first phase of the project.

Since 2009, The EAC has been working with the World Bank Group to implement a regional financial market integration project which forms part of the Common Market Protocol. This project is well outlined in a paper, "Scaling-up Regional Financial Integration in the EAC."[107] It also features in a much more elaborate and powerful IMF Working Paper, *Capital Market Integration: Progress Ahead of the East African Community Monetary Union*.[108] The project has five components: financial inclusion and strengthening of market participants; harmonisation of financial markets laws and regulations and the mutual recognition of supervisory agencies; integration of financial market infrastructure; development of the regional bond market and capacity building of both the EAC Secretariat and the regulatory bodies in the EAC Partner States. The output of the project is the realisation of an integrated EAC capital market regime which allows capital to flow easily across borders and participants to operate freely in the EAC region. As part of the whole process, it should be possible for the EAC to establish a Regional Stock Exchange and financial market intermediaries to offer and deliver services in all the five EAC Partner States.

As noted earlier in this chapter, Tanzania and Burundi are yet to fully liberalise their capital accounts. However, as the process of financial markets integration moves apace and as the negotiations process towards a Monetary Union gains momentum, it is expected that Tanzania and Burundi would ease restrictions on capital flows across the EAC borders.

---

[107] See WAGH, Smita Wagh, Andrew Lovegrove, and John Kashangaki, *Scaling-up Regional Financial Integration in the EAC* (Africa Trade Policy Notes - Note #22), Washington, D.C.: International Bank for Reconstruction and Development, July, 2011.

[108] See YABARA, Masafumi, *Capital Market Integration: Progress Ahead of the East African Community Monetary Union* (Working Paper – WP/12/18), Washington, D.C.: International Monetary Fund, January, 2012.

Free Movement of Persons and Right of Establishment

The right of citizens of East Africa to move freely and reside in another EAC Partner State encapsulated under Article 7 of the Common Market Protocol remains a nightmare. The acceptance of the EAC Travel Identity Card and mutual recognition of the national Identity Card of Partner States also remains elusive and a source of sensitivity. If one issue had the potential of dislodging the agreement reached over the Common Market Protocol, it was the question of free movement of persons and the right of establishment. It conjured the en masse migration of citizens of one country to another in search of land. Tanzania was particularly against this aspect of 'free movement' forming part of the Common Market Protocol and was only embraced as part of the Protocol when consensus was reached to subject it to national laws.

To the extent that the right of establishment and residence, which falls under Article 123 of the Common Market Protocol, is embedded in the free movement of persons, it is equally confronted by similar negativity associated with free movement of persons. It is important to note, however, that what justifies the EAC being called a 'community' is precisely the notion that the citizens of East Africa would enjoy the right of cross-border movements and settlement. It could not be envisaged that such an allowance would engender wholesale migrations of people. The whole ethos of free movement of persons, in my view, is the promotion of economic and business socialisation that would contribute to economic growth, job creation and improvement in the quality of lives.

Unfortunately, free movement of persons has come to be seen as a source of struggle over the utilisation of scarce natural resources such as land whose acquisition is, after all, governed by strict laws that apply even to nationals of a country host to immigrants. The negative fallout of a strict control on free movement of persons is the isolation of free movement of self-employed persons who are able to sustain themselves and even create jobs in a host country outside the investment framework. Since the 1970s, the European Court of Justice has contributed important thinking in clarifying the disjuncture between free movement of labour and free movement of persons. The Court has been able to give a broader interpretation of Article 39 of the Treaty of Rome by underscoring the social and individual dimension of free movement outside the specificity of the construction of a Common Market.[109]

---

[109] See BALDONI, Emiliana, *The Free Movement of Persons in the European Union: A Legal-historical Overview*, (State of the Art Report PIONEUR Working Paper No. 2), Centro Interuniversitario di Sociologia Politica (CIUSPO) – Università di Firenze – Italy, July, 2003, pp. 5-6.

Indeed, the Treaty of Maastricht and the EU Report of the High Level Panel on Free Movement of Persons of 1997 foster a broader idea of an individual as a fully-fledged citizen of Europe. In the final section of this chapter, an examination is made of the institutional framework and arrangements for the promotion of the Common Market.

Institutional Framework and Arrangements

Articles 46 to 54 of the Common Market Protocol outline the institutional framework and institutional arrangements needed for the implementation and management of the Common Market. These provisions cover the following aspects: approximation and harmonisation of policies, laws and systems (significant progress has been made in these areas); safeguard measures and measures to address imbalances (the measures also feature under Articles 77, 78 and 88 of the EAC Treaty); monitoring and evaluation, Council of Ministers' powers to make regulations and issue directives (which is also pursuant to Article 14 of the EAC Treaty) and settlement of disputes.

Whilst seemingly comprehensive on paper, the EAC institutional framework and arrangements outlined in the Common Market Protocol are weak with regard to making the Common Market work. They merely restate the provisions of the EAC Treaty, provisions which reflect the challenges that confronted the drafters of the Treaty in the late 1990s. The challenges revolved around what remains as a harsh debate about the nature and dynamics of EAC integration given its past history which saw the Community break up in 1977. It is a debate, if you like, between institutionalists who seek to see strong supra-nationality in the EAC and inter-governmentalists who wish to see the Partner States as the dominant decision makers over the direction, character and pace of EAC integration.[110]

This debate is tacitly captured in the thinking of the late Mwalimu Julius Nyerere who, in reflecting on the thesis of unanimity in decision making in regional cooperation, observed that:

> the requirement of unanimity ... is not easy to achieve despite our great will to cooperate. Each of our three governments is answerable to the people of its own country. Each of our three Governments is answerable to the people of its own country. Each of them is beset with the urgent needs of one part of the total East African area.[111]

---

[110] See DONALD J. PUCHALA, Donald J., "Institutionalism, Intergovernmentalism and European Integration: A Review Article," Vol. 37, No. 2 *Journal of Common Market Studies*, June, 1999, pp. 317-331 at p. 330.

[111] NYERERE, Julius K., "Problems of East African Cooperation," op. cit. at p. 63.

Thus, not only do most of the key areas of cooperation outlined in the EAC Treaty require decisions to be made by the Partner States through the Summit of Heads of State, Council of Ministers and other organs in which the Partner States are represented, but also that those decisions must be reached by consensus (Articles 12(3) and 15(4) of the EAC Treaty).

It is the tension between institutionalisation and intergovernmentalisation of the EAC that has impeded the transformation of the EAC into a more effective institution in the delivery of the integration agenda in the past decade. Little wonder that though the Council of Ministers is empowered by the Treaty under Articles 75(3) and 76(3) to establish and confer powers and authority upon such institutions as it may deem necessary to administer the Customs Union and the Common Market respectively, it has so far failed to exercise its authority because of the consensus decision making rule.

The idea of Partner States ceding some decision making powers, even if of an administrative character (for example over appointments of junior staff) is still anathema to some Partner States. Indeed, in the recent past, there has been a creeping, probably successful attempt by officials of the Partner States (notably those of the Ministries responsible for EAC Affairs) to usurp even those powers of the EAC Secretariat that are conferred upon it by Article 71 of the Treaty. Those powers include the general administration and financial management of the EAC and the mobilisation of funds from development partners and from other sources for the implementation of EAC projects.

It is of note that between 2009 and 2011, and particularly in the context of the on-set of the Common Market, the EAC Secretariat embarked on a major exercise of reviewing the EAC institutional arrangements. Through the support of UK's DFID, Adam Smith International was hired to review the EAC Institutional Framework and recommend institutional changes that would fit the effective operationalisation of the Common Market. In their Final Report dated March 2010, the consultants made several observations and recommendations. However, I shall only make reference to those that have a bearing on the Common Market. First, that the EAC Secretariat lacked authority to initiate, monitor and evaluate policies and programmes "which is a key requirement if the Common Market is to be successful." It was recommended that the Secretariat be given sufficient resource, competence and authority to enable it to act as the executive arm of the EAC, "acting independently in the Community's best interests."

In this regard, it was proposed that the EAC Secretariat be substantially restructured and transformed into a Commission" with increased authorities and decision-making powers," thus necessitating the Partner States ceding some sovereignty to EAC organs and institutions. Given the sensitivity about this question of ceding sovereignty, it needs to be clarified that what is transferred is not sovereignty but 'sovereign rights.'[112]

The Adam Smith Report noted that the experience of the European Commission is that making the Common Market work hinges on the existence of appropriate rules, an empowered organisation and effective processes.[113] It has to be observed that in the EU, the Single Market Act of 1992 clearly spelt out such rules and processes including the authority of the European Commission in managing the Common Market. The EAC Protocol, in contrast, has not incorporated similar provisions. In this vein and of particular significance, it is proposed in the Adam Smith Report that the EAC Commission should have authority to initiate programmes and projects, to enforce protocols and empower the East African Court of Justice to allow appeals where Partner States violate or infringe the requirements enshrined in protocols and Community laws, to implement EAC policies backed by enabling legislation and administer its own finances and finally represent the EAC Partner States in major trade and economic fora where the Partner States have to negotiate as a bloc.

The second recommendation focused on strengthening the East African Court of Justice to enable it to exercise jurisdiction over settlement of disputes between Partner States and individual companies seeking redress on Common Market related issues. Presently, the EACJ has no such remit.

The third recommendation revolves around the centrality of the EAC Competition Act in the Common Market. It is clear that the working of the Common Market will give rise to anti-competitive behaviour and abuse of market position through measures such as state support. It has already been seen in the operationalisation of the Customs Union that some Partner States do contravene the Customs Management Act by extending exemptions to selected investors in their countries. As such, there has to be a way to ensure that economic players in the EAC Common Market enjoy a level playing field. Where the EAC Competition Law, which has to be overhauled, because it is weak and unresponsive to the dynamics of a Common Market, having been drafted largely to fit trade in goods under the Customs Union, is violated, enforcement should lie with the EAC Secretariat and the EACJ.

It is thus critical that the ongoing process within the EAC of amending the Treaty be speeded up and should include not only extending the jurisdiction of the EACJ to cover settlement of disputes that arise both from the operationalisation of the Customs Union and the Common Market but also making the Court a permanent one in the same manner that the African Court on Peoples' and Human Rights and the SADC Tribunal are. It is of

---

[112] See, Edward Bust, Supranational Institutions and Regional Integration – www.eclac.org.

[113] This point is also captured in BOYFIELD, Keith and Tim Ambler, *EUtopia: What EU Would be Best and How Do We Achieve It?* London: Adam Smith Institute, 2006.

significance to note that EAC Summit of Heads of State in November 2011 decided, that as a start to making the EACJ permanent, the President of the Court as well as the Principal Judge who heads the Court of First Instance be made permanent officers of the Court with full time pay and perks. This development is highly commendable.

The fourth recommendation focuses on the overall capacity of the EAC Secretariat particularly in monitoring and evaluation of how the Partner States are implementing various Common Market Protocol provisions. In this context, building and strengthening the Secretariat's capacity in research and statistics is an important area requiring urgent attention, particularly following the enlargement of the Community and the entry of the Common Market. Reliable and timely data on trade flows, cross-border investments and their impact on jobs and tax revenues; the impact of climate change on food security, cross-border student enrolments, etc is presently a serious deficit and can explain why it is often difficult to show the tangible benefits that accrue to the EAC Partner States.

The fifth recommendation is on the authority of the East African Legislative Assembly. It is proposed that the EALA should have more members, greater financial and management authority and that more time and resources be extended to it if it is to enhance its effectiveness over legislation work, legislative oversight and outreach roles. In the EU, the extended powers of the European Parliament marked by co-decision by which the Parliament and the European Council must agree on a legislative act, have been viewed as a means of 'democratising' a supranational decision-making process. However, the EU Parliament, in contrast to the EALA, is directly elected by the citizens of Europe in their member states and, ostensibly, it garners its legitimacy and authority from such electoral system. There is thus the hanging question whether EALA should be given additional powers when it is not a directly elected Parliament.

Conclusion

The EAC has made significant progress in its integration agenda. There are clear signs that the Customs Union has leveraged not only intra-EAC trade but also confidence in the investment area with significant cross-border investment activity taking place in the past few years. In taking the bold step to usher in a Common Market even when the Customs Union still faces a number of challenges is indicative of EAC's high level political commitment in putting the regional economy on a higher trajectory. The EAC is of course mindful of the fact that the Common Market and especially the liberalisation of services trade is more complex than the liberalisation of merchandise trade under the Customs Union. This is largely because services trade as well as capital movements demand rigorous regulatory systems and processes.

Crafting such regulation both at the levels of a legal regime and that of establishing appropriate enforcement and monitoring mechanisms that effectively balance the authority of supranationality and respect for subsidiarity and consensus decision making requires a great deal of care.

It is in this context that making the Common Market work can neither be rushed nor achieved within a brief space of time as in the case of the Customs Union. Even after 18 years of Single Market operation, at the end of 2009, some "74 single market directives had not yet produced their full effects in the EU due to lack of national transposition measures in one or more Member States. In other words, the single market is an engine that works at around 95% of its potential."[114]

Of course the EAC is much smaller than the EU and does not have the complexity of the EU trade and economic dynamics. However, the Common Market presents enormous opportunities for the EAC to realise higher economic growth and standards of living and making it work is thus of great significance. The Common Market also constitutes a strategic pillar for the next stage of EAC integration, namely the establishment of the Monetary Union. A high degree of integrated markets of goods, services and capital is an important underpinning for the single EAC currency and for fostering productivity and competitiveness. What all this means is that the Partner States must strive to comply and enforce all the Common Market Protocol provisions with zeal.

One question that stands out in integration processes is whether the common market to work well it needs to be supported by a monetary union. In the EU there was a strong thesis that the Single Market needed a common currency to realize its full potential. Yet with the Euro-Zone crisis that has engulfed the EU in recent times such thesis has been shaken to its foundations. The EAC is engrossed in the negotiations process for the establishment a monetary union and single currency. No doubt the Euro-Zone crisis will aptly inform and shape the thinking and decisions of political leaders. In the next two chapters the process and the challenges the EAC faces in realizing this stage of integration are critically examined.

---

[114] See MONTI, Mario, *A New Strategy for the Single Market – At the Service of Europe's Economy and Society: Report to the President of the European Commission José Manuel Barroso*, op. cit. at p. 95.

CHAPTER EIGHT

Hard Questions about the Monetary Union[115]

On behalf of the East African Community, I join the Governor of the Bank of Uganda in welcoming you to this meeting of the EAC Monetary Affairs Committee. The presence of all the five Central Bank Governors at this meeting testifies to the importance you attach to this Forum. It also clearly manifests your personal interest and commitment to promoting deeper integration in the EAC.

May I take this opportunity to extend a special warm welcome to Professor Benno Ndulu to this august Committee and meeting and to congratulate you, Governor, most sincerely on your recent appointment as Governor of the Bank of Tanzania. Personally, having known you closely for several years, I have total confidence that, under your leadership, the Bank of Tanzania will quickly recover the crucial trust of the Government of the United Republic of Tanzania and of the people of Tanzania following the recent damaging report on the management of the External Payments Arrears Account.

I am beholden to extend EAC's deep appreciation to the Bank of Uganda and to the Government of the Republic of Uganda as a whole for hosting this meeting; for your warm hospitality and for the excellent facilities that have been put at our disposal.

This meeting, Distinguished Governors, takes place against the backdrop of a disturbing and tragic environment in Kenya, EAC's main economic powerhouse. The EAC is deeply concerned by the post-general elections violence, loss of lives, wanton destruction of property and the continuing political impasse in Kenya. The economic dislocation that has so far emerged and which would deepen, if return to normalcy delays, is most worrisome to all the five partner states, some affected more than others. Indeed, the very viability of the EAC project has now been put under heavy test. As you meet and deliberate on deepening our integration process, we cannot be obvious of these testing events and of the hard lessons we must draw there from.

Evidently, the EAC political leadership has all along been seized of the difficult situation engulfing and confronting this important sister Partner State of the EAC. Last Friday, I was in Bukoba where I met the Tanzanian President, His Excellency Jakaya Mrisho Kikwete, and was able to learn

---

[115] Opening Remarks at a meeting of EAC Monetary Affairs Committee, Kampala, Uganda, 23rd January, 2008.

about his discussions with the Chairperson of the EAC Summit, His Excellency Yoweri Kaguta Museveni on how to deepen EAC's engagement in bringing about a *modus vivendi* and a rapprochement in the Kenya political stalemate. On Monday this week, I had occasion to meet President Museveni at State House, Entebbe and received assurance about what the EAC political leadership is doing in resolving the Kenyan political impasse. As you may be aware, President Museveni is now leading this effort from the frontline and on the ground.

Much as this is my first meeting with you, at this level, and thus the temptation is high, I am not going to act historian by recollecting the excellent work that this Committee has done in recent years in putting in place some of the key policy benchmarks and actions focused on monetary integration. Suffice to state that it is your commendable achievements, to date, that have prompted the EAC Heads of State to believe that an EAC Monetary Union can be fast tracked and realized by 2012. Indeed, there is a directive by the 6th Extra Ordinary Summit of EAC Heads of State that met in Ngurudoto, Arusha on 20th August, 2007 that requires the EAC to explore how best we can move expeditiously towards the establishment of the Monetary Union by 2012.

In this context, I am aware that the Monetary Affairs Sub-Committee, comprising Senior Technical Officials from the Central Banks of the Partners States and from the EAC Secretariat, met in October last year to begin some ground work that would lead to the formulation of a strategic framework for fast tracking the establishment of the Monetary Union. The same Committee met over the last two days to further refine the work it undertook last October and which constitutes your working document at this meeting. I wish to pay tribute to this Sub-Committee for the hard work it has put in and the excellent document it has produced.

My hope, in this whole process, is that, as professionals, you will be bold enough to recognize that political will should always be ideally tested against realities on the ground. Monetary integration is complex and often shrouded in sensitive issues of sovereignty and economic preparedness. We should not, therefore, seek to re-invent the wheel. For instance, the experience of the European Union in moving towards and realizing the Monetary Union, which remains a quasi Union in that some key EU members still remain outside it, should constitute a useful lesson for our thinking and approach. As you know, the EAC is still grappling with the consolidation of the Customs Union. Yet, the process towards the establishment of the Common Market has already been launched with the aim of putting it in place, come January, 2010.

So, yes, we must run while others walk, to cite a famous mantra of the Late Mwalimu Julius Nyerere.[116] However, some hard realities clearly stare us in the face, especially since we live in complex and challenging times, globally and in our region. As a start, EAC's enlargement with the recent accession of Rwanda and Burundi into the EAC does not make our vision and resolve for deeper integration any easier.

One should pose the question, for instance, whether we should have a two-speed EAC on the Monetary Union issue? And if so, how then do we respond to the current Treaty requirement for the Council of Ministers and the Summit of Heads of State to make decisions on the basis of unanimity or consensus? In turn, should the decision to establish a Monetary Union be taken by the Summit or should it, as is the case in the EU, be subjected to a referendum in the Partner States?

But the hard realities that stare us in the face have other bearings outside politics. These are fundamentally economic. In fact, the Economic Affairs sub-Committee of the Monetary Affairs Committee addresses some of them quite well in their Report before you. They largely centre on the wide variation in the desired macro-economic convergence criteria that has been set out for the EAC Partner States. At the same time, the state of economic development and of preparedness to embrace a single currency and being subjected to a central fiscal and monetary authority lies at the heart of the challenge of fast tracking the Monetary Union.

Even in the EU, the desired convergence as set out in the Growth and Fiscal Stability Pact remains a nightmare several years of its being put in place. Thus, compliance to laid down benchmarks on issues such as inflation rates, budget deficits, State subsidies and protection of the so called "national champions" - strategic state and private industries - remains fluid in the EU.

On our part, centralized enforcement of a similar pact under the EAC would require, as a start, the development of a robust and well managed database and system of macro-economic fiscal and financial statistics. This remains a major deficit in the EAC organizational system. There will also have to be an East African Central Bank working closely with what will necessarily have to be an EAC Commission. In the EU, such a relationship has consolidated after sometime. All these dimensions constitute onerous challenges. They can be met; but we need to work on the basis of accepting complex realities on the ground.

I hope that my hard sobriety about the way forward in this work shall not dent our spirits and resolve. I personally believe in the benefits of a monetary union and, in a related context, I am presently working earnestly to have an

---

[116] This is captured in SMITH, William Edgett, *We Must Run While They Walk: A Portrait of Africa's Julius Nye*rere, New York: Random House, 1992.

East African Capital Markets established at the earliest moment. In this regard, I truly hope that Governor Ndulu will quickly make sense of the need for Tanzania to fully liberate its capital account.

Finally, I commend the proposals of the technical team to you as the basis for the way forward. The journey to our economic liberation through deeper integration through monetary union must go on and the first step, probably not a hop and step one, is crucial and urgent.

CHAPTER NINE

Negotiating the Monetary Union[117]

I am pleased to join you this morning at this historic inaugural meeting of the High Level Task Force representing appointees of all the EAC Partner States on the EAC Monetary Union. I congratulate Burundi for taking the mantle of leadership of this Task Force.

Allow me, in welcoming you to Arusha, to express my profound appreciation to the Investors of this most beautiful hotel, Mt Meru. This hotel is a vivid expression and manifestation of the economic vibrancy of our region and of the clear direction we are taking towards an economically prosperous future which the EAC is committed to building. Indeed, the context of our meeting today is proof of our determination to construct this new future for our region. We meet here to fundamentally embark on a new phase in our process of integration, an integration that is deeper.

It is deeper because it also constitutes a form of political integration. As you can imagine, one of the important symbols of political integration is a common currency. So you could say that today, as we begin these deliberations which will usher in the formal negotiations for the establishment of the East African Community Monetary Union in March this year, we begin a serious journey, whatever the length, towards the East African Political Federation.

The task before you is not an enviable one. It is complex in its political overtones and its sheer technical character. I do believe though that having been chosen to lead this process speaks volumes about your competences and your commitment to the goal that underlies your work.

I also know that you have the benefit of a great deal of preparatory work that has been done and which should help lessen your burden of thought and, probably, of the national political overhang! You have with you the Draft Monetary Union Protocol; a Draft East African Monetary Institute Bill; a Draft East African Central Bank Bill; and several other documents and literature of benefit to your work. A Draft Road-map to guide your process of negotiations has also been prepared for you and you will be required, at this meeting, to review it and agree on how you think you can proceed bearing in mind that the Summit expects you to be expeditious in coming up with final proposals.

---

[117] Statement at the opening of the meeting of High Level Task Force to draw up a Framework for Monetary Union Negotiations, Arusha, Tanzania, 18th January, 2011.

I need not be the political mobiliser for deeper EAC integration to draw your attention to the reality that the eyes and ears of the East African citizens are, from today, centred on this Task Force. These people, across the age difference, have not lost their sense of history; that once upon a time, in the 1960s, this region had the most developed common market and monetary union in the world. The bravery and resolve of our independence political leaders made that possible. But they also let us down for reasons probably justified at the time.

However, the realities of the brave new world today demand that some of us lead a major consciousness change; that we need to integrate our economies more deeply and that the introduction of a common currency will provide a stronger and more solid basis for investment and economic growth. Certainly, for an efficient and effective common market to operate, a monetary union, and not simply the free movement of capital, is essential. This is because a monetary union helps to eliminate price instability and exchange rate volatility. And as a result, a competitive business environment that spurs investment flows and growth is garnered.

The EAC Heads of State at their Summit meeting in Arusha on 3rd December, 2010, were unequivocal about the integration stage we have reached in the EAC and of the need to expedite the process towards the establishment of the Monetary Union. They called upon the Partner states to fast track macro-economic convergence that constitutes the basic criteria for the monetary union. Yet, we know, as monetary specialists and as informed citizens that this is one of the challenging tasks that the High level Task Force will have to face and confront in the next 12 months of negotiations.

The reality is that some of the EAC Partner States have only recently emerged from years of turmoil and are only beginning to construct robust instruments of State. In the European Union, the process of monetary integration was hampered by varying degrees of convergence criteria - compliance which gave way to the adoption of an opting-out formula, call it variable geometry. But then, the EU was a significantly large family even before the later enlargement process. For the EAC, on the other hand, it is an issue of five members, at least for now! But this is clearly one of the critical issues that will have to be dispassionately considered in determining the pace and timing of the on-set of the monetary union.

Can only few of the EAC members move alone into the monetary union and allow others to join later? What would be the costs and benefits of such a move in a small integration family?

The EAC Council of Ministers has already set up a special Sectoral Council of Ministers on Monetary Union to be directly involved in ensuring that your work as a High Task Force receives constant political oversight and direction. You will be assisted by the relevant statutory organs comprising officials, technical and Permanent Secretaries, cutting across sectors such as Ministries of Finance, Central Banks, Capital Markets, Pension Funds, and Revenue Authorities. In other words, you have all the support you need to complete your work within one year.

Let me end my welcoming remarks by saying that it has been a privilege for me to work closely with the Governors of the EAC Partner States' Central Banks on this enterprise of great importance to our region. I have always found them to be a highly patriotic group, full of passion for regionalism but also always carrying a weighted frame of mind about the sensitivity of this next stage of EAC integration. We must thus continually engage these Governors as you proceed in your work to ensure that we finally create an institution that would be solid, robust and sustaining; not one that, in the face of the kind of crises the European Monetary Union finds itself in today, would spell disaster. As I complete my term of office at the end of April this year, be certain that as an ardent East African committed to deeper EAC integration, I will continue to be watchful of how you undertake your work.

Postscript on the Monetary Union

If there is a particular stage of integration in the EAC that is extensively covered by the Treaty it is the process towards the realization of the Monetary Union. It is important for critics of this process to be cognizant of the fact that the process of establishing the Monetary Union did not start with the negotiations of the Protocol for its establishment. Thus, apart from its being mentioned as a subsequent stage of integration under Article 5(2) of the Treaty, the various fundamental aspects that underpin and which constitute the bedrock of a monetary union are well stipulated under Articles 82 - 86 of the Treaty. These provisions extensively cover cooperation in monetary and financial matters including maintaining the convertibility of the currencies of the Partner States as a basis for the establishment of a Monetary Union, harmonization of macro-economic policies in relation to exchange rate, interest rate and monetary and fiscal policies, taking measures that would facilitate trade and capital movement within the Community and promoting capital markets. What comes out clearly here is that the quest for the monetary union was not deemed to be a stand-alone phase, exclusively governed by protocol negotiations. Rather, it is an end product of various build up processes.

In all these processes, significant progress has been made, particularly in the past six years, with the Governors of the Central Banks being at the helm. Of course, the entry of Burundi and Rwanda into the EAC fold in July 2007 meant that the progress that had been realized had to take into account the state of their macro-economic policies in order to realize their convergence with those of Kenya, Uganda and Tanzania. Rwanda is almost there in achieving macro-economic convergence with the old EAC members. Burundi, on the other hand, is fast working on such convergence but may be the cause for a delay in the establishment of the Monetary Union.

Implications of the Euro Zone Crisis

The crisis in the Euro Area in the recent past has inevitably also raised concerns about the pace of the East African Monetary Union. Such concerns are apt. However, they should not be viewed as sacrosanct for the EAC region. As the respected French political economist Jacques Attali recently observed:

> We should not have let Greece enter the Economic and Monetary Union with falsified figures. We should not have left the debt grow so large given the country's weak economic fundamentals. We should have forced the Greeks to establish effective fiscal and economic institutions long ago.[118]

The EAC would not rush to establish a Monetary Union nor would it allow a Greek-type situation to happen in its Monetary Union. Rather, the EAC will learn from the Euro Area crisis. However, learning cannot necessarily mean postponing the early establishment of the Monetary Union. Such a prescription would clearly be illogical because the situation and complexity of the economies of the Euro Area and EAC do not correspond.

In my view, the fundamental question about the EAC Monetary Union corresponds closely with the stance taken by the Harvard economist, Professor Kenneth Rogoff. In an article in the *Financial Times* of 7th June, 2011 titled, "The Global Fallout of a Euro Zone Collapse," he posits, "having a small number of currencies is a phenomenon that makes a lot of sense economically, economizing on transaction costs and leveraging economies of scale. The real question is whether common currency is sustainable politically." He goes on to conjecture that "if the current slow patch in global growth does not quickly subside, we will not have to wait long for an answer."

What Professor Rogoff implies is that a common currency would work best where economies experience sustained robust growth. The EU economies are not experiencing such growth. Indeed, the global economy is undergoing yet another crisis which could be worse than that of 2007/2008. The richer Euro countries have established Bailout Funds to help out the poor performing EU economies. Whether such funds will in time help to sort out what are fundamental structural economic problems of some of the EU countries remains a conjecture. Clearly, economic growth that shores public

---

[118] In an interview with the German TV Station Arte on 16th January, 2012 he said that the entry of Greece into the Eurozone was a huge hypocrisy of Germany and France.

finances from getting under pressure and making the public debt manageable will prove to be the determining factor.

Will the EAC avoid an EU or Euro area type of crisis? This is the large question and it has to inform the whole process of monetary union negotiations. Of course, Article 84(2) of the EAC Treaty calls upon the Partner States to evolve policies designed to improve their resource and production base as a basis to realize balanced development in the Community, an important factor in hedging against the Euro type of crisis where the EU Growth and Stability Pact could not be rigorously enforced in the context of hugely varying national fiscal performances. Already with the contraction in budget support from donor countries, some of the EAC partner states are already going thorough serious budget deficits and growing public debts. According to Tanzania's Budget Speech for fiscal year 2012-2013, Tanzania's national debt stock, for example, increased by 15.4% between March 2011 and March 2012. Kenya's total public debt has also grown by 22.2% between June 2010 and June 2011.

It is for these reasons that the EAC is promoting a number of regional projects to ensure that the national economies are robust with healthy fiscal policies and conditions. The following projects are important in this particular process.

Regional Projects Supporting Economic Growth

First, there is infrastructure development: This encompasses a number of roads which open up the regional economic space, the Arusha-Namanga-Athi River Road being the flag bearer; the modernization of railways from the present single metre gauge to an international gauge and building a railway extension that links Isaka on the Tanzanian Central line with Rwanda and Burundi as well as an extension from Arusha to Musoma to link Tanzania and Uganda via Lake Victoria. The estimated cost of the roads infrastructure alone in the next 10 years is in excess of US $ 25 billion.

The modernization of the railway systems is estimated at US $ 20 billion excluding the cost of the Isaka railway extension and the Arusha-Musoma extension. Equally, in the area of broadband technology, the infrastructure network to interconnect the five EAC Partner States via a high capacity fibre optic link under the support of the African Development Bank is estimated to cost US $ 30 million. A number of infrastructure projects involving railways, roads, ports and harbours development are also planned under the COMESA-EAC-SADC Tripartite arrangement whose main thrust is to establish a grand free trade area embracing 26 countries in Africa.

Linked to infrastructure development are efforts being undertaken by the EAC to promote an EAC Cross-Border Electrification Programme driven through current and new hydro, natural and methane gas, thermal and geothermal power plants as well as through a natural gas pipeline from Mtwara to Mombasa. Through the COMESA-EAC-SADC Tripartite framework, efforts are underway to connect the East African Power Pool with the Eastern Africa Power Pool and the Southern Africa Power Pool.

The discoveries of oil in Uganda, more natural gas in Tanzania and the potential entry of South Sudan into the EAC present positive opportunities for the EAC power industry to develop beyond optimality. It is important and urgent to address the energy challenge because it has been identified by business in the EAC region as a major constraint to business operations, investment promotion and competitiveness.

It is important to point out though that promoting joint infrastructure projects, in my experience, has suffered from the lack of an effective regional approach to financing of such projects. There is still too much national focus and thrust to infrastructure development. Indeed, part of the challenge facing NEPAD's effectiveness has precisely been this lack of a clear regional dimension to infrastructure development. At the EAC level, it has even been difficult to raise counterpart funds to leverage grants available, for example, from the African Development Bank Group, because the Partner States are not well disposed to coughing up contributions to an EAC fund for the purpose. Above all, even though in theory, going by the provisions of the Treaty establishing the EAC (Article 4), it is possible for the EAC to borrow funds for undertaking various projects, in practice this has not been possible and largely because of a dominant national interest mindset.

In June, 2008, the EAC Secretariat organized a half day retreat in Kigali, Rwanda, for the EAC Heads of State to discuss regionalisation of infrastructure development. Regrettably, no consensus was reached on the matter because national chauvinism in promoting infrastructure projects at national levels was too deep seated in some of the President's mindsets. Yet, the success of the EAC integration hinges a great deal on promoting infrastructure and energy connectivities. Indeed, the principal providers of infrastructure funding such as the African Development Bank and JICA are now more disposed to offering long term soft loans to infrastructure projects of a regional nature than to those that are simply national. It is only the US Millennium Challenge Corporation that still extends loans and grants to national projects and this is largely because of the bilateral character of the funding conditions.

Second, is the need to promote deeper industrialization in the manufacturing front. The EAC Heads of State in December 2011 adopted an industrialization policy and strategy whose main thrust is to promote the realization of a larger EAC internal market within which there are optimizations of both comparative and competitive advantages of each of the partner states. It is clear that the EAC countries remain heavily import oriented even for items that could easily be competitively manufactured or processed in the region. In support for the realization of this industrialization project is the EAC Small and Medium Enterprises Programme which forms part of a Regional Programme on Industrial Upgrading and Modernization supported by UNIDO.

Of course, the foregoing infrastructure and industrialization programmes cannot alone stimulate sustainable higher economic growth and competitiveness. Therefore, working closely with the East African Business Council (EABC), the EAC has since 2008 been holding Annual Investment Conferences to promote both domestic investments and foreign direct investment.

The EAC -EABC co-operation coupled with the Partner States are also presently engaged in promoting the establishment of a more conducive business environment in the region in line with recommendations from the *World Bank Doing Business Reports* and the *Global Competitiveness Reports* of the World Economic Forum. The EAC is seized of the fact that, as a collective economy, in 2011 its position was 111 out of 139 countries in the *Global Competitiveness Matrix* compared to the Sub-Saharan Africa average of 91. It is thus imperative that the Doing Business Environment is urgently improved throughout the EAC.

Third is the challenge of improving the quality of education. It is evident that for the EAC region to become globally competitive and achieve sustainable high economic growths it will have to more seriously address the state of its education system and particularly primary schooling which is worryingly poor. *The Uwezo Report,* [119] published in 2011 has, through large scale household surveys in Kenya, Uganda and Tanzania focused on literacy (English and Kiswahili; Uganda was not tested in Kiswahili) and numeracy competency of children aged 5-16 years, brought out shocking results. The assessments were all based on Standard 2 level competency. In Tanzania, for example, which is the worst case in the English competency level, only 51% of children in Standard 7 passed the Standard 2 level English test. In numeracy, 12% of Kenyans in Standard 7 failed the Standard 2 level; 15% of Ugandans and a disturbing 32% of Tanzanians in Standard 7 failed to reach the Standard 2 level.

Little wonder that in the *Global Competitiveness Report 2011*[120] these three large EAC economies do not score well under the sub-pillar of quality of

---

[119] See UWEZO EAST AFRICA, *Are Our Children Learning? Numeracy and Literacy Across East Africa,* Nairobi and Dar es Salaam: UWEZO East Africa and Twaweza East Africa, July, 2011

[120] See SCHWAB, Klaus (Ed.), *The Global Competitiveness Report 2011 – 2012,* Geneva: World Economic Forum, 2011.

primary education though Kenya, as indeed shown in the *Uwezo Report*, scores better. Kenya is positioned at 61 out of 139 countries; Uganda is at 100 whilst Tanzania is positioned at 115. Rwanda is the best in the pack, positioned at 56. Apart from Kenya, the performance on the sub-pillar of enrolment in primary education, Tanzania leads at 13 followed by Uganda at 38, then Rwanda at 50 and Kenya at a shocking low of 118 which clearly explains the huge state of inequality in access to education in Kenya. The challenge for Uganda and Tanzania is how to match the excellent gross enrolment rates with quality. Numbers do not count in a world where competition rests on talent.

In sum, for both the common market and the monetary union to make meaning, social and economic factors embracing infrastructure, growing the internal market through deeper industrialization and improvement of the quality of human capital must be prioritized both at national and at EAC level.

In the following chapter, we end the analysis of the four stages of integration as encapsulated in the EAC Treaty by examining the process towards a political federation.

CHAPTER TEN

The Case for Political Federation[121]

We are extremely honoured, Your Excellency, by your important gesture in gracing this occasion of launching of the National Consultative Process on the Political Federation of East Africa. This is yet another practical reaffirmation of your powerful vision and relentless championship of a united and prosperous East Africa. You have consistently articulated the cause of East African unity with formidable logic and unstinting commitment to Pan Africanist ideals. As the East African regional integration process intensifies, Your Excellency has come out clearly with strong advocacy of the consolidation of the EAC Customs Union, realization of the East African Common Market as well as bold measures in the development of regional economic infrastructure, hence acceleration of the process towards the Political Federation of East Africa.

- We recall with great appreciation, the Special Summit held in Nairobi on 27-29 August, 2004, during which Your Excellencies, the Heads of State of the EAC Partner States made the historic declaration on fast tracking the Political Federation of East Africa; and established the Committee on Fast Tracking East African Federation. The Committee submitted its report to the Summit in November 2004 recommending, among others, the establishment of the East African Federation by the year 2010.

- The EAC Secretariat has been seized of the Summit's directives on the process of accelerating regional integration, and the Summit's emphatic declaration that the process must be centred on the deep involvement and participation of the East African people in all its facets and throughout the process from the decision making to the implantation stages. Following the Extraordinary Summit held in Dar es Salaam on 29-30 May 2005, the Department of Political Federation has been established at the EAC Secretariat, among whose first activities

---

[121] Remarks during the Launching of the Consultative Process on East African Federation, Kampala, Uganda, 13th October, 2006.

is the co-ordination of the National Consultative Process that Your Excellencies have agreed to simultaneously launch in the three East African capitals today.

Today is therefore a historic day for East Africa. It marks the beginning of a process to wipe out the colonial and imperial legacy of the partition of Africa. For too long, East Africa and Africa as a whole have continued to be enslaved by a mental condition emanating from the colonial past. And as years have gone by, the sanctity of the post colonial state has consolidated thereby frustrating and undermining the fundamental cause for real political and economic liberation. This is an untenable position. It is untenable because globalization has catapulted the need and urgency for nation states to build viable, robust and competitive economic structures.

Indeed, experience from more developed countries such as those of the European Union shows that stand alone nation states cannot realize economies of scale and scope, let alone of competition to be able to survive the acute economic pressures unleashed by globalization. In our specific case, the road towards realizing a critical mass of economic competitiveness is often affected by strong parochial political interests. As a result, the path for realizing deep economic integration has suffered. No doubt, even the EU countries face similar hurdles, albeit of lesser political extent much as the EU Constitution Treaty suffered serious damage last year. But EU countries can afford some of the setbacks. We cannot. We lack the wherewithal to withstand such setbacks.

We therefore need stronger political will to underpin economic integration. Little wonder the founding fathers of the Treaty for the establishment of the East African Community, a Treaty that was drafted following a gradual treaty making process involving a wide spectrum of participation of East African constituencies, equally saw such position as untenable. Inevitably, the Treaty under article 5, the Treaty encapsulates the political Federation of the partner States as the ultimate objective of the EAC.

Inasmuch as the EAC Treaty recognizes this ultimate objective, having a Political Federation, East Africa's leaders, as I have observed, have emphasized the necessity that such objective be put to a test involving wider and deeper participation of the East African people. The East African people have to pronounce themselves not only on what the Treaty provides but also on the form of the

Federation and the time scale for its realization.

This is the context that brings us together this afternoon. Getting East Africans started on the right footing with the right message, a powerful message, is pivotal in ensuring that the dialogue and consultative process about Political Federation, being officially launched today throughout East Africa, achieves the intended objective. It is in this regard that we thank Your Excellency, not only for the great inspiration which you consistently and constantly provide to the cause of East African, indeed African unity and development but also for gracing this occasion intended to focus the attention of all East Africans on this most important issue of our time - the Political Federation of East Africa. Beyond rhetoric, we at the EAC Secretariat hail this development as a major milestone in the quest of the East African people to realize their vision of a strong, united and prosperous East Africa.

The EAC has succeeded in the past six years to develop a number of close relationships with several foreign countries and international organizations. These relationships have been highly beneficial to the EAC in terms of budget and project funding support. In the following part of the book I present two cases of such cooperation as examples. Support from organizations such as the African Development Bank, the World Bank and JICA have been covered in much of the body of this book. It has to be acknowledged that the EAC is a model amongst RECs in Africa in crafting a working Partnership Fund modelled on the Paris Declaration Principles. Whilst these principles have lately been admonished at the Fourth High Level Conference on the Paris Declaration in Busan, South Korea, at the end of November 2011, as a failure within the overall framework of the ostensible failure of ODA, the same could not be said of the EAC Partnership Fund.

Postscript on Political Federation

Article 5(2) of the Treaty establishing the EAC invokes the attainment of an East African Political Federation as the ultimate stage of integration. There are conflicting views about this political integration objective being relegated to the end of the EAC integration process. On the one hand, a Ugandan Professor, the late Dani Wadada Nabudere who in the 1970s taught Law at the School of Law of the University of Dar es Salaam, advances the view, founded on what he describes as the failure of the erstwhile EAC Common Market because the forces struggling for a national economy" were much stronger, that any effort at either 'reviving of the East African Community or the 'Fast Tracking of the East African Federation' cannot succeed to bring about the integration of East African economies at a time when economic globalization is driving these countries in the opposite direction by being integrated into the global economy through other structures.[122] Clearly, Nabudere's view is a wildly extreme one and totally devoid of the political and economic realities of a new world order of which the EAC countries are intimately part of.

The old and tired Marxist ideas propagated mainly by Samir Amin and close associates such as Issa Shivji[123] and Dan Nabudere[124] focused on 'centre and periphery' global economic relations have seen their day.[125] In my view, they remain an intellectual exercise in futility. In similar wild pessimistic fashion, Professor Issa Shivji posits the view that Africa is yet to gain *"Uhuru"* in the absence of African Unity. In his paper titled "Pan-Africanism or Imperialism? Unity and Struggle towards a New Democratic Africa,"[126] Shivji presents the argument that Africa's territorial nationalism is equivalent to what Mwalimu Julius Nyerere described as "tribalism" within the context of separate nation states. In my view, both Nabudere's and Shivji's arguments are

---

[122] See NABUDERE, Dani W., "The Fast Tracking of Federation and Constitutionalism in East Africa," a paper presented at the 10th Annual Sir Udo Udoma Symposium, Makerere Law Society, Makerere University, Kampala, Uganda, April, 2006.

[123] Some of the seminal works of Prof. Shivji include: SHIVJI, Issa G., *Class Struggle in Tanzania*, London: Heinemann, 1976; SHIVJI, Issa G., *Let the People Speak: Tanzania Down the Road to Neo-Liberalism*, Dakar: CODESRIA, 2006; SHIVJI, Issa G., *Pan-Africanism or Pragmatism? Lessons of Tanganyika – Zanzibar Union*, Addis Ababa and Dar es Salaam: Organisation for Social Science Research in Eastern and Southern Africa (OSSREA) Mkuki na Nyota, 2008.

[124] On some of the views of the late Professor Nabudere see NABUDERE, Dani Wadada, *The Crash of International Finance Capital and Its Implications for the Third World*, Harare: SAPES Trust, 1989; and NABUDERE, Dani Wadada, *Essays on the Theory and Practice of Imperialism*, London and Dar es Salaam: Onyx Press and Tanzania Publishing House Ltd, 1979.

[125] On a spirited debate among them see TANDON, Yash (ed.), *The University of Dar es Salaam Debate on Class, State & Imperialism*, Dar es Salaam: Tanzania Publishing House, 1982. See also SHIVJI, Issa G., *Intellectuals at the Hill: Essays and Talks 1969 – 1993*, Dar es Salaam: Dar es Salaam University Press, 1993.

[126] See SHIVJI, Issa G., "Pan-Africanism or Imperialism?" Published in Issa G. Shivji, *Where is Uhuru? Reflections on the Struggle for Democracy in Africa*, Dar es Salaam: E&D Vision Publishing, 2009.

romantic at best.[127] They fail the test of political realities on the ground in Africa.

On the other hand, however, there is another view that the relegation of a political federation to the last stage of integration could be deemed logical precisely because the people of East Africa are well aware of past dysfunctional lessons of integration and would wish to offer a new opportunity for social and economic integration to prove their worth before the political federation project is ventured into. Indeed, it is for this reason that whilst political federation is prescribed as the *ultimate* objective of integration, the EAC Treaty yet outlines a number of areas of political cooperation which are exercisable, in the interim, as necessary building blocks for the viable realization of the political federation. Article 123(1), for example, spells out that:

> in order to promote the achievement of the
> objectives of the Community as set out in Article 5
> of this Treaty particularly with respect to the
> eventual establishment of a Political Federation ...
> the Partner States shall establish common foreign
> and security policies.

In the context of the provisions of Article 123 supported by Articles 124 on regional peace and security and Article 125 on defence cooperation, the EAC has been able to make significant progress in laying firm foundations that are supportive of a process towards the establishment of the East African Federation. These foundations include:

- deepened defence cooperation involving frequent joint military exercises by the armed forces of all the Partner States. These joint exercises have promoted not only a sense of community amongst the EAC military establishment but have also injected into the citizens of East Africa the confidence about peace and stability of their region. It is also important to note that the EAC Defence Chiefs work closely in addressing the challenges of terrorism and of piracy in the Indian Ocean. Defence

---

[127] On the same line of thinking see TANDON, Yash, *In Defence of Democracy*, Dar es Salaam: Dar es Salaam University Press, 1993; BABU, Abdulrahman Mohamed, *African Socialism or Socialist Africa?* Dar es Salaam: Tanzania Publishing House, 1981; BABU, Salma and Amrit Wilson (eds.), *The Future that Works: Selected Writings of A.M. Babu*, Trenton, NJ and Asmara, Eritrea: Africa World Press, Inc., 2002; and OTHMAN, Haroub (ed.), *Babu: I Saw the Future and It Works – Essays Celebrating the Life of Comrade Abdulrahman Mohamed Babu 1924-1996*, Dar es Salaam: E & D Limited, 2001.

cooperation has now moved from the level of a Memorandum of Understanding executed in 1998 to a Protocol that is legally binding. This Protocol was signed by the EAC Heads of State at its Summit in December, 2011 in Bujumbura. However, Tanzania objected to an article on mutual defence pact by the Partner States which was excluded from the Protocol, ad interim.

- the conclusion of a Protocol signed in December 2010 on foreign policy co-ordination. This Protocol, which awaits ratification by the Partner States, will guide co-ordinated actions of the Partner States in international organisations and international fora; it will foster and preserve peace and strengthen security among the Partner States and develop and consolidate democracy, the rule of law and respect for human rights and fundamental freedoms, and will foster peaceful resolution of disputes and conflicts between and within the Partner States. The ratification of this Protocol will enable these processes to have legal basis and thus avoid dispute impasse of the *"Migingo"* Island- type. Already, through the Sectoral Council on Foreign Policy Co-ordination, the Ministers of Foreign Affairs of the Partner States meet at EAC level to decide on matters relating to status on immunities and privileges of the EAC, the EAC Headquarters and persons employed in the service of the Community pursuant to Articles 73 and 138 of the Treaty;

- the conclusion of a Protocol on Peace and Security which should be adopted by the EAC Summit later in 2012. This Protocol will integrate the roles of defence, intelligence, police and immigration of the Partner States in undertaking joint operations in pursuit of criminals and terrorists, establishing common border security communications systems, combat money laundering and drug trafficking, establish common mechanisms to manage refugees and internally displaced persons and exchange training programmes for security personnel;

- the conclusion of a Protocol on Good Governance which will constitute a key pillar of best practices in matters relating to constitutionalism, the rule of law, accountability and transparency, respect for human rights and fundamental freedoms, gender equality and equal opportunities. The Protocol, in effect, seeks to encapsulate Article 6(d) of the EAC Treaty. The Draft Protocol is yet to be adopted by the EAC Summit.

Along with the construction of these building blocks for the viable attainment of the political federation, the EAC has been bold to test the thinking of the East African citizens about the federation project and whether it should be fast tracked. Following the astute recommendations of the *Wako Committee Report on Fast Tracking of the East African Federation* and which was tabled before the EAC Summit on 23rd November, 2004,[128] it was decided by the Summit that those recommendations be put before the citizens of the EAC countries through a national consultation process, to gauge their views.

The Wako Report itself had proposed 2013 as the year when the Federation President could be elected. The results of the national consultation process, which later also involved Rwanda and Burundi after their accession to the EAC in July 2007, showed that an average 80% of citizens interviewed support a political federation. On the other hand, support for fast tracking the federation as proposed by the Wako Committee was an average of 59.6%. This figure could have been higher but for the fact that the Tanzanian support was a mere 25.4%. Strangely, Uganda's support was next lowest at 56.3%.

Reports of the National Consultative Process brought out a number of useful concerns and fears about fast tracking the political federation project. Those from The United Republic of Tanzania were of a particular burning nature and have more recently been well articulated in a Report of Kituo Cha Katiba titled, *Federation Within Federation.*[129] They touched mainly on issues relating to:

- the enduring problems facing the Union between Tanzania Mainland and Zanzibar;

- what the status of Zanzibar would be in the East African Federation;

- the lack of respect for constitutionalism in Uganda with specific reference to the lack of fixed terms for the Presidency;

---

[128] See EAST AFRICAN COMMUNITY, *Report of the Committee on Fast Tracking East African Federation,* Arusha: EAC Secretariat, 2004.

[129] See JJUUKO, Frederick W. and Godfrey Muriuki (eds.), *Federation Within Federation: The Tanzania Union Experience and the East African Integration Process: A Report of the Kituo Cha Katiba Fact-finding Mission to Tanzania,* op. cit.

- divergent national visions of development;

- the trend towards *"Majimboism"* in Kenya which are largely fuelled by deep seated tribal considerations for what Professor Mahmood Mamdani recently described as the entrenchment of "tribal homelands,"[130]

- continuing and potential national strife and conflicts in Uganda and Burundi;

- uncertainty about the state of reconciliation and sustainable peace and stability in Rwanda post-genocide of 1994;

- Pursuant to these fears and concerns, the EAC Summit in November 2009 directed that a Team of Experts be constituted by the Council of Ministers with three representatives drawn from each Partner State to examine such fears and concerns in detail and propose measures that can be adopted to address them.

The Report of the Team of Experts which was constituted in April 2010 was tabled before the Summit in April 2011. The Summit rejected the Report for dwelling on the very fears and concerns which were common knowledge and for failing to propose robust recommendations on how to tackle the same. Whilst the terms of reference for the work of the Team of Experts seemed clear enough on the expectations of their work, it would appear that national interests injected some form of fear in the team thereby undermining boldness in tackling difficult issues. The Summit directed that the work be re-done, possibly involving a new team of experts.

The Team of Experts tabled a new set of proposals at the 13th EAC Summit meeting in Bujumbura, Burundi at the end of November, 2011. Tanzania had vehemently rejected the new report at the Ministerial level arguing that it sought to re-introduce land ownership and use of Identity Cards as means for intra-EAC travel by citizens of the EAC partner states, issues that had been rejected at the stage of negotiations of the Common Market Protocol. It needed the Tanzanian Vice President's diplomatic skills to calm tensions and enabling the Ministerial report to the Summit to be signed by Tanzania by omitting

---

[130] MAMDANI, Mahmood, "The East African Federation: Challenges for the Future," keynote address to the East African Legislative Assembly Symposium, "A Decade of Service towards Political Federation," Arusha, 30th June, 2011.

any references to land and ID issues. If there is a point of departure from past difficulties in moving the political federation agenda forward, it was the agreement by the Summit that the EAC Secretariat proposes an Action Plan on and a *Draft Model of the Structure of the East African Political Federation* at the 14th EAC Summit to be held at the end of November 2012.

The growing sensitivity of the political federation agenda has, however, led to an interesting conjecture about the relevance of the principle of variable geometry in the EAC integration project. This ferment is partly triggered by the flexibility that exists in the European Union with respect to membership of its Monetary Union and to various opting-out clauses including on issues of immigration. As it is known, there are a number of EU member countries including the United Kingdom that did not join the Euro. In turn, Denmark, UK and Ireland opted out of the Single Market clause that allows free movement of persons, asylum and immigration.

In this vein, there is a burning question within certain quarters of EAC's intellectual discourse whether the principle of variable geometry which is enshrined in Article 7(1) (e) of the EAC Treaty, cannot be applied to the political federation objective. That Article stipulates that "the principle of variable geometry which allows progression in cooperation among groups within the Community for wider integration schemes in various fields and at different speeds" shall be one of the principles that govern the practical achievement of the objectives of the Community.

This is an interesting point for debate in the EAC. But it has sensitive legal ramifications in the sense whether a decision to proceed for or with variable geometry is not, in itself, governed by the principle of consensus as spelt out under Article 12(3) with respect to Summit decisions. On the face of it, it would appear that where variable geometry is invoked, say in deciding that two or more members, but not all of them, proceed to establish a political federation, a Partner State or Partner States not ready to join the bandwagon may allow the other states to proceed.

Such outcome may, however, raise a number of difficulties in terms of the whole decision making structure and process within the EAC, probably with dire consequences. For example, what would the implications be of the federated members *vis a vis* the non federated ones in so far as the workings of the monetary union? What is interesting though is that the question relating to consensus and variable geometry was a subject of an application by the EAC Council of Ministers to the EACJ for an advisory opinion within the ambit of Article 36(1) of the Treaty. The application sought the Court's opinion on three matters: first, whether the principle of variable geometry was in harmony with the requirement for consensus in decision making and, second, whether the principle of variable geometry can apply to guide the integration process, the requirement on consensus in decision making notwithstanding; and third, whether the requirement on consensus in decision making implied unanimity of the Partner States.

The submissions made by learned lawyers representing the governments of the Partner States reflected varying, if not opposing, thinking on the questions before the Court though there was a predominant view that sought to preserve the sanctity of sovereign interests assured by a strict adherence to the principle of consensus. The EACJ in its opinion delivered on 24th April, 2009, found that the principle of variable geometry "is a strategy of implementation of Community decisions and not a decision making tool in itself". Its purpose is to "guide the integration process". The Court found "no reason or possibility for it to conflict with the requirements for consensus in decision-making." It is significant to note the finding by the Court that variable geometry "actually allows those Partner States who cannot implement a particular decision simultaneously or immediately to implement it at a suitable certain future or simply at a different speed while ... allowing those who are able to implement immediately to do so." This would imply that consensus is irrelevant where Partner States exercise the right of variable geometry.

The political federation idea faces an interesting environment given the fast changing national political culture in the EAC Partner States with the entry and consolidation of multiparty political systems. This is a political system that seems to be more engrossed in national political and economic issues than on EAC matters. In some respects, this is understandable when you consider the years of monolithic political party systems (*de jure* and *de facto*) that pervaded the "old" EAC Partner States. The struggles for political visibility, relevance, legitimacy and power have demanded a dominant national thrust. It was in this context that former Kenya President Daniel Arap Moi during the 10th Anniversary Symposium of the East African

Legislative Assembly in Arusha in 2011 surmised that East African Unity should be about strength and not about power.

It is thus axiomatic, that apart from the National Resistance Movement (NRM) of Uganda, none of the political parties in the other EAC Partner States have had an election manifesto or party programme that outlines a policy on East African integration and least of all on the East African Political Federation. Mainstreaming and deepening the political federation idea within the EAC's political culture and processes may well underpin and determine its legitimacy and acceptance to the broad citizenry of East Africa.

CHAPTER ELEVEN

Uncharted Waters in Political Federation

*Do not fear to imagine a nation called East Africa with a
Parliament, Judiciary, President and a Commander in Chief. I
think it is only when you start entertaining the idea that you
realize it is possible to reach there. A country stretching from
Abyei in Southern Sudan, to Mtwara in Southern Tanzania,
cannot be anything else other than a super-power.*

Daniel T. Arap Moi, CGH[131]

Political Leadership and Mindset Change

The role of the top political leadership in pushing forward the agenda of the
East African Political Federation is an imperative. In this context, it is
important to examine the state of mind of the EAC Heads of State when they
met at a Retreat in Nairobi in August, 2004 to discuss how best to fast track
EAC integration and, particularly, political integration and contextualize it
within the overall perception that exists in East African society about the
idea of the political federation. This is important because the general
thinking about the East African Federation seems to be based on mistaken
ideas about I; ideas which have to be debunked and corrected. In my view,
you need a powerful and consistent political message to achieve this type of
objective.

There is a sense, for example, that the East African Federation would be a
'big bang' event and not the product of a well-planned and structured
evolutionary process. Often this perception has been the main source of
apprehension and even of denigration of the federation project. What the
Heads of State did at their Nairobi meeting which gave rise to the
appointment of the Wako Committee on Fast Tracking the EAC Political
Federation was principally to try and 'exorcise' such a 'devil' from the
minds of many East Africans by launching a dialogue process on the
federation; a process which, since 2006, has informed a broad consultative
process in the EAC partner states pursuant to the proposals and
recommendations of the Wako Committee.

---

[131] Former President of the Republic of Kenya, addressing the 10th Anniversary of the East
African Legislative Assembly, Arusha, 30th June, 2011.

High level political leadership role constitutes an important area of the uncharted waters in the quest for the political federation. It is evident that a broadly shared, right thinking, about the federation could only properly emanate from the top political leadership. However, this is one area of serious weakness at present. Of course, President Yoweri Museveni has always stood up to champion the cause of the federation and to celebrate the benefits which would accrue to East Africans therefrom. Unfortunately, for playing such a role, President Museveni has often been misunderstood as to his intentions. There has been a mischievous view in certain quarters of East Africa's political elite that Museveni actually aspires to become the first President of East Africa and that his ostensible celebration of the federation is, at heart, self centred. What baffles the mind, however, is how such thinking could make sense when a democratic constitutional process would inform how the President of East Africa would be elected!

Changed Political Dynamics

Yet the role of the political leadership in propelling the political federation idea has to be considered against the changed political dynamics in East Africa. It is notable that whilst the federation project suffered serious damage in the early 1960s following Mwalimu Julius Nyerere's crusade to make it happen, there is little doubt that East Africa's top political leadership constituted the major bulwark in its quest. The leaders popularized the idea to the point of making it romantic amongst the citizens and the educated youth in particular. And even when the theme for the federation had faded, Mwalimu Nyerere could still make references to the missed opportunity. In a speech to the Liberian Parliament in January, 1968, titled "Unity Must be Worked For," Nyerere stated:

> When Tanganyika and Zanzibar decided to form the present United Republic of Tanzania, only the most basic questions of principle were settled between the two governments. The detailed negotiations about unification of tariffs, division of tax revenues, etc, were carried out later – and in some respects are still unfinished. But in the case of the East African Community, all these detailed discussions have taken place without a decision for political unity. We settled for something less than federation because we were not all equally ready to make a merger.[132]

That speech of Mwalimu Nyerere raises a fundamental uncharted question, namely, why, in recent discussions about the East African federation, could the East African States not settle the most basic questions of principle and

---

[132] NYERERE, Julius K., "Unity Must be Worked For" in *Freedom and Development*, Nairobi and Dar es Salaam: Oxford University Press, 1973 at p. 21.

leave the detailed negotiations for later? Could the formation of the Tanzania Union not be a useful model for informing the partner states how best to constitute the East African Federation?

This question goes to the heart of what I describe as the changed political dynamics in the region. For whilst President Julius Nyerere and Sheikh Abeid Amani Karume could, in 1964, meet and agree on the Union of Tanganyika and Zanzibar and carry other leaders and their people with them, the same probably could not happen today. Nyerere and Karume's era was, after all, not only governed by political oligarchy of one political party systems, but was also heavily animated by ardent romanticism about Pan-Africanism. No doubt there was more to it.[133]

We should not be overly simplistic about these sentiments because the 'Tanzania Union' logic may in fact beg the question why similar political oligarchies in Kenya and Uganda and in equally strong Pan-Africanist

---

[133] On the Union between Tanganyika and Zanzibar forming the United Republic of Tanzania see AYANG, Samuel G., *A History of Zanzibar: A Study in Constitutional Development 1934-1964*, Nairobi: Kenya Literature Bureau, 1970; BAILEY, Martin, *The Union of Tanganyika and Zanzibar: A Study in Political Integration* (Eastern African Studies IX), New York: Syracuse University, 1973; BAKARI, Mohamed Ali, *The Democratisation Process in Zanzibar: A Retarded Transition*, Hamburg: Institute of African Affairs, 2001; BURGESS, G. Thomas (ed.), *Race, Revolution and the Struggle for Human Rights in Zanzibar: Memoirs of Ali Sultan Issa and Seif Sharif Hamad,* Athens: Ohio University Press, 2009; FENGLER, *Wolfgang, Tanzania at Cross-roads: The Conflict of the Union, Its Reasons and Its Consequences*, Munich: University of Augsburg, 1995; JJUUKO, Frederick and Godfrey Muriuki (eds.) *Federation Within Federation: The Tanzania Union Experience and the East African Integration Process*, Kampala: Kituo Cha Katiba and Fountain Publishers, 2010; JUMBE, Aboud, *The Partner-ship: Tanganyika Zanzibar Union - 30 Turbulent Years*, Dar es Salaam: Amana Publishers, 1994; OLOKA-ONYANGO, Joseph and Maria Nassali (eds.), *Constitutionalism and Political Stability in Zanzibar: The Search for a New Vision*, Kampala: Kituo Cha Katiba, 2003; OTHMAN, Haroub, *Zanzibar's Political History: The Past Haunting the Present?* Dar es Salaam: Institute of Development Studies, 1993; PETER, Chris Maina and Haroub Othman (eds.), *Zanzibar and the Union Question*, Zanzibar: Zanzibar Legal Services Centre, 2006; SHIVJI, *The Legal Foundations of the Union in Tanzania's Union and Zanzibar Constitutions*, Dar es Salaam: Dar es Salaam University Press, 1990; VONHOFF, Y., *Union Without Unity: The Case of Tanganyika and Zanzibar*, A Master of Laws Dissertation, University of Leiden, The Netherlands, 1987; BAKARI, Mohamed A., "The Union Between Tanganyika and Zanzibar Revisited," in ENGEL, Ulf et al (eds.), *Tanzania Revisited: Political Stability, Aid Dependency and Development Constraints*, Hamburg: Institute of African Affairs, 2000, p. 133; BAKARY, Abubakar Khamis, "The Union and the Zanzibar Constitutions," in *Zanzibar and the Union Question*, Zanzibar: Zanzibar Legal Services Centre, 2006, p. 1; DOURADO, Wolfgang, "Whither the Tanzania Union?" in SOCIETY FOR INTERNATIONAL DEVELOPMENT (TANZANIA CHAPTER), *Towards 1995: Proposals for a New Constitutional, Electoral and Union Order*, Dar es Salaam: Friedrich Naumann Stiftung, 1995; OTHMAN, Haroub and Leonard P. Shaidi, "Zanzibar Constitutional Development," Volumes 11-14 *Eastern Africa Law Review*, 1978-1981; and OTHMAN, Haroub, "The Union between Tanganyika and Zanzibar – Tanzania: The Withering of the Union," in PETER, Chris Maina and Saida Yahya-Othman, (eds.), *Haroub Othman: Farewell to the Chairman*, Zanzibar: Zanzibar Legal Services Centre, 2009.

environments, did not leverage similar fervour and drive for the formation of the East African Federation in the early 1960s? It is important to recognize that Tanganyika and Zanzibar historically comprise largely the same people and that the same does not apply with the other East African Community states.

But, to revert back to the core question, namely why the EAC partner states could not first settle the most basic questions of principle in so far as political federation is concerned rather than postponing the idea to some largely indeterminate date, the answer clearly lies in the changed political dynamics of the region. The emergence of deeply entrenched multi-party politics in the EAC partner states has meant that "the most basic questions of principle" about the political federation are no longer within the exclusive purview and decisions of the Heads of State. They are questions that require a broad engagement and decision of the citizens, partly represented by a diverse character of political parties and partly by a better organized, informed and increasingly well networked citizens. Put differently, the drive for the East African Federation today must become a broad based, people-centred and driven project.

Whilst the federation project must importantly be championed by the political leaderships in power, the need to mobilize and galvanise a popular support for the project across the political divides and involving the broad masses, faith leaders and civil society could not be over-emphasised. These new political dynamics have to be given greater attention particularly now that national politics are increasingly coming under pressure from people's growing concerns about enduring poverty, unemployment and growing inequalities. New constitutional and development models that can better respond to these challenges are, unfortunately, taking the wind off the sails of the East African federation agenda. In such an environment, the role of a regional citizenship in clarifying the link between national constitutional and development change and the East African federation emerges as the strategic uncharted area requiring effective mobilisation and galvanization.

The recent "Uamsho" group in Zanzibar that ostensibly fights for Zanzibar's sovereignty but from an Islamic "sheep skin" cover cannot be viewed simply as outlandish or isolated from mainstream sentiments about the Tanzania Union and, connectedly, about the East African political federation. Nothing must be left to chance in delving what the East African citizens think about the nature of the federation being conceived. The decision taken by the Warioba Tanzania Constitution Commission that Tanzanians must feel free to give their views about the Tanzania Union even if it is about the breakup of the union is, in this vein, laudable. In turn, the decision of the EAC Heads of State that the EAC Secretariat should work out a Model and Structure for the East African political federation is very apt. It will be recalled that when East African citizens were asked to offer their views about the WAKO recommendations on fast tracking the East African political federation many had actually wondered what form of political federation was being touted. Thus, it is such a model when subjected to a broad and extensive discussion by the citizens of EAC that could bring about a consensus on what a viable constitutional dispensation actually entails. The EAC Secretariat has already constituted a Team of Eminent East Africans to work out such a model and structure which will be tabled before the EAC Heads of State in November, 2012 for further direction. The role of the East African citizens in determining what they want in this regard cannot be overemphasised.

The Role of Regional Citizenship

When inaugurating the University of East Africa in June, 1963, Mwalimu Nyerere observed that the realization of one identity and culture of East Africanness constituted a strategic factor in the quest for the East African federation. In effect, Nyerere was thinking about the creation of regional citizens; of individuals sold to and who champion the cause of a larger East African political entity. The day when East Africa can achieve the realization of a critical mass of citizens and of organisations who identify themselves as citizens of East Africa and not citizens of their countries, that is when East African federation will become inevitable.

I am of the view that the viability of the EAC federation project hinges on building a broad based vision about the benefits of such a federation. There is a need to cultivate regional activism as driver and igniter of a deep passion about political integration. In this connection, the internet is an important tool for enabling such regional citizens to exchange views about their shared vision and for strategizing on how best to execute the vision. It is important though, that regional citizens are as broadly representative of the society at national and regional levels as possible. Getting the youth, women, politicians, businesspeople and firms, academics, the media, progressive bureaucrats and professional civil society professionals involved in advancing the cause of the political federation is of strategic importance. East African regional business champions like East African Breweries, Vodafone, Lafarge, Equity Bank, KCB, Azam, Nakumatt, Transcentury, Serena Hotels, Sameer and Bidco should also use some of their resources to promote the benefits that would accrue from an East African federation. For ultimately, EAC integration will effectively benefit the citizens of East Africa when it becomes a truly single market and single economic community. It is only through a political federation that such deeper integration can sustainably be realized.

How to mobilize and galvanise a broad based peoples' engagement in the EAC integration project and political integration in particular is thus the larger question going forward. Evidently, some progress has been achieved in getting the East African business to organize on a regional basis and pursue a regional agenda. It is unfortunate though that the EAC has so far failed to realize the benefits of giving statutory recognition of the East African Business Council and allowing it to enjoy the status of an organ of the EAC. Such status would have given a huge stimulus to the EABC to foster political integration. Some civil society bodies in fields as diverse as law, youth, agriculture, local authorities and the informal sector have also fostered regional frameworks with varying degrees of success in promoting regional programmes.

Since 2007, the EAC Secretariat has also worked closely with the media in the EAC region to create a platform that promotes a vision of a politically integrated East Africa. The EAC mantra,' One people, One Destiny' has helped to shape a regional identity. However, much more needs to be done overall in getting ordinary folks to understand and appreciate the purpose of regional integration and why the federation idea is of such paramount importance. It could be posited that this challenge probably constitutes the main area of uncharted waters in EAC's integration.

Considering the fact that a federation would always require a referendum to be undertaken, it is critically important that the broad electorate is made to know what they would be voting for and why. Going by what happened in the European Union in 2005 when the Constitutional Treaty was subjected to a referendum and the French and Dutch electorates were first to reject the treaty, for different reasons, it could not be over-emphasised that it is the people who ultimately matter over decisions of great political import. The EU Constitutional Treaty debacle was in fact blamed on a 'disconnect' between the grand wishes of the political leadership and the basic concerns of ordinary citizens about perceived implications of the treaty on their social and economic interests at national levels.

In several respects, the EU lessons point to the special importance alluded to earlier of the centrality of political leadership in mobilizing and galvanizing a shared vision about political integration. As I have pointed out, there is a vivid yawning gap in East Africa with respect to a political leadership that is genuinely hungry about political integration. The depth of the Nyerere federation fervour of the 1960s is clearly missing in the current leadership in East Africa. Without such a forthright leadership, it will always be difficult to secure a critical mass of support for a political federation especially given the changed political dynamics in the region.

Conclusion

The quest for an East African federation is not a romantic idea; neither is it a means for anybody to secure higher political power beyond the nation-state. I am not sure if the Union between Tanganyika and Zanzibar would have materialized had the thinking behind it been to create a structure for someone's quest for additional or higher political power. The quest for the East African federation must thus be viewed from the context of a shared fate and future of East Africa in a complex global environment. Such shared fate – extreme poverty, fragmented small markets, artificial borders, the lack of economies of scale and scope for infrastructure and industries, trans-boundary ecological systems and natural resources, the demographic transition manifested in a worrisome youth bulge – requires a shared political sovereignty framework to promote effective solutions. National chauvinisms will not provide effective solutions to these challenges.

The national governments have a role to play in constructing a regional shared vision and purpose provided a dynamic political leadership takes the reins and leads the process. Ultimately, however, it is the citizens of East Africa and especially individuals and organisations that embrace a regional perspective who must become the blood and sinews of political integration. The challenge is to how best engage these citizens.

PART 4

The Roles of EAC Organs and Institutions

Context

In the following part four of the book, I turn to examine the role of EAC Organs and Institutions. As observed earlier, EAC's strength largely flows from the types of institutions that have been established to drive the integration agenda. In his recent book titled *Civilization: The West and the Rest*[134] Harvard history Professor, Niall Ferguson celebrates the role of institutions in making the West realise the level of prosperity it has achieved since the 16th century in contrast to the rest of the world and especially the East. Examining the dimensions that constitute the institutions that Ferguson articulates, such as competition, science, property rights, medicine, consumer society and work ethic and which, in his view, incorporate issues of freedom, democracy and rule of law, you cannot but agree that any political integration venture- national, regional or global has to be underpinned by such institutional values and processes. And because of their very centrality, such institutions often constitute the battleground in forging consensual agreement in realizing supra national objectives.

EAC Organs and Institutions are established under Articles 9(1) and 9(2) of the Treaty. They include the Summit and the Council of Ministers which we have already dealt with under Part two above. In the following chapters, I will dwell on two organs namely the East African Court of Justice (EACJ) and the East African Legislative Assembly (EALA) as well as examine the roles of EAC's institutions.

---

[134] See FERGUSON, Niall, *Civilization: The West and the Rest,* London: Penguin Group, 2011.

CHAPTER TWELVE

The East African Court of Justice

The role of the EACJ is outlined under Article 23 of the Treaty to be the judicial body that shall ensure the adherence to law in the interpretation and application of and compliance with the EAC Treaty. The court is divided into two chambers: a court of first instance and an appeal court. The head of the EACJ is President and is assisted by a Principal Judge who heads the court of first instance. The judges of the Court are appointed by the Summit and their membership reflects a democratic representation by all the Partner States. The Court is so far ad hoc in its work but in the past ten years of its existence it has shown remarkable output in legal decisions that have shaped regional jurisprudence. Indeed, because of the intensity and growing work of the court the EAC Summit of Heads of State have decided that effective July 2012, the President of the Court and the Principal Judge of the Court of First instance be full time and based in Arusha, Tanzania where the court is presently seated.

One of the serious shortcomings of the EACJ is its limited jurisdiction even though through a number of its rulings an element of judicial activism has been manifested showing the boldness of the Court to give broad interpretation and application of the rule of law that is enshrined in several provisions of the Treaty especially those dealing with the objectives, fundamental principles and operational principles of the EAC together with the provision relating to general undertaking as to implementation of Community's objectives. Thus, one of the hottest subjects in EAC legal fraternity is the desire to extend the jurisdiction of the EACJ beyond what is prescribed under Article 27. In particular, there are strong recommendations to the effect that the EACJ should have express jurisdiction on human rights and fundamental freedoms as well as on commercial disputes arising out of the Customs Union and the Common Market.

It is argued, for instance, that it is inconceivable that commercial disputes of a cross-border nature should be adjudicated under municipal law when the transactions fall within the ambit of the Customs Union and or the Common Market. Indeed, a test case arose through the case of *Modern Holdings (EA) Limited v. Kenya Ports Authority*,[135] based on Article 30 of the Treaty, the East African Community Customs Management Act of 2004 and it's Regulations of 2006. The Claimant averred that its containers with imported

---

[135] East African Court of Justice at Arusha, Reference No. 1 of 2008. This case is reported in East African Law *Society Law Digest 2005-2011*, p. 49.

fruit juices and mineral water from Dubai were not cleared in time at the port of Mombasa due to the post election violence in Kenya in 2007/2008 and that the perishable goods with limited shelf life, known to the respondent, were affected with serious loss of business. The Court was faced with two questions: first, whether it had jurisdiction to entertain the reference, and second, whether the respondent had the capacity to be sued in the Court. The Court ruled that it had no jurisdiction to entertain the reference and that the Kenya Ports Authority was not of the respondents envisaged under Article 30 of the Treaty.

In a paper titled, "An Overview of the East African Court of Justice,"[136] the President of the EACJ, Hon. Mr. Justice Harold Nsekela, has argued that the EAC is witnessing a number of Protocols that are:

> contradicting the position of the Treaty. Other parallel dispute resolution mechanisms (national courts and quasi-judicial bodies) are being established. For instance, Article 41(2) of the EAC Customs Union Protocol that deals with dispute settlement establishes committees to handle disputes arising out of the Protocol and gives these committees finality in determining the disputes. The Court (EACJ) is left out and therefore denied a role in all this process except if a party challenges the decision of the committee on grounds of fraud, lack of jurisdiction or other illegality. Again, under Article 54 (2) of the Common Market Protocol, jurisdiction to entertain Common Market related disputes has mainly been given to national courts. This Partner States' tendency of ousting the jurisdiction of their joint Court is not conducive to the integration agenda. It has the effect of undermining the Court itself and causing confusion to the development of uniform regional jurisprudence.

> In reference to EACJ Reference No. 3 of 2007, between the East African Law Society and the Attorney Generals of Kenya, Tanzania and Uganda and the Secretary General of the EAC where the EALS joined by the then country Law Societies of the three partner states petitioned the EACJ to declare Treaty amendments undertaken by the EAC Summit in 2006 as unlawful and unconstitutional, Justice Nsekela has posited that the Treaty has to be amended to give effect to the declarations

---

[136] See NSEKELA, Harold R., "Overview of the East African Court of Justice," A Paper for Presentation During the Sensitisation Workshop on the Role of the EACJ in the EAC Integration, Imperial Royal Hotel, Kampala, Uganda, 1st - 2nd November, 2011; see also East African Court of Justice Reference No. 3 of 2007, between East African Law Society and Attorney General of Kenya, Uganda and Tanzania and the Secretary general of the East African Community. The Court declined to invalidate the amendments but declared that the amendments undertaken "are capable of rectification".

of the Court on how the Treaty should be amended. In the reference under discussion, the EACJ had ruled that the amendments done to Articles 27, 30(3) and 45 of the Treaty had eroded the supremacy the EACJ over the interpretation and application of the EAC Treaty for ensuring harmony and predictability and had to be re-amended to restore the status quo ante position.

These are fiery comments which reinforce the point that political will have to allow some element of supranationality to emerge in order to dynamise EAC's integration.

Put in context, it may be asked: how could East Africans aspire for a political federation when they see, for example, important organs such as the EACJ having their powers chipped off, as evidenced by the amendments done to the EAC Treaty in 2007 following the *Anyang Nyong'o Case*[137] and now a reference issue before the court as to the legality of those very amendments?

The East African Centre for Trade Policy and Law based in Uganda has petitioned the EACJ that the amendments undertaken in 2007 erode the basic supranational powers of the EACJ as provided in the Treaty establishing the EAC. Whilst the original Article 30 has been retained as a new Article 30 (1), two new subsections were added following the court decisions on the *Anyang Nyong'o Case*, the controversial one being Article 30(2) which stipulates that the EACJ shall have "no jurisdiction under this Article where an Act, regulations, directive, decision or action has been reserved under this Treaty to an institution of a Partner State." The effect of this amendment is to erode the EACJ's jurisdiction on matters that had already been vested on it from the start. Political expediency based on Kenya's electoral politics unfortunately took command and thereby undermining EAC's supranationality on certain key areas of law which underpin the realization and sustenance of integration objectives.

More fundamentally, how could the EAC be serious about the process towards a Political Federation when it inhibits, at a lower stage of integration, the rights of East African citizens to petition their own regional court for redress on matters that are already governed by Protocols that form an integral part of the Treaty or are governed by EAC laws which, pursuant to the Treaty, take precedence over national laws? I return to this subject about the constrained role of the EACJ in the chapter dealing with the role of national politics on EAC integration.

---

[137] See *Prof. Peter Anyang' Nyong'o and 10 Others v. Attorney General of Kenya and Others*, Application No. 1 of 2006.

However, and in sum, I should point out that over the past four years the EAC Secretariat has been working with the Sectoral Council on Legal and Judicial Affairs on amending the Treaty to extend the court's jurisdiction and address several deficits in several treaty provisions. One area of focus is on the extended jurisdiction of the EACJ involving commercial disputes that arise from the Customs Union and the Common Market operations. This delay gave rise to a Reference before the EACJ. This is the case of *Hon. Sitenda Sebalu v. The Secretary General of the East African Community and Three Others.*[138] Interestingly, the Court held that there was indeed undue delay by the EAC in determining the issue of extended jurisdiction of the court. It is also concluded that such delay "contravenes the principles of good governance as stipulated in Article 6 of the Treaty."

EAC Partner States have to come to terms with this reality that their national courts should not adjudicate on matters that are or should be governed by a regional law. Not to accept such reality would simply frustrate and undermine the very meaning of the Customs Union and the Common Market and the whole integration process and purpose.

---

[138] At the East African Court of Justice at Arusha, Reference No. 1 of 2010.

CHAPTER THIRTEEN

The East African Legislative Assembly

Established under Article 9(1) of the Treaty, the basic role of the EALA is defined under Article 49 of the Treaty. EALA came into force in 2001 and its original membership of nine members from each Partner State was extended to cover Rwanda and Burundi in 2007. In its principal functions as a legislative organ of the Community, as an oversight body for approving the EAC budget and examining the audit of the EAC (organs and institutions) and as an organ that liaises with National Assemblies and discusses all matters pertaining to the Community, EALA is a unique legislature in the whole of regional communities in Africa.

There have been varying views about the extensive role of EALA in the context of a new inter-governmental institution that has been at the stage of institution building and implementing a robust mandate of integration. Some observers hold that there has been greater flexibility in ECOWAS, COMESA and SADC Secretariats in executing their tasks, responsibly and accountably, to their Councils of Ministers, without having to be "encumbered" by legislature breathing on their necks.

The opposing view is that the EAC is a different regional entity from other regional economic communities in Africa. The Treaty extols the EAC Partner States from day one to cooperate in several political matters "to enhance the eventual establishment of a Political Federation of the Partner States (Article 123(3) (f)). In this regard, the EALA is one vehicle of political cooperation that can facilitate the application of this particular Treaty prescription. Moreover, even in the erstwhile EAC, there was a regional legislature, probably with even wider powers than the present one.

In the past ten years of its existence, EALA has played a signal role in ensuring that the EAC finances are well allocated to priority business and are also well accounted for in terms of value for money. In its legislative work, EALA has so far passed thirty four Bills though some are yet be assented to, like the EAC Tourism Bill. In recent years, EALA has taken up more and more legislative activism, much as this role is governed by Article 59(1) of the Treaty, in tabling Private Member Bills. None of these, except the EAC Joint Trade Negotiations Bill of 2007, have been assented to by the Summit, reflecting a serious divide in thinking between the Council of Ministers, which is the primary initiator of Bills pursuant to Article 14(3) of the Treaty, and the Legislature.

In my view, given the consensus rule under the EAC Treaty, it seems that the idea behind Article 59 (1) of the Treaty which allows a Member of EALA to introduce a Bill in the Assembly is self defeating. The fact that the private members bill, the Trade Negotiations Bill was assented to by the EAC Heads of State should not be seen as a generic circumstance. No other Bill initiated by the assembly has received assent. You need all the five Heads of State to assent a Bill for it to become law. Under such circumstances the ideal process is for EALA to pass resolutions calling for the Council of Ministers to initiate Bills it considers of great importance in promoting deeper integration. Short of that, you end up with endless gridlocks between the Assembly and the Council of Ministers.

There have also been occasions where there has been a gridlock between the Council of Ministers and EALA with respect to the form and content of Bills initiated by the Council. Two bills, the Lake Victoria Basin Commission Bill and the EAC Civil Aviation Safety and Security Oversight Agency, have faced such gridlock with EALA proposing changes to the Bills that are unacceptable to the Council of Ministers. In the case of the Lake Victoria bill, EALA sought to totally change the governance structure of the Commission which would have conflicted with the provisions of the Protocol that created the Commission in the first place. In the case of CASSOA, the Assembly wanted the term of office of the Executive Director to be extended to two terms of five years each which would have conflicted with the standard contract offered to all such executives in other EAC institutions. It would also have undermined the policy of geographical rotation of top executive posts in the EAC. As a result of such unnecessary gridlocks, the two institutions have had to continue operating on the basis of the Protocols that established them.

The EALA has also over the years passed various Resolutions some of them with serious policy implications. For example, in 2010, it passed a resolution stopping the EAC from proceeding with negotiations of the Economic Partnership Agreement (EPA) with the European Union. EALA then proceeded to reject the inclusion of SIDA grant to the EAC to support EPA negotiations and other capacity building measures related thereto in a supplementary budget. These actions brought the negotiations to a halt because EAC did not have other funds from the Partner States to support the negotiations.

EALA's decision raised a fundamental question regarding EAC negotiating as a block for which idea the legislature was the brainchild through its Private Members' Bill on EAC trade negotiations. The larger question is whether EALA has legal mandate to disenable the EAC to receive grants which are supposed to enable the Partner States, as legal negotiating state parties to the Cotonou Agreement, to negotiate EPAs under the EAC framework. The Summit that met in April 2011 was seized of this situation which could have been resolved through an Advisory Opinion of the EACJ but chose instead not to be offensive. It instead directed EAC Secretariat to negotiate with SIDA for the grant to be directly allocated to the Partner States instead. It is one of those issues that should not be shoved under the carpet. They should be brought before the EACJ for an opinion lest the legislature elects to be the dominant organ in the EAC.

Probably the most interesting feature of EALA's role relates to how the EAC can realize the Treaty requirement under Article 7(1) (a) that the EAC shall be "people-centred". Ordinarily, at national levels, such a requirement is captured in the representativeness of the National Assemblies. By virtue of being directly elected, Members of the National Assemblies are deemed to represent the people. Indeed, they are rejected at polls when the people feel they have not been well represented. In the case of EALA, however, its members are not *directly* elected by the people in such manner in which Members of the European Parliament, for example, are. Instead, they are elected by Members of the National Assemblies. Thus a question looms large whether the EAC has, indeed, realized the goal of people centredness.

A new dimension has also cropped up with respect to EALA's "representativeness". On the face of it, Article 50 of the EAC Treaty envisages a broad representation of "various political parties represented in the National Assembly". However, the electoral process favours numerical strength of political parties with evident disenfranchisement of minority parties. This situation gave rise to a Reference before the EACJ by the Uganda Democratic Party which argued that the Rules of Procedure applied in Uganda Parliament to elect EALA members contravened the letter and spirit of Article 50 of the EAC Treaty.[139] In spite of arguments presented by the Uganda Attorney General that amendments of the Rules in question was in process, the Court ruled, in accepting the applicant's reference and arguments, to refrain the amendment process pending judgement. Basically the judgement was to the effect that the Rules of Procedure applied in Ugandan parliament did in effect "disenfranchise" minority political parties represented in Parliament.

More fundamentally, it could be questioned whether EALA indeed has the legitimacy to determine priority activities which the EAC should budget for as is the case presently. Under Article 49 (2) (b), the EAC Treaty provides that the EALA shall debate and approve the budget of the EAC. This provision is reinforced by article 132 (5) wherein it is stated that the resources of the EAC shall be utilized to finance activities of the EAC as

---

[139] See the case of *Democratic Party v. The Secretary General of the East African Community and The Attorney General of the Republic of Uganda,* East African Court of Justice at Arusha, Reference No. 6 of 2011.

"shall be determined by" the EALA on the recommendation of the EAC Council of Ministers.

The burning point here is how does a regional parliament that is not directly elected by the citizens of East Africa exercise so much power? As the EAC proceeds to give closer and deeper attention to the process towards the realization of an East African Federation, it is imperative that the form of how representation in the East African Legislative Assembly is structured is reviewed. The EAC Treaty invokes the principle of "people centredness" in the assumption that the organs of the Community shall translate such objective in their structures and operations.

Indeed, EALA is probably the organ to best translate that objective in both its representation and operations. However, the Members of EALA are elected by the National Assemblies. This means that there is a disconnect between the EALA Members and the citizens of East Africa to whom they should rightly be accountable and responsible for the realization of deeper integration, more especially when political federation is involved. Recent elections of EALA members by the Tanzania National Assembly, in April 2012, could not reflect anything more glaring that this disconnect; that people get elected by Parliamentarians largely through political corruption and not the ability to represent Tanzanians in an important regional project.

In the context of the foregoing, and as the EAC ponders on the process towards a political federation and as it embraces more complex integration projects relating to the Common Market and the Monetary Union, projects of the type that find heated debate in the European Parliament, for example, it may be time, especially when the Third Assembly has started its work in June 2012, to seriously consider how the EALA could be transformed to become an organ that truly represents the people of East Africa. The advantage of this course of action is that the politics of integration can be sparked and stimulated at national levels, across the political divides, represented by different political parties, independents and by civil society.

I realize that this issue has its controversies from the experience of the European Union. There is growing thinking that an elected European Parliament is now increasingly exerting the kind of influence that is symptomatic of a Federal Europe. With the constant crises facing the European Union especially within the Euro Area, the role of the European Parliament is taking greater attention. It should be realized that until 1979, the European Parliament comprised of delegates nominated by the Parliaments of member states and it merely exercised an advisory function unlike the East African Legislative Assembly.

However, since 1979, the European Parliament has been directly elected. And with such aura of authority extending to authority over the EU budget as well as enactment of legislation without the requirement of assent by EU

Heads of State and Government, in contrast to EALA's enactment of bills which requires such assent, the EU Parliament has significant teeth. Moreover, since 1992, the EU Parliament has powers to approve the appointment of the President of the European Commission. It would also be recalled that in March, 1999, the entire European Commission was forced to resign when it lost the confidence of the European Parliament.

In the light of such extensive legislative powers, the tension between the benefits of cooperation and coordination in an integration project and the sustenance of national interests and sovereignty is becoming accentuated and there are genuine feelings that the EU is taking a federalist mode by default. This tension should not escape our minds in the EAC as we ponder the future dispensation of integration and especially the movement towards a political federation.

In my view, the realization of a political federation will be best tested and ensured when the citizens of East Africa are enabled to exercise the right to vote for its representatives to the EALA. This system is applied in the European Union in the election of their Members of EU Parliament. Taking such a course would help to stimulate greater sensitization and conscientisation in the East African people about the EAC generally and about the rationale for a political federation in particular. The process would also force political parties at national levels to view the EAC integration project as one deserving their attention and for which they can advance their positions within national electoral and governance processes, a situation that does not exist presently and thus making regional integration a periphery issue in the manifestos of national political parties.

CHAPTER FOURTEEN

EAC Institutions

A unique feature of the EAC which marks a major departure from other Regional Economic Communities in Africa is the establishment of specialized institutions to deal with various developmental matters that impinge on regional integration. There are five notable EAC institutions whose roles will be briefly highlighted:

- Lake Victoria Basin Commission (LVBC);

- Inter-University Council of East Africa (IUCEA);

- Lake Victoria Fishers Organisation (LVFO);

- East African Community Civil Aviation Safety and Security Oversight Agency (CASSOA); and

- East African Development Bank.

There are several other institutions in the offing. They include, East African Health Research Commission; East African Science and Technology Commission; East African Kiswahili Commission; East African Culture, Youth and Sports Commission and few others. Their establishment will largely depend on EAC's resources capacity.

Lake Victoria Basin Commission (LVBC)

The LVBC is a specialized institution responsible for co-ordinating the sustainable development of the Lake Victoria Basin. Established in 2006, LVBC was founded as a result of the 2nd EAC Development Strategy (2001-2006) which designated the Lake Victoria as an economic growth zone to be exploited in a co-ordinated manner. In the past five years, LVBC has put the Lake Victoria and its basin at the heart of EAC integration; promoting it as a shared resource of the EAC Partner States including Rwanda and Burundi which form part of the broader basin of Lake Victoria. In this regard, the LVBC Environmental Management Project (LVEMP) I and II have focused on:

- elimination of hyacinth from the lake;

- promotion of sustainable use of natural resources and maintaining the Lake Victoria eco-system and thus improving the sustainable livelihoods of the people;

- reducing environmental stresses within the Lake and the littoral zone;

- improving the quality of trans-boundary natural resources and eco-systems especially along the Mara River and Mt. Elgon;

- undertaking hydrographical analysis of the Lake Victoria for purposes of determining the quality of water as well as charting out new and safe navigation systems on the lake;

- addressing the main threats to the lake especially in relation to use of water lake and quality of water. In this context, early this year, the African Development Bank gave the EAC a grant of close to US $ 120 million to support a Water and Sanitation Programme in fifteen satellite towns that are within the basin or lie in proximity of the Lake Victoria basin, three towns selected from each of the five EAC Partner States. This programme will go a long way in supporting other measures directed at effective reduction of excessive use of the lake water and of toxic products spill; and

- promoting a maritime communications system for search and rescue operations.

In all these interventions, many of which are well supported by a number of development partners including the World Bank, SIDA, Norway, France and Finland, the primary goal is to ensure the sustainability of the Lake Victoria and the reduction of poverty which is very high in the Lake Zone, contributing to equally high levels of HIV infection and AIDS for which the LVBC has an elaborate intervention programme being implemented jointly with African Medical and Research Foundation (AMREF).

The LVBC has more recently embarked on a bold undertaking to promote the Lake Victoria and its basin as an investment area. Supported by the EAC Lake Victoria Transport Act which provides a supportive legal framework for opening up the lake to investments in various lake modes of transport, in fishing and water sports, as well as investments on the lake basin such as tourism, the LVBC launched an Investment Forum in December, 2010 to promote investments on the lake and its huge basin that includes some of the most attractive tourist attractions in Tanzania, Kenya, Uganda and, with a short hop, in Rwanda and Burundi.

The Inter-University Council for East Africa (IUCEA)

The Inter-University Council for East Africa (IUCEA) is a creature of East African Community history. It survived the breakup of the Community in 1977 and has found a new legal life beyond the Treaty establishing the EAC by having a specific legislation passed by the EALA. It has been an autonomous institution of the EAC but effective EAC financial year

2011/2012, it has become mainstreamed in the EAC's budget framework. Its principal role is to promote and develop mutually beneficial collaboration among universities in East Africa, both public and private, and between them and the governments of the EAC Partner States in transforming tertiary education into the highest global standard. In this vein, the IUCEA co-ordinates cooperation to:

- promote collaboration between member universities and governments and other organizations, public and private;

- strengthen regional and international communication in higher education;

- co-ordinate state of art research in the region;

- promote exchange of academic staff and students between member universities;

- encourage and propel development of EAC higher education institutions of learning;

- promote the use of best practices in education delivery through ICT and using ICT to leverage the promotion of ICT in region-wide education delivery; and

- advance a regional accreditation system for tertiary education to foster investments in the establishment of regional education institutions.

As in the case of the European Union where the Bologna Process has for several years been promoting a European system of education that can exploit the benefits of the Single Market, the IUCEA, whose members is presently 87 universities in the EAC region, is equally in the process of harmonizing the educational systems of the EAC Partner States all the way from primary school level to university. It should be remembered, nostalgically, that in the 1960s and 1970s the EAC had a common curricula for its schools, primary and secondary, and had a common examination, even after the fall out of the Cambridge School Certificate for 'O' and 'A' levels examinations. The East African School Certificate for 'O' and 'A' levels subsisted until 1977 when the erstwhile EAC collapsed. All these systems were administered by the East African Examinations Council.

EAC need not therefore re-invent the wheel. It is only a matter of political will to revert to *that* old system. Indeed, with the present huge congruence in political and economic philosophies, the sensitive issues about the viability, relevance and appropriateness of a harmonized curriculum for East Africa should not hold sway. It would be remembered also that even during the Cambridge School Certificate Examinations, the sensitive papers were largely centred on the history paper which always covered several questions anyway that offered comfortable options to students from different countries in the Commonwealth.

Clearly, in the context of the EAC's Common Market objective of free movement of labour, it is critical that the process of putting in place a viable system of mutual recognition of qualifications from tertiary institutions should be predicated on enabling such movement, lest an unfortunate situation of unnecessary clashes is triggered by employment applicants wondering why their qualifications are considered secondary or not up to the mark.

A critical challenge in the role of the IUCEA also lies in how the EAC, in the same manner it is seeking to promote the region as a single tourism destination, can also promote investments in tertiary education with the EAC being treated as one regional education space. Presently, an investor, such as the Aga Khan University, that seeks to establish an East African University with specialized facilities and schools in the EAC Partner States, has to apply for separate accreditations in each country. Such procedure is bureaucratic, it is an unnecessary cost and it undermines the whole ethos and thrust of developing a regional university of the type that existed in the 1960s and 1970 in the form of the University of East Africa. Sovereignty powers that have little benefit to the promotion of advancement of education in East Africa should be discarded. This is a policy area that needs a progressive mindset and the reform of national laws in its regard is both urgent and imperative.

The IUCEA should be conferred with the authority to liaise with national accreditation authorities to offer accreditations to organisations that seek to establish region-wide tertiary institutions. The EALA has proposed an amendment of the IUCEA Act to allow regional accreditation. However, there is a gridlock with the EAC Council of Ministers on the amendment. Tanzania in particular is against the proposal with the other four partner states seemingly supportive. Interestingly, EALA passed the amendment at its sitting in Bujumbura in April, 2012. It is doubtful though that the amendment will be assented in Tanzania.

Lake Victoria Fisheries Organization (LVFO)

LVFO was established in 1994 through a Convention signed by the old EAC Partner States of Uganda, Kenya and Tanzania because of the need to better and collectively manage the fisheries resources of Lake Victoria. The principal objective of the LCFO is to harmonize, develop and adopt conservation and management measures for the sustainable exploitation of fisheries resources of Lake Victoria for socio-economic welfare of over 30 million East Africans who live on the basin of the lake. LVFO is unfortunately still being run directly by the Ministries responsible for fisheries of the EAC Partner States and is thus outside the EAC decision making framework. Its budget depends on contributions of those Ministries with the result that its capacity has been undermined. There are new moves to change this ownership structure to give LVFO the importance envisaged under Article 9 of the EAC Treaty and thereby mainstream LVFO into the EAC programmes and operations including budget allocation, control and oversight by EALA. Side by side with this move, is the new direction being conceived at the EAC level to integrate LVFO and LVBC and extending their mandates to cover all the lakes in the EAC region.

The East African Development Bank (EADB)

The EADB was established in 1967 under the Treaty of the then East African Cooperation. Following the break-up of the erstwhile EAC, the Bank was re-established under its own Charter in 1980 which subsists to-date. Under that Charter, the Bank's role and mandate were expanded to offer a wide range of financial services to the original EAC member states. The mandate now extends to Rwanda upon its joining the EAC and acceding to the EADB Charter. Burundi is yet to accede to the EADB Charter. The Bank is primarily owned by the EAC Partner States but has other shareholders such as the African Development Bank, the Netherlands Development Finance Company, the German Investment and Development Company and few leading global Commercial Banks.

Because of this diverse shareholding structure, the EADB has found it difficult to be an overly East African Development Bank supportive of the strategic objectives of EAC integration. Moving forward, it will be crucial for the EAC Partner States to transform this Bank into one that is 100% owned by the EAC Partner States. The Bank can then relate to some of the current external shareholders in the form of securing long-term credit lines. The independence of the EADB in promoting the interests of EAC integration is critical. Presently it is not and this is a matter for further reflection within the EAC decision making organs whether time has not come for the EADB to be a wholly owned bank by the EAC Partner States.

East African Civil Aviation Safety and Security Oversight Agency (CASSOA)

This agency was established in April, 2007 by the Civil Aviation Authorities of Kenya, Uganda and Tanzania. Thereafter, it received the endorsement of the EAC Summit in June, 2008. The Agency, which is about to be established by an Act of EALA, has been set up on the basis of a Protocol ratified by the original three EAC Partner States. Its main function is to promote a co-ordinated development of an effective civil aviation safety and security oversight infrastructure in the EAC fitting the model or best practice establishment by the International Civil Aviation Organisation (ICAO). This infrastructure embodies:

- creating harmonized regulations that ensure that EAC civil aviation regulations meet international standards;

- development of standardized procedures for licensing, approval, certification and supervision of civil aviation operations; and

- providing guidance and assistance to Partner States on civil aviation matters.

Since its establishment, CASSOA has developed a Five Year Strategic and Organisation Development Plan to guide its operations. At the core of this plan is to transform the EAC main airports into ICAO and US Department of Transportation standards in terms of safety and security and thus open up the EAC skies to direct flights from North America. This development would have positive impacts in the EAC tourism industry.

PART 5

Enlargement of the EAC

Context

One of the defining moments in EAC's integration process has been the integration of Rwanda and Burundi through a highly structured and legalistic process. Ordinarily, states join the AU and RECs at pleasure. In the EAC, however, membership enlargement is governed by the Treaty and involves laborious accession negotiations which can take as much as a whole year. Acceding members are then required to abide to several principles and conform to laws and protocols in place. In the following part eleven the enlargement of the EAC through the accession of Rwanda and Burundi is examined on the basis of these fundamental principles. However, I should observe the following at the outset.

The entry of Rwanda and Burundi into the EAC from July 2007 is a major milestone in EAC's integration. Whilst not considered a stage of integration as defined in the EAC Treaty, it is so in effect because it corresponds to EAC's core objective of widening and deepening integration as spelt out under Article 5(1) of the Treaty. The Customs Union has become more vibrant as a result of the entry of these two countries in the EAC. Intra-EAC trade has grown and so have cross-border investments. More importantly, EAC's objective of promoting peace, security and stability within and good neighbourliness among the Partner States has been given a shot in the arm by Rwanda and Burundi joining the EAC. The days of Burundi refugees being a constant menace in the bordering countries, especially Tanzania, are now history. Through the EAC, Burundi is being stabilized from different angles: constitutional, governance, electoral and economic.

The EU was formed to make the spectre of war history. EAC's enlargement, and with the hope of South Sudan joining soon, the East African region is equally entering a new era of peace, stability and prosperity that would be enviable in the whole of Africa. The role played by Tanzania and Rwanda in Darfur peace keeping and of Uganda and Burundi in Somalia's peace keeping evidence EAC's leading role in promoting peace and stability in

Africa, in itself, a reflection that the EAC region is at peace with itself. Recent intervention by Kenya armed forces in Somalia to confront the *Al Shabaab* insurgency that is *Al-Qaeda* linked is also a clear manifestation of the region's quest to stabilize the region and create the conditions supporting investments and trade to prosper.

With the integration of Burundi and Rwanda, and especially Burundi which is predominantly French speaking, the question of EAC's official language has inevitably become an issue. The EAC Treaty provides that English shall be the official language and that Kiswahili shall be the lingua franca. This Treaty clause merely reflects the history of the EAC as an organization that bound together Kenya, Uganda and Tanzania. There is no magic about it. It can be appreciated that Rwanda has transformed significantly from its French language past and English is now the official language though French remains the second language.

Experience shows that since Burundi's accession into the EAC, its officials have found it difficult to fully participate in official proceedings, some of them of a highly complex nature like negotiations of the Common Market and Monetary Union Protocols. It is neither right nor fair to be simplistic that a condition precedent to Burundi's accession was its acceptance of English as the official language of the EAC and it must thus fulfil the condition. The real issue is how to secure Burundi's best participation in critical integration discussions in the EAC. Moreover, by strictly adhering to English as an official language, a wrong signal could be sent out to countries like the Democratic Republic of Congo that may wish to join the EAC. How does a country join an institution where its role and effectiveness may not be fully felt due to a language limitation?

It is important, therefore, as part of EAC's objective of widening and deepening integration, that the Treaty is amended to incorporate French as a second official language. There is a financial cost to such a decision but it is worth its while. Of course, ultimately, the EAC must promote Kiswahili to become the official working language.

CHAPTER FIFTEEN

Negotiations on Accession of Rwanda and Burundi[140]

I am very pleased to welcome you on this occasion of the Launching of the High Level Negotiations on the Admission of the Republic of Burundi and the Republic of Rwanda to the East African Community. This is indeed a happy and historic occasion considering, if not anything else, the long process and protracted preparations that have finally led to this definitive moment.

The Republic of Burundi and the Republic Rwanda have close historical and geographical links as well as longstanding cultural, social and economic ties with the East African Community countries - Kenya, Uganda and Tanzania. On account of this, it is to be recalled that the applications of Burundi and Rwanda to join the Community remained on the agenda throughout the life of the first East African Community.

Indeed, just as it had been unfortunate when the first East African Community collapsed in 1977, it was also unfortunate that the issue of the admission of Burundi and Rwanda was never resolved by the former Community. It is also significant to note that the resumption of East African co-operation in 1993[141] led promptly to the resumption of the applications of Burundi and Rwanda to join the Community. Thus Burundi formally applied to join in 1993 and, as soon as the Treaty for the Establishment of the East African Community was signed in 1999, Rwanda also applied to join.

The rest, as one would say, is history. The processing of the applications, in accordance with the provisions of the EAC Treaty, has gone on for now over a decade. This is no doubt a long time but it is also important to note that several factors, particularly the political environment prevailing in the sub-region at the time, also contributed to the delay. Coupled with this was the need to consolidate the revived Community among the core EAC Partner States before meaningful negotiations could be entered into with the new applicants. Among these was the need to establish the EAC Customs Union

---

[140] Statement during the Launching of the High Level Negotiations on the Admission of the Republic of Burundi and the Republic of Rwanda into the East African Community, AICC, Arusha, 8th July, 2006.

[141] For a chronology of major events in economic integration in East Africa see MSAMBICHAKA, L.A. et al, "Economic Co-operation in East Africa: Lessons Learnt and Prospects for Tanzania," in MBELLE, A.V.Y. *et al* (eds.), *The Nyerere Legacy and Economic Policy Making in Tanzania*, Dar es Salaam: Dar es Salaam University Press, 2002, p. 248.

which, as the entry point of the East African integration process was finally launched last year.

Be that as it may, the applications by Burundi and Rwanda have all along been positively received by the EAC Partner States. The overriding concern has been to engage due diligence in determining the applications within the stipulations of the EAC Treaty and to ensure that the ultimate decision on the matter is arrived at in the best interests and mutual benefit of all the States Parties on a sustainable basis.

It is on this account that, as consultations and verification missions were continued, the longstanding interactions and exchanges were maintained and intensified between EAC on the one hand and Burundi and Rwanda on the other. These co-operation activities, particularly in infrastructure and energy development, Lake Victoria Development Programme, social and cultural activities as well as in trade and investments continue to thrive and form the basis for further progress and deepening of co-operation among the five Partner States.

The EAC Treaty aims at effective participation of the Partner States in the regional integration process and establishing regional competitiveness in the international markets. Thus the strategic interests of the EAC take into account the positioning of the EAC as a centre around which a wider and meaningful Community could be built.

With a larger East African Community in which Burundi and Rwanda are enjoined, the resource base for the Community, in terms of human and physical resources would be greatly strengthened. A wider East Africa, incorporating Burundi and Rwanda, would form a viable regional economic bloc and become a force to reckon with in a globalizing world.

On the whole, the desirability to bring on board Burundi and Rwanda is generally felt in the EAC as testified to by the pronouncements which both the EAC Summit and Council of Ministers have made over the years. The challenge is now to get it right in the details to ensure that enlargement of the Community, by bringing in Burundi and Rwanda contributes further to the promotion of the wellbeing and enjoyment of human rights, good governance, peace and prosperity by the people of our five countries.

It is not too much to hope, therefore, that the high level negotiations which we launch today will lead to a positive outcome and further reinforce the solidarity among the countries of our sub-region in the spirit of East African and, indeed African continental unity that we all cherish.

CHAPTER SIXTEEN

Accession of Rwanda and Burundi[142]

Let me first of all express, on my own behalf and on behalf of my delegation, our great appreciation for accepting to meet with us and for the warm welcome you have extended to us. We are indeed honoured and pleased to have this meeting with you.

This is a historic meeting, the first working meeting between officials of the East African Community and high ranking officials of the Republic of Rwanda and the Republic of Burundi since the decision last November by the EAC Heads of State to admit Rwanda and Burundi as full members of the East Africa Community.

Before proceeding with my remarks, allow me, Honourable Ministers, distinguished members of the Rwandese delegation, to introduce to you senior officials of the East African Community Secretariat who have accompanied me to this meeting: Hon. Wilbert Kaahwa, Counsel to the Community; Dr. Nyamajeje Caleb Weggoro, Director, Productive and Social Sectors; Mr. Philip Wambugu, Director, Planning and Infrastructure Development; Mr. Magaga Alot, Head, Directorate of Corporate Communications and Public Affairs; and Mr. Henry Jabbo-Obbo, *Chef de Cabinet*.

As you are aware, the decision to admit Rwanda and Burundi to the East African Community was the culmination of a process of intensive consultations and negotiations. This process gained momentum after the signing of the Treaty for the Establishment of the East African Community in 1999 and the Custom Union Protocol in 2004.

The relations between Rwanda and Burundi and the three East African countries however, go a long way back to almost time immemorial. Indeed, the five East African countries have always been inextricably linked in social, cultural, trade and other exchanges, their peoples sharing one economic and social space that predates the colonial invasion and partitioning of Africa.

With the attainment of independence in the 1960's, the clamour for re-unification came to the fore. The formation of the East African Community in 1967, involving the integration of Kenya, Uganda and Tanzania was a

---

[142] Statement at meetings with High ranking Officials of the Governments of the Republics of Rwanda, and Burundi during Working Visits to Kigali and Bujumbura in February 2007.

pioneering and shining example of a break with the colonial past and the re-creation of Africa's continental unity, peace and development. Rwanda and Burundi applied as early as then to join the Community. After all, the two countries had, under the colonial state, been enjoined with the then Tanganyika as German East Africa. Although the former East African Community collapsed in 1977 before Rwanda and Burundi could join, the traditional links between the two countries and East Africa were continued. These were expressed particularly in the areas of trade and commerce, communications as well as cooperation in environmental management of Lake Victoria.

We could go on and on recounting this past history, this memorable history of our countries. What is important however is that this occasion has brought us together to engage in the process of finalizing the integration of Rwanda into the East African Community. I will be undertaking a similar mission to Burundi.

The process we are now engaged in is in line with the decision of the EAC Summit in November, 2006, namely to work out the operationalization of the accession effective 1st July, 2007. This visit will enable us to share ideas on how to proceed with the completion of the Accession Treaty. Evidently, the legal experts from Rwanda will shortly be invited to Arusha for detailed discussions in this area.

A lot of work has already been done to ease the process. We at the EAC are already working on a Draft Treaty of Accession which will be availed to the Republic of Rwanda by end of March, 2007. The Draft Treaty takes care of the necessary amendments to the Treaty, other Community instruments, projects and programmes.

It is my hope, and indeed, that of my delegation that this task will be accomplished in the best interest of a renewed, reinvigorated, enlarged and empowered East African Community to benefit the present and future generations of our people. In this regard, we are gratified that Rwanda brings to the East African Community a number of comparative as well as competitive advantages that will add value to our new enlarged economic bloc for mutual benefit. I would mention among these the great achievements that Rwanda has made in communications technologies (ICT). Indeed by hosting the EASSy network, Kigali is destined to become the hub of EAC's information and communications technologies. EAC's ongoing e-government project also stands to gain from Rwanda's experience and achievements in this area in providing efficient service delivery and improved interaction between Government and the citizenry and Government and the business community in the East African Community.

The major challenge confronting the EAC Partner States is the diversification of its agriculture and industry to fit both the comparative and competitive advantages given the impact of climatic change and the resultant extreme vagaries of weather that have afflicted our sub-region in recent years not only in the agricultural but also the energy sectors. We have to search for innovative ways of boosting more sustainable agricultural production able to address our growing food insecurity.

Increasingly, we need to promote a higher level of industrialization focused on adding value to our agricultural conditions through agro-processing in line with the East African Community Industrialization Strategy.

You will be aware that the EAC Heads of State at their Summit Meeting held on 30th November, 2006 launched the EAC Development Strategy 2006-2010 to guide the implementation of the EAC priority projects and programmes in a targeted and systematic manner over the next 5 years. In light of the decision for the admission of Rwanda and Burundi to the EAC, we will be undertaking a review of the programmes therein to ensure that the interests of Rwanda and Burundi are incorporated. The interests of Rwanda and Burundi will also be taken on board within the framework of the EAC Power Master Plan, the EAC Railway Master Plan, the EAC Road Network Project as well as other regional infrastructure projects.

Honourable Ministers will also wish to note that we recently commissioned a study to guide the preparations for entry into a Common Market. The consultants have since been directed to visit both Rwanda and Burundi to undertake consultations with key stakeholders on the establishment of the EAC Common Market.

During the negotiations for entry into the EAC, both Rwanda and Burundi expressed readiness and unreserved commitment towards the attainment of this important goal. I am also glad to report that the national consultations on fast tracking the establishment of the East African Political Federation are progressing well in Kenya, Uganda and Tanzania and we hope to initiate the same process in the two acceding countries at an appropriate time.

Only last week I led a High Level Mission to the African Development Bank in Tunis during which we held discussions on ways of deepening collaboration between the Bank and EAC. The Mission, which was extremely successful in terms of achieving our goal, consulted on ongoing and proposed projects with specific reference to sector programmes that EAC proposes to extend to both Rwanda and Burundi. I will be circulating a copy of the Aide Memoire of the Mission for your information and reference.

We are faced with a few challenges in the EAC integration project one of which is the court case regarding the election of Members of the East African Legislative Assembly from Kenya. We only hope that this matter will be resolved as soon as possible.

Lastly, I would like to inform you that an Extraordinary Summit of EAC Heads of State will be held in April 2007 to, among other things, effect the rotation of the chair of the Summit from President Kibaki to President Museveni and also to appoint a new Deputy Secretary General from Kenya.

In addition, a Strategic Meeting and Working Summit of EAC Heads of State is also scheduled for the third week of June 2007 to, among other things, consider the outcome of the national consultations on the East African Political Federation as well as finalize the process of the accession of Rwanda and Burundi to EAC. I look forward to us meeting again during the Strategic Meeting and Working Summit in June 2007.

CHAPTER SEVENTEEN

The Dynamics of EAC Enlargement[143]

Introduction

I am pleased to address this group of young East Africans attending the East African Uongozi Institute School for the year of 2007. I would like to thank the organisers of this important annual programme for the interest consistently shown in the East African Community. As an East African Institute, this collaboration is imperative and we need to investigate how best we can transform it into an EAC Centre of Excellence on issues of politics, governance, human rights, the environment, and development.

The topic you have requested me to address: "Regional Integration and Development: the Dynamics of Enlargement and the Fast Tracking of the East African Federation" is highly topical. It seeks, on the one hand, a discussion on the impact of enlargement on the integration agenda with its focus on development. It also seeks to contextualize, on the other hand, the debate and the vision of a political federation in the regional integration agenda, a rather fuzzy idea but important anyhow in the light of an uninformed perception that has emerged that a negative response on fast tracking political federation may damage the fundamental building blocks of deeper integration.

Fast Tracking Political Integration

Allow me to begin my remarks by examining the basic question in the topic, namely integration and development. This question is important of itself; in other words, important even without considering the dynamics that impact it as a result of enlargement of the EAC and of fast tracking the process towards political federation or, as others have put it, fast tracking political federation.

I have been criticized in some East African literary quarters for distinguishing the two "fast trackings" describing the issue "as not being semantic". My critics posit that my distinction is, in fact, semantic; in other words, they posit that that they do not see the difference. Maybe I should use this occasion to clarify my view of what I meant by the distinction. Fast tracking the process towards a political federation puts emphasis, in my

[143] Speech to the East African students attending the East African Uongozi Institute for the Year 2007 Arusha, Tanzania, 26th July, 2007.

view, on fast tracking the Customs Union, the Common Market and the Single Currency in order to realize the Political Federation much faster. I believe that it is this view that lay at the heart of the decision of the EAC Heads of State taken in Nairobi in 2004 that led to the appointment of the Wako Committee. The Wako Committee went forward to recommend the compression of time in moving towards the building blocks; that is, in EAC's quest to realize the different stages of integration much faster, in order to realise the political federation more speedily.

Fast tracking the political federation, on the other hand, regrettably and again in my humble view, has been interpreted, in several quarters in the public domain, especially in Tanzania, to "seek ye first the political kingdom and all other things shall be added unto it."- the Kwame Nkrumah thesis. In the light of this clarification, is my distinction of the two "fast trackings" still semantic? I leave it to your judgment.

Integration and Development

Now let me revert to the basic question about integration and development. I mentioned that this is an important question. Let me explain why. In his speech at the OAU Summit in Cairo in July 1964, the late Mwalimu Julius Nyerere said, in the context of Africa, and I quote:

> The major problems that we now face as a continent, whether united or balkanized is one of development. It is the problem of realizing the standards of living of our people, to a level that is considered reasonable in terms of the possibilities of this scientific age.[144]

Nyerere seemed to say that development is paramount with or without integration. However, in March 1965, Nyerere wrote in the first issue of the magazine, *African Forum,* that "if we (Africans) remain separate it will take an intolerably long time before our economic growth be such as to bring the standard of living of our people to acceptable levels."

On the surface, one could interpret Nyerere as saying that integration does not infer higher development than what is achievable under a state of balkanization. Yet in the same 1964 Cairo speech, referred above, Nyerere had posited, in the context of the East African situation, that a Common Market, a higher stage of integration, is meaningless unless it can be equally exploited by all those who form it. The Common Market that existed then was what East Africa had inherited from the East African Common Services

---

[144] See NYERERE, Julius K., *Speech at the O.A.U. Cairo Conference,* Dar es Salaam: Tanganyika Information Service, 1964. See also MWAKIKAGILE, Godfrey, *Nyerere and Africa: End of an Era: Biography of Julius Kambarage Nyerere (1922-1999) President of Tanzania,* Atlanta, Georgia: Protea Publishing Company US, 2002.

Organization (EACSO), a colonial legacy. Put differently, Nyerere was saying that integration has to promote social and economic equity.

For us in the EAC, this idea about promoting social and economic equity is the fundamental challenge. We need to determine how to ensure that the Customs Union and the Common Market, now under formulation and due for negotiation, create a win-win environment and build economies and societies that equally share the costs and benefits of integration. It is this philosophy of equity that informed the Treaty for East African Cooperation of 1967.[145] Its failure to respond to that objective partly contributed to the EAC's collapse. This challenge of equity is now even greater following the EAC enlargement.

Integration and the Impact of Globalization

However, it is equally important to recognise that the challenge of equity is much more formidable in an environment where globalization is unleashing new rules of trade, environment, health standards and competition. This is an environment where the Most Favoured Nation (MFN) arrangement, for example, which underpins regional integration systems, is being put to question by the WTO. Indeed, come January 2008, the MFN is supposed to be history! The burning question that emerges then is whether the intensifying multilateralism will undermine regional integration and thereby the envisioned higher development subsumed in integration arrangements. This is a question for all of us to ponder. I do not believe that there are easy answers.

Suffice to state though, that the logic about development linked to integration is reinforced by what Nyerere described, in 1977, as the "trade union of the poor." Clearly, Integration at regional levels enhances the scope and leverage of negotiating power at the global level. This is probably the reason why the WTO last year described the EAC as the most successful illustration of regional integration in Africa. The EAC working Customs Union has undoubtedly leveraged this position and may have led to the accolades showered upon it because the EAC has succeeded to promote a coordinated trade policy with a well structured and operating Common External Tariff. At the same time, the introduction of Standards, Quality, Metrology and Testing law, as well as the Competition law, as part of the EAC legal regime, have bolstered EAC's collective strength vis-à-vis third parties. More importantly, the growth of an enlarged market, following the

---

[145] On this earlier East African Community see *inter alia*, ROTHCHILD, Donald S., *Politics of Integration: An East African Documentary*, Nairobi: East African Publishing House, 1968; EZE, Osita C., *The Legal Status of Foreign Investments in the East African Common Market*, Leiden: A.W. Sijthoff, 1975; and NKONOKI, Simon R., *The East African Community in Retrospect: The Context of Regional Co-operation in Eastern Africa*, Bergen: Chr. Michelsen Institute, 1983.

accession of Rwanda and Burundi into the EAC, acts as a spur for promoting EAC domestic investments and for attracting Foreign Direct Investment.

However, what we must take care against is for the EAC integration through the Customs Union and later the Common Market to lead into a fortress EAC where trade diversion, in other words, an environment where competitively lower cost imports from third parties are displaced, becomes the dominant feature rather than trade creation. Evidently, the EAC, as an integration project, would be able to become a competitive trade creator, not diverter, where and when it promotes robust competition and develops the infrastructure (energy, roads, railways, telecom, civil aviation, ports and harbours) that unlock the supply-side constraints thereby bolstering improved production and higher levels of productivity. Integration only becomes synonymous with development when such economic objectives are focused upon and implemented.

Dynamics of EAC Enlargement

I will now turn to examining the second part of the topic before us, namely the impact of enlargement on the integration agenda with specific focus on the dynamics of enlargement and of fast tracking the process towards political federation.

EAC needs to show greater imagination and thinking about how the enlarged EAC will function. There is little doubt that enlargement and the greater diversity it fosters will strain the current EAC decision making structure and process. Evidently, enlargement will precipitate qualitative change in EAC's ambitions, its responsibility and, above all, political dynamics. Let me ramify these points with a number of examples.

First, the enlarged EAC will become a more ambitious institution in Africa; in our relations with the AU, the EU and the WTO. Its bigger size should surely leverage its negotiation capacity as earlier alluded to.

Secondly, enlargement will also result in new responsibilities for the EAC. Whereas Rwanda has succeeded to come out of the era of the tragic genocide and is on an economic growth path, Burundi poses some unique challenges to the EAC – challenges of development, security and stability. It is unrealistic not to anticipate these threats. Specifically, on security threats, we have to be realistic that they still bedevil even the core members of the EAC, namely Kenya, Uganda and Tanzania. I need not over emphasize the spate of cross-border violent crime taking place in our region, recently in Uganda, and here in Tanzania, involving the NMB robbery in Mwanga which led to a wild-west type of shoot-out, but with modern weapons being used at Njiro in the Arusha Municipality.

Thus, whilst a critical dynamic of EAC's enlargement centres on bringing Rwanda and Burundi into the development policy sphere of the EAC, a critical one centres on the security policy sphere. In this context, defence, police and security cooperation will constitute an important and urgent area of cooperation to be structured and enforced.

Thirdly, there is the fundamental question about how the EAC makes its decisions. As you may know, as per the Treaty, EAC's decisions are presently based on consensus or unanimity. If this process has been a challenge for three Partner States, you can understand what would face the EAC with five Partner States. Effectively integrating five countries into the EAC's various policies and programmes will inevitably hinge on the ability and willingness of the Partner States to be more committed to such policies and programmes. There is little doubt that greater diversity of views, perceptions and interests, over various policy matters, much as Rwanda and Burundi made commitments to accept current policy positions as part of their Accession Treaties, will precipitate varying decisions.

Reforming the Decision-making Structure

The ideal direction of course is for the EAC to review its present decision making system based on consensus and shift to a qualified majority voting system. In other words, policies that are politically sensitive to the Partner States should be left for consensus or unanimity decision, whilst those that are not politically sensitive should be decided upon based on majority decisions. How to delineate what is politically sensitive and what is not requires calm and rational minds. The Partner States must be informed by the big picture in this task. But, at all costs, the EAC must avoid a gridlock in its decision making system.

Let me also emphasize that this political dynamic takes a more critical dimension where a Partner State fails to attend a meeting where a decision is to be taken. The meeting then becomes ineffectual. Not only would such outcome be dysfunctional to the development of the EAC; it would also prove costly to the Partner States which bring Officers and Ministers to Arusha and elsewhere for meetings.

The EAC could learn from the EU in this critical issue. In the EU, Member States do not have to reach decisions on consensus on some key policy matters. For example, the UK is not part of Schengen, the European Visa system. The UK, and few other EU member states, are also not members of the Euro. They retain their own currencies. Such exception, however, what you could describe as ala carte choice, does not necessarily harm the EU. Even in the WTO, there are no uniform or one type of agreements tying every member. In fact, there are two major types of agreements: one that is *multilateral* which covers everybody and, the other, is *plurilateral* which covers only those countries that decide to participate in specific agreements. For example, liberalisation of telecommunications is a *plurilateral* issue. Such flexibility of decisions needs to be examined in the EAC as part of the reform programme of its decision making system.

Fourthly, enlargement also raises another dynamic that relates to locking in the new member states into the EAC legal and regulatory framework. Rwanda and Burundi will immediately enjoy membership in the East African Legislative Assembly and participate in the oversight responsibility of the Assembly over the EAC Secretariat. So will they also be entitled to appoint a Judge each to the two Court Chambers of the East African Court of Justice. But these entitlements come with obligations which are well enshrined in the EAC Treaty. They centre on democratic consolidation, promotion of good governance and human rights, peace and security and embracing a market economy. It would be dangerous for the new Partner States to shoot themselves on the foot!

Fifthly, a key dynamic of enlargement, particularly in respect of Burundi, but probably of Rwanda as well, is the huge hope and expectation of the people of the two new Partner States that their membership of the EAC will result in faster reconstruction and development of their economies and societies, including the re-establishment of viable and robust institutions essential for promoting governance, democracy, rule of law, peace and reconciliation and stability. In the EU, there are special funds called "Structural Funds" for enabling new members to achieve critical transitions as members of the EU. The EAC lacks such funds and this would be a huge challenge.

Finally, an important dimension in promoting an East African identity and a key dynamic in the integration process is the mainstreaming of Kiswahili as East Africa's lingua franca along with English. It has just been reported from Uganda, for instance, that all MPs and school going children shall receive Kiswahili instructions to prepare, notably, for the East African Federation. Rwanda and Burundi will have to follow suit. Burundi has fortunately already introduced compulsory Kiswahili as a subject from primary school level since September 2006.

Dynamics of Political Integration

As I have alluded to earlier in this discussion, there is little doubt that political integration is what would secure economic integration. Mwalimu Nyerere was right when he wrote in the July 1965 issue of the *Journal of American Society for African Culture*, that if you do not soon enough move forward to political integration, the result would be a backward movement into reduced economic cooperation. His reference point was the East African experience. The EAC should be well seized of Nyerere's thinking going by the experience of the collapse of the erstwhile EAC in 1977. Interestingly, the EU is well seized of the importance of political integration in its vision of sustaining the single market and creating shared freedoms and other values in Europe. This is why it continues to be seriously concerned about the fate of its Constitutional Treaty. After the 2005 debacle of the Treaty, the recent EU Summit under the German Presidency has moved closer to promoting a semblance of political integration. More challenges remain but there is a clear direction.

For us in the EAC, we cannot afford the luxury of not realizing, soon enough, the imperativeness of political integration as the locking mechanism for ensuring the sustainability of our economic integration. However, when we should go for such political integration can be the burning question. Its necessity, on the other hand, is clearly without question. At the same time, the EAC should remain mindful of the dynamic of fast-tracking; what some East Africans, and especially many Tanzanians, view as a move to simply fast track the political federation.[146] The dynamic crucially centres on the question: how would such fast tracking respond to what is perceived to be existing different and inequitable levels of development in the region. The fears and concerns that centre on issues of land, jobs and even varying commitments of the Partner States to democracy, good governance and the state of national security in the different Partner States cannot simply be swept under the carpet even when some committed East Africans in Tanzania regard these issues as inconsequential in the integration vision. These concerns are important dynamics of integration and development and should seriously be examined.

Conclusion

Let me conclude by saying that EAC integration and the enlargement that has recently taken place and which may further arise in the future, is a triumph of African economic liberation. It must be celebrated. It must be consolidated and protected.

---

[146] In charge of fast-tracking the East African Community to a Federation was Ms. Beatrice Kiraso, the Deputy Secretary General of the Community. See KIRASO, Beatrice, *Making a Difference*, Central Milton Keynes, UK: Authorhouse, 2011.

PART 6

Building an Effective Organisation

Setting the Stage

In this part of the book I turn to addressing some of the critical challenges that impinge on EAC's efficiency and effectiveness as an organization. As noted in several sections earlier, the Treaty establishing the EAC was drafted at a time when there were concerns about past integration mistakes and how they could be mitigated or avoided. To that extent, the 1999 Treaty has created mechanisms of decision making which, whilst supportive of the need to assure the survival of the EAC for posterity, they also introduced bottlenecks that impede the realization of greater efficiency and effectiveness in the integration effort. In the following chapters under this part five of the book, the challenges the EAC faces in the areas of decision making are particularly examined including how the relationships among the different Organs need to be better clarified to support the pursuit of a shared mission.

As in any organization, efficiency and effectiveness in the delivery of the organizational mandates crucially hinges on the structure and processes of decision making. In inter-governmental organizations this dynamic is even more complex especially where decisions are largely vested in organs that are controlled by partner states and where ceding of some sovereignty to a central body like the EAC Secretariat, the EALA and the EACJ is constrained by zero sum game sensitivities and the state of national politics. It is argued in the following chapters that EAC's future prospects of deeper integration will depend significantly on how these decision making challenge as are resolved and how organs like the EACJ are quickly given additional jurisdiction consistent with the advanced stages of integration that the EAC has realized.

CHAPTER EIGHTEEN

EAC Efficiency and Effectiveness

The EAC Treaty places the Secretariat at the heart of the organization's day to day management of integration affairs. Article 71(1) outlines the functions of the Secretariat which are quite broad in nature, the key ones being:

- the strategic planning, management and monitoring of programmes for the development of the Community;

- the general administration and financial management of the Community;

- the mobilization of funds from development partners and other sources for the implementation of projects of the Community;

- the implementation of the decisions of the Summit and the Council;

- the establishment of practical working relations with the Court (EACJ) and the Assembly (EALA).

What is of legal importance about the role of the Secretariat with respect to the functions allocated to it is the authority placed on the Secretariat by Article 71(1). The Article reads, "The Secretariat *shall* be responsible for." In other words, in the exercise of the functions listed under that Article, the Secretariat's authority is exclusive. It is important to appreciate the implications of this legal position in the context of Article 14 of the Treaty which spells out the functions of the Council of Ministers, the organ that works closely with the Secretariat. Article 14 stipulates that the Council shall, among other functions, be the policy organ of the Community and, in that vein, shall make policy decisions for the efficient and harmonious functioning and development of the Community.

The only functions vested in the Council that are of administrative character relate to making Staff Rules and Regulations and Financial Rules and Regulations of the Community (Article 14(3)(9)). The logic behind this particular administrative function is that these rules and regulations have a budgetary implication and it is the Council that is empowered to consider the budget of the Community. Ideally though, the Council should not *"make"* staff rules and regulations and financial rules and regulations. Its authority should properly be to *approve* such rules and regulations as made and proposed by the Secretariat.

As it stands, this function by the Council has unleashed an unwarranted role by those organs made up of representatives of Partner States, notably the Sectoral Committees, dominantly of an administrative nature. Officials from Partner States have been allowed an unnecessary opening to be engaged in many administrative activities to the extent of increasingly micro-managing the EAC Secretariat. These officials have in recent years insisted in being closely involved in the preparation of the EAC budget, in strategic planning, recruitment of staff, determining the agenda for the meetings of the organs of the Community and even in the mobilization of funds from development partners, functions which are exclusively within the mandate of the Secretariat.

The trend by Partner States to micro-manage the EAC Secretariat defeats the spirit enshrined in Article 72(4) of the Treaty which provides that "the Partner States agree to cooperate with and assist the Secretariat in the performance of its functions as set out in Article 71 of this Treaty." It is upon the Secretariat to enlist the support of the Partner States, when so needed, and not for the Partner States to impose such support and cooperation especially when the support turns into control. As alluded to earlier in this paper, micro-managing the Secretariat within the context of the challenges the EAC faces and of issues relating to statutory meetings of different organs failing to take place due to quorum and consensus requirements, has often undermined the efficiency and effectiveness of the EAC's integration programmes.

On the face of it, the idea behind the establishment of Ministries directly responsible for EAC Affairs in every Partner state was intended to ensure that the EAC is enabled to better fulfil its mandate. However, these Ministries are merely co-ordinating institutions. They do not represent the Partner States in all the activities that take place at the EAC level. Indeed, the EAC presently has several Sectoral Councils of Ministers established under Article 14(3) (j) of the Treaty and whose decisions are deemed to be decisions of the Council of Ministers (Article 14(3) (i). These are specialized Ministerial Councils covering a broad spectrum of EAC's cooperation mandates – defence, legal, education and health, trade, industry and investment, finance, foreign affairs, monetary, inter-state security, agriculture and natural resources, tourism, etc.

Thus, to secure constant quorum for all these sectoral meetings that enables decisions to be reached on consensus basis can often be a nightmare and the Ministries responsible for EAC Affairs cannot and are not the solution. For example, the Sectoral Council on Legal and Judicial Affairs *must* have, in attendance, the Ministers responsible for Justice and Constitutional Affairs and where such Ministers are not also Attorney Generals (as in Kenya), the Attorney General must attend.

A concrete case of how the lack of quorum can undermine the efficiency and effectiveness of the EAC is the failure of the Sectoral Council on Legal and Judicial Affairs to meet for a whole year in 2010 and part of 2011 thereby delaying important work of finalizing proposed amendments of the EAC Treaty which, after a decade, reflects serious flaws and is thus much in need of improvement to fit changed circumstances on EAC's integration. The tourism sector has equally faced challenges due to failure of its Sectoral Council to meet for long periods of time.

These challenges of quorum have been brought before the Summit in search of a political solution given the fact that the Partner States are hesitant to cede more authority to the Secretariat. The Summit had directed in June 2008 that a solution be sought through amendment of the Treaty and the Rules governing statutory meetings. To what extent any proposed amendment of the Treaty to adjust the strict quorum requirement would be acceptable to the Partner States is a highly volatile issue. What is more important is for the Partner States to come to terms with the reality that the EAC has matured and it has developed greater internal capacity and competencies to be able to discharge more responsibilities and exercise greater authority.

Ceding of more powers to the Secretariat and reducing the role of the Partner States in EAC's decision making process is the right answer. This is what has happened in ECOWAS which has seen its organisation being transformed from a Secretariat to a Commission more in line with the European Commission. What would be needed is to strengthen the structure of the reporting relationship with the Council of Ministers and extend EALA's oversight role. In extending the powers and authority of the Secretariat as proposed in the Institutional Review Study Report undertaken by the Secretariat with the support of Adam Smith International in 2010/2011, it would also be imperative to amend the Treaty and give the Secretary General an independent power to request an advisory opinion from the EACJ on any matter falling within the Treaty.

Presently, this power is vested in the Council of Ministers (Article 14(4)) and in the Summit and Partner State (Article 36(1)). Restricting this authority to these organs and Partner States means that the Secretary General can never be able to bring before the Court a matter that specifically touches on the roles of the Council and the Partner States which frustrate the functioning of the Community. This is a serious anomaly in the Treaty.

There is another broad area of concern with respect to the efficiency and effectiveness of the EAC as an institution. This has to do with the EAC budget resources. The EAC budget is deemed to depend on equal annual contributions from the Partner States. Whilst these contributions have been increasing by about 10% annually in the past five years, the resources available have largely been adequate to meet personnel emoluments, gratuity fund payments and some recurrent or operational costs. In the financial year 2011/2012, for example, out of a total budget of US $ 109,680,319, personnel emoluments take a share of 19% and recurrent 15%. The budget has never been adequate to cover the costs of carrying out programmes and projects of the Community whose share in financial year 2011/2012 is 67%.

In this regard, and as an example, the whole budget for the negotiations of the Common Market Protocol of over 18 months had to be underwritten by donors. The costs of the on-going negotiations of the Monetary Union are also largely being met by development partners. The whole process of improving the capacity of the EAC to better manage and control its resources, human and financial, has equally been funded under the Capacity Development Action Plan whose benefactors are DFID and Trademark East Africa.

Thus, overall, the EAC budget support by development partners has grown from US $ 6,558,800 in financial year 2006/2007 compared to contributions from Partner States of US $ 7,818,397 to US $ 75,807,769 (a 1056% growth) in 2011/2012 compared to contributions from the Partner States of US $ 33,666,700 (a 331% growth). This huge donor dependency is not sustainable. It is imperative and urgent for the EAC to develop an alternative financing mechanism which will ensure that the EAC budget is funded largely by the Partner States themselves. In this regard, attempts have been made by the EAC Secretariat since 2005 to propose new alternative financing mechanisms which have a bearing on the varying sizes of the economies of Partner States.

Whilst the Summit of Heads of State has reflected political will in supporting, in principle, a new budget financing system and which could be based on a percentage of customs revenue or VAT from intra-EAC trade collected by each Partner State, there has been a consistent tongue in the cheek support from the bureaucrats representing the Partner States. Continuous postponements to deliberate on the Secretariat's proposals in this context have been the order of the day.

In the light of the foregoing, the EAC continues to depend heavily on the support of development partners. Fortunately, this dependency has not led to the EAC losing a grip on pursuing its priorities. This has been ensured through the establishment of an EAC Partnership Fund in 2007 within the framework of the Paris Declaration on Aid Harmonization and Co-ordination. This Fund has elicited strong commitment and support of development partners for the EAC. Donors and the EAC now agree on a broad framework of priority activities proposed by the EAC with budget indications. Donors then decide to what extent they would each be able to contribute and, normally, irrespective of their specific interest in any particular project.

The Fund is well accounted for and the EAC-Donors' Joint Steering Committee undertakes a twice a year evaluation of the utilization and performance-related outcomes of the Fund. The challenge, as noted earlier, remains, namely, for how long will the donors continue to sustain such huge support to the EAC. For example, on the political federation project, donors are reluctant to extend any support arguing, logically, that for a serious political matter as this, the Partner States should surely be passionate enough to cough up the required funding.

Broad Conclusion

As a broad conclusion of the chapters under part two of the book, it would be noted that in spite of the challenges that would normally face an inter-governmental agency like the EAC, there have been tremendous achievements that the EAC has realized since its formal establishment in mid 2000. Accolades have been showered on the EAC from different quarters, the US government, the World Bank and the World Trade Organisation. Yet the EAC faces a number of challenges as elaborated in these chapters. None of them are insurmountable. They only need greater political will, ceding of more authority from the Partner States, changing the culture of work and attitudes of public officials at border posts, developing key infrastructures, clarifying roles of organs and improving self reliance over budget resources. The need to enhance sensitization and conscientisation of the citizens particularly on the political federation project cannot be overemphasized.

The EAC clearly holds the best promise in making African regional integration a reality. It is the pace setter and, because of its stature, it cannot afford to fall back. It must sustain and scale up its momentum. This it can partly do by providing closer leadership in the COMESA-EAC-SADC Tripartite, a unique project that can transform Africa into a sizeable internal market that would contribute to higher economic growth and living standards of the people.

In the following part three of the book, from chapter eight to thirteen, I offer a historical perspective of the EAC; it's past, present and future and I also examine some of the key developments in the EAC, notably the on-set of the Common Market and the negotiations of the Monetary Union. An important contribution in this part is my reflections on my tenure in the EAC and what I deem to have been the milestones realized. There is also a reflection on what I see as the next stages of EAC's integration and the challenges to be faced.

CHAPTER NINETEEN

Institutional Cooperation and Collaboration[147]

Hon Mr. Speaker Sir, I beg to second. The Budget that the Honourable Minister has just tabled before the House is a momentous one. Though the EAC Development Strategy (2006-2010) will only come on stream sometime later in the year, this Budget launches this Development Strategy whose thrust is truly path-breaking in terms of enhancing the development of the Community. The Strategy seeks to consolidate the Customs Union, address the infrastructure deficits that hamper and slow down economic growth, set the stage for negotiations of the Common Market and, above all, reach out, more closely, to the East African citizenry by sensitizing and galvanising them better on the delicate but critical directions our Community is destined for. It is thus imperative that I thank Honourable Minister John Arap Koech and his Ministerial colleagues for commending before the House a well thought out budget that is consistent with our priorities and mindful of our resource constraints.

Allow me, Honourable Speaker, to avail this opportunity to say a few words. First of all to use the platform of this august Assembly to thank their Excellencies, the Heads of State of the East African Community, for their trust in appointing me Secretary General of the East African Community. I accepted the appointment with great humility and I commit to devote every effort to the advancement of the regional integration programme. I wish also to thank Honourable Members of this House for their congratulatory messages and for their heartening words of warmth and friendship. There is a powerful Kiswahili adage that says *"nyota njema huonekana alfajiri"*. (A blessed day is gathered at dawn). I believe that in a brief three days of my close encounters with Honourable Members of the House, a new dawn has set that will define and set a new path in the relationship between the Secretary General and the key organs of the EAC and its Members, individually and collectively. I want to assure the Honourable Members of the Legislature that they will not find me wanting in developing a close and friendly working relationship. I appeal for reciprocation.

Hon Speaker Sir, allow me also to use this opportunity to pay tribute to my predecessors, Ambassador Francis Muthaura, the first Executive Secretary/Secretary General of the Community, from 1996-2001; and Honourable Amanya Mushega, my immediate predecessor. Cumulatively,

---

[147] Maiden speech to the East African Legislative Assembly at the EALA Chambers, AICC, Arusha on 25th May, 2006.

under their successive administrations, a solid foundation has been laid on which to build our Community. The vision and mission of East African regional integration has been well defined. The institutional mechanisms for the realization of the mission of our lofty goals continue to be put in place and consolidated. The EAC Customs Union as well as a significant number of regional projects and programmes have been launched and are at various stages of implementation. There is much that I can benefit from lessons of experience and from all those that continue to serve the EAC with passion and commitment.

Honourable Speaker Sir, The regional integration process would largely be unsustainable if it is not built on a collaborative effort of all its constituencies and stakeholders. This is why, the Treaty for the Establishment of the East African Community charges the Organs and Institutions of the Community with crucial roles in promoting regional integration and development. A primary challenge in the effective execution of our regional programmes is to manage harmonious relations and bolster complementarity of roles and functions of the Organs and institutions of the Community. The evolvement of strong organs of the Community – a decisive and enabling Executive, a vigilant Legislature, an independent, impartial and authoritative Court of Justice, a highly professional and well equipped Secretariat as well as efficient and effective institutions of the Community – together constitute the prerequisites for successful regional integration and development. These organs and institutions have to foster a shared collective response and judicious application of synergies to respond and muster the challenges of regional integration and development.

Honourable Speaker Sir, I have keenly followed the developments in the Community, right from its inception. One of the salient observations that I am proud to speak about is the role that this Assembly has played, with significant success in energizing the regional integration process. If the EAC today is poised on a fast tracking and pragmatic orientation, it is largely because this Honourable House has been valiant in its role and its oversight responsibility. It is thus befitting to thank you, Honourable Speaker and Members of this Assembly, for the dynamic role you have played, which you continue to play in giving meaning and purpose to EAC's lofty vision. The House should rest assured that the Secretariat that I lead will double up commitment to its work and chart out more effective interfaces and collaborative working methods that will translate into making the EAC a more robust and vibrant institution. This is what the East Africans expect of us. We cannot fail them.

Hon Speaker Sir, East Africa has great advantages in forging regional integration. I believe that this organisation provides the most pragmatic and ideal framework and conditions for realising a comprehensive and strategic regional integration in Africa. Though its economic space, in population and gross domestic product is still small, yet its regional cohesion, based on history and shared cultural values, is a critical source and driving force for a natural people driven economic integration. I believe that the leadership of East Africa, working in close harmony with the people, will work in making this Community a beacon of hope for the economic integration of the whole of Africa. I wish to reiterate, once again, my avowed commitment to use my energy and resourcefulness to lead the EAC to a higher trajectory of success. I count on this esteemed House for support.

CHAPTER TWENTY

Building Capacity of Organs to Deliver[148]

This Retreat comes at a time when the Community is faced with a big challenge to meet the expectations of the people of East Africa. The launching last year of the East African Community Customs Union had heightened these expectations for increased productivity and trade within the region and, on the whole, for tangible benefits of the Community in terms of wealth creation, and improvement of their living standards.

These hopes and expectations pinned on the Community stem from the provisions of the EAC Treaty which touch on virtually every aspect of human endeavour. The Treaty vests in the Secretariat initiative role in spearheading the regional integration and development process. Not only is the Community expected to deliver on the integration and development objectives, it is also expected to do this within the agreed and reasonable timeframes. Planning, monitoring and evaluation thus assume a critical dimension in the management of the Community.

With the past performance of the EAC in perspective, a time has come to look at ourselves critically and review our strengths and weaknesses with a view to improving performance and maximizing the benefits of the Community. We need to look at the existing structures and processes and see how they hinder or facilitate the achievement of our objectives. During this Retreat we shall therefore be looking at some of the challenges that we face and see how far and at what pace we are making progress in attaining our set targets, if any.

In about a week's time, I shall have completed my first 100 days in office as Secretary General of the East African Community. I have therefore had sufficient time to observe and examine closely the workings and other dynamics of the Community. At the same time, I have embarked on various measures to define some of the action oriented and focused approaches I intend to institute in the period ahead as Secretary General, and which I would like to share with you in this Retreat.

---

[148] Keynote address to EAC Executive and Professional Staff at the EAC Strategic Retreat held at the Zanzibar Beach Resort, Zanzibar, 20th July, 2006.

Human Resource Dimension

One of the most salient observations I made upon taking office was the low morale and uncertainty within the work force in the EAC. I observed a dispirited mood among the staff across the board, the situation stemming from lack of concrete measures taken in the last decade to restructure the organization such that there would be a fit between structure and manning levels as well as competencies.

Related to this, no major review of the terms and conditions of service of employees had taken place over the last decade of the EAC's existence whereby the terms and conditions accorded to EAC staff remained static and the lowest of all the regional economic communities (RECs) in Africa. Even intergovernmental organizations that are not as powerfully defined in terms of their roles, structures and mandate, have better terms and conditions of service for their workers than EAC. Quite perplexing too, EAC Partner States offer to staff in the diplomatic missions, including those diplomatic missions within the region, better terms of service way beyond those they are prepared to grant the staff of the EAC.

Indeed, part of the reason there is lacklustre implementation and overall tardy delivery of the regional programme, is that the EAC Secretariat is too thin on the ground, as far as technical support, follow-up and monitoring and evaluation mechanisms are concerned. Hence there is a proliferation of conference, seminar and workshop and little to show of concrete achievements, which is leading to genuine disenchantment about the EAC project.

Needless to state, this is a matter that we have to address quickly in order to reconstruct staff morale as prerequisites for a performing, if not competitive regional organization. Already, I have engaged the efforts to come up with a new organization structure as well as to propose new compensation packages which are comparable to similar organizations in Africa and the rest of the world. Also, some urgent recruitment is considered within the current ongoing job evaluation exercise.

Information and Communications Dimension

Coupled with this, I intend to institute new measures with specific reference to giving the EAC greater visibility in the region and beyond as well as branding the EAC as a viable and robust institution for achieving the lofty goals that have been enshrined in the EAC Treaty.

There is need not only to push projects through to concrete implementation stages but also at the same time to put in place a more robust strategic communication and publicity strategy to sensitize East African people about what is taking place in EAC and galvanize their sense of ownership and commitment to the regional organization and what it stands for.

Thus in the new organization structure we are upstaging the role of our division for public information and communication so that it takes a frontline position in the promotion of EAC's image and identity. As we embark on this phase of deepening and concretizing regional integration and indeed the process of fast tracking East African Federation, it is critical that the role of this division be given its vantage position.

Relations with the Assembly and other Organs and Institutions of the Community

Another big challenge relates to rebuilding our bridges between the Secretariat and the other organs and institutions of the Community, particularly the East African Legislative Assembly. The EALA is too important an organ of the EAC to find itself in a state of fractured relationship with the Secretariat and particularly with the Secretary General, who is the Chief Executive of the whole EAC.

We all learn from our mistakes and, without apportioning any blame, in the short period that I have been Secretary General I have tried the best I could to regain the confidence of EALA as well as that of all the other organs and institutions of the EAC, including the Court of Justice and the Senior Officials of the Partner States responsible for EAC affairs. In the next period it is important that we consolidate these relationships.

The Treaty for the Establishment of the East African Community provides for the roles and functions of the various organs and institutions of the Community. And in the institutional development of the Community, the Partner States have appointed ministers solely responsible for EAC affairs. But it is one thing to have institutions in place and another to make these institutions work to the full benefits of EAC. Our main challenge right now is to reconfigure how best we want to work with these institutions because, if well utilized, we can improve significantly the decision making processes within EAC.

We should therefore in the next few months work out more elaborate mechanisms to shorten and speed up these decision- making processes. And this should not be a one way challenge or initiative. We call upon the Partner States Ministries to also come out with concrete proposals on how best we can work together beyond the statutory decision making structures which are static and could drastically stymie the integration process.

It is important to note that whereas one of the causes of the failure of the former Community was the concentration of decision making in the Authority, the problems with the current one may yet turn out to be the concentration of decision making and implementation on the bureaucrats of the Partner States, such that we might be trying to fix square pegs in round holes in the attempt to implement integration programmes through more or less rigid, pre-ordained and otherwise entrenched national state priorities, programmes, processes and systems which wouldn't work for regional integration.

Another major plank of the EAC focus in the period ahead will be the private sector, and in particular the EABC. The EABC's present and potential membership in the private sector contributes about 80% of the gross domestic product of the East African Community, thus has high stakes in the Community.

I have therefore already entered into discussions with EABC intended to deepen EAC's relationship with the private sector and, specifically to speed up EABC's incorporation as an institution of the EAC. In my view, we cannot seriously talk about the EAC being market-driven when the key institutions that drive the market are only peripherally engaged in EAC's mission and work.

Civil Society Dimension

The EABC, along with other strategic partners within East Africa's civil society, should be formally mainstreamed in EAC's decision-making structures and processes, if our region is going to timely transform into a competitive economic powerhouse.

The launching by the Society for International Development (SID) Eastern Africa of their State of East Africa Report 2006, which I was honoured to officiate in April this year, is a major development and contribution by the EAC civil society. As we embark on the establishment of the Civil Society Forum as required by the Treaty, SID would be a building block to such EAC Civil Society Forum. I am glad to note that the directors of SID are participating in this Strategic Retreat. We also have other resourceful civil society organizations in the region, such as Economic and Social Research Foundation (ESARF), African Centre for Economic Growth (ACEG) and Development Policy Management Forum (DPMF) which should be involved in intellectual work, which is critical to modern competitive regional organization, and indeed form a Think Tank or Think Tanks to inform the East African regional integration process.

Relations with the Development Partners

This last week, the EAC was privileged and honoured to have a meeting with the President of the World Bank. EAC is the only regional economic community (REC) that the President of the World Bank is visiting during his current visit to Africa. As such, and in itself, the visit and the meeting signified strong confidence of the World Bank in the EAC.

The discussions were very fruitful and they focused on regional infrastructure development; EAC Customs Union and trade liberalization; Lake Victoria Development Programme; Regional Poverty Reduction Strategy and Programme (PRSP); Regional Mechanism on Anti-Corruption and Good Governance; and capacity building for the East African Community organs and institutions.

However, as far as the World Bank President's sense is concerned, he believes that the EAC, ambitious as it may wish to be, should seek to engage development partners around three main areas, i.e. the Lake Victoria Development Programme, Infrastructure development, mainly roads and railways and Energy and power development for the region.

The meeting was the culmination of a series of current re-focused consultations between World Bank and EAC on support to the EAC regional integration and development process. As a result, in the next few months, EAC and Word Bank officials will be working out a project proposal that will relate the identified priority areas to specific projects for implementation in the short, medium and long terms. These parameters will also constitute the basis for a Memorandum of Understanding that is planned to be signed between EAC and the World Bank.

Strategic Financial Plans

I am pleased to report that we are moving along similar lines in the targeted engagement with our development partners to support the new action oriented and focused approach for the regional organization. Thus, I have been able to obtain the support of the Director General of United Nations Education, Social and Cultural Organisation (UNESCO) to second a top Specialist in the UN system to our Headquarters to review our strategic financial plans, budget systems and audit as well as our financial monitoring and evaluation systems. Mr. Martin Shio, a director in UNESCO and advisor to the Director General with wide experience in finance, budget and audit is already in Arusha and will be with us for three months. His assignment to us is without cost to EAC.

In this context also, I have been consulting closely with Ambassador Conrad Mselle, who has served as Chairman of Advisory Committee on Administrative and Budgetary Questions (ACABQ) of the United Nations for decades, on the best way in which the EAC can have a sustainable financing system. This is a subject which has engaged EAC for a long time but never been put to fruition. Ambassador Mselle has offered his services, also without cost to EAC, to work with us in developing a financing mechanism for the EAC that would assure us of a more sustainable financing arrangement. Ambassador Mselle has already put up a short memo to me which will inform the terms of reference for his work with us.

Investments and Trade

Similarly, useful contacts have been established with the President and CEO of the Whitaker Group, USA, Ms Rosa M. Whitaker. The Whitaker Group is comprised of industry and government experts with a track record of achievement in trade, investment and economic development. Indeed, the Whitaker Group is a premier US consulting firm that facilitates trade, investment and commerce in Africa and currently works with African governments and US, African and multinational corporations to forge alliances and capitalize on commercial opportunities.

Rosa Whitaker, as you may be aware, served as the first Assistant US Trade Representative for Africa in the administrations of Presidents George Bush Senior and Bill Clinton. In this capacity, she developed and implemented the African Growth and Opportunity Act (AGOA) and other bilateral and multilateral trade policy initiatives toward Africa. She started the US Trade Representative Office for Africa and was the lead US negotiator for trade agreements with African countries. The initial contacts made in June this year with the Whitaker Group have set the stage for a long and elaborate engagement between the Group and the EAC with prospects of investing in the production of ethanol as an alternative source of energy as part of the overall strategy to address the prevailing power shortage in the region and wider issues of trade capacity building and facilitation.

There is tremendous potential for US investment in the EAC which remains unexploited and we should engage in focused negotiations to attract meaningful investment in the region. We would therefore be following up this initiative in exploring the production of ethanol as an alternative source of energy as part of the strategy to enhance more power production and usage in East Africa. Indeed, the EAC region has high potential and capacity for sugar production and the bi-products could be used in the production of ethanol for energy. EAC could then be marketed as the *ethanol hub* of the region and Africa as a whole.

Political Commitment

Finally, during these first days, I was honoured by the invitation last May to attend the inauguration of H.E. President Yoweri Kaguta Museveni in Kampala which gave me first hand insight of the political commitment at the highest levels to regional integration. This was demonstrated by the recognition and limelight which the Secretary General was accorded at the ceremony and in the context of the Speech which the President made on the occasion in reference to deepening East African integration through bold investment in infrastructure and other major capital intensive projects and programmes that have significant impact on the socio-economic transformation of our region. I believe, therefore, that we can count on the continued support of our leadership, both the Council of Ministers and the Summit in pursuing the radical approach required to make the East African giant stir, rise and move.

Conclusion

Honourable Ministers, in making these observations, it is my wish to serve notice of my intention, during the coming few years of my term, to put our Secretariat fully at your disposal in taking EAC to the high ground it was meant to occupy in the first place. I believe that with a common purpose, we should, at the end of the day, emerge with pride that our efforts have contributed to the strengthening of the Community. This, I believe, is what is expected from this important forum – to set our targets with bold purpose and start on our journey towards a new, highly performing, focused and demonstrably achieving East African Community.

CHAPTER TWENTY ONE

Dynamising the EAC Organisation System[149]

It is an honour for me to be invited to this august EAC Inter-Parliamentary Relations Seminar for 2006 to talk about EAC's prospects. I wish to thank the leadership of the East African Legislative Assembly for associating me, not simply in the deliberations that have featured in this Seminar, but also in contributing this Statement. Inasmuch as my Statement features at the concluding end of the Seminar, it remains my earnest belief and hope that it will add value to this important process of interaction, engagement and dialogue.

Although I was invited to talk about EAC'S Prospects, I realize that my EAC colleagues who have spoken before me have covered a lot of ground in this particular area and I would not like to sound repetitive. Thus my statement will not cover some of the more mundane issues relating to the Customs Union, infrastructure development or Fast Tracking East African Federation. Rather the thrust of my statement will be on how I see the EAC evolving into a more robust and dynamic organization following its extended mandate and the challenges it faces.

Importance of "Nanyuki Series" of Conferences

The series of meetings that bring together the Members of the EALA and those of the National Assemblies of our three Partner States, now popularly known as the "Nanyuki Series" are of landmark importance. They constitute an umbilical cord that enjoins the national and supranational legislators in the lofty service of the East African people. They represent a unique and constructive platform for exchange of views, insights and experiences on how best our legislators can collectively address the challenges the EAC confronts as well as respond to the opportunities that surround us and whose strategic seizure can have a liberating impact on our lives.

It is a central task of our legislators to continuously respond to the rising expectations of East Africans in their quest to improve their quality of lives and realize the dream of an economically powerful East Africa.

This meeting, the third in the series, is clearly taking a new momentum. The Partner States are now called upon to be more conscious about the need and

---

[149] Presentation to the Inter-Parliamentary Relations Seminar (Nanyuki III), Kilimanjaro Kempinski Hotel, Dar es Salaam, Tanzania, 14th August, 2006.

urgency to transform the East African Community into a more effective organization for realizing the EAC Treaty objectives. Whilst the EAC has made steady progress since the signing of the Treaty in November 1999, and one may cite the establishment of the EALA and the East African Court of Justice as well as the launching of the Customs Union and several projects, much remains to be done if the East African people are to draw meaning out of this institution.

Slow Progress in Integration

Indeed, the Special Summit of the EAC Heads of State that met in Nairobi in September 2004, whilst appreciating the gains realized by the EAC, reflected dissatisfaction with the performance and pace in forging EAC's central objectives. That historic Summit was held against the background of a lacklustre record of implementation, by the Partner States, of important decisions taken by the Council of Ministers. Decisions such as the Liberalization of the Capital Account, Agreement on Avoidance of Double Taxation and Prevention of Fiscal Evasion, unratification of Protocols etc, which had remained (some continue to remain) unenforced or not implemented.

In sum, the Nairobi Summit expressed serious concern about the slow delivery of EAC's programmes and, in the same breath, launched the process to fast track the regional integration process. With that Summit's Communiqué, the EAC, had, so to speak, crossed the Rubicon. A distinct re-awakening was ushered in; there was in the air a sense of renaissance, the urgent need to refocus and to engender a fresh, action-oriented, almost business-like momentum. The EAC was being challenged to deliver tangible results and benefits, for all to see and feel. Put differently, EAC's credibility was on the line.

Little wonder, a flurry of bee-hive type of activity in the EAC emerged thereafter. The Wako Committee was appointed, its task accomplished in record time. And only then did the Partner States rush to ratify most Protocols, then kept in abeyance. They also proceeded expeditiously to finalise the Customs Union negotiations, which, hitherto, had been like a ship without a captain.

This change in mental thrust is critical, but so is its sustenance and reinforcement. For whether we like it or not, there is a prevailing perception in East Africa that the EAC has little to show to justify some of the more radical proposals it is now flagging and putting into motion. Even President Jakaya Mrisho Kikwete, as recent as August 2005, and Foreign Minister at the time, in an address at the EAC High Level Retreat in Arusha, observed, and I quote: "Policy documents and reports of studies, bound in elegant stationery are all well and good. But we shall never convince the East

African people that the Community is making progress by simply enumerating the studies that we have carried out or the Protocols that we have signed. The proof of the pudding is in the eating. Our strategic plan should be a bold and focused statement of objectives and processes towards targeted and measurable achievements within specified time frames."

A New Dynamic to Move EAC Forward

Yet there is a new momentum in the air. It is a momentum that has to be seized and translated into forging a more robust and results-oriented EAC. The recent appointments of Ministers solely responsible for East African Community Affairs, in Tanzania and Uganda, following Kenya's earlier precedence, are a solid manifestation of this momentum. Clearly, these appointments could not simply be symbolic. They represent, in my view, a bold and purposeful commitment and direction in putting in place a political lynchpin for not only co-coordinating and promoting a national ethos about the EAC and what it stands for but also for providing some semblance of executive authority at the EAC level. As Members of EALA in their own right, these Ministers should raise the level of deliberations in EALA to a more vibrant and robust level.

In this vein, we should witness, more than ever before, EAC affairs, in the form of programmes, projects, activities and budgets, being tabled and discussed in the National Assemblies of the Partner States. In turn, the nationals, whom our legislators represent, should now be better placed to hear and learn more and discuss more about the East African Community. In fact, one would expect that the EAC Ministers will henceforth play a wider and deeper role at national levels in involving MPs in promoting the objectives and activities of the EAC.

The timing of these changes could not be more apt since the EAC today suffers from what we can unashamedly describe as a visibility deficiency syndrome. In your earlier Nanyuki Series, you clearly observed that many East Africans lack a shared perception of the benefits of integration and that a number of East Africans are even sceptical of such benefits. Needless to underscore, as the EAC, by its presently defined responsibilities, is not an implementation agency, the role of the EAC Ministers and of the Legislators, at EALA and National Assemblies' levels, in promoting EAC's visibility, image and identity is highly important.

Let me also add that the appointment of East African Community Ministers should catalyse a new dynamic at the East African Community Secretariat. As you know, the EAC Secretariat presently operates, not as an executive decision-making organ but largely as an agency for generating thinking, ideas, projects and programmes for the consideration of the Partner States. If there is one serious drawback to the functioning of the EAC today, it is precisely the lack of any form of executive authority on the part of the Secretariat. In saying this, I am not in any way interrogating or questioning the original rationale behind the Treaty provisions.

My point is this: ten years after the birth of the Secretariat, much water has surely flowed under the bridge. The EAC has learnt from useful lessons and experiences. New insights have been gained. What is clear is that no organization, even of the EAC intergovernmental type, can be or can be allowed to be static. Left so, it inevitably atrophies. Thus, much as I am adequately seized of the rationale and even necessity to ensure that the interests and priorities of the Partner States in the EAC are secure and protected, a probable price an EAC-type organization must pay to assure a win-win transition dispensation, yet there should be a time-planned limit to it.

Today, we can reasonably question whether the EAC can adequately respond to the challenges it faces and manage its complex tasks with the decision-making structure and processes in place. To cite one example: A Draft 3rd EAC Development Strategy (2006-2010) has been lying with the Partner States awaiting their reactions way beyond agreed time-lines. This Strategy defines the EAC's work in the next five years. Without it, you could say the EAC lacks a programmatic focus and direction. Should such a situation be allowed to exist?

Put it this way: does it not beg logic to appoint Ministers solely responsible for EAC affairs if such appointments do not bring about a demonstrable change in the way the Partner States make decisions pertaining to the EAC? What then is the role of these Ministers; what delegated powers do they enjoy? Do they add value to the decision making structure and process presently in place?

I have noted, for example, that in the Nanyuki I and II Summary of Proceedings, you take the view that the Council of Ministers should facilitate EALA to legislate on concluded Protocols so as to spur implementation at national levels. Yet in the same proceedings you also observe that the EAC Ministers should drive the integration process instead of relying on the Council of Ministers and Heads of State. An excellent idea but where would these Ministers derive their authority from to drive the integration process? This conjures some debatable scenario.

Assuming that the EAC Ministers are to become a Sectoral Council, what would such Council be in respect of? But more importantly, and in line with your Nanyuki II thinking cited above, would such Council then exercise overriding authority? But how, when you have a Council of Ministers under the Treaty? Moreover, have we also considered how to transform the EAC Secretariat to give it teeth? At a High Level Staff Retreat in Zanzibar last month, an idea emerged that time had probably come for the Secretariat to be transformed into a Commission, a smaller equivalent of the AU-type Commission. The implication is that as a Commission, the EAC would be able to exercise some executive authority, which would then help to speed up decisions. Is this an idea whose time has come?

Priorities for Leadership Focus

I have recently completed 100 days in office. This is too brief a time to behave as if I know everything in the EAC; I do not. Yet in management, a new Chief Executive Officer is often evaluated on the basis of what he or she accomplishes in the first 100 days. It is said that the first 100 days constitute the litmus test of what one seeks to achieve. If you fail to use those days to chart out a path you believe in and begin to seriously getting other key people in the organization to walk that path, you blow away the unique opportunity to effect needed change. Allow me, Chairperson, to share with you the path I am beginning to pave for the EAC. I believe that this path responds to the topic you have requested me to dwell on, namely EAC's prospects.

First and foremost, I wish to underline that the key driver of any organization is its human resources. However, these resources do not emerge from or operate in a vacuum. They have to be well organized. This task demands developing a well conceived organization structure that fits the strategy to be implemented. Yet whilst the EAC has made some headway in implementing the objectives of the Treaty, its organization structure has remained largely static representing the EAC mandate as it was determined in 1996. Today, not only is the EAC as a whole too thin on the ground human resource-wise, but its key people are also overworked, underpaid and in an acute state of low morale and productivity.

A mechanistic operating environment has crept in undermining creativity, new thinking and strategic management. Today, as we await the approval of an ambitious 3rd EAC Development Strategy, we are confronted by this passive environment that has fuelled diversionary pursuits centred in travels to conferences, seminars and workshops, often of little value to the realization of EAC's objectives. One is thus not surprised about the general disenchantment over EAC's performance in terms of producing tangible results.

Given this background, my first priority has been to transform the existing organization culture; re-generate staff confidence and morale, and give the EAC Staff a new sense of hope, belonging and direction. The EAC is now in a position to propose to the Council of Ministers a new EAC organization structure that fits EAC's present status, its demands and challenges. At the same time, a new salary and compensation package that closely corresponds to and which is commensurate with applicable terms similar regional economic communities in Africa as well as in the Public Service of our Partner States is being proposed.

It cannot be equitably argued that Partner States lack resources to fund the EAC's budget to meet higher staff compensation when these same States separately pay, for instance, their diplomats in East Africa more than what they pay EAC staff. If anything, the EAC staff should be better paid if the EAC is to attract the best and the brightest of East Africans. I truly hope that these proposals will be approved, thereby paving the way for EAC's organizational renewal and vitality.

The second priority, which defines EAC's credible and plausible prospect, relates to giving the EAC greater visibility in East Africa and abroad. This measure crucially involves branding the EAC as a viable and robust economic community able to transform the East African region into a competitive and prosperous region in Africa whilst sustaining peace and stability. But as earlier observed, the vision and mission of the EAC is yet to be shared by most East Africans. Merely to say that the formulation of the EAC Treaty involved many East Africans is not sufficient for the vision to be a shared one.

The EAC as a project has to be effectively sold to the people of East Africa in terms of its goals, its programmes, its strategies and its dreams. East Africans have to be informed, sensitized, mobilized and galvanized about EAC's lofty objectives. And failure to do this could cost us the future of our organization. EAC's prospect, in this direction, therefore crucially hinges on how we allocate adequate resources for reaching out to the citizens of East Africa. On our side, the new EAC organization structure is elevating the role of communication and public affairs, giving it a frontline position in EAC's affairs. Indeed, as we hit the road on promoting the entry of the Common Market and Fast Tracking East African Federation, the role of communication and information takes a higher priority position.

The third priority, in tandem with the first and second, is the challenge to promote close linkages between the Organs of the Community. I realize that this has been a topical subject in the Nanyuki Series. It is a rude reality that there have been serious fractures in relations among the EAC Organs and especially between the Secretariat and EALA. This would not be the first time I pronounce that such estrangement is a recipe for divorce. It cannot be allowed to continue.

I have made a commitment to bring about a radical change in relationships, not out of populism but in the genuine belief that EALA is a pivotal organ in promoting EAC's interests. So is the role of the Court of Justice. Specifically, it is critical that the legislation programme of EALA is deepened. Until recently, there has been some ambivalence about the role of

Protocols *vis-a-vis* Legislative Bills, leading to unnecessary misunderstandings between EALA and the executive arm of the EAC.

I am happy to report that the recent Sectoral Council on Legal and Judicial Affairs has charted out an objective path that better clarifies which EAC matters would be covered by Protocols and which matters would fall within the ambit of Bills. Protocols will henceforth be restricted to matters of cooperation relating to policy harmonization by the Partner States whilst matters pertaining to operational issues such as institutional development, will be subject to enactment of appropriate legislation. This clarity will remove the sources of misunderstanding that have hitherto bedevilled the relations between EALA and the EAC Council.

With respect to the East African Court of Justice, it is gratifying to note the positive steps being taken to extend the Court's jurisdiction in line with the Treaty provisions. This Court, which as you may be aware, is presently hearing the first reference to it, is now set to be very busy as the Customs Union consolidates and as the integration process deepens and widens. In this context, the 3rd EAC Development Strategy addresses the centrality of the Court's extended jurisdiction and this objective will be put in the front burner of the EAC's agenda.

The fourth priority will centre on the consolidation of the Customs Union, notably its full implementation. There are two related issues in this important pillar of the EAC. First, is the task of harmonization of laws relating to the Customs Union and the Customs Management Act, 2005. The need for accessible, predictable and transparent laws at both national and EAC levels is imperative if an enabling environment that spurs optimum private sector participation in business and economic development is to emerge.

The 3rd EAC Development Strategy has identified this legal issue as of strategic priority and the EAC is working closely with the World Bank to effect appropriate interventions. The second issue is connected with the removal of non-tariff barriers, adopting centralized collection of duties, elimination of internal taxes and negotiating as a bloc. The latter issue, that of negotiating as a bloc, is particularly worrisome as pressure mounts on conclusion of the EU Economic Partnership Agreements and as the WTO deadline on membership of Customs Union being restricted to one membership draws close. In April 2002, the EAC had taken a bold decision that it shall negotiate regional and multilateral agreements as a bloc.

The Nanyuki Series have taken bold stands on this issue to the extent of calling on the EAC Partner States to disengage themselves from other trading blocs like COMESA and SADC. Which way forward remains a puzzle or was Shakespeare right when he wrote in Macbeth that it is darkest before dawn?

An important question connected with consolidation of the Customs Union and especially as we commence the process towards the creation of a Common Market, is the centrality of promoting productive investments. It is investments that drive trade in the globalization era, not vice versa. Consolidation of the Customs Union thus hinges on how the East African economies are best able to attract both domestic and foreign investments. Today, about 30% of East Africa's economic competitiveness is eaten away by high costs of doing business – across all sectors of the economy.

Unless serious attention is focused on improving physical infrastructure: roads, telecoms, ICT, railways, ports and harbours and, above all, energy, the Customs Union will be more of a shell than a vibrant market promoting vehicle. My understanding of the perception of international multilateral financial institutions like the World Bank and the African Development Bank about investments in these infrastructure sectors is that East Africa will be better placed to attract funding if its projects shift from national to regional. These institutions now view East Africa as a geographical and economic entity and that shared development of infrastructure projects is the right approach to take. I am posing this trend in thinking to reinforce the approach we are taking at the EAC level. But more importantly, to influence a mindset change in project planning which, today, is primarily national focused.

It is thus important that we attach greater importance to the regional projects under EAC, namely, the Lake Victoria Development Programme, East African Power Master Plan, East African Road Network Project, East African Railways Development Master Plan, East African Submarine Cable System (EASSY) Project etc. Our serious concern with development infrastructure would also focus on soft infrastructure whereby equal emphasis would be put on human resource, health, HIV/AIDS and Information Communication Technology (ICT) projects. The success of all these projects, in terms of funding and fast tracking depends a lot on how they are conceived, packaged and sold for funding. It is also crucial that these projects be made open to private sector participation as well as to public-private partnerships.

The role of the private sector in deepening economic integration in East Africa cannot be overemphasized. The EAC Treaty recognizes this role in stating that the EAC shall be "market driven". During the last five years, the cross-listing of stocks in the three East African stock exchanges has fertilized a new development in the form of mergers and acquisitions. Though Tanzania is yet to liberalise its capital account fully to allow free movement of capital in East Africa, Kenya and Uganda have taken the lead.

The creation of East African companies as opposed to Kenyan, Ugandan or Tanzanian irrespective of national ownership is a psychological mindset booster to those that cry wolf about one country "swallowing" another. When you have a Kenyan company, for example, East African Cables acquiring Tanzania Cables and transforming it into East African Cables (Tanzania) Limited, then proceeding to improve its technology, create new jobs, train and pay the workforce better, where would the fear of being swallowed emerge from? I believe that Shelly's of Tanzania, a Tanzanian pharmaceutical giant has also acquired a leading Kenyan pharmaceutical company making Shelly's (part of the Sumaria group) the largest pharmaceutical company in East Africa. Uganda's Casements Ltd has also acquired a Mombasa-based Casements company. These cross border mergers and acquisitions must be bolstered and the full liberalization of the capital account in Tanzania will be a shot in the arm for Tanzanian firms seeking to invest in East Africa.

Conclusion

Let me conclude my remarks by restating my popular message. As the EAC consolidates the Customs Union, as it begins a process towards the creation of a Common Market and allows ideas to contend about the fast tracking of East African Federation, the question of putting the East African people at the heart of EAC's agenda is critical. We cannot simply be rhetorical about the EAC being people-driven when the people occupy the backseat of the bandwagon. Evidently, the structure for enabling direct people's participation in EAC's affairs and programmes is nebulous and ineffective. Yes, to some extent, success has been achieved in engaging the East African business community, especially in the negotiations involving the Customs Union Protocol and the Customs Union Management Act. In fact it is in order to salute and pay tribute to the East African Business Council for its leading and effective role in many EAC's programmes.

The role of the EABC in the next three and a half years as the EAC makes the transition from the Customs Union to the Common Market will be as important as it will be arduous and challenging. I need not overemphasize the need for the business lobby to reflect less zero-sum economic nationalism and boldly embracing the logic of deeper integration, learning from the experiences of the European Union where Europe's hitherto backwater countries like the Republic of Ireland have come to achieve phenomenal economic performances.

The challenge, however, is to move beyond the participation of these well organized groups like the EABC and the East African Law Society (EALS). As you know, the Treaty provides for the establishment of an East African Civil Society Organisations Forum (EACSOF). Unfortunately, this call has escaped us so far. We have to work together to determine how best to constitute this Forum.

All of us here constitute an important segment of the East African Society with a bold mission to realize the ambitious dreams East Africans have set for themselves. I am confident that we are up to the task. I know that we enjoy the full support of the East African political leadership. In my recent visits to Uganda and Kenya where I had long audiences with Presidents Museveni and Kibaki, I obtained first hand insight of the high level political commitment that exists on the EAC. I received great encouragement and assurances of total support in leading the EAC to higher outcomes. In particular, the Presidents were very positive about the measures I am taking to restructure the EAC with a view to strengthening its Organs, improve the terms and conditions of service of staff and promote EAC's image and visibility.

CHAPTER TWENTY TWO

Decision Making Structure and System[150]

Introduction

When my term as Secretary General of the East African Community commenced at the end of April last year, I did not hesitate to put the Staff on notice that they should be prepared for a new leadership mindset and direction in transforming the EAC into a more robust, vibrant and results-oriented organization. During the EAC Strategic Retreat for Executives and Professional Staff in Zanzibar, I urged that we examine ourselves critically and review our strengths, weaknesses, opportunities and threats with a view to improving the performance of the EAC. That Retreat was my first serious encounter with the top leadership of the EAC. I used the platform to begin a conversation about my own perceptions of the EAC and how this important institution could be transformed to respond better to the wishes and aspirations of East Africans. Two issues were at stake at the time: the need to concretize the new EAC Development Programme and the urgency to deepen positive awareness about and visibility of the EAC.

At the subsequent General Staff Retreat that took place in Jinja, Uganda in July 2006, we focused greater attention on one of the aspects that I addressed in the Zanzibar Retreat, namely how we can transform the EAC into a more results-oriented organization. In this context, we examined some of the latest management tools that can assist us achieve this goal. Results-Oriented Management or ROM was introduced to all of us and has since been mainstreamed in EAC's operational activities. The speed at which we have implemented ROM in our operations is a clear reflection of our deep commitment and resolve to transform the performance of the EAC Secretariat and of the administrative support functions in the Court and EALA. Of course we are yet to finalize performance management contracts for each one of us. But we are getting there.

The Jinja General Staff Retreat was also historic in its focus on how best we can engender team spirit across the organizational hierarchies in the EAC administrative agencies. We all agreed that team spirit could only be nurtured and nourished if we collectively determined what constituted the core values that lay at the heart of our institution and of the people who work in and for the EAC. We took time to toss up the values we shared which

[150] Speech at the EAC Annual Staff Retreat, Mkonge Hotel, Tanga, Tanzania, 8th August, 2007.

could then become the driving forces of our resolve to effectively achieve the objectives of the EAC Treaty. Since Jinja, work has been done to synthesize and refine the identified core values. We are now in the process of printing, prominently displaying and boldly disseminating these core values to all of us and to other key actors in the East African integration process.

But there is another dimension that I reflected upon at the Zanzibar Retreat for the Executive and Professional Staff. It concerned how the EAC organization structure could be adapted to fit the changed circumstances in and demands of the EAC. It is a cardinal principle in organizational management that structure follows strategy. Yet, whilst efforts to review the EAC organization structure had started in 2004, little headway had been made in terms of results. It was not a surprise therefore to find in the EAC, in mid 2006, a mood of gloom and frustration. Staff were overworked and underpaid. There was low morale and motivation. Career development was uncertain. Moreover, the relationship between some organs of the EAC, notably between the Secretariat and the East African Legislative Assembly, was polluted by mistrust and even lack of shared direction.

Today, one year on, we can look back with some nostalgia and guarded satisfaction at some of the transformations that have taken place; notably in our organization structure, the new recruitments of professionals and the introduction of new and better terms and conditions of service. These transformations have not only affected the EAC Secretariat; they have also embraced the whole EAC family; that is including the Court and the Assembly. The members of the Assembly remain dissatisfied by the new terms. As the Secretariat, we cannot be blamed for not trying to push for better terms for the Assembly members, or for that matter, for the Judges. In the case of the Assembly, we involved a selected group of EALA members to move with us around the Partner States to justify new terms. Could we do more when it is the Partner States that make decisions on matters of this kind? Going by the proverbial adage, should the messenger be hanged?

Following the transformations we have effected in the past year, the central challenge before us now is how to apply them to realize greater efficiency and effectiveness. At the same time, we cannot be oblivious of the reality that organizations are dynamic. They must constantly be adjusted and adapted to fit new challenges and tasks. In particular, organizations like the EAC, which are inter-governmental, face myriads of challenges of change, co-ordination and decision-making. These challenges become more complex and onerous as these institutions enter into higher levels of integration and expand their memberships. Moreover, the EAC is experiencing vast changes in its external and internal environment.

Emerging Challenges

Let me mention only three challenges.

Enlargement

First, there is the enlargement of the EAC following the admission of Rwanda and Burundi. The size and scope of our activities and decisions will inevitably increase and even take a more complex form.

Globalisation

Secondly, intensifying globalization will manifest itself in new global rules for trade and investment with effect from January 2008 when the WTO abolishes the Most Favoured Nation (MFN) treatment that partly underpins regional trading arrangements. In other words, a borderless world is coming and will put to severe test the basic meaning and purpose of regional integration. Innovative and creative minds at regional levels will thus have take pre-eminence in such competitive environment.

Uncertainty

Thirdly, the hopes of the poor world, pinned on the promise of the rich world to make poverty history, rest, at best, on uncertainty. The rich world has not lived to its promise. And regrettably, developing countries are nowhere close to being able to achieve the Millennium Development Goals by 2015. In other words, our problems of development, in the EAC and in the rest of the poor world, are not abating; on the contrary, they are increasing.

Clearly, such a grave economic landscape calls for improved quality of institutions like the EAC, with new capacities and innovative methods and practices. It is these capacities that can help make regional integration more effective in mastering the challenges that confront us. The EAC has in place policy and programmatic framework and direction to make regional integration the key vehicle in bolstering our economies and improve the living standards of East Africans. The EAC Development Strategy, 2006-2010, clearly outlines the strategic interventions to be taken to realize these gains.

It is these challenges that centre on capacities which I will focus upon today, by examining how our Organs and Institutions can be made more effective in achieving the EAC Treaty objectives. However, you will appreciate that this effort is merely path breaking. I do not underestimate its complexity and sensitivity. In fact, it involves venturing on a path where most angels fear to tread! Therefore, my role is to simply highlight few ideas and insights. My aim is to provoke thinking and stimulate ideas. After all, if there is a central purpose of these Staff Retreats, in my view, it is to promote an environment where each one of us can ask questions of one another and assess the complex pros and cons of alternatives. In other words, this is an environment that cultivates an ensemble of minds; destroys hierarchy and hopefully promotes buy-in of ideas and, maybe, even of decisions we take or proposals we make.

The Decision Making Challenge

I believe that an effective institutional framework is pivotal to promoting successful integration. Indeed, the whole idea about economic integration is founded on a fundamental principle of liberalized decision-making. What is thus crucial in reinforcing regional economic integration is the ability and willingness of the constituent partners to unpack some of their core dimensions of sovereignty and embrace the objectives of supra-nationality insofar as social and economic development interests are concerned. I believe that the building agenda of any regional economic body is easily susceptible to retrogression where such unpacking of some elements of stateness is shunned or avoided.

This is the particular context which led the late Mwalimu Julius Nyerere to observe, at the OAU Summit in Cairo in July 1964, that:

> For Africa, the lesson of East African experience is that economic cooperation can go a long way without political integration, but there comes a point when movement must be either forward or backward – forward into the political decision, or backward into reduced economic cooperation.

Political integration need not be viewed, necessarily, as an act of political federation, much that is the ideal, indeed as well captured in the letter and spirit of the Treaty establishing the EAC. However, in my view, political integration can also be viewed in the context of the gradual but deliberate unpacking of state authority in the decision making process of a regional economic organization like the EAC. In fact, Mwalimu Nyerere was seized of this *form* of political integration insofar as decision-making authority in the East African context is concerned. In July 1965, he wrote in the Magazine, *African Forum:*

> although each of the three governments (as they existed then) concerned has to look at each question from the point of view of its country first and only secondly from the point of view of the whole area, every major relevant decision has to be a unanimous one. Such a system is inevitably slow and means

that developments which one country regards as urgent can be held up by a decision of another.[151]

Yet, it would be foolhardy to question the logic and imperativeness of political authority of the Partner States in EAC's decision-making process. After all, this is the essence of sovereignty. What is questionable, however, is the extent to which such authority should be exercised and in what spheres of activities. The current requirement, pursuant to the EAC Treaty, that consensus is the exclusive determining factor in decision making by the Sectoral Councils and the Council of Ministers potentially poses complex conditions if we go by the above cited Nyerere's postulation and, of course, going by our own experience. For the Summit, however, one does not see similar difficulty because its meetings are few and the areas of policy that demand its decisions are equally few after delegating significant authority to the Council of Ministers.

In the case of Ministerial meetings, two central difficulties arise: First, quorum may be difficult to secure. Given the numerous meetings the EAC has at ministerial levels, and following EAC's enlargement, the quorum requirement for meetings to take place and for enabling consensus of decisions to be reached may be elusive. Secondly, the enlargement of the Community, with the admission of Rwanda and Burundi, has catapulted a broader diversity of national views and interests. Unanimity of decisions may therefore not be easily achievable. The burning question is: can the EAC, at the current stage of integration, afford to have a gridlock in its decision making system? This question should be confronted dispassionately. To borrow Albert O. Hirschman's phrase, the EAC must "let voice trump loyalty."[152]

Towards A New Decision Making Dispensation

As we begin today a discussion on how to make the EAC Organs and Institutions more effective in achieving EAC objectives, the starting point should be on how to improve the present system of decision-making in the

---

[151] For this work see also NYERERE, Julius K., "The Nature and Requirements of African Unity," in NYERERE, Julius K., *Freedom and Unity*, Nairobi and Dar es Salaam: Oxford University Press, 1966 at pp. 339-340.

[152] This is in reference to Albert Otto Hirschman, the influential economist whose major contribution was in the area of development economics where he emphasized the need for unbalanced growth. He argued that because developing countries are short of decision making skills, disequilibria to stimulate these and help mobilize resources should be encouraged. Key to this was encouraging industries with a large number of linkages to other firms. His later work was in political economy and there he advanced two simple but intellectually powerful schemata. The first describes the three basic possible responses to decline in firms or polities: *Exit, Voice, and Loyalty*. The second describes the basic arguments made by conservatives: perversity, futility and jeopardy, in *The Rhetoric of Reaction*.

EAC, mindful of the sovereignty sensitivities. If we examine what takes place in the European Union, as an example, we observe that the Member States do not have to make all decisions on the basis of consensus, even over some key policy matters. It is for this reason that the UK is not part of the Schengen Visa System. Moreover, the UK and few other EU Member States are not members of the Euro. There are also differential approaches by Member States to some of the EU Directives, for example the one on services. Even the implementation of the EU Fiscal and Stability Pact experiences varying approaches by Member States.

How then should the EAC respond to its own decision-making challenges? How does it seek to strike a delicate balance between matters that are of extreme political sensitivity as to demand consensus in decision-making (for example deciding on the Protocols for the Common Market and the Monetary Union) and those that are not politically sensitive and which a majority voting system could underpin decision making? Put differently, how to balance legitimate national concerns with the risk of subjecting the EAC to decision making paralysis should take the centre stage. Which authority should determine this balance? Should it be formalized, or should it be left for decision whenever an issue or issues arise at meetings?

A related question is the devolution of decision-making authority to the Secretariat. Presently, there is a wide array of mundane issues and activities that engage the Partner States which result in a highly skewed cost structure for the Partner States; issues that could probably be easily dealt with and determined upon by the Secretariat without harming the national interests of the Partner States. Going by the current structures which involve numerous meetings of Senior Officials and Sectoral Committees, and now involving five countries where even quorum becomes a precarious issue, the EAC may find it difficult to transact its business efficiently if some devolution of decision making powers to the Secretariat is not sanctioned. What this devolution should embrace is a matter for discussion when the principle is accepted.

Time has come for bold decisions to be taken by the EAC leadership to delineate these issues, both in the interest of time-effectiveness and cost, especially cost to the Partner States. You simply have to imagine the cost of round trip travel from Kigali and Bujumbura, given the numerous meetings EAC holds annually, to appreciate the cost enormity involved if this overall decision making issue is not addressed dispassionately. No doubt, democracy is expensive; but it should be cost-effective democracy, especially where national interests would not suffer.

Building Synergies with the Court and Assembly

Let me now turn to examine issues relating to relations between the organs of the Community; in particular, those relating to the East African Legislative Assembly, the East African Court of Justice and the EAC Secretariat.

Role of the Court

In so far as the Court is concerned, there is little link between it and the Secretariat apart from the fact that, pursuant to Article 67(3), and Article 67(3) (b), the Secretary General is the Principal Executive Officer and the Accounting Officer, respectively, of the Community. This relationship arises by virtue of Article 9(1) which defines the Court as an Organ of the Community. However, the Court retains its independence.

The Court's independence is importantly underlined by what Article 45(4) stipulates, namely that the Registrar shall be responsible to the President of the Court for the day to day administration of the business of the Court. In some respects, this reporting relationship has weaknesses due to the fact that the Court (and its President) presently operates on an ad hoc basis even though the Treaty does not subsume such ad hoc character. Thus, in the context of the question about how the Court should be made a more effective organ in achieving the objectives of the EAC, this weak reporting relationship between the Registrar and the Court is an area of concern. In turn, the relationship of the Registrar with the EAC's Executive, serviced by the Secretariat is unclear. Put differently, what role does the Registrar of the Court have in proposing changes deemed necessary in making the Court a more effective organ in advancing EAC's objectives? What is the relationship between the Registrar and the Secretary General and the EAC Counsel in matters of this character? Does the principle of separation of powers in any way feature in this relationship?

Be that as it may, short of extending the jurisdiction of the Court, as presently provided for under Article 27 of the Treaty, and thus subjecting the Court to more work, the ad hoc character of the Court may not change. Let me state though that some work is being done by the EAC Sectoral Council on Legal and Judicial Affairs in this direction. At the same time, the East Africa Law Society (EALS) and especially Kituo Cha Katiba (KCK), an EAC Centre of Excellence based in Kampala, have submitted to the EAC robust and insightful proposals for transforming the Court into a more effective contributor to the achievement of EAC objectives, especially following the EAC becoming a Common Market. The EAC Secretariat is also working out a system whereby the Court would enjoy greater autonomy in the management of its finances. This autonomy will further be enhanced when the EAC Secretariat, through the Sectoral Council on Legal and

Judicial Affairs, finalizes work on review of the Treaty to accommodate a better structured system of separation of powers in the EAC. This exercise would also affect the EAC Legislature.

Role of the Assembly

As regards the role of the East African Legislative Assembly, the Assembly itself has done considerable work in visioning its own transformation so as to make it a more effective organ in achieving EAC's objectives. Some of its proposals have been reiterated in the Draft Report on the Common Market Protocol. Key proposals centre on the following:

- Expansion of membership from the present nine per Partner State;

- Extending the period of sittings of EALA. Whilst Article 55 of the Treaty provides that the Assembly shall meet at least once every year, it is silent on the number of days of its sittings. Presently, the EALA budget is worked out on the basis that the number of sitting days is limited to sixty; and

- Expanded powers, where EALA would:

  - consider and adopt its budget estimates which are thereafter integrated in the EAC overall budget;

  - exercise veto over the appointment of the EAC Executives;

  - co-decide policy decisions that are now exclusively reserved for the EAC Council of Ministers and Sectoral Councils;

  - co-decide all draft legislation introduced by the Council of Ministers; and

  - approve all development grants.

However, what EALA has not proposed but the Draft Common Market Protocol has, is that extended powers as those listed above, have to emanate from a directly elected East African Legislative Assembly like the European Parliament is. The logic rests on the force of democratic legitimacy and grassroots representativeness. Can EALA become a more effective contributor to the realization of EAC's objectives, within the framework of the above cited powers, without being directly elected by the people? Should EALA then be a full time organ the way National Assemblies are? Who should propose answers to these questions? I am led to believe that EALA members favour the current system of election of Members through the National Assemblies. But another key question, can EALA, as presently constituted, in form and in numbers, be able to effectively reach out to East Africans, as electorates and as citizens, on matters that are important to them on the EAC?

Another dimension to be considered in making EALA a more effective organ is to make it necessary for the Chairperson of the Summit to deliver to the Assembly a State of the EAC Address annually. The Address should embody important directions of EAC policy and legislative programme for the Assembly.

Inter-Organ Relations

As we discuss the challenges to make the EAC Organs more effective in achieving EAC objectives, we would be remiss if we do not address the question of inter-organ relations. These relations are important if EAC's overall objectives are to be effectively realized. In a recent book, *Five Minds for the Future*,[153] Harvard Professor of Cognition and Education, Howard Gardner, posits:

> It is evident that organizations and communities work more effectively when the individuals within them seek to understand one another (despite their differences), to help one another, and to work together for common goals.

And yet this is one area that has been a cause of misunderstanding, mistrust and even friction, especially between the Secretariat and EALA. Whatever its background and cause, it is important that this relationship is improved. To cite Gardner again: "In the long run, rule by fist, fiat, fear, and fury is destined to fail." But then, improvement of such relations calls for some bold realizations about certain realities. For example, whilst the Secretary General is described as the Principal Executive Officer of the Community, the Treaty is silent on Secretary General's relations with the Assembly, apart from being:

- an ex officio Member of the Assembly;

- causing every Act of the Community to be published in the gazette; and

- receiving from the Clerk of EALA, on a timely basis, all records of debate in the Assembly.

In this specific context, allow me to cite an interesting development. Recently, I received a copy of a letter from the Honourable Speaker of EALA addressed to the Chairperson of the Council. The letter cites Article 67 of the Treaty that outlines the powers of the Secretary General. The Speaker seeks clarification as to whether the Secretary General is "Head" of the Assembly because sub-section (a) of that Article states that the Secretary General shall be "Head of the Secretariat". In other words, the assumption

---

[153] See GARDNER, Howard, *Five Minds for the Future,* Cambridge, MA: Harvard Business School Press, 2007.

mooted is that, to the extent that Article 67(a) specifically makes reference to the Secretary General being Head of the Secretariat, he cannot be subsumed to be Head of the other Organs, namely the Court and EALA. Yet Article 66 of the Treaty also stipulates that the Secretariat shall be the executive organ of the Community. The Secretary General is the head of the Secretariat.

Clearly, these circumstances raise interesting jurisprudential questions particularly in the context of separation of powers. At national levels, the Chief Justice is Head of the Judiciary and the Speaker is Head of Parliament or National Assembly. The difference, if at all, is that, in the case of the EAC, the Treaty does not clearly provide for separation of powers and the two organs, the Court and the EALA, are not full time bodies. Whether these distinctions are of material importance is a matter for debate. But they are issues that sometimes cause unnecessary tensions and the collective quest for promoting and realizing common goals can suffer unnecessarily.

Another area of concern, in the context of EALA, relates to the reporting relationship of the Clerk. Whilst in the case of the Court Registrar, the reporting relationship is stipulated in the Treaty as alluded to earlier, the same is silent insofar as the Clerk is concerned. Should it be assumed that the Clerk reports to the Speaker on the day to day activities of the EALA?

I raise these points and questions because, first, they go to the root of some of the difficult and sensitive inter-organ relations that presently exist. Second, because they may constitute some of the constraining factors to both the Court and the Assembly to rise to the pinnacle of their roles in achieving EAC objectives. But above all, these questions also relate to the onerous challenge as to how the EAC can construct more harmonious inter-organ relations that help to bolster more effective achievement of EAC's objectives.

The Role of the Council of Ministers

In the Treaty, the most important policy organ of the EAC is the Council of Ministers. Yes, the Summit is the highest Organ in determining the direction of the EAC. But it overly relies on the Council for advice. Thus, the challenge of transforming the EAC into a more effective regional organization crucially hinges on the Council. But how does this Council, and the Sectoral Councils which derive authority (Article 14 (3) (1)) from it, work? Can its effectiveness be improved and how? This organ is responsible for giving direction and impetus to the development and achievement of the objectives of the EAC. And at this critical juncture, as the EAC moves into deeper and higher levels of integration, notably the negotiations and adoption of the Common Market Protocol and moving forward the other building blocks of integration, namely the monetary union and political federation, how best to improve the Council's operations and decision making is critical.

The importance of the Council of Ministers has now been reinforced by the establishment, in all the Partner States, of Ministries specifically responsible for East African Community Affairs. In deciding to establish these Ministries, the Summit, I believe, was cognizant of the need, first, to speed up the decision making process in the EAC. Secondly, and probably more importantly, to bring EAC agenda and issues before National Parliaments, and, in turn, through the direct representativeness of the National Members of Parliament, get such agenda and issues before the citizens – the electorate – in the Partner States. In positing this perception, I am not in any way attempting to belittle the role of EALA. I want to underscore this point because I know it may arouse emotive and misplaced sentiments. But certain things are better said. It is in the interest of building the EAC.

Thus, the decision to establish EAC Ministries was a decision driven by the need to cause political accountability on what is happening at the EAC before the highest organs of national representativeness: the Houses of the People. This is why EAC Ministers present budgets of their ministries in Parliament and face questions of Parliamentarians in the same way that Ministers of other portfolios face. By doing so the Ministers responsible for EAC Affairs, which now legally constitute Sectoral Councils that exercise some of the powers of the Council of Ministers, are now able to reach out to national citizens through the directly elected representatives. That way, they are better able to promote sensitization and galvanization of the citizens of East Africa on the goals and the work of the EAC. Through this system, the Council of Ministers has been strengthened and its role in the EAC given even greater legitimacy.

In the same vein, the authority of the Co-ordination Committee of Permanent Secretaries has equally been reinforced by the establishment of EAC Ministries. For this reason, the role of the Retreats for the Permanent Secretaries should be better planned, be more focused and rigorous in the future. The EAC Secretariat can in fact secure mandate for greater autonomy in decision making when its programme of activities and what it want to do is cleared well in advance at such Retreats.

Role of EAC Institutions

The question about the roles of EAC institutions is an easier one. We have two types of institutions: First, there are those whose budgets form part of the EAC budget; a good example is the Lake Victoria Basin Commission (LVBC). In the next few months, the Inter-University Council for East Africa (IUCEA) would fall in this mould. We are proceeding expeditiously to present the bills for the establishment of these two institutions before EALA which will make both the LVBC and the IUCEA part of EAC in most respects. The EAC, through the Secretariat and the Council of Ministers, will thus be able to determine the strategic directions of these institutions and ensuring that they effectively work towards the realization of EAC objectives.

Second, there are institutions which are recognized under Article 9(3) of the Treaty and are "deemed" institutions of the EAC. But pursuant to Article 132(i), they do not fall within the EAC budget framework. They are described as self accounting institutions. These include the East African Development Bank (EADB) and the Lake Victoria Fisheries Organization (LVFO). In fact, these institutions are surviving institutions of the former East African Community. Whilst it may not be that difficult to bring LVFO into the EAC budget fold because it does not have external shareholders, the same would be difficult with EADB whose Charter allows non-East African Partner States or institutions, to be shareholders. EADB does have such external shareholders.

Thus, the challenge of transforming the EADB to become a more effective contributor to the achievement of EAC objectives is complex and onerous. Be that as it may, the Partner States may consider transforming the EADB into a 100% owned development bank of the EAC Partner States. Alternatively, and this is part of the proposal EADB put before the Summit in November, 2006, the EADB may develop specific financial products that could exclusively be funded by the Partner States with support from external financial institutions. Such financial products may focus funding on what the EAC regards as priority development projects, infrastructure, for example. The EADB proposal was adopted by the Summit but awaits decisions of the Treasuries of the Partner States on funding viability.

As for the LVFO, it is important to open up discussion on its future direction within the broad context of how to make it more effective in achieving EAC objectives. There is a view presently being mooted about creating an apex body under the EAC to be responsible for all programmes and projects involving the Lake Victoria and its basin. Such body may provide the strategic framework for determining the future role of LVFO.

At the same time, as we all know, the EAC recently launched a number of new institutions, namely the East African Science and Technology Council, the East African Health Research Commission; The East African Kiswahili Commission, the East African Community Civil Aviation Safety and Oversight Agency (CASSOA) and the Nyerere Centre for Peace Research. Apart from CASSOA and the Health Research Commission, which have commenced operations, the others have not taken effect. The challenge for the EAC is to enable all these institutions to hit the ground running by developing strategic road maps that would enable them to quickly contribute to the achievement of EAC goals. Experience shows that finance is the limiting factor. We must therefore ensure that through the Partnership Fund, we are able to bring all these institutions on board and mobilize adequate resources to enable them take off.

Conclusion

In concluding my remarks and putting my above views in perspective, I would like to underline that successful regional integration, in the context and experience of the EAC, is crucially defined by the collaborative and collective effort of all its stakeholders. The Treaty Establishing the East African Community charges the Organs and Institutions of the Community with crucial roles in the regional integration and development effort. A primary consideration in the effective execution of the regional programme is ensuring the promotion and maintenance of harmonious relations and complementarity of roles and functions of the Organs and institutions of the Community.

Building quality organs of the Community – a decisive and enabling Executive that is highly seized of how decisions can best be taken, a vigilant Legislature that is highly representative of people's views, an independent, impartial, authoritative and even activist Court of Justice, a highly professional, well equipped and independent minded Secretariat and institutions of the Community that put the EAC development agenda on the front burner - is a prerequisite for successful regional integration and development. However, the quality of these Organs and institutions highly depend on how they foster discipline, trust, ethics, creativity and respect among and between themselves. A balanced and judicious application of synergies to the challenges of regional integration and development is paramount.

I must admit that I have been quite excited by the urge of the Court Justices to meet me and exchange views about the role of the Court and EAC's development in general. I must also mention that during the five weeks of my absence from Arusha when I was undergoing treatment in Dar es Salaam, the current Speaker of EALA twice flew from Nairobi to Dar to see me. He has also been in constant touch with me on the phone, from Nairobi, Kampala and Kisumu, to touch base and exchange views. This is the ideal working relationship that I look forward to intensifying. It is the type of relationship that will make the EAC a more effective and results-oriented organization.

Such a closely-knit organization with well defined structures and processes, giving no cause at all for inter-organ or inter-institutional mistrusts and tensions that would normally hamper progress, must be our vision for the EAC. Going by the regrettable past experiences, in particular relating to the conduct of relations between the Secretariat and the East African Legislative Assembly, the EAC organs and institutions should strive to maintain constant dialogue and consultation in managing the issues and dynamics of regional integration. We owe it to the East African citizens to ensure that the EAC excites their hearts and minds about unity, peace, stability and prosperity.

In this Retreat, I urge you to be candid, objective and constructive in your contributions. I hope that at the end of the Retreat, we will all be in a position to have absorbed, internalized and unified a winning strategy to deliver on our mandate. Let this serene and peaceful City of Tanga be the catalyst for us to come up with proposals that embody its spirit. I wish you fruitful deliberations.

PART 7

EAC Partnership with Business

In this part seven of the book I turn to examining the centrality of the business sector in the EAC region in making the EAC integration project work and succeed. At the end of the day, it is the private sector that is the motive power of the overall integration effort. Yes, the role of ordinary citizens is important in sanctifying the project and giving it sustainability. However, it is trade and investment that dynamises the whole system and makes regional integration bear the tangible fruits that legitimize the purpose of the EAC. In the EAC, this dynamisation of integration has been well orchestrated and ensured by the East African Business Council working closely with the EAC Secretariat and other Organs of the EAC.

The EABC has succeeded to secure legitimacy as an honest partner in the integration process. And its role and contribution should be accorded greater recognition that is evident. Making the EABC one of the Statutory Organs of the EAC, without budgetary implications on the part of the EAC, as otherwise that would flout the very ethical purpose of the partnership between the two and may even compromise EABC's independence, would give the EABC a more powerful platform than presently to engage the EAC on the role and contribution of the private sector in the integration project. As a business organization, the EABC should be financially capable to take care of its institutional advocacy needs.

CHAPTER TWENT THREE

Challenges to the East African Business Community[154]

I am pleased to have this opportunity to address you on this important occasion of the East African Business Forum. It is indeed apt that the forum is being held here in the beautiful surroundings of the Ngurdoto Mountain Lodge, itself an icon of the brave new spirit of enterprise that is fast taking root in East Africa.

As most of you know, I remain one of you, my absence in Paris as Tanzania's Ambassador from July 2002 until my appointment as Secretary General of the EAC at the end of April this year, can neither diminish the reality that business runs in my blood nor my commitment to putting the private sector at the heart of the East African project. I continue to cherish my past connections with the East African Business Council (EABC), having been one of its architects and its Chair for the period 1999-2000.

In establishing the EABC, the founding members had the vision of its role as an integral part of the EAC programme. I am glad to note that in the past decade, EABC has, with modest resources, championed its role with vigour and great commitment. EABC's resourceful participation in the successful negotiation of the East African Community Treaty,[155] signed in 1999, and the East African Customs Union Protocol, concluded in 2004 as well as the continuing mobilization of its membership on the regional integration and development effort are well documented and appreciated. With the EABC's present and potential membership in the private sector that contributes about 80% of the gross domestic product of the East African Community, you have high stakes in the Community. This means that you must always be alert and engaged in what goes on in the Community.

Given my intimate association with the EABC, it is inevitable that I should flag my statement with a clear reinforcement of my avowed commitment to do the best I can to deepen EAC's relationship with the EABC and, specifically, to work with new vigour, energy and speed, for EABC's acceptance as an institution of the EAC. In my view, we cannot seriously talk about the EAC being market-driven when the key institutions that drive the market are only peripherally engaged in EAC's mission and work.

---

[154] Keynote address to the business community at the East African Business Forum at the Ngurdoto Mountain Lodge, Arusha, Tanzania on 27th May, 2006.

[155] See LUBEGA-KYAZZE, Jean, "Legal Implications of the East African Community Treaty," Volume 1 No. 1 *The Uganda Living Law Journal*, 2003, p. 43.

The EABC, along with other strategic partners within East Africa's civil society, should be formally mainstreamed in EAC's decision-making structures and processes. This Business Forum and the important themes it is addressing indeed attest to how imperative it is that the EABC becomes an institution of the EAC as soon as possible. This Forum is a clear manifestation of EABC's responsiveness to fundamental policy questions that underlie EAC's programmatic direction and the challenges it must confront head on, and urgently, if our region will timely transform into a competitive economic powerhouse.

The East African region is today going through one of its most challenging phases in the process of transformation to a vibrant economy. The region needs at this time, more than ever before, to marshal its full capacity to manage its enormous resources and potential in establishing its competitiveness in the new world economic order. With over a decade behind us of mainly the conceptualisation phase of the Community, we need to embark with earnest on translating the vision of the Treaty for the Establishment of the East African Community into reality. With so many of these already long identified in the key areas, the critical projects of the Community should be taken from the drawing boards to the implementation status on the ground.

People-Centred Integration

The first step in actualizing the Community, indeed in implementing the Treaty is to unleash the potential of the East African people in the regional integration and development process. The people are at the centre of the development process, being the actors and the beneficiaries of the process. They should be empowered to participate in the EAC's projects and programmes - right from the policy setting stage to the implementation processes.

As you are aware, I have been on my job as Secretary General of the East African Community for only a few weeks now. One of the top priorities that I have identified is the empowerment of the broad section of the East African people to participate in the regional integration agenda and programme. We therefore intend to strengthen and intensify the programme of marketing and publicity of the Community among the people. The EAC presence should be seen and felt across the entire East African region, from the central business districts of our cities and towns to the hamlets in the farthest corners of the vast expanse of the region. Related to this, we should fast track the ongoing process of establishing an effective consultative forum for civil society participation in the activities of the Community; and as I have stated, do the same for the private sector with respect to the East African Business Council.

The viability of the Community, the concrete outputs of the Community, will depend on the inputs which all its constituencies, its broad range of stakeholders, civil society, the public and private sectors and the development partners, contribute to the Community. A synergy should, in this respect, emerge between the public and private sectors in contributing towards the achievements of the objectives of the Community and in demonstrating tangible benefits of regional integration.

Both with regard to the role of governments in creating the enabling environment and the role of the private sector as the driving force, a system of positive measures, beyond rhetoric, should be instituted that take the Community forward. Thus, once the governments have provided the enabling policies and conducive environment, the private sector should operate with confidence, undertaking long-term business investment plans which impact on the socio-economic transformation of the region. Armed with a new paradigm, we should set out to be action-oriented and move faster in concretizing the benefits of regional integration. Much talk has been necessary and has taken place to get the Community where it is today. The worst risk we run is to have the EAC branded as a "talking shop". Therefore, we must, so to speak, begin to walk the talk.

Within the 3rd East African Community Development Strategy (2006-2010) which is to be launched soon, we want to set deliverable targets with respect to modernization of the East African highway network and railways system, realization of region-wide energy sufficiency and reliability, agricultural development and food security, as well as scale up the promotion of industry, investments and trade. Realization of this no doubt ambitious vision, will of necessity involve re-organization and refocusing of the operations of the EAC bureaucracy as well as institution of measures in smart partnership with and between the public and private sectors of our region.

EAC Customs Union

I would now address the key themes of your Forum, namely the enhancement of the Customs Union and the vital importance of the energy sector in East Africa's development. With regard to the challenges of enhancing the Customs Union, my view is that such enhancement hinges probably not so much on opening up and deepening cross border trade but on bolstering productive output among the EAC Partner States. The critical aspect of trade is less linked to *how* countries trade than *what* they may trade. Whilst the adoption of the Common External Tariff (CET) charts out levelling of the playing field, insofar as imports of our raw materials are concerned, the strength of the Customs Union will increasingly depend on how speedily the Partner States are able to create conditions supportive of economic symmetry and thus competitiveness.

Presently asymmetry rules tend to revolve around several costs of doing business and other transaction costs. These costs, which embrace differing taxes and duties, power tariffs, including availability of reliable power, trade supporting interest rates and burdensome bureaucracy, have to be addressed if the Customs Union is to be consolidated. Enhancement of the Customs Union cannot also escape appreciation of realities about the limits of regional co-operation versus national priorities. Finding robust ways to strike a delicate balance between these objectives is a challenge not only of political leadership but of business as well. Often zero sum economic nationalism that underlies enhancement of regional integration, such as open ended disputes over the application of CET and NTBs, is driven by the business lobby.

Indeed, as had been anticipated, the most immediate shocks of opening up the regional market and ushering competition are being felt by those industries that formerly enjoyed protection and which operated more or less as monopolies. Open competition has been intensified among various producers, hence the resistance often encountered from those groups which, for various reasons, continue to harbour distaste for, or fears of competition. Those States whose industries were insulated from competition now have to bear a higher cost of economic restructuring to enable them achieve sustainable industrialization.

These problems may linger but what we ought to acknowledge is the fact that with the launching of the Customs Union, East Africa has made a great leap forward in promoting competitive advantage that should foster a more rapid attainment of our development objectives. There is great potential for effective utilization of resources and bolstering higher productivity flowing from the restructuring and privatization of industries and benefiting from economies of scale that the Customs Union engenders.

Above all, the Customs Union, and subsequently the Common Market for East Africa, provides the critical mass necessary to attract new domestic and foreign investment, bringing with it innovations in the form of new technological processes and new products. Moreover, the larger regional market that these developments bring about opens up not only enormous opportunities but also challenges to the private sector.

The setbacks that may be experienced in the Customs Union today, barely 17 months after its launch should therefore be viewed for what they are; isolated and temporary in the initial stages of establishing a single market and investment area. What we need to be mindful about is that there are vast potential benefits of regional integration that lie ahead. The private sector should be at the forefront in championing regional integration, which is in its best strategic interest. The private sector should go out of its way to ensure the success of the Customs Union. It should build strategic alliances across the borders. It should be proactive in planning ahead rather than reacting to the forces and challenges posed by the roll out of the Customs Union. The developments in cross listing of stocks in the regional stock exchanges are very encouraging in this regard. Cross listing of stocks and building strategic alliances as well as mergers and acquisitions among the traders and manufacturers in the region should be encouraged as definitive steps towards the realization of a fully fledged East African Customs Union.

Trade expansion, both intra-regional and international, is to a good extent the logical spin-off of the consolidation of the Customs Union. However, deliberate and bold efforts should be made to strengthen the region's productive and supply capacity, taking advantage of the operations of the Customs Union and subsequently the Common Market. To this extent, the private sector is expected to play its part to the fullest. On its part, the EAC is committed to pursue concrete measures to bolster the region's productive sector. Specifically, we intend to fast track a number of key projects that have for long been at various formulation stages. Among these are the East African Agricultural and Rural Development Strategy, the East African Industrialization Strategy and the East African Private Sector Development Strategy, all of them of great interest to the members of the EABC and the business and investing community in general.

Infrastructure Development

As regards the pivotal importance of the energy sector and indeed of infrastructure generally, the EAC faces serious challenges as witnessed by the slowing down of the East African economies in the last one year in particular. Countries like Tanzania have seen growth rates decline from targets of 7.2% for fiscal year 2005/2006 to 5.8%. Inflation is also on the rise as a consequence of these declining growth rates. Clearly, the serious energy deficit prompted by a long drought and over reliance on hydropower has major and devastating implications on the productive sectors of the EAC's economies.

Whilst the EAC Partner States are now more seriously engaged in finding sustainable ways of assuring availability of reliable power, the role of the private sector, on its own and in partnership with governments, at national levels, and regionally, takes precedence. The overwhelming success of the recent initial public offer by the Kenya Electricity Power Generation Company (KenGen) has shown how much domestic resources are available within the Partner States to finance what is normally viewed as capital intensive investment. The KenGen case has amply demonstrated that we can mobilize our own resources in East Africa to finance the high profile projects that we have identified in the energy and other priority areas in the infrastructure sector such as those in roads, railways, airways and civil aviation.

Your Forum's focus on the energy issues is therefore timely, considering the centrality of energy resources in the regional integration and development process. Luckily, in the EAC countries, we have the advantage of abundant potential in a mix of energy resources including hydropower, natural gas, coal, and geothermal energy. All the three countries have considerable hydroelectric potential, Uganda a great abundance of it, while, in addition, Kenya has geothermal resources and Tanzania has natural gas deposits. Indeed, there exists good opportunities for achieving an efficient and relatively low cost type of pooled power supply system through regional co-operation in East Africa. The East African Power Master Plan, which is one of the priority projects of the Community, envisages the expansion of a combined power generation system of the region and a comprehensive system of interconnected power generation and supply, incorporating electricity grid interconnections. Needless to state, this is one of the projects that we would be placing on the fast track in the period ahead, working closely with the private sector.

Conclusion

In conclusion, I would like to mention a few of the broader and essentially strategic issues of which the EAC is also seized at the moment, namely the ongoing processes in fast tracking the Political Federation of East Africa, the active involvement of the EAC in the AU initiatives with respect specifically to the NEPAD and the International Conference on the Great Lakes processes as well as the applications of the Republic of Burundi and the Republic of Rwanda to join the Community. These initiatives have significant bearing on the EAC's future direction and, on the whole, hold great prospects for expansion of trade and investments in the East African region with immense benefits to the business community, among others.

Therefore in commending the EABC and the business community at large for the support that you have very ably, and with great dedication and commitment, extended and continue to extend to the East African regional integration process, I would urge you to remain ever close to the EAC in the days ahead. You should continue to make your contribution which is definitive in the transformation of the East African region into a solid economic block and a fast modernizing, thus a competitive investment and trade area and destination.

It is clear that the private sector working closely with the public sector charged with the responsibility of promoting investments both from within countries, regionally and from abroad, will be critical in the overall task of transforming the EAC region into a low cost, job creating and competitive production and trading block. In the following chapter I examine the important role of public East African Investment Institutions in realizing these objectives.

CHAPTER TWENTY FOUR

Drivers of Regional Investment Promotion[156]

Welcome to Arusha and even though we are meeting in a hotel I still would want to welcome you to the East African Community Headquarters. It is an honour and a privilege for me to open this inaugural meeting of Chief Executives of our Investment Promotion Agencies and those of our major business associations. We meet today against a worrisome regional backdrop. The Kenyan political impasse imposes a difficult and complex environment for the EAC; for investment promotion and for business players alike in the region. Following the Kenyan political situation, trade flows have been negatively affected and so have exchequer and business revenues. Movement of raw materials and fuel has also been seriously impacted, threatening not only industrial competitiveness but also the retention of existing jobs. Tourism in particular has suffered greatly. Thank goodness, there is a silver lining before us. Kenya is quickly returning to normalcy.

However, there are serious lessons that we must all learn from what has happened in Kenya in the context of promoting our region as a destination for investment and tourism and, in particular, in our quest to promote the EAC region as a single investment and tourism destination. We have also seen, for example, that whilst poor infrastructure has all along constituted a major barrier to doing business in our region, and thereby eroding our competitive edge, civil strife has a devastating economic impact even where infrastructure is good. The lesson we learn is that we can only promote and attract investments sustainably as well as assure effective intra-regional trade, if we have enduring peace and stability.

In turn, it is the core values that underpin peace and security that assure sustainable development. These values embrace democracy, good governance, rule of law and respect for human rights. In other words, we can no longer afford not to address these core values that need to be commonly shared in all the EAC countries as we continuously deliberate on how best to work together as promoters of investment and as business actors. In April this year, from the 10th-11th, the East African Community and the East African Business Council will stage the Second East African Media Summit in Dar es Salaam, hosted by IPP Media of Tanzania, and the core theme will be on these particular issues.

---

[156] Statement at the Opening of the Meeting of East African Chief Executives of Business and Investment Promotion Agencies, Arusha, 22nd February, 2008.

Let me also underline that the Kenyan political situation has heightened the importance of addressing the key strategic factors that constitute the bedrock of business confidence and competitiveness. In this area, the availability of reliable and robust infrastructure, in alternative routes in our region, is of critical importance. At the EAC level, steps are already underway to address our infrastructural deficits in railways, ports and harbours, roads, energy, civil aviation, and lake transportation both on Lake Victoria and Lake Tanganyika. The EAC Master Plans for roads, railways and energy are under review in order to mainstream Rwanda and Burundi in the Master Plans. Progress is also at an advanced stage in promoting an East African Civil Aviation Regime that meets international standards in air safety and security oversight.

All this work is being done in the realization that good infrastructure is what unlocks the potentials for economic growth and development. In as much as our governments, in some Partner States, have concessioned the railways and ports, this remains inadequate as experience has shown. What is at stake is the injection of investments in improving the railway permanent ways and the handling capacities of our ports. In view of the challenges that lie in these infrastructure areas, the EAC has decided, over the next four months, to give them central attention. Thus Retreats for Permanent Secretaries and for Ministers of our key infrastructure ministries will be held in Mwanza early March and in Kampala in April, respectively.

Globalization has been the driving force behind market-driven economic integration in the world. The challenges of globalization are best responded to and mastered when efforts toward regional cooperation and integration are undertaken. The reason is simple. Regional integration assures better sharing of opportunities as well as management of risks. Since the onset of the EAC Customs Union in January 2005, our region has reaped benefits through the growth of intra-regional trade and business confidence. As a result, we have also witnessed growth in intra-regional investments. Indeed, the liberalization of the capital account in Kenya and Uganda and part liberalization in Tanzania has catalysed growth in the shares market through the process of cross-listing of company shares in the three stock exchanges. There are efforts to extend the process to Rwanda and later to Burundi.

More importantly, the EAC is fast moving towards the promotion of an East African Capital Market with a Central Stock Exchange. The international Finance Corporation (IFC) of the World Bank is funding a major project in this regard and work is in progress. Once developed, the East African Capital Market would act as a spur and a catalyst of vibrant mergers and acquisitions and of greenfield investments that reflect an East African character. Already, we are seeing a growing Initial Public Offering (IPO) activity as well as a Bond Market in the East African Partner States. The cumulative effect of these innovative financial products and instruments is improved liquidity in our region that can be available to fund capital investments and grow our various businesses. This is as it should be because the urgency to forge public-private partnerships, especially in the field of capital investments, in areas such as infrastructure development is real and critical. Our governments are well focused on creating the enabling environment to support Public Private Partnerships (PPPs) and the business sector, so well represented here by the investment promotion agencies and the leaders of private sector business associations.

The centrality of PPPs could not be overemphasized at a time where there is growing concern, especially in Tanzania, about the letter and spirit of mining contracts. The jury is still not out on the exact character of these contracts. Â Suffice to state, that the ethos of economic empowerment of our citizens in the EAC region is growing in importance and sensitivity. Ownership by the citizens of their national economic resources, even whilst we seek to forge closer collaborations with foreign capital, technology and skills, is what economic liberalization is all about.

I was thus moved by a report published in the Daily News of Tanzania yesterday which reported that Mbeya has huge deposits of high grade phosphate able to produce 30,000 tonnes a year. The Mbeya authorities, quite rightly and commendably, are moving in the direction of floating an IPO to raise funds for investing in the exploitation of the deposits and the production of fertilizer. In my view, this is the correct route to take towards achieving the economic empowerment of East Africans. It is a route that our Investment Promotion Agencies and our indigenous private business sector should pursue and develop. Moreover, it is a route that will importantly mitigate the presently heightened fears and concerns about corruption and malfeasance in the high circles of the government, public sector and business. In sum, it is the best route that can create the enabling conditions for a broader ownership of our resources on an East African scale.

As I mentioned earlier, our region must quickly move towards creating a platform for the mobilization of people' savings that can go towards funding not only strategic infrastructures but strategic businesses as well such as that represented by the Mbeya phosphate and fertilizer case.

What I have so far said points to the importance of our working together and, I believe, that this we can attain through joint investment promotion conferences and forums. Two years ago, we were about to start an annual East African Investment Conference. It was slated for Nairobi, Kenya with the collaboration of the Commonwealth Business Council (CBC). It did not take place for reasons that are now historical. Now we are better focused and organized. Thus, the first annual East African Investment Conference will take place in Kigali, Rwanda from 26th-27th June this year. Contacts are being made with the EABC, the Investment Promotion Authorities and all business associations in our region to ensure that we have a successful inaugural investment conference. The Commonwealth Business Council has already been approached to render a helping hand. We also plan to use the Leon Sullivan Business Summit which President Jakaya Kikwete is hosting in Ngurdoto Arusha from 2nd to 6th June as a platform for promoting our own Investment Forum slated for Kigali.

You have a unique opportunity before you to discuss how best we can work together in our region in order to achieve the EAC vision of promoting a secure, competitive and prosperous East Africa. I have every trust and confidence in your wisdom, experience and commitment in making this vision possible. As the late Mwalimu Julius Nyerere put it, "it can be done, play your part."[157] The EAC will extend to you every support in this important venture.

At the Commonwealth Heads of State and Government that took place in Kampala, Uganda in November, 2007, the EAC had the opportunity to address the Commonwealth Business Forum and promote itself as an area of preferred investment. In the next chapter, the story why the EAC region offers unique opportunities for foreign investment is outlined.

---

[157] On this famous quote from Mwalimu see MWAKIKAGILE, Godfrey, *Tanzania Under Mwalimu Nyerere: Reflections on an African Statesman*, Dar es Salaam and Pretoria: New Africa Press, 2006.

CHAPTER TWENTY FIVE

Expanding Business Horizons[158]

I am very pleased to address this important Commonwealth Business Forum and to share with you my perspectives on the strategic direction that the East African Community is taking in supporting business initiatives in our region.

Overview

In setting the context to my address, I would like to give a brief overview of the East African Community covering its history, goals and objectives. As you are aware, the East African Community has a long history; its genesis going back to the 19th century.

The construction of the Uganda Railway, 1897-1902 opened new economic and social interactions across the borders, eventually dovetailing into the common services across the sectors in education, civil aviation, railways, ports and harbours, customs, post and telecommunications, agriculture, forestry and fisheries amongst others under successive regimes - both during the colonial and Independence phases of our region's history.

Most memorable throughout the successive regional integration arrangements that the region has experienced , was the erstwhile East African Community that lasted from 1967 to 1977 when it collapsed due to the various reasons that have been cited, mainly the ideological and political differences; disagreements over the sharing of the costs and benefits of the jointly owned common services and investments.

Subsequent to the collapse of the Community, however, fresh negotiations were sustained leading to the revival of regional integration, the harbinger of the 1999 Treaty establishing the current East African Community. With a determination to avoid the pitfalls of the past, today's EAC jealously guards a system of governance characterized by sharing decision-making power and equitable management of the costs and benefits; as well as involvement of the private sector and Civil Society in the integration process.

Why East Africa?

Pursuant to the Treaty provisions, the Community has made steady progress and today boasts the only Customs Union in Africa was formally established

---

[158] Address to the Commonwealth Business Forum 2007 at Kampala Sheraton Hotel, Kampala, Uganda on 20th November, 2007.

on 1st January, 2005. On the basis of a phased-down implementation arrangement, the EAC Customs Union is expected to culminate in a fully-fledged zero-rated internal tariff regime by 2010. Under the EAC Customs Union, the EAC applies a common external tariff that defines trading relations with third countries and is working to eliminate internal tariffs among the Partner States. By the same token, negotiations have begun for the establishment of a Common Market by 2010 to provide for the freedom of movement of the factors of production.

Currently, the EAC Partner States are pursuing a comprehensive private sector development strategy with the aim to create an enabling environment for the business community. Similarly, the EAC is pursuing a regional industrialization strategy, preparations for which are at an advanced stage in tandem with moves towards the establishment of a Common Investment Area Agreement (CIAA), ensuring, among others, a transparent operating environment for investors where rules, regulations and administrative procedures as well as processes are harmonized across the region.

Coupled with these developments, the East African Business Council (EABC), formed in 1997 as the apex body of business associations in the EAC Partner States, continues to play a catalytic role in fostering dialogue among the private and public sectors in a unique partnership to drive the EAC integration process. The EABC has observer status in all the organs of the East African Community, hence participates at all levels of the decision making process in the EAC where the agenda of the private sector is constantly highlighted. This position and role of the EABC is particularly important at a time when the EAC governments are implementing public sector reforms to allow the private sector to play a greater role in the management of business. To ensure a level playing field for investors there is continuous review and implementation amendment of national Investment Codes/Acts to conform to international best practices.

The success of this approach and focus is demonstrated by the rapid GDP growth levels registered in all the five countries at above 5% on the average in the recent years. Similarly, the Partner States have maintained macroeconomic variables within prudent levels affecting both the rates of inflation and stable exchange rates; and they have fully liberalized the foreign exchange market as well as fairly liberalized their capital markets.

With the accession of Rwanda and Burundi, the East African Community now has a population of 124 million people with a combined GDP of US $ 44 billion. All the Partner States of the Community are signatories to international/multinational arrangements such as World Trade Organisation

(WTO),[159] Multilateral Investment Guarantee Agency (MIGA),[160] and International Centre for Settlement of Investment Disputes (ICSID)[161] which underscores the fact that the region is also integrated within the global trading system. All in all, the EAC Partner States have well managed economies and good governance systems in place with international interveners, among them the World Bank acknowledging the achievements the EAC Partner States are making in this regard.

---

[159] On WTO see STOLL, Peter-Tobias, "World Trade Organization," in BERNHARDT, Rudolf (ed.), *Encyclopaedia of Public International Law* (Volume III), Amsterdam: North-Holland, 1992, p. 1529.

[160] On MIGA see ALSOP, R.B., "The World Bank's Multilateral Investment Guarantee Agency," Volume 25 *Columbia Journal of Transnational Law*, 1986, p. 101; CHATTERJEE, S.K., "The Convention Establishing the Multilateral Investment Guarantee Agency," Volume 36 *International and Comparative Law Quarterly*, 1987, p. 76; PETER, Chris Maina, "MIGA and GRIP: Two International Investment Insurance Programmes," Volume 12 No. 3 *World Competition: Law and Economics Review*, 1989, pp. 95-103; SHIHATA, Ibrahim F.I. and Antonio R. Parra, "Multilateral Investment Guarantee Agency," in BERNHARDT, Rudolf (ed.), *Encyclopaedia of Public International Law* (Volume III), Amsterdam: North-Holland, 1992, p. 473; SHIHATA, Ibrahim F.I., "Eligibility Requirements for MIGA's Guarantees," Volume 2 *ICSID Review: Foreign Investment Law Journal*, 1987, p. 373; and VOSS, J., "The Multilateral Investment Guarantee Agency: Status, Mandate, Concept, Features, Implications," Volume 21 *Journal of World Trade Law*, 1987, p. 5.

[161] On ICSID see BROCHES, Aron, *Selected Essays: World Bank, ICSID, and Other Subjects of Public and Private International Law*, Dordrecht/Boston/London: Martinus Nijhoff Publishers, 1995; AMERASINGHE, C.F., "Jurisdiction of the International Centre for Settlement of Investment Disputes," Volume 15 *Indian Journal of International Law*, 1979, p. 166; AMERASINGHE, C.F.,, "Investment Disputes, Convention and International Centre for the Settlement," in BERNHARDT, Rudolf (ed.), *Encyclopedia of Public Internanational Law* (Volume II), Amsterdam: North-Holland, 1992, p. 1447; SOLEY, D.A., "ICSID Implementation: An Effective Alternative to International Conflict," Volume 19 *International Lawyer*, 1985, p. 521; SUTHERLAND, P.F., "The World Bank Convention on Settlement of Investment Disputes," Volume 28 *International and Comparative Law Quarterly*, 1979, p. 367; and SZASZ, P.C., "Using the New International Centre for Settlement of Investment Disputes," Volume VII No. 1 *East Africa Law Journal*, March, 1971, p. 128.

MACROECONOMIC CONVERGENCE INDICATORS FOR EAC (2006-2007):

	KENYA	TANZANIA	UGANDA	RWANDA	BURUNDI
GDP (US $ Billion)	18.78	13.1	8.7	2.2	0.8
Real GDP Growth Rate (%)	6.1	6.2	6.2	6.5	5.1
GDP Per Capita (US $)	547	316	303	238	106
Population (Million)	36.9	39.4	30.2	9.9	8.4
Population Growth (%)	2.8	2.1	3.57	2.8	3.6
Annual Inflation Av. (%)	15.6	6.7	11.3	11.9	2.7
Debt to Official Creditors as % of GDP	20.6	48.4	41.4	14.8	158.8
Current Account Balance as % of GDP	-4.3	-16.1	-6.7	-18.8	-36.8
Forex reserves in months of Imports	3.6	5.3	6.8	7.6	3.2

Sources: Regional Economic Outlook – Sub-Saharan Africa, IMF (2007); EAC Database.

Investment Climate

As the East African region positions itself as the land of opportunity, its natural resource base, which is yet to be optimally exploited, remains its truly big trump card. The region has surplus arable land which offers huge potential for commercial agricultural investments in livestock farming, horticulture, floriculture and agro-processing, for both the regional and international market. The niche industries include rice, tea, coffee, sugar, sisal and cotton farming as well as manufacturing, processing and trade in hides and skins, and bio-fuels and other growth industries. The region has huge potential in mining with sizeable deposits of soda ash, cement, fertilizers, gold, tanzanite, diamond and other gemstones. There are also prospects for oil in Uganda, Kenya and Rwanda as well as huge deposits of natural gas in Tanzania.

In addition, EAC offers some of the best tourist destinations and boasts a wide array of flora and fauna as well as magnificent mountains, craters, lakes and rivers that guarantee attractive returns on investments in the hospitality and other service industries. The world renowned Maasai Mara and Serengeti national parks, the Mountains of the Moon, the Mountain Gorillas, the Source of the Nile and indeed, Lake Victoria - the second largest freshwater lake in the world and largest fisheries habitat - are unique endowments of diverse natural beauty. There is similarly, an amazing collection of scenic attractions including the sandy beaches of the vast East African coastline and many world heritage and cultural sites.

To optimize the benefits of such abundance in the gifts of nature, the region has developed reasonable supporting infrastructure, both soft and hard, as well as various sector Master Plans for the expansion of the existing facilities. Tremendous growth has been recorded in financial services, health care and education and ICT is among the fastest growing and most profitable sector of the regional economy with mobile telephony exceeding initial projections.

Other opportunities abound in the privatization and commercialization of state enterprises in all the Partner States. A major development in terms of doing business is the evolution of the capital markets in the region. Apart from tremendous response to Initial Public Offers (IPO's) for Kenya Electricity Generation Company (KENGEN) in Kenya and Stanbic Bank in Uganda, there has generally been strong performance in all the three stock exchanges in the EAC Partner States. The trend suggests even stronger growth over the years with bond markets, first initiated by the East African Development Bank, now on the threshold of expansion. Both KENGEN of Kenya and Tanzania Electricity Supply Company (TANESCO) of Tanzania are in the process of issuing bonds to raise capital for their operations. Plans are underway to set up an EAC Regional Securities and Capital Markets Authority by 2009.

The region has succeeded in cross listing of shares among the stock and securities exchanges in the Partner States. Evidence of growth in market liquidity is exemplified by the oversubscription of KENGEN and the Stanbic Bank IPO's. A new wave of interest has also emerged amongst the leading Banks – Citibank, Standard Chartered Bank, Barclays Bank, Stanbic Bank etc to extend syndicated loans of significant amounts to promote private sector infrastructure development projects. TANESCO is a beneficiary of this type of syndicated loan arrangement whilst KENGEN is pursuing a similar loan arrangement.

Enshrined within the vision for the Community is an understanding that peace and stability are crucial for development. It is on this basis that the

EAC has a strong programme to address the question of peace and security in the region including cooperation in defence. The region enjoys relative stability and peace - both of which are crucial for business – and the prospects for peace in Burundi are encouraging.

Likewise, political stability has been well established in the region. The EAC Partner States have a long and rich cultural, political, social heritage which forms a common bond providing a strong foundation for the integration process. Kiswahili is widely spoken in the region and English is common to educational, judicial and commercial life in all the five Partner States. Most importantly, the sanctity of private property is guaranteed in all the national constitutions of the EAC Partner States. In the offing however, is an effort to develop a comprehensive policy and promulgate an EAC Bill of Rights to guarantee these and other freedoms at the regional level.

A major strength of the EAC region lies in its large pool of human resources, both skilled and trainable and, on the whole, resourceful and competitive. The good performance of some hitherto state-owned enterprises which are managed by local expertise on the stocks and securities exchanges is a reflection of the capabilities of the locals in the management of business. There is also growing confidence in the ability of the labour force at the technical level that has recently led to massive wave of exportation of skilled labour to the neighbouring sub-regions.

Similarly, with regard to infrastructure development as a vehicle for business development and growth, there exists a commitment by the Partner States for undertaking improvements in existing transport systems as well as investing in new infrastructure facilities. Major projects are to be found in civil aviation, energy, roads, railways, ports and telecommunications. A large proportion of national budgets is allocated to infrastructure development. At the Community level, Master Plans are been developed in energy, rail and road sub-sectors to guide the development of these areas in the medium to long-term. In the medium term, it is envisaged that several opportunities will be available for the public-private sector partnership in infrastructure investments in the region.

The benefits of integration have indeed begun to be show across the business landscape. Some of the success stories of foreign companies that have made it serve as an inspiration to others including the experiences of South African Breweries, UNILEVER, British American Tobacco, Coca Cola, Brooke Bond Tea, MTN, CELTEL (now Airtel) and others.

Challenges

I would like now to turn to some of the challenges that EAC faces. Indeed, the challenges of doing business in the East African region are similar to those experienced in most sub-Saharan Africa. They mainly hinge on inadequate physical infrastructure, some governance issues and human resources constraints in some specialized fields. One may also add the cost of transportation of goods, bureaucratic shortcomings and delays in clearing of goods at the ports of entry and exit, significantly raise business costs. However, and this is where the EAC comes in with the various interventions I have outlined above to address the bottlenecks and put in place strategies aimed at reducing red tape in the licensing of business enterprises and other hindrances to the smooth and low cost operations of business in the region.

For instance, the EAC is implementing the World Bank/Africa Development Bank funded Trade and Transport Facilitation Project whose main objective is to establish one-stop border posts and the reduction of transportation bottlenecks in the region. To this extent, the border posts of Malaba (between Kenya and Uganda) have been remodelled to conform to the one-stop border post operation. The border post of Namanga (between Tanzania and Kenya) is in the process of being re-designed to incorporate aspects of the one-stop border post operation which should drastically reduce the time spent at the border points.

Similarly, the high costs of utilities such as telephones, water, and electricity which have raised some concerns to investors in the past and are being addressed. It is gratifying, in this regard, to note that the most recent World Investment and Development Reports and other international interveners have acknowledged the successful efforts being made by the EAC to address this issue. For example, Kenya and Uganda have been recognized as some of the fastest reforming countries in the continent while credit rating for purposes of official borrowing have gone up considerably among the EAC countries. Indeed, Uganda Investment Authority (UIA) and Tanzania Investment Centre (TIC) have been acclaimed as some of the best performing Investment Promotion Agencies (IPAs) in Africa. Further, at a recent regional trade policy review exercise, EAC was acclaimed by WTO as the best illustration of successful regional integration on the continent.[162]

The issue of non-tariff barriers involving the administration of certificates of origin and the valuation of goods is an area of concern as well. This will however, change as we progress into a fully functional Customs Union and the Common Market. All this, however, can be sustained where the effects of external shocks such as the unprecedented rise in oil prices in recent times, which have adversely affected the performance of our economies, pushing up domestic inflation rates to untenable limits remain in check. Uncertainties in the world trading arrangements, like the stalled WTO Doha Round of Trade Talks, and the uncertainties surrounding the EPA

---

[162] See IBRAHIMU, Ngabo Patrick, "Perspectives and Reflections on the WTO: Participation of Developing Countries and its Challenges," Volume 8 No. 1 *The Justice Review*, 2009, p. 27.

negotiations with the European Union, also pose threats to the EAC integration and development efforts. These issues I believe provide justification for holding investors forums such as this one where there are open exchanges of ideas and experiences.

Way Forward

As I have tried to highlight, the EAC is making intensive efforts to improve the conditions necessary for businesses to flourish in the East African region. We have in place a Model Investment Code to align and harmonize the investment codes of the Partner States for mutual benefit. Plans are underway to transform this Code into a Common Investment Area Framework Agreement (CIAA) which will bind the Partner States to a more uniform code of conduct desired by investors.

The EAC Private Sector Development Strategy is also being implemented to enable the private sector reap the full benefits of regional integration. All the challenges which have been identified are being addressed within the context of Sector-based Master Plans of the Community. We are not only encouraging FDI's but also East Africans in the Diaspora to participate by investing directly in the investment opportunities provided by our region. We are focused on the agenda of global development partnership and will intensify our application and contribution in the period ahead.

Conclusion

In conclusion, I would like to state that if one is looking for a region where there is a warm population and beautiful climate, where there are enormous investment opportunities in about all the sectors of the economy, abundant, efficient and affordable human resources, investments are guaranteed, assured huge market access, stable macroeconomic variables, then the EAC is such a place. Indeed, East Africa is fast changing and modernizing. There is a clear and definite commitment to a new direction in the management of the affairs of the region that provides a peaceful and stable environment for productivity, trade and investment, hence a good investor destination.

The adage that charity begins at home had to constitute, at some point, as the central mantra of EAC's integration through investment promotion. After considerable discussions with the National Investment Promotion Agencies of the EAC partner states, a decision was finally taken that the EAC, in collaboration with the EABC, organizes Annual Investment Promotion Conferences to be hosted in the EAC countries on rotation basis. The first of such conferences was held in Kigali, Rwanda in August, 2008, coinciding with the meeting of the Summit of EAC Heads of State. The following chapter celebrates the birth of this Conference.

CHAPTER TWENTY SIX

Promoting EAC as an Investment Area[163]

His Excellency President Mwai Kibaki had an idea of hosting this first investment conference. However, circumstances intervened and the idea was not fertilized. But little did we know that a young and vibrant East African Partner State would later be challenged to take leadership and fertilise the idea. And so, here we are. For the first time in the history of our Community, what until now has been captured in theory in the Treaty establishing our community, namely Article 7(1) (a) that the EAC shall, *inter alia*, be market driven, is being given a shot in the arm.

For coming to this achievement, we should thank the leadership of Rwanda and particularly of its illustrious and visionary leader President Paul Kagame. But equally, we must thank the brilliant and young foot soldiers in President Kagame's government, and especially the dynamic leadership in the Rwanda Investment and Export Promotion Agency (RIEPA) for the excellent planning work that has gone into making this conference possible and successful. RIEPA has effectively partnered the East African Community Secretariat, the other Investment Promotion Agencies in all the Partner States and the East African Business Council in ensuring that this inaugural East African Investment Conference takes off with a bang and proves a good benchmark for future annual conferences which will rotate in the EAC Partner States.

I want to make my statement brief. At the outset, allow me to salute and hail our East African Investors who are so well represented at this Conference. As they say, charity begins at home and we are witnessing it today. So whilst I recognize and appreciate the presence of investors and business firms and executives from outside our region, who are also here and to whom we extend a very warm welcome and appeal to them to invest in our region, I wish to address myself specifically to our own regional investors. Here today we have business firms that are flag bearers in promoting not only East African economic growth but also an East African business identity and image. Without them, our region would not have a track record. Without them, the East African citizens may not understand the underlying vision and mission of our integration. It is these investors who ensure that the East African people touch and feel the fruits of integration because they are the ones, in their various activities that provide goods and services that fuel not

---

[163] Statement at the Opening Ceremony of the First EAC Investment Conference, Kigali, Rwanda, 26th August, 2008.

only our economic growth, the exchequer revenues but also job creation. They are also the investors who respond to social responsibility demands that cut across sectors like education, health, water supply, housing, sectors whose demands are well beyond the resource capacities of our governments.

Allow me to name some of these East African firms that have invested and operate on an East African wide basis, firms that make the difference to our quest for higher economic growth and improvement in the living standards of our people. I will mention them without reference to importance or country of origin: Nakumatt, Gapco, Madhvanis, Kenya Commercial Bank, East African Breweries, Bakhresa, Sumaria Holdings, Sopa Hotels and Lodges, Mukwano Group of Companies, Kenya Airways, Precision Air, Jubilee Insurance, IPP Limited, Heritage Insurance, Sameer Group of Companies, Comcraft or Chandaria Group, East African Cables, Equity Bank, CFC Bank, Kobil, Alam Group of Companies and Bidco. This list is not exhaustive. Let me also mention some of the regional and international investors that are equally participating in growing our economies. They play a fundamental role and we should recognize their presence and contribution at this conference.: Lafarge, Unilever, Celtel, Vodafone, MTN, Stanbic Bank, Barclays Bank, Standard Chartered Bank, Citi Bank, Brooke Bond, AON, Alexander Forbes, Maersk Line, Ilovo, South African Breweries, Coca-cola, Pespi, Reliance Industries of India, TATA of India, Serena Hotels and Lodges, ABSA of South Africa, Guinness Africa, Bata Shoes and Bank of Baroda. Again, the list is not exhaustive.

Let me also use this platform with a call to arms for our regional investors and business players. Yes, we do appreciate their focus on deepening investments in what we normally regard to be the traditional economic sectors in our economy. However, in a global economy where knowledge is increasingly taking the lead and pre-eminence, particularly in so far as competitiveness is concerned, it is difficult to realize effective integration of our economies in the global economy if we do not quickly invest in skills development. By skills development I do not infer university or tertiary education. What I have in mind is technology skills that are central to promoting higher productivity especially in agriculture, agro processing, industry and services.

Regrettably, our higher education system is yet to sufficiently cater for producing these types of skills. Yet it is these skills that leverage the competitiveness of emerging economies such as India, China and the East Asian countries. In order to address this skills deficit, it is imperative that the Partner States invest in Skills Academies particularly those that are technology-education focused. The economic future of our region lies in technology adaptation, and their application in our different productive sectors.

It is my hope that this three day investment Conference will provide the platform for our business leaders and executives to foster closer cooperation and exchange of ideas on how best to boost cross- border business ties, partnerships and investments. Our region offers a huge potential in opening up new economic spaces that can lead to higher economic growth and prosperity of our countries. This potential can be seen through the vibrancy of the Capital Markets in the region. Kenya, for example, has now achieved a stock market capitalization of Kenya Shillings 1 trillion or USD 16 billion. On the other hand, Tanzania and Uganda's stock market capitalizations which are, respectively, slightly about one fifth of Kenya's, are fast growing considering that they are new comers in this field. I believe though that the growth of this capital markets sector will leapfrog when Tanzania liberalizes its capital account.

Such development will give impetus to greater cross- border and green field investments as well as mergers and acquisitions. It is also notable that Rwanda has moved into this stock market field with the launch of the Rwanda Stock Exchange in January this year. There is every hope that this country will soon become a new tiger in the capital markets sector in our region. Burundi, on the other hand, is a challenge to the investment community. It is fast realizing peace and stability, the key pillars for attracting investments including the development of a capital market.

As with most conferences of this type, there is a group of highly dedicated people who have worked tirelessly to ensure that this Conference succeeds. I thank them all for a job well done. But the success of this Conference has also hinged on the huge support the organizers have received from many business firms in our region and abroad. Later today, at the interactive luncheon, special recognition will be made of these firms that have underwritten various costs of this Conference.

Finally, I wish to take this opportunity to thank you, our Heads of States, for being with us here; for gracing this historic occasion and for the wisdom that you will share with us that will inspire us to sustain this path that we have taken to promote our region as a preferred one for investment.

The EAC is well seized of the reality that the realisation of a large African market crucially hinges on the role of business exploiting open borders. How businesses collaborate to realise such an objective depends on how public policy at the level of regional economic communities creates the supporting environment. The emergence of the COMESA-EAC-SADC Tripartite with its core objective of establishing a grand free trade area provides a shot in the arm for such business collaborations. In the next chapter, I examine the potentials that exist for businesses to expand trade across regional blocks.

CHAPTER TWENTY SEVEN

Role of Business in Deepening Integration[164]

Thank you for honouring me and the East African Community as Guest of Honour at this historic Expo. As a former business leader, in Tanzania and in East Africa, I could not hope for anything more apt and transformational than this path breaking event. For too long, the African business sector has, wittingly or otherwise, taken a back seat in promoting expositions of the type mounted here. The common lament that the African private sector is still nascent (some critics even contend that Africa lacks a truly indigenous private sector); that it is inadequately recognised, appreciated and empowered and is thus incapable of taking the lead in organising major trade and industry Expos should be debunked. Of course, African governments and their Trade and Industry Promotion Agencies retain a primary role in galvanizing and catalyzing Expos of different types to promote exports and showcase domestic market capacities and products. Yet time is nigh for the African business sector to begin a process of taking command and forging what is fundamentally a business responsibility.

We in the East African Community have since the last three years been seized of the importance of putting the East African business sector at the heart of promoting intra-regional trade and investments. The Annual Investment Conferences, organized in close collaboration with the East African Business Council epitomise the centrality of making the private sector the principal driver of regional economic development. And the EAC can point at a number of achievements made from this thrust, supported by the enabling environment created by the Customs Union established in January 2005. Suffice to state that there has been a surge in cross-border investments in the EAC region, with Kenya becoming Tanzania's second largest investor.

It is important to recognize and appreciate the role of our regional investors in taking the lead in promoting intra-regional investments. For as Maria Ramos, Chairperson of ABSA Bank has put it, "we forget that in order to attract investment, we have to be investing ourselves. So we need to show the confidence in our own capability, in our own country, in our continent. I think it is important to say that, because sometimes we think FDI alone is going to generate the growth that we need. It isn't. It will add to that growth.

---

[164] Speech at the Opening of the Eastern and Southern Africa Trade and Industry Expo, Diamond Jubilee Hall, Dar es Salaam, Tanzania, 20th September, 2010.

It's going to enhance it ... But as Africans, we need to be confident that we have a great story."

Therefore, allow me at the outset, to salute and commend the Confederation of Tanzania Industries and the East Africa Speakers Bureau for collaborating to organise this first Eastern and Southern Africa Trade and Industrial Expo. I am specifically excited by the fact that the ethos and spirit of this Expo is regional integration cutting across the COMESA, SADC and EAC geographic space. This is an ethos that resonates well with the emerging regional integration paradigm which has seen the decision of the COMESA-EAC and SADC Heads of State to establish a Task Force of Chief Executives of these regional organisations to work out the mechanics of establishing a Grand Free Trade Area and, later, a Customs Union. Indeed, from tomorrow, I am hosting here in Dar es Salaam a crucial five days meeting of this Tripartite Task Force, of which I am Chair. Significant progress has already been made by the Task Force in formulating the framework for the Grand Free Trade Area and the accompanying rules of origin.

The COMESA-EAC-SADC Free Trade Area fits in well with the theme of this Expo: Tapping Business Opportunities in the Expanded Market. This Free Trade Area will create a market of 26 African countries with a population of 527 million people, half Africa's 1 billion population, a GDP of US $ 624 billion and an average GDP per capita of US $ 1,184 per annum. This potential vividly contrasts with EAC's 130 million people with a GDP of US $ 80 billion and an average per capita of US $ 600 per annum. Estimates show that exports among the tripartite countries stood at US $ 27 billion in 2008 whilst imports stood at US $32 billion in the same period. Clearly, the grand free trade area would present new business possibilities for economic players in this broader African region. What is important to note is that the establishment of such large economic space is being conceived hand in glove with addressing some of the fundamental challenges that impede and frustrate the growth of an African internal market.

Fifty years since most African countries gained political independence, Africa continues to largely consume what it does not produce and produce what it does not consume. This is why the share of intra-African trade in total trade remains a paltry 10%. In contrast, the share of intra-ASEAN trade to total trade is 46% whilst that of the European Union is above 60%. Africa thus faces a huge challenge in creating its own internal market.

If Africa is to succeed to create a robust and vibrant internal market, it has to do more than simply create trade-promoting regional integration mechanisms. It must first of all address its low capacity in agriculture. Africa still cannot feed itself on a sustainable basis. Secondly, Africa must add value to its commodities whether agricultural, metal or mineral. Above all,

Africa must connect itself better with reliable infrastructure-roads, railways, air, telecommunications, ICT, maritime (both sea and inland waterways). It must exploit its renewable energy sources (hydro, geothermal, methane, solar and wind) which are plentiful. It is these infrastructures, along with improving trade facilitation, especially at border posts through the introduction of one Stop Border Posts and streamlining customs procedures that the business opportunities in an expanded market can be profitably tapped.

The costs of doing business in Africa and in the Eastern and Southern Africa region are higher largely because of the paucity and weaknesses of these hard and soft infrastructures. The expanded market has to spur competitiveness if it is to be attractive enough to investors and traders. Through the Tripartite Process, COMESA, EAC and SADC are working together through Aid for Trade mechanism and other financing mechanisms to develop several transport corridors in the broad region. Along with IGAD, the Tripartite RECs will hold an Infrastructure Conference in Nairobi from 28th -29th October this year to deepen discussions and planning on the development of four key transport corridors in Eastern and Southern Africa. The EAC has also finalised a model law for the establishment of several One Stop Border Posts within the EAC region.

This Expo is taking place at a time when there is hope in the recovery of African economies following the global financial and economic crisis of the past three years. Indeed, estimates show that Africa has greater promise in the world in moving back into a higher economic growth trajectory, averaging 5.6% in 2011 and much higher for the EAC region which, according to the African Development Bank *Economic Outlook Report of 2010,*[165] experienced the highest growth performance in Africa in 2009.

This good performance has been spurred by macro-economic prudence and the introduction of micro-economic reforms geared at creating a better and supportive business environment. Countries like Tanzania and Kenya could, however, realise even higher growth performances had they seriously addressed shortcomings in their business environments. Both the *World Bank Doing Business Report of 2010*[166] and the recently released World Economic Forum *Global Competitiveness Report 2010-11*[167] paint adverse pictures about Tanzania and Kenya on business environment issues. Improvement in the predictability and consistency of rules and regulations

---

[165] See AFRICAN DEVELOPMENT BANK, *African Economic Outlook 2010*, Tunis: AfDB, 2010.

[166] International Bank for Reconstruction and Development, *Doing Business 2010: Reforming through Difficult Times*, Washington, D.C.: World Bank, 9th September, 2009.

[167] See SCHWAB, Klaus (Ed.), *The Global Competitiveness Report 2010 – 2011*, Geneva: World Economic Forum, 2011.

relating to investments, licenses and labour market are crucial in changing this adverse scenario.

This Expo is also taking place at a time when commodity prices - oil, minerals, metals and food grains are either surging or offer profitable returns. Africa has a particularly huge potential in putting agriculture at the forefront of its economic growth and wealth creation. It controls 60% of the global uncultivated land but only 15% of the arable land is currently in use compared with 60% in Asia. Countries like Tanzania have as much as 44 million hectares of arable land largely lying fallow. With Asia accounting for half of the global population and in much need of food, the global food market will increasingly become buoyant. However, tapping this huge food market opportunity demands both re-thinking commercial farming policy and the application of biological sciences in agricultural production.

Such re-thinking is vital and urgent given the frequent droughts experienced in East Africa, a clear consequence of climate change. For instance, the last three years of serious drought in East Africa, presented a bitter lesson for the EAC region necessitating this re-thinking process to be given serious attention by the EAC Heads of State.

In 2009, over 10 million Kenyans were without adequate food and Kenya had to import grains from abroad, not from the region which had food shortages as well. I am thus in agreement with Oxford Economics Professor Paul Collier when he argues in his article, the *"Politics of Hunger: How Illusion and Greed Fan the Food Crisis,*[168] that "commercial agriculture may be irredeemably unromantic; but if it fills the stomachs of the poor, then it should be encouraged". Tanzania should particularly take heed of such view and allow *"Kilimo Kwanza"* to be a more robust policy which, for the first time since independence, can enable Tanzania achieve a green revolution.[169]

This Expo is equally taking place when the East African Community, which has been described abroad as the most promising regional economic community in Africa, is moving into a higher level of social and economic integration. The on-set of the Common Market from 1st July this year ushers in a new market opportunity that is much broader than what the Customs Union offers through the free movement of goods.

The Common Market is going to scale up the achievements realised from the Customs Union which have been phenomenal by African standards. Total intra-EAC trade (the data is only applicable to Kenya, Uganda and Tanzania) in 2008 increased by 37.6% over the 2007 figure. The value was US $ 2.7

---

[168] See COLLIER, Paul, "The Politics of Hunger: How Illusion and Greed Fan the Food Crisis," op. cit.

[169] On the ten pillars of *Kilimo Kwanza* see
http://www.tzonline.org/pdf/tenpillarsofkilimokwanza.pdf.

billion. Tanzania recorded the highest trade growth rate of more than two folds, from US $ 279.5 million in 2007 to US $ 735.8 million in 2008. This surge is partly explained by the automation of trade data compilation at Tanzania's border points with Uganda and Kenya.

Overall, Kenya continued to dominate the EAC regional trade, accounting for 44.8% of total value of trade in 2008. Uganda and Tanzania accounted for 28.1% and 27.1% of total intra-EAC trade respectively during the same period. It is also notable that Rwanda's total trade with the EAC Partner States grew from US $ 237.8 million in 2007 to US $ 337.6 million in 2008, an increase of 27%. Burundi's trade with the EAC Partner States, on other hand, slightly increased from US $86.6 million in 2007 to US $ 94.0 million in 2008, an increase of 8.7%.

With the onset of the EAC Common Market, new business opportunities are being unleashed in a broad spectrum of services-financial, capital markets, wholesale and retail trade, construction, shipping, transport and logistics, air transport, media, tourism, medical, education, consultancy, accounting and audit, ICT solutions, telecommunications and several others. Of course effective tapping of these business opportunities hinges on a number of legal and regulatory reforms that need to be effected at both the EAC level and at the level of the Partner States. Kenya is leading in this reform process in the region. Working closely with the private sector it has identified several laws and regulations that need to be amended to fit the requirements of the Common Market Protocol. In fact, Kenya's approach is to have all such legal reforms undertaken through a single Miscellaneous Amendment Bill.

Now that Rwanda and Burundi have finalised their electoral processes, they should also be proceeding to determine how best to implement the Common Market Protocol. Tanzania is in the throes of a general election and we can only expect necessary reforms being undertaken from early 2011. The same applies for Uganda whose general election process has started rather early considering that the elections will only take place in February 2011. At the EAC level, on the other hand, the EAC Secretariat is working closely with the Investment Climate Advisory Services of the World Bank Group to generate regulatory capacities of the EAC organs including identifying the reforms that need to be undertaken at the EAC level to assure effective realization of the Common Market Protocol objectives.

The African expanded market is well captured by recent data from the *Africa Investor* Magazine and The Africa Group (TAG). In a report titled "Richer than You Think" published in the *Africa Investor Magazine of July-August 2010,* it is outlined that Africa's market potential in energy, minerals, agriculture, tourism, water, forestry, fisheries and human capital is US $ 16.17 trillion. Excluding energy, oil and minerals, the remaining sectors have a potential of about US $ 1.7 trillion as against the current market size of US

$ 909 billion. Here then lies a huge business opportunity to be tapped. Africa clearly is the most fertile investment area in the world today.

But Africa is also witnessing, Co-Chairs, the emergence of a new phenomenon that augurs well for business opportunities. In 2000, Africa had 50 million households earning more than US $ 5,000 a year. This is the amount which is about the threshold where a person begins to enjoy discretionary spending. In 2008, there were 80 million households – a 60% rise in eight years that earned more than US $ 5,000 a year. In other words, Africa now has about 220 million people emerging as a middle class. Moreover, 40% of Africa's 1 billion people now live in cities and urban towns.

Urbanisation will increasingly be a key driver of economic growth because of higher levels of consumption. Already, the explosive buoyancy of the mobile telephone industry in Africa and especially in the EAC region is clear testament of the growing urban consumption appetite. And with 62% of the African population aged below 24 years, well educated and culturally savvy with diverse modern consumer tastes, business opportunities can only expand in response to this new market. It is critical in this context that businesses appreciate the changed logic of wealth creation. What drives consumption today is centred on the individual end user rather than the old logic of wealth creation that was driven more by organizational-centred interests of efficiency, costs, revenues and returns on investment. Expos like this one should help to provide the testing ground for determining who the customers are, what the needs are and how their needs could be met.

Equally important in tapping business opportunities in an expanded market is the pursuit of a business model that defies the current traditional, nation-based and nation focused model. It is evident that the capacity to take advantage of an expanded market requires that manufacturers and producers move across borders and set up local businesses. Two industries in the EAC region have been path breakers in defying the traditional business model; Azam of Tanzania in food processing and Bidco of Kenya in the oil-seeds processing industry. Both firms have established, not trading, but manufacturing processes in several countries in Eastern and Southern Africa (in the case of Azam) and in the EAC region in the case of Bidco. At the retail trading level, Nakumatt of Kenya has also been a pioneer in defying the traditional business model by establishing retail or supermarket chains in Uganda and Rwanda.

All these companies have also importantly embraced branding as a strategic tool for promoting their products and services. The Azam, Bidco and Nakumatt brands have attained household recognition and acceptance in the EAC region and beyond.

Countries that have succeeded to develop strong internal markets, like the United States, China and India have been able to secure competitive confidence to trade globally. Indeed, Michael Porter's central thesis of competitive advantage of nations is that the achievement of national competitiveness is a key test for venturing into regional and global markets. An Expo like the one staged here by CTI and the East Africa Speakers Bureau offers a unique opportunity for businesses in Eastern and Southern Africa to showcase industrial products that stand the test of regional and global acceptance and competitiveness. It is such Expos that can spur greater intra-African trade, so crucial in leveraging Africa's economic growth.

The inclusion in this Expo of conferences and symposia around the products exhibited, technology, branding and marketing will provide a rare exchange of information and experience that can only bolster improvements in the quality of products and services offered. The regional economic communities, notably EAC, COMESA and SADC support this effort and will wish to be directly involved in the organisation of future Expos. As part of getting such tripartite process engaged in putting business at the centre of dynamising the tripartite envisaged Grand Free Trade Area, the East African Business Council has been approached to lead a process towards the establishment of a COMESA-EAC-SADC Business Council. EABC will be given full support in fulfilling this lofty objective.

We live in interesting times that are rich with unique opportunities for businesses to tap and exploit. Africa offers such a market potential. But it is only African businesses that are dynamic enough to decipher this market and respond to emerging demands that will bring about the much needed growth of Africa's own internal market. It is a challenge to be celebrated. This Expo provides the structure to make the celebration possible.

How EAC business firms prosper depends on the state of the national and regional environments. In recent years this environment has become heavily polluted by counterfeits and pirated goods. These counterfeits have distorted the business level playing field and in many instances have led to some industries either closing down or scaling down their operations and employment. The implications of this business menace are examined in the following chapter.

CHAPTER TWENTY EIGHT

Confronting Counterfeits and Piracy[170]

The East African Community Secretariat is deeply honoured to be associated with this Anti-Illicit Trade Conference, the first of its kind in the EAC region. I wish to express the EAC's gratitude to the Government of Kenya for both hosting this Conference and for playing an important part in its organization. I also wish to commend the East African Business Council for the intellectual capital that has gone into the conceptualization, design and logistics of this Conference. I am proud, Mr. President, to have personally been involved in the establishment of the East African Business Council back in 1997 and to have served as its Chair from 1999 – 2000, my friend Mr. Manu Chandaria having been the founding Chair. Today, the East African Business Council (EABC) has come of age. This Conference and many other programmes and activities promoted and undertaken by the EABC, including the partnership with the EAC Secretariat in the organization of the Annual EAC Investment Conferences and the EAC Media Summits, are indeed credible testaments of how this EAC Voice of Trade, Industry and Services; the Voice of Business, has become an important translation of the EAC being truly private sector driven.

Let me add my voice to thanking you for gracing this historic Conference. On every occasion when I have had the noble privilege to meet you, I have been mesmerised and deeply touched by your steadfast strong passion and resolute commitment to the lofty goals of the East African Community. You never stop, Mr. President, to reminisce of your Makerere University Days and how you and fellow students, like your Tanzanian friend, Cleopa David Msuya, former Prime Minster of Tanzania, became militantly ardent about East African economic integration and political federation. Indeed, Mr. President, you are probably one East African Community President whose National Address in Kenya (maybe elsewhere as well) always captures the centrality of the EAC in Kenya's development. Mr. President, thank you for this important leadership contribution you provide for our region's future.

This Conference on Anti-Illicit Trade is taking place against a historic background. The EAC Common Market came into force on 1st July this year ushering in a new epoch making history in Africa. The EAC is the only Common Market in Africa today; the third in the world after the European Union and that of the Caribbean Economic Community. However, it is

---

[170] Remarks at the Opening Ceremony of the Regional Anti-Illicit Trade Conference, Windsor Golf and Country Club, Nairobi, Kenya, 6th October, 2010.

important to recognize that the Common Market has not emerged from a vacuum. In the past five and a half years, the EAC Customs Union, born on 1st January, 2005, has witnessed a catalyisation of confidence in the East African people and in our business and economic players, as well as in the engraining of a more positive mindset about our collective quest to make regional trade a strategic driver of economic development, job creation and improvement in the lives of the citizens of this region.

Thus intra-EAC trade has, in the past five years, grown by 50%. Intra-EAC investment has equally grown, propelled by growing trade in goods. It is thus no surprise that Kenya has now become Tanzania's second largest investor. This trend will continue because it is the belief in ourselves, as the primary developers of our economies, that matters most when it comes to investments.

With the entry of the Common Market, the pattern of trade in the EAC will inevitably change and dramatically so. Trade in goods will now extend to trade in services, providing a new business potential embracing tourism, ICT, construction, transport, trade logistics, retail trade (or supermarkets of the Nakumatt type), banking, insurance, financial services, professional services, petroleum and energy, media, education, (especially tertiary education), medical etc. Opening up of all these services at a regional economic space will trigger a robust flow of investments, regional and foreign direct ones. Indeed, our region is already a centre of attraction for leading firms – in mobile telephony, railways, petroleum refinery and oil pipelines, ICT, computer software, internet broadband, university education, specialist medical services etc. Yet, we cannot be oblivious of the reality that trade drives investments. Where trade, in goods and services, is undermined, investments stay away. This is the point about this Conference.

Illicit trade and especially trade in counterfeits, substandard goods and piracy of products undermine the viability of manufacturing firms in the EAC region. We have a number of cases where leading industrial firms in East Africa have come close to total closure. How could it be otherwise when it is reported, for example, in *Africa Investor Magazine* of July- August 2010, that the value of counterfeits in Kenya in 2009 was US $ 642 million. Compare it with South Africa where the value was US $ 402 million and Nigeria where it was US $ 219 million. Moreover, the same Magazine reports that the EAC Partner States lost US $ 500 million in annual tax revenues because of counterfeit products.

Our region has a close and strong trade relationship with countries of Asia, especially China and India, for good reasons, not mere romanticism about South-South trade. Yet, most of the counterfeits and sub-standard goods imported into our region originate from Asia. Recently, I read a media piece published in the Qatar Newspaper *The Peninsula*[171] titled "India Becomes a Hub for Fake Medicines". After reporting that the global fake drug industry is worth about US $ 90 billion, it goes on to say that the Indian Government has disclosed that 0.4% of India's drugs are counterfeit and substandard, though independent estimates put the figure at between 12 – 25%. India's annual exports of pharmaceutical products to Africa and Latin America are now worth US $ 8.5 billion. In 2009, Kenya Bureau of Standards impounded containers of Panadol Extra and, when tested, it was all chalk powder.

The EAC Partner States are doing the best they can to arrest the growing menace of illicit trade through counterfeits and substandard goods. At the EAC level, there is a proposed legislation, thanks for the support of the Investment Climate Facility for Africa, represented here by Dr. William Kalema, to counter the menace. But it is a huge problem, of global scale and proportions. If we fail to counter it effectively, we will inevitably spur a process of de-industrialization, loss of investments, jobs will disappear, exchequer tax revenues will falter and innocent lives would be lost due to fake medicines. At this Conference, we will focus on these burning issues and propose measures, national and regional, that can help to arrest what is a highly a grave situation.

In the following chapter, a specific case of an investment area within the EAC is examined in the context of how a regionally shared resource like the Lake Victoria and its basin could be transformed into a huge investment opportunity for the 40 million EAC citizens who live around and depend on their basic livelihoods on the lake and its environs.

---

[171] Issue of Sunday, 12th September, 2010.

CHAPTER TWENTY NINE

Investing in the Lake Victoria Basin[172]

Welcome to the Rock City of Mwanza, Tanzania's second largest city, home to cotton, cattle, lake fish and gold. I am always proud to disclose that I was born here, spent my early years here and on the largest island on Lake Victoria, Ukerewe, where I received my first four years of primary education. Mwanza is home to me and I believe it will also be to many of you now and more in the future.

Our investment Forum is one of a kind and thus one of historic value to the East African Community. For the first time in EAC's history, we have devolved our focus on investment promotion; from a general regional perspective to a specific project level dimension. And what better investment area could we have started with than the Lake Victoria and its basin. This lake is the 2nd largest fresh water lake in the world. Its basin is home to around 38 million people whose sustainable livelihoods are largely dependent on the lake and the soils and soil cover around it. It is this lake which, in many ways, defines why the EAC's mantra and brand is "One People, One Destiny". Indeed, the catchment area of the lake extends deep inwards into Burundi and Rwanda making these two EAC Partner States strategic stakeholders of the lake as well.

Allow me to commend Dr. Tom Okurut and his colleagues at the Lake Victoria Basin Commission Secretariat in Kisumu for fertilizing the idea behind this Forum. Working closely with our National Investment Promotion Agencies and the EAC Secretariat, LVBC today stands tall to see the fruits of shared labour. And today, and the coming two days, we shall together lay the critical foundations for making the Lake Victoria geographical space an area of profitable business opportunity. One can be as nostalgic as you could wish to be about the economic vibrancy of Lake Victoria of yesteryears. The port cities of Kisumu, Port Bell (and Jinja) Mwanza, Bukoba and Musoma, once upon a time in the 1950's, 60's and 70's, used to be major centres of commercial activity in the EAC region. Passenger ships, cargo ships and wagon ferries dominated the means of transport. Road transport was negligible and not much thought about. This efficient marine transport was linked to equally efficient railway systems. But that was once upon a time!

---

[172] Statement made at the official opening of the 1st EAC Lake Victoria Investment Forum, Malaika Hotel, Mwanza, Tanzania, 6th December, 2010.

Overtime, all that could be thought about in the broad Lake Victoria zone is fishing and fish processing, modern and traditional. But times have changed. This lake zone is now rich in gold; it interfaces with some of the world's famous tourist attractions; the Customs Union has moreover catalyzed fertile cross-border trade and movement of people in the area. Mwanza, Kisumu and Entebbe have international airports. There are flights linking these airports and others in the lake circuit. Bujumbura and Kigali are only a stone throw away from the Lake's epicentre. And with 38 million inhabitants, very urbane and comparatively earning higher incomes, consumer appetite for goods and services is equally higher.

I am reaching out to you and other potential investors to take advantage of what this lake zone offers. Just look at this amazing Malaika Hotel where we are meeting at. Look around you: the beauty, splendour and serenity of the environment. It is the same story around the whole lake zone, in Kenya and Uganda. Go to Akagera in Rwanda, same story. In Burundi, there are outstanding sites overlooking Lake Tanganyika, an investment area which the EAC will be promoting next. And if you were to ask me what I have in mind for investment in this lake zone, my list would include:

- Ship and boat building including high quality maintenance thereof;
- Fish farming of prized fish species;
- Passenger boat and luxury liners for tourists who wish to visit numerous islands and islets rich in flora, fauna, bird life and rare monkey species;
- Cargo ships, passenger ferries and wagon ferries;
- Exclusive hotels and lodges on islands and offshore which would form part of a tourist circuit linking Masai Mara, Serengeti, Murchison Falls, Rwenzori, the major tourist Mountain Gorilla areas of Rwanda and the Lake Tanganyika in Burundi;
- Lake water sports and marina;
- Tourist air charters etc.

In addition, and especially for social entrepreneurs of Bill Gates types, there is much to invest on the lake and its basin to ensure the lake's sustainability. It should be appreciated that Lake Victoria is a public good, nationally, regionally and globally. At a time when there is global focus and heightened concern about climate change, there is need to put Lake Victoria at the heart of this global concern. This lake influences the climate of a huge geographical area. If its survival is threatened, the resulting effect would be devastating to millions of people. Thus investing in its sustainability is much more than the conventional commercial profitability attached to it. This role cannot be left to governments alone or to regional institutions such as the EAC and the LVBC. It is important that this Forum gives special attention to this aspect of investment.

Before I end my remarks, allow me to express my deep appreciation to the members of the LVBC Partnership Fund Agreement. These include: Sweden, Norway, the World Bank, the East African Development Bank and the African Development Bank. I wish also to inform this gathering that the Government of Finland has joined the Partnership Consultative Committee with an initial contribution of 3 million Euros. Indeed, most of the initiatives we see today under LVBC have been supported through the Partnership Fund.

For those who are familiar with the Lake Victoria Basin, you may be aware of the Lake Victoria Environmental Conservation project where the World Bank and the Government of Sweden have provided US $ 257.2 million towards addressing environmental concerns in the basin for a period of eight years. I wish also to single out the Lake Victoria Water and Sanitation project II where the African Development Bank has provided a grant of US $ 120million to support three towns in each of our Partner States and within the basin in addressing water and sanitation concerns. The Bank has also made substantial commitments to support the Lake Victoria Maritime Communications and Safety Project.

For purpose of time management, I would not wish to enumerate all the projects that are being coordinated under the Lake Victoria Basin Commission. I believe that the Executive Secretary of the Commission, my friend Dr. Tom Okurut, will go into greater details during his scheduled presentation to this Forum. Suffice for me at this moment to acknowledge the support from the Government of the United States of America extended to the EAC/WWF Mara River Basin project and on trade matters as we work towards a strong and vibrant EAC Common Market.

Please join me in thanking Dr. Tom Okurut for providing the leadership that has contributed immensely to the people in the basin and to the EAC. As his immediate supervisor for the last five years, I can state with much confidence that he scored highly in providing the required leadership in all aspects including resources mobilization to support the commission's activities. As his term at LVBC comes to an end early next year, Dr. Okurut leaves behind a strong institution which he single handled started in 2001 at the EAC Secretariat. From that humble beginning, it is gratifying to note that the LVBC currently has a workforce of about 48 staff and a budget portfolio of US $ 13 million contributed by Development Partners and US $ 2 million contribution from the EAC Partner States.

Once again, I extend a very warm welcome to you all. I have every confidence that this conference will result into profitable and worthwhile investments that will create wealth, jobs and sustainable life of this beautiful lake.

PART 8

Role of Media and Civil Society

In the same way as Karl Marx recognized that popular power and the collective will required a commonality of perspective to be effectively mobilized, the regional integration process requires a similarly shared perspective. Information and Communication are the vehicles by which we arrive at that point; that point where our collective consciousness, despite the isolation of individuality, recognizes the common cause, and rises to a single, larger, unifying purpose. As caretakers of information and communication, the regional media is at the centre of this process. They share the responsibility of educating the people of this region about the commonality of our circumstances, the similarities that bind rather than divide us, and the common solutions we might apply to our own development.

Dr. Kenny D. Anthony[173]

In the ensuing part of the book, I turn into a critical review of the role of the media in the EAC integration agenda. Evidently, the role of the private sector is closely intertwined with that of the media. Both sectors have close affinity with the interests of the people. Business caters for wealth and jobs whilst the media ensures that the people are not only well informed about what the private sector is doing in an era where the market is on the ascendancy, but also instils into them their rights and responsibilities in determining the direction of development that impacts them.

Evidently, objectivity becomes a central issue, if not a concern, when it comes to the role of the media. Having put that caveat, the role of the media as gate keeper and as the fourth estate in society, whether national or regional, in the case of this contribution, stands out as one of the most

---

[173] Address to the AGM of the Caribbean Broadcasting Union, 27th August, 2003.

important preoccupations of the EAC. Indeed, the Treaty establishing the EAC clearly spells out that the EAC shall be "people-centred". However, how the EAC as an institution is able to reach out to the citizens of East Africa and make them appreciate that they are the principal shareholders of the integration project and must therefore expect tangible benefits to accrue to them has been one of the key challenges for the regional organization. In working out a structured cooperation with the East African media, the EAC has somewhat succeeded to advance a people-centredness culture in the East African media. Clearly, much more needs to be done. However, as reflected in the following chapters, it can be seen that attempts have been made to realize this objective.

CHAPTER THIRTY

The Media in Regional Integration[174]

First of all, let me thank you, dear colleagues, for setting aside other pressing demands on your time in order to attend this first East Africa Media Summit. As you are aware, the Summit is jointly organized by the East African Community and the East African Business Council. This collaborative undertaking reflects our recognition of the key and central role of the Media and the business community in the regional integration and development process.

At the outset I wish to hail and commend the EABC for the visionary partnership it has shown in contributing to the realization of this Media Summit that has brought together the top leadership and cadre of the region's information industry. EABC's insight and commitment to making the EAC truly market driven is well recognized and appreciated by us in the EAC. A partnership based on mutual trust and confidence between us is taking root. Our shared quest for making the private sector the central driver of deeper integration must be reinforced. It is for this reason that the EAC is searching for juridical ways of making the EABC an institution of the EAC pursuant to the EAC Treaty.

We meet at an interesting moment when the Media in East Africa is slowly but steadfastly taking an East African shape and form. This imagined identity is inevitable as economic players in our region respond to the logic of the market. Recent trends in media consolidation in the Partner States marked by mergers and acquisitions are clear pointers to the transformation of the Media into a powerful tool for deepening democracy, good governance as well as for bolstering development for the common good.

The East African media identity today has been charted out by several players. Indeed, I should salute all our media owners and the journalists in general for the role they are playing in promoting this identity. Our national newspapers and magazines have taken wings and now ply the pavements of our towns and cities. However, two players stand out. First the Kenya Nation Group whose media ownership now extends to Uganda and Tanzania.

The birth of the Nation Group's weekly newspaper, "The East African" has had a phenomenal impact in ingraining the ethos and spirit of East African-

---

[174] Keynote Address to the Media at the East Africa Media Summit, Grand Regency Hotel, Nairobi, Kenya, on 27th April, 2007.

ness. Second, Tanzania's IPP Group which, through its East Africa TV and East Africa FM Radio, have transformed trans-boundary terrestrial broadcasting. The impact of East Africa TV in promoting East Africa's own unique music, a major cultural coup, is of particular significance. Gone are the days when East Africans wholly embraced Congolese music as their own. Today, the youth of East Africa proudly share home-grown music, from *Bongo Flava* in Tanzania, *to Luga Flow* in Uganda and *Hip-Hop* in Kenya. Even *Taarab* music has found a hip-hop innovation in *"Taarap"*! The cultural spirit of East Africa is truly coming alive.

I also believe that this Summit is meeting at an interesting moment in another perspective. Around the world, the quest for integration at corporate and nation-state levels, is deepening. Globalization has debunked the mantra that small is beautiful. Size now matters. The logic of corporate consolidations that I referred to earlier in the context of the East African Media is now the survival kit globally. The same applies to countries. I know that I speak to the converted here and will not therefore belabour this point about the imperativeness for us in East Africa to deepen integration and ensure that the East African project succeeds. Yet it is clear or should be clear that this project can only make meaning if it is connected to the real lives of ordinary East African citizens, to their aspirations and to the future of East African children.

In this context, it is important to be clear that the EAC project is not an ideology, an idea that is dogmatic or puritanical. Rather, the EAC project is founded on a philosophy which the founding fathers of our independence movement enunciated. That philosophy is well encapsulated in the Treaty establishing the EAC. It is a philosophy that visions a collective direction for East Africa; but it is a direction that is not dogmatic. Rather this is a philosophy that is constantly subject to interpretation, dialogue and debate. After all, there are always contentious issues on any form of integration. Experience drawn from the European Union clearly shows that even after 50 years of integration differences of opinion remain over issues such as the Monetary Union, the rigid application of the fiscal and stability pact, the Services Directive and subsidies extended under the Common Agricultural Policy.

The point I am making is that while size matters, it is always critical that the integration process is legitimized. Such legitimization requires the constant involvement and consensus of citizens. This is the supranational democratic imperative. It is illusionary to behave and, worst, to believe that it is the political leadership or the political class that drives the agenda and strategic direction of any integration. The EU learnt a bitter lesson, in this context, when its Draft Constitutional Treaty was rejected in a Referendum in France and the Netherlands in 2005.

The disconnect between the political establishment and the citizens was all too clear in that Constitution debacle.

But here lies the rub. How does one ensure the legitimization of an integration process? How do ordinary citizens get involved and engaged in a continuous conversation, debate and dialogue over the policies and strategies of an institution like the East African Community? Liberal democracy would point out, in this case, that the elected organs of the State perform the role of representative-ness. In other words our Parliamentarians, national and supranational as well as civic leaders in Local Authorities thus represent the citizens.

In the EU, there was a vigorous debate whether the Draft Constitutional Treaty could simply be tabled before National Assemblies for decision. However, the public view and response, in contrast, was vigorously for referenda to be applied. Imagine, in our immediate context what the response would be where the issue about fast tracking East African Political Federation reserved for decision by our Parliaments?

The question thus remains: how to legitimize the integration process. Clearly, there is a democratic deficit within the EAC today in the sense of the lack of an effective public sphere for enabling citizens to offer their views and opinions on the EAC project. On its part, the EAC has structural limitations for promoting a social dialogue and connect with East African citizens. There are efforts underway to create a robust civil society forum under the EAC framework which would provide a platform for the social dialogue to take place. However, you will appreciate that such a forum would operate more or less like a meeting and would not provide the kind of continuous consultative process that needs to be promoted to assure a functional democratic environment.

Thus the EAC needs a platform that is more robust in reaching out, sensitizing and galvanizing East Africans around the policies and strategies it formulates and implements. Importantly, such a medium has to operate as a feedback loop that enables the EAC to constantly hear and consider what the people say. In my view, such platform and medium can only be provided by the Media.

The Media represents a public sphere for our citizens to express their opinion and to be listened to. It plays several roles: It is a medium in the sense of being a provider of information; it is a mediator because it promotes discourses, deliberations and activism; and it is a political actor through the features its professionals write. To this extent the Media can and is able to influence the social interaction of our citizens by promoting the East African Agenda. Such role when undertaken with passion would help to create societal integration, shared values and also address the critical factors that underpin successful integration. It follows therefore that our Media should at all times be well informed about EAC's policies, strategies, programmes and projects. In turn, the quality of EAC's own relationship with the Media would determine the quality and quantity of reporting and critique. This relationship evidently needs much improvement and the EAC is cognizant of the need to revamp its media strategy, a project we are now poised to undertake with the soon to be launched EAC Re-Branding Project.

I realize though that the Media today, as opposed to a few decades earlier, and this comparison may not wholly be objective given the dominant state ownership of the Media in the 70s and the 80s, is run more by business bottom line than by a societal utilitarian philosophy. The burning question is whether our Media has become so dominantly commercialized as to belittle issues of societal importance such as regional integration which may not sell well with the readers. Specifically and in the EAC's perspective, it is notable, with the probable exception of The East African Newspaper that our Media is largely nationally oriented. Its responsibility is more towards national society and little on the East African supranational society. Could it be that I am begging the issue? Is the supranational delinked from the national? No; what is at issue is basically what the Media competes on.

The competition today is largely on national content. The East African content, whilst driven by national attitudes and perceptions, is not a battleground. Yet, and if I may revert to my earlier theme, I believe that size matters. Our national futures in East Africa hinge largely on the success of the EAC project. Numerous examples can be adduced to show how some of the European countries which were backwaters in terms of development have become vibrant and prosperous economies upon their becoming Members of the European Community. Why therefore can't our Media sell this reality, the reality that size matters, more powerfully? Where lies the problem?

Where lies the problem, in my view, is the challenge before this Summit. It is my earnest hope that this Summit that brings together Media owners, Executives, professionals, business players, policy makers and EAC Executives will open new spaces for a candid and powerful conversation as well as a frank exchange of views and opinions on how best the East African Media can rise to the challenge of arresting the existing democratic challenges through the promotion of a more robust citizen participation in EAC's affairs. I hope that this historic event will mark a new watershed for a strong coalition between the EAC and the East African Media for our collective quest to bridge the gap between the vision of a prosperous, competitive, secure and politically united East Africa and its concrete realization.

In conclusion, I would like to reiterate EAC's great appreciation for the important role of the media in the regional integration process. We look forward to the successful outcome of the Summit and to working closely with you on the implementation of the proposals that have a bearing on our common objectives. With these remarks, I thank you all for your attention, and wish this Media Summit great success.

Evidently, the main drivers of the media revolution in the EAC region are the private sector media institutions. Yet, in a region that is going through a huge democratisation transition, the role of public or state owned media is crucial. The people need a balance between the force of the market and those of the state in order to make well informed choices about the preferable direction of their societies. In the next chapter, the role of public broadcasters is outlined in the context of the foregoing quest for balance.

CHAPTER THIRTY ONE

Public Broadcasters and Regional Integration[175]

Let me start by thanking you for the honour you have accorded me and, for that matter, the East African Community, to officiate at this Closing Ceremony of your important Conference on the Role of the Public Broadcast Media in the EAC Integration Process. It is indeed commendable that your Conference has brought together some of the top professionals in the Public Broadcast Media of our region, among them Top Management and other leading Media practitioners in the field.

For this achievement, I would like to pay tribute to the organizers of the Conference, Sponsors, participants and resource persons, who have, in one way or another, contributed towards making the Conference the success it has been. We, in the East African Community, have been encouraged by your recognition of the need for collaborative approach to Media development within the regional framework. This will go a long way to promote the objectives of the East African Community of regional integration and accelerated economic development.

I have been informed that the papers presented in your Conference have been of a high quality and the discussions that have ensued have been frank and constructive. This is, no doubt, as a result of the long experience of some of you who have been in the Broadcast Media for a long period, some scanning over several decades. In the circumstances, your views cannot but be given the most serious attention by those who are in a position to contribute, in any way, towards strengthening of the role of the Broadcast Media in this region.

In making this observation, I have taken into account the emerging trends which are increasingly impacting the Media of our region as, indeed, the rest of the world. One of these trends relates to the changing patterns of ownership and, therefore, control and content of the Media. Enlargements and mergers of Media institutions across the borders are slowly but steadily creating regional audiences and media propensity towards projecting and promoting regional issues and agenda. The other trend relates to the increasing technological sophistication and, therefore, flexibility, efficiency and effectiveness of the Media in packaging and transmitting information to wider (regional) audiences.

---

[175] Remarks during the closing of the First East African Public Broadcasters Conference, Kibo Palace Hotel, Arusha, Tanzania, 22nd May, 2007.

Indeed, technological innovation, emphasizing, in the case of Broadcast Media, installation of FM stations, worldwide/region-wide instantaneous satellite television network, and the advent of digital radio transmission are leading to more and more user expectations and satisfaction. These are developments/benefits which we would all like to tune into, and indeed the broadcast media can become a major force for socialization of East Africans along the common identity and forging a common destiny that the EAC is working for.

As you are aware, the East African Community exists with the primary objective to realize the socio-economic transformation of the East African region. In order to achieve this objective, it is imperative that the general East African citizenry is involved and fully participates in the process of regional integration and development. Indeed, as stipulated in the Treaty for the Establishment of the East African Community, the emphasis is on a people-centred regional integration.

Unless the people are responsive to the policies and programmes being formulated by the governments of the EAC Partner States, within the framework of EAC integration, and unless the governments themselves are responsive to the people's views and needs in relation to the integration process, the EAC mission would be virtually a mission impossible.

The challenge, therefore, for the Broadcast Media, for the other Media as well, at this critical juncture in the evolution of the East African Community, when the regional integration process is intensifying, widening and deepening, is to get the debate and discourse going on about the issues of regional integration and, indeed, to lead the crusade for strengthening the spirit of East African unity.

I would like, therefore, to take this opportunity to make a special appeal to the East African Media, and in particular, the broadcast Media, to embrace the support to the East African Community as their patriotic duty. The broadcast Media, which have the widest reach of all the Media of our region, should act as a creative source of inspiration and unity for the people of our region in the process of shaping their common destiny and brighter future.

There is another role for you in strengthening the friendly and fraternal ties that have bound together the people of our region in cultural, trade and other interactions and exchange from time immemorial. There is a need for you to project to the regional and world audience the role which the East African Community is playing in deepening integration and accelerating economic growth and development. The EAC Secretariat extends its readiness to work hand in hand with you for the realization of this objective.

In this regard, I should inform you that we have launched the EAC Re-Branding Project that will involve the implementation of a robust EAC

Marketing and Publicity Strategy through a revamped new EAC Directorate of Corporate Communications and Public Affairs established at the EAC Headquarters. Among the features of the EAC Re-Branding Project is the planned installation at the EAC Headquarters of modern facilities for Radio and TV production that will link with your stations in spreading the EAC message. On the whole, we would make available to you information, on a continuous basis on the events and developments of interest to regional integration and facilitate your coverage of the EAC activities.

Having said this, I should like to state, once again, our appreciation and support to the Broadcast Media of our region. We look forward to receiving the final Report of your Conference and to working closely with you in the collaborative effort to promote East African unity and development.

PART 9

Education in Regional Integration

In the Hybrid Age, what distinguishes societies from one another is not just their geography, their culture, their income level, or other traditional factors, but their capacity to adapt to exponentially changing technological circumstances. We don't live in different places so much as we live in different stages of Technik.

Ayesh and Parag Khanna[176]

Part nine of the book examines the role of education both in bolstering regional integration and in making the EAC a competitive region. As in the European Union, where the Bologna Process has been a defining policy dimension in promoting an education system that is not only harmonized but which also supports the whole endeavour of free movement of labour, so has the EAC seen the importance of leveraging the quality of its overall education system on a regional basis. There is little doubt that the quality of the region's workforce is the crucial determinant of the prosperity of EAC's member states. But there is a worrying crisis in the overall quality of education. A number of efforts are underway, led by the Inter-University Council of East Africa, to harmonise the education systems in the region and put in place a quality assurance system that enables qualifications to be evaluated objectively and thus allow a system of mutual recognition of such qualifications also to be objectively undertaken. Some countries like Kenya have already realized that they need to move fast to overhaul their total education systems in response to a fast emerging world driven by a knowledge economy where skills and talent have become the main factors of competitiveness. Talent and vocational schools that aim at providing life-long learning are being proposed.[177]

---

[176] "Technology Will Take on a Life of its Own," *Foreign Policy Special Report*, 15th August, 2011.

[177] *Daily Nation* (Nairobi), 2nd February, 2012, pp. 4-6.

255

The following three chapters discuss the importance of harmonizing the regional education systems and improving the quality of education and training. Developing partnerships with the developed world research institutions is presented as one way in which EAC institutions of higher learning can leapfrog into twenty first century education standards of excellence.

CHAPTER THIRTY TWO

Mission of the University in the EAC[178]

This is a historic meeting for me as Secretary General of the East African Community. I am attending the meeting of the Executive Committee of the Inter-University Council for East Africa (IUCEA) for the first time since taking up my appointment as Secretary General in April 2006. However, my absence all this time, even though I have been represented in most of your meetings, should not be interpreted in any negative light. As some of you know, throughout my private life I have been very close to the vision and mission of the University in East Africa and particularly so of the University of Dar es Salaam. For a record 15 years between 1988 and 2003, I was President of the University of Dar es Salaam Convocation and also served as an elected Vice Chair of that University's Governing Council for 12 years between 1990 and 2002. You can thus rest assured that my passion and commitment about the University and its role in our region is deep and sacrosanct. I will therefore try the best I can to attend many future meetings.

The mission of our universities in the East African region is now increasingly challenged by the enlargement of our community as our borders continue to open up thereby enabling a huge movement of our students. In this context, issues about standardization of university fees as well as harmonisation of curricula are becoming urgent. More importantly, our universities and institutions of higher learning are challenged to produce graduates who are East Africans as opposed to being nationals of the different Partner States within the East African Community. We should take the cue in this context, from the birth and growth of the European University with campuses throughout Europe and with a focus on a curriculum that is pan European.

The mission of our universities is equally challenged by the onset of a new liberal economic model wherein the market rather than social justice takes command. The days of public enterprise management and control are becoming history. And as the East African Community begins the process of becoming a Common Market, other challenges are emerging with the advent of free movement of people, labour, goods, services, capital and technology. Increasingly, our region shall witness the growth in domestic and foreign investments particularly in the knowledge sector notably in banking, insurance, ICT, financial services and the broad area of hospitality

---

[178] Address to the Inter-University Council for East Africa, Executive Council meeting, Kigali, Rwanda, 23rd June, 2008.

embracing tourism, hotels and lodges, medical services and education. These emerging economic sectors will necessarily require our universities and institutions of learning to readjust as well as to retool themselves if they are to adequately match the educational requirements that fit the new environment.

But it is not a mere question of responding to the development of new skills needed for these knowledge based economic sectors. The greater burden that we face at our universities is how to attune the educational programme to develop new mindsets that are capable to provide the requisite leadership in the changed environment.

It is also important to recognize that our public institutions, the public services as well as the regulatory institutions that have emerged as a result of a new liberalized market economy, will equally been challenged to respond to this new environment which calls or demands a fair rule of law, transparency, democratic pluralism, good governance and above all social justice. A public service management system that responds to these new demands following the demise of socialism and of the one party state is yet to be deeply embedded in the curricula of our universities and institutions of higher learning. Indeed, our region lacks effective institutions that specifically cater for public service management training. Yes, we do have a plethora of business schools around but their curricula do not adequately cater for institutions that are not of a typical business character. Hitherto, specialized institutes that had been created specifically for providing public service management programmes, for example, the former Institute of Development Management (IDM) Mzumbe in Tanzania, have now become fully fledged universities and therein have lost their erstwhile focus on training public service officials at the highest level.

In contrast, in the developed world, you see within universities specialized institutes, colleges and schools that cater for the specific need to cater for public service management. One can cite the example of the John F. Kennedy School of Government at Harvard University. Similarly, many of these developed countries have used institutions of higher learning to provide omnibus and capsule human resources development programmes that respond to new demands for improving the performance of public service institutions. Many of these programmes are within the continuous education centres where there is great flexibility in impacting knowledge particularly in terms of evening training facilities.

The rapid expansion of the private university in our region is a welcome positive development. Many private universities have been constituted particularly in the last decade. However, it is an expansion that poses serious challenges on quality, in both teaching and research, key attributes of a good university. It is feared that an academic qualification deficit within the university teaching cadre is visible. What with many of academic deans not possessing doctorate degrees! It is clear that if we are not careful, we many end up having universities as symbols rather than as centres of excellence with a low calibre product being unleashed.

Herein lies a critical role for the IUCEA to play particularly at this stage when we are going to experience significant movement of skills across the borders of our region. Issues of how applicant universities get accreditation as well as the mutual recognition of degrees and other qualifications like diplomas will have to be closely monitored and determined. I know that the IUCEA is already seized of the deficits that exist in these areas and you are on the road to promoting a quality assurance scheme that will go a long way in ensuring that we do not end up with a poor calibre of young people coming out of our universities, notably from private universities.

I realize that there is a global debate today about the marketisation or commercialization of university education. Indeed, there is growing literature on this subject in the United States as well as in the United Kingdom. In the US, the former President of Harvard University Derek Bok wrote in 2003 a pioneering book titled *Universities in the Marketplace: The Commercialization of Higher Education*.[179] This book unleashed a tirade of criticisms about how higher education is increasingly geared at satisfying the needs of business and jobs as opposed to focusing on the learning dimension. In the EAC region there have been similar criticisms about the commoditization of education with students largely becoming the consumers of such commodity. Prof. Issa Shivji[180] at the University of Dar es Salaam and Makerere University Prof. Mahmood Mamdani[181] and several others have written on how the University of Dar es Salaam and Makerere have become victims of such commoditification of higher education not only in these two institutions of higher learning in East Africa but also elsewhere in the African continent.[182]

---

[179] BOK, Derek, *Universities in the Marketplace: The Commercialization of Higher Education*, Princeton, New Jersey: Princeton University Press, 2003.

[180] On Shivji see NYAMNJOH, Francis B., "Intellectual and Social Responsibility in Scholarship: Lessons from Professor Issa Shivji," Issue 343 *Pambazuka News*, February, 2008.

[181] See MAMDANI, Mahmood, *Scholars in the Marketplace: The Dilemmas of Neo-Liberal Reform at Makerere University*, African Books Collective, Oxford, 2007.

[182] On this theme see also BENNEH, George *et al* (eds.), *African Universities, the Private Sector and Civil Society: Forging Partnerships for Development*, Accra: Ghana Universities Press, 2004; KASOZI, A.B.K., *University Education in Uganda: Challenges and Opportunities for Reform*, Kampala: Fountain Publishers, 2003; and AJAYI, J.F. Ade *et al*, *The African Experience with Higher Education*, Accra: The Association of African Universities, 1996; MBWETTE, T.S.A. and A.G.M. Ishumi (eds.), *Managing University Crises*, Dar es Salaam: Dar es Salaam University Press, 2000; LUHANGA, Matthew L. *et al*, *Higher Education Reforms in Africa: The University of Dar es Salaam Experience*, Dar

Whatever your views may be about this debate and these criticisms, we cannot be oblivious of the centrality of the role of the university as a centre of learning as opposed to being reduced to becoming a business organization.

I think I have made a contribution to what I regard to be an important role of the Inter-University Council for East Africa at this critical juncture in the evolution of the East African Community. I have tried to outline some of the challenges that face our universities and institutions of higher learning and I have every confidence and trust in the Inter- University Council for East Africa doing what is in its capacity to ensure that our region is able to promote institutions of learning that we can be proud of and which, through its products, can contribute to the kind of development our countries and our region expect.

es Salaam: Dar es Salaam University Press, 2003; LUHANGA, Matthew L. *et al*, *Strategic Planning and Higher Education Management in Africa: The University of Dar es Salaam Experience*, Dar es Salaam: Dar es Salaam University Press, 2003; MWAMILA, Burton L.M. *et al* (ed.), *Financing of Higher Education in Eastern and Southern Africa: Diversifying Revenue and Expanding Accessibility*, Buffalo and Dar es Salaam: State University of New York and University of Dar es Salaam, 2002; MUGERWA, David, *Political Penetration and Primordial Attachment at Makerere University: A Study of Organisational Effectiveness*, Kampala: MK Publishers (U) Ltd, 2002; MKUDE, Daniel *et al* (eds.), *Higher Education in Tanzania: A Case Study*, Oxford and Dar es Salaam: James Currey and Mkuki na Nyota, 2003. Also relevant is KIMAMBO, Isaria N. et al (eds.), *In Search of Relevance: A History of the University of Dar es Salaam*, Dar es Salaam: Dar es Salaam University Press, 2008.

CHAPTER THIRTY THREE

Harmonising Higher Education for Regional Integration[183]

We meet exactly two weeks since the commemoration of Mwalimu Julius Kambarage Nyerere's 10th death anniversary which took place on 14th October. Coincidentally, the East African Community is celebrating 10 years since the signing of the Treaty that established it. These two commemorations have an interesting connection particularly in the context of this Symposium held with the main theme: *Strategic Development and Management of Higher Education for Socio- Economic Development of the East African Region.* For there cannot be a proper examination of the development of higher education and especially of University Education in the East African Community Region which fails to make reference to the role of Mwalimu Nyerere.

Nyerere and East African Consciousness

Mwalimu was the first Chancellor of the University of East Africa. In that capacity, he presided over the inauguration ceremony of the University of East Africa in Nairobi on 28th June, 1963. It was at that historic ceremony that Mwalimu Nyerere spoke of the imperative for the University of East Africa to develop an "East African consciousness" and to be an active participant in what he referred to as the "social revolution" which the then East African States of Uganda, Kenya and Tanzania were engineering.[184] There is little doubt that the highest attribute of the University of East Africa was indeed the achievement of an East African consciousness. Many of the products of that University remain strong advocates of the East African Federation.

But what is of particular interest about Nyerere's speech of 1963 is its focus on the role of the University in its generic sense and not necessarily in specific reference to the University of East Africa. Nyerere underscored that role as being centred on the pursuit of what he termed "that elusive thing", the truth. Over time, Nyerere may appear to have veered from this central ethos about the University role given the dominance of his thrust that "a University – any University has to be relevant to the society within which it exists, it must relate its thinking and its teaching to the needs, the aspirations,

---

[183] Paper presented at the Inter-University Council for East Africa 10th EAC Anniversary Universities Symposium, New Africa Hotel, Dar es Salaam, Tanzania, 28th October, 2009.

[184] See NYERERE, Julius K., "Inauguration of the University of East Africa," in NYERERE, Julius K., *Freedom and Unity*, 1966, op. cit. at p. 218.

and the problems of that society." This is the thrust that came out powerfully in the last speech Nyerere made at any university before he died. In his address titled "The Link between the Economy, the Society and the University," delivered during the 25th Anniversary of the University of Dar es Salaam on 1st July, 1995 Nyerere underscored the dominant ethos of the University in a developing society.[185]

However, it would be simplistic to think, in the context of this emphasis on the importance of the University to society, that Nyerere departed from his earlier thinking about the core role of the University being the search or the pursuit of truth. Indeed, in the same speech of July 1995, Nyerere postulated that a university could only fulfil its societal role "if it is the hub of, and stimulus for, the kind of scientific thinking which is a necessary preliminary to constructive action." And in that context, he makes reference to the students and staff of the University having "untrammelled freedom to think and to exchange thoughts even if the thinking leads to some of its members to become unorthodox in their conclusions." And whilst orthodoxies change in the light of expansion of knowledge, Nyerere noted that "the understanding of truth develops."[186]

Harmonisation of Education: Historical Perspective

It is important to examine Mwalimu Nyerere's views about the role of the University and thus of higher education as we proceed to a discussion on harmonization of higher education for socio-economic development. This is so because Article No. 102 of the Treaty establishing the East African Community calls for the East African Community Partner States to harmonize curricula, examination, certification and accreditation of education and training institutions amongst other areas of cooperation in the field of education and training. This Treaty provision could be more informed by the historical realities that partly ruled in our region during the Community that collapsed in 1977 during the prior cooperation framework under the East African Common Services Organization. Our region not only had a University of East Africa since 1963, but also had an East African Examinations Council which was responsible for issuing Certificates of Education for Form IV and Form VI leavers. In other words, our secondary schools had common curricula.

The University of East Africa, on the other hand, was structured in such manner that there was no exchange of students as such from the then three East African countries including during the period before establishment of the first East African Community in 1967. There were three Constituent

---

[185] On this speech see NYERERE, Julius K., "The Link between the Economy, Society and the University," Volume 3 Nos. 5-7 *Change Magazine*, 1995, pp. 46-51 at pp. 49 and 50.
[186] Ibid.

Colleges of the University of East Africa with a division of academic labour or specialization faculties. A student who wanted to study law had to go to Dar es Salaam University College; you went to Makerere if you wanted to study medicine, to University of Nairobi if you sought to pursue engineering and so on and so forth.

Moreover, students attending the University of East Africa enjoyed a choice to which University College they wanted to go to pursue general degrees, for example, a degree in Political Science. Thus a student named Yoweri Museveni chose to study political science at the University of Dar es Salaam largely because of its radicalism fame due to the presence of Marxist academics such as Walter Rodney[187] in contrast to a liberal political scientist like Ali Mazrui who was at Makerere.[188] Such contrast of the constituent colleges speaks volumes about the nature of the University of East Africa.

Challenging the thrust of Harmonisation

In the field of general degrees especially in Arts or Humanities the curricula was not harmonized. It was significantly influenced by the teaching faculty. Indeed, even the curriculum of the Faculty of Law at Dar es Salaam was not comparable to the curricula of many other African University Law schools. This situation rules even today, when you examine the curricula, for example of political science and law at the University of Dar es Salaam *vis-a-vis* that at Makerere and Nairobi. The pursuit of truth in these various fields of intellectual discourse is different because it is informed by varying ideological perspectives even when all the East African Community polities are now deemed to enjoy a great deal of convergence in social and economic policies. This is because non-conformism to obtaining national ideological social and economic philosophies by academia is not necessarily of a regional character. It thus begs a fundamental thesis of academic freedom to think of harmonization of curricula. In fact, in his 1995 Address, Nyerere noted that:

> an understanding of the 'market' and indeed usefulness in the 'market'' may well be aspects of relevance in the determination of University courses or teaching; but I fail to see how the prime purpose of making a profit is consistent with the

---

[187] It is while at the University of Dar es Salaam that Walter Rodney wrote his classic book *How Europe Underdeveloped Africa,* Dar es Salaam: Tanzania Publishing House, 1971.

[188] Professor Mazrui proceeded to hold prominent academic positions at various Universities across the globe. Among others, he an Albert Schweitzer Professor in the Humanities and the Director of the Institute of Global Cultural Studies at Binghamton University in Binghamton, New York and is also the Chancellor of one of the local Universities in Kenya – the Jomo Kenyatta University of Agriculture and Technology, Nairobi, Kenya.

academic freedom and excellence which is an intrinsic part of being a University.

In the light of the foregoing analysis, it is important that we are clear about the type of harmonization of higher education we have in mind and whether such harmonization has any impact on socio- economic development. But first of all, let us examine the context of this harmonization idea. It is quite clear that the idea has been inspired by the development of regionalism around the world specifically by the so-called *Bologna Process* born at Bologna, Italy in 1999 when twenty nine European countries signed a joint declaration to move towards increasing the compatibility and comparability of European Higher Education systems. Now integrated within the European Union Framework with over forty European countries signatories of the Bologna Process, its principal aim is to establish a European Higher Education Area by 2010. Key elements of the system are recognition of course structures, mutual recognition of degrees and providing the mobility of academic faculty and students. The driving force of harmonization of higher education is principally the quest for quality and excellence in research and academic programmes in the light of globalization.

Higher education institutions are viewed as critical factors in the realization of national economic competitiveness and thus of integration of national economies in the global economy. This concept has now being embraced by UNESCO which, in 2005, launched the Global Forum on International Quality Assurance, Accreditation and Recognition of Qualifications. The African Union has also adopted the idea in its Second Decade of Education for Africa Programme. The key mechanism for Africa's operationalization of the harmonization strategy is the Arusha Convention, a UNESCO initiative for promoting Africa Cooperation of mobility of lecturers and students.

Harmonisation of Education in the EAC

At the level of the East African Community, there are efforts in a similar direction as well. The Inter-University Council for East Africa is now properly constituted by a special law passed by the East African Legislative Assembly in 2008. Under the Act, the Council is mandated to spearhead the harmonization of higher education amongst the member Universities with collaboration of National Regulatory Agencies dealing with Higher Education. Focus of this harmonization is the promotion of comparability of qualifications, setting standards of higher education through quality assurance and promotion of mobility of lecturers and students. The overall aim, as in the Bologna Process, is to establish an East African Higher Education and Research space that fosters mobility and employability of human resources. It is a timely thrust in the context of the establishment of the EAC Common Market next year which will allow free movement of labour in the region.

But the idea of harmonization is easier said than done even when it excludes harmonization of curricula. As a start, there is growing delivery of higher education through distance learning and e-learning. These forms of delivery open opportunities for unregulated systems as well as unfettered competition especially from private higher learning institutions. Through the Africa Council for Distance Education, some effort is being undertaken to create a continental quality assurance framework and an accreditation body. But it remains a huge challenge.

Secondly, there is the challenge of comparing the performance of universities against commonly agreed criteria. How do you establish such criteria and benchmarks? As Professor Mary Evans quizzes, in her book *Killing Thinking: The Death of the Universities:*[189] is it possible to recognize the relationship between ideas and how to evaluate them?

Third, achieving political commitment on harmonization at national levels could also be a huge challenge even when the Treaty establishing the EAC provides broad policy architecture.

Fourth, EAC Partner States themselves are yet to develop adequate capacity for undertaking quality assurance and quality accreditation of higher education institutions. This challenge is made more onerous when you consider the present state of low funding of public universities and lack of state funding for private universities. There is thus an overall inadequacy in infrastructure supportive of quality teaching and research in most universities both public and private. As such the question, when is a University "a University" is a huge paradox.

Fifth, there is the challenge of developing a broad based template for information gathering from institutions of higher learning and at the same time creating the conditions for transparent and undistorted information to be given to higher education regulatory institutions.

Sixth, the EAC region now faces barriers to language and communication which affects mobility of both students and lecturers. Burundi is still predominantly French speaking and the language of teaching at all levels of education remains French.

Finally, as to the question of the relationship between harmonization of higher education and socio-economic development, the jury is not out as yet. There is still much debate around this relationship. Professor Alison Wolf has opened a wide debate on this subject in her landmark book, *Does Education Matter? Myths about Education and Economic Growth.*[190] She

---

[189] EVANS, Mary, *Killing Thinking: The Death of the Universities*, London and New York: Continuum International Publishing Group, 2004.

[190] See WOLF, Alison, *Does Education Matter? Myths about Education and Economic Growth,* London: Penguin Group, 2002.

posits that education, education, education has become a mantra of government officials and politicians who see it as the key to economic growth and prosperity. Yet, in her view, there is lack of empirical evidence to support the mantra. If anything, the purported linkage between education and economic performance is what has contributed to marketization of universities, to the transformation of universities from being centres of learning to becoming purveyors of skills. The growth of the private university "as an end in itself" and "self-evidently desirable" is viewed by Professor Wolf as a threat to the "symbiosis between education and economy that currently exists."

In similar vein, Professor Mary Evans argues that "what universities have become is a distortion of the values of academy". She goes on to point that the university has shifted "from a collective world at which independent and critical thought was valued, to a collective world in which universities are expected to fulfil not their values but those of the marketplace and the economy". These views have also been advocated in our region by leading academics like the late Professor Seithy Chachage, Professors Issa Shivji and Mahmood Mamdani. What emerges from all these critiques is precisely the question whether the products coming out of our universities, indeed even from universities in the West, where both have increasingly become production lines that churn out commodities to suit the market, are able to contribute to improved economic performance or economic growth. And as a corollary, it is also questionable how harmonization of higher education in such circumstances could bolster economic development?

Conclusion

It would thus appear that the critical challenges we face in our higher education system centre firstly on re-positioning the universities to play their core role, namely that of promoting learning and knowledge. Secondly, they centre on improving the quality of academic scholarships and the restoration of scholarly integrity. Harmonization of higher education should thus give focus and priority in promoting or assuring achievement of these core objectives.

The other tasks, within the broader context of the vision encapsulated in the Treaty establishing the East Africa Community and of the Bologna Process, are, in my view, of lesser priority. It also follows that the challenge before the Inter University Council for East Africa, as the EAC proceeds to craft its 4th Development Strategy for the period 2011 – 2016, is to promote a deeper debate about three central themes: first, the rationale for a University; second, the relationship between the University, class and culture and third, the appropriate form of organizing Universities. It is a rigorous treatment of these themes that would provide a solid and insightful framework for the process of harmonization of higher education in East Africa.

However, the EAC's institutions of higher learning can leap frog in realizing world class status if they forge close collaborations with foreign universities and research institutions. Our universities do not have to re-invent the wheel. In the following chapter, an example of such collaboration, which has already delivered positive results, is examined.

CHAPTER THIRTY FOUR

Building Research Partnerships for Regional Integration[191]

Thank you for inviting me as Guest of Honour at your Conference on the CREATING Project. Let me first of all welcome you to Arusha, the seat of the East African Community. I hope you will find the climate and the surrounding environment supportive of your intellectual engagement. Secondly, I wish to commend the joint work by the Inter-University Council of East Africa (IUCEA) under its able but departing Chief Executive, Prof. Chacha Nyaigotti-Chacha and the French Institute for African Research represented here by Prof. Bernard Calas, on the one hand, and the *CREATING* Project Coordinator, Prof. Bernard Charlery, Professor at Toulouse University, on the other hand.

The two years Cooperative Research for Eastern Africa Territorial Integration under Globalization (CREATING) is on its final leg at this Conference. During this period, European Union based scholars from the countries of the East African Community have been able to foster cooperation, collaboration and partnership around the themes of climate change, population mobility and rural-urban dynamics and identity. I believe that this Conference will make an assessment of the profitability of the CREATING Project and, hopefully, determine a new framework for extended cooperation.

There is much to commend the CREATING Project because it fundamentally and concretely responds to the centrality of knowledge as the principal resource and driver of globalization. In the Cape Town Statement, which arose from an international gathering of Adult Educators at the University of the Western Cape in 2001, it was pronounced that "international partnerships and linkages occur when life-long learning institutions in the globalizing world forge a broad exchange on teaching/learning systems, and collaboration across national boundaries. This is for sharing knowledge and knowhow; partnerships and alliances based on common interest, mutual respect and desire to attain social justice, globally and locally; enhancing the sharing of skills, research opportunities and staff and student development." The CREATING Project fits in well into this Cape Town Statement ethos and thrust.

---

[191] Statement at the Opening of the CREATING Conference, Arusha, Tanzania, 23rd March, 2010.

Recently, Prof. Jeffrey Sachs has further expounded the critical importance of global cooperation. In his book titled *Common Wealth: Economics for a Crowded Planet*,[192] he argues that:

> the defining challenge of the 21st Century will be to face the reality that humanity shares a common fate on a crowed planet. That common fate will require new forms of global cooperation, a fundamental point of blinding simplicity that many world leaders have yet to understand or embrace.[193]

He goes on to elaborate that:

> the barriers (to attaining sustainable systems of energy, land, resources use, biodiversity, climate change related issues, population growth, ending extreme poverty as encapsulated in the Millennium Development Goals and new approach to global problem solving) are in our limited capacity to cooperate, not in our stars.[194]

Apparently his ending words citing Shakespeare's play *Julius Caesar*.

We in the East African Community have not been blinded by any such simplicity that Prof. Sachs refers to. Indeed, we meet here to celebrate the attestation and proof of how we have embraced global cooperation in the important and strategic sector of knowledge creation and knowledge sharing. In fact, as recent as the 15th of this month, the EAC Secretariat hosted a Global Panel of some of the world's leading minds involved in the field of Agricultural Innovation in Africa, a project funded by the Bill and Melinda Gates Foundation. The Chair of this Panel is a distinguished East African, Prof. Calestous Juma who teaches at Harvard Kennedy School.

It is of interest that some of the CREATING Project thematic issues correspond to those of the Agricultural Innovation in Africa Project; notably, agricultural research, environment, human capacity and business development. I wish to note, in particular, the work that the IUCEA is doing through the BIO-EARN project which has involved research work in bio-technology policy development. I could not underscore greater importance and urgency for our universities and research institutions to delve deeper into agricultural research and bio-technology in particular.

According to the 2008 World Development Report, Africa has only increased its agricultural research investment by 20% since 1998 compared to a three-fold increase in Asia. Our leaders have evidently been partly to blame in resisting GM technology. However, it would appear that change is

---

[192] See SACHS, Jeffrey, *Common Wealth: Economics for a Crowded Planet,* op. cit.

[193] Ibid., at p. 3.

[194] Ibid., at p. 5.

on the way in embracing bio-technology as witnessed by the statement of the Tanzania Prime Minister last week in which he debunked the fear about GMO and fervently expressed the need for Tanzanian Scientists to quickly move into the development of genetically engineered crops.

It is of interest to note that this statement came a week after my hosting the Global Panel on Agricultural Innovation in Africa, which was well covered by the Tanzania media. Indeed, one of the Panellists, who was part of the delegation that visited the EAC, Prof. Robert Paarlberg, is the author of the influential book: *Starved for Science - How Biotechnology is Being Kept Out of Africa.*[195] It is my hope that together, through this CREATING network, our universities and research institutions in the EAC region will lead the much needed change in this field of bio-technology which has been responsible for keeping our agriculture backward. It is imperative that we reap the full benefits of knowledge in a highly competitive global landscape and in an era where climate change will disrupt food security.

It is our abiding faith in the EAC which also informs the principal rationale behind the establishment and empowerment of the IUCEA, that cooperation and collaboration in education, research, trade, health, infrastructure and even migration should have a regional dimension. It is partly for this reason that the EAC has lately established close working relationship with the UNHCR and the IOM to address both forced migration and ordinary migration issues from a regional perspective and focus. This development has had to come because the EAC is proceeding expeditiously to establish a Common Market in July this year, one of whose pillars is the free movement of persons and labour. The EAC is also moving ahead to establish regional research institutions to deal with issues related to health, science and technology and Kiswahili as a unifying language for East Africans.

At the level of the IUCEA, a number of regional research programmes have also been unleashed with positive outcomes on the livelihoods of the people. We have already made reference to BIO-EARN. Another project in this line is the Lake Victoria Research Initiative – VIC-RES, an inter and multi-disciplinary research programme geared at the restoration of ecological balance on the basin of Lake Victoria and at poverty reduction through improvement of sources of sustainable livelihoods. This project, which is undertaken in collaboration with SIDA/SAREC of Sweden, has so far resulted in some cutting edge scientific research output, an example being on Bruchid Pests on beans.

The IUCEA has recently come up with a new Strategic Plan which outlines academic thematic clusters in various professional areas, sectors and economic activity. These clusters have attracted scholars and graduate

---

[195] PAARLBERG, Robert, *Starved for Science: How Biotechnology is Being Kept out of Africa,* Cambridge, Massachusetts, Harvard University Press, 2008.

students both from the EU countries and the EAC Partner States. They cover training, research and information sharing in the following areas: Forestry and Agriculture; Environment Management; Arts and Social Sciences; ICT; Library Services and Business Studies. The EAC Secretariat will strive to support the IUCEA more concretely in implementing its Strategic Plan.

Presently, the EAC is in the process of developing its 4th Development Strategy for the period January 2011 to December 2016. It is important that the IUCEA submits its Strategic Plan for incorporation into the new EAC Development Strategy. It should be noted, however, that the Council of Ministers recently decided that prior to a Strategic Plan being drawn, it is crucial that the policy framework that would inform such strategy be developed. In this respect, the IUCEA will have to provide a background policy framework that informed the development of the Strategic Plan.

Allow me to conclude by reiterating EAC's full support to the CREATING Project. The global economy today is knowledge and information-intensive. It is clear that we need international cooperation and collaboration if we are to take advantage of such a resource. Globalization is not a tide that necessarily lifts all boats; indeed it could be a major source of social and economic destabilization. However, if and when effectively mustered and the CREATING Project is one way in which we can muster globalization, we should be able to turn the tide into our favour. You have an important two days workshop before you which should provide the EAC Partner States with the reason to believe in what you plan and do. Give us that hope and inspiration.

CHAPTER THIRTY FIVE

Universities as Fountain of East Africanness[196]

It is an honour and a privilege for me to receive an honorary doctorate from this distinguished University. When I first visited this University two years ago, I was struck by its acronym, NUR (for National University of Rwanda). In Arabic and in Kiswahili, NUR stands for 'light'. Little wonder that since its founding in November, 1963, and particularly so after its re-opening in March 1995 following the atrocities of genocide, this university has indeed become Rwanda's source of light; light for renewal and regeneration; light for liberating Rwanda from the ugly and savage past.

University's Excellence Linked to National Environment

It is a past of the type that the Nigerian Poet Ben Okri so powerfully captures in his book, *Mental Fight, An Anti-Spell for the 21ˢᵗ Century,*[197] as:

> a world without hope, without wholeness, without moorings, without light, without possibility for mental fight, a world breeding mass murderers, energy vampires, serial killers with minds spinning in anomie and amorality with murder, rape, genocide as normality.

In the powerful mental fight role that this University is distinguishing itself in and for, one could not, evidently, be oblivious of the contextual environment that NUR has found itself in. It is the environment that Stephen Kinzer lucidly romanticizes in his book, *A Thousand Hills: Rwanda's Rebirth and the Man Who Dreamed It.*[198] In that book, whilst referring to Rwanda's dense web of challenges, Kinzer is quick to point out that Rwanda is a thrilling and exciting place whose story is still unfolding. And it is Paul Kagame, Rwanda's awesome President, who occupies the centre stage of the unfolding new Rwanda; its enviable modernization and the excitement it exudes.

---

[196] Acceptance Speech of an Honorary Doctorate of Political Sciences from the National University of Rwanda, Butare, Rwanda, 27ᵗʰ January, 2012.

[197] OKRI, Ben, *Mental Flight: An Anti-Spell for the 21st Century*, London: Phoenix House, 1999.

[198] See KINZER, Stephen, *A Thousand Hills: Rwanda's Rebirth and the Man Who Dreamed It,* Hoboken, New Jersey: John Wiley & Sons, Inc.2008.

Clearly, the new Rwanda under the leadership of President Paul Kagame is not simply the land of a thousand hills – delinked, desolate, though a huge characterization of the country's beauty, serenity and a source of vitality.

New Rwanda is more fundamentally a land of hope, of economic resurgence and of the drumming spirit to build a national identity that is driven by tolerance and trust and a collective pursuit of shared prosperity. We need to recall that pre-genocide Rwanda was a country characterised by violence and where identity was not a source of pride, trust and confidence but rather, to use Amartya Sen's words, an instrument to kill "and kill with abandon."

In his seminal book, *Identity and Violence: The Illusion of Destiny*,[199] the Nobel Economics Laureate, Amartya Sen captures the Rwanda-type violence whose epicentre was the 1994 genocide as being "fomented by the imposition of singular and belligerent identities on gullible people, championed by proficient artisans of terror."

Role of Inspirational National Leadership

It is Paul Kagame who has avidly created the fundamental social foundations upon which Rwanda is regaining and reclaiming its traditional past; the pre-colonial past when Rwanda was a nation of people united by a strong and homogeneous cultural identity. This is not an easy task. It is a task of great enormity and, in managing it well and effectively, Kagame has often been misconstrued as undemocratic and even authoritarian. Yet effective leaders are those that are bold enough to take prudent risks and accept criticisms even when they are unfair, misplaced or simply lack an intimate understanding of national historical contexts.

How could any reasoning person fail to appreciate that a poor country committed to taking giant leaps forward, socially and economically, needs a political leadership that is prepared to cause social and economic disruptions and creative chaos and which puts itself on the line for its revolutionary actions? Yet, paradoxically, it is the avowed democratic developed world that often quickly jumps up to characterize such actions in developing countries as symptomatic of un- democratic-ness! In fact, such bold actions and transformations have often been labelled Singapore's Lee Kuan Yew-authoritarian leadership- type.

In his book, *Fortune Favours the Bold: What We Must Do to Build a New and Lasting Global Prosperity*,[200] MIT Professor Lester C. Thurow has observed that "fearful societies are not rich societies. They won't make the

---

[199] See SEN, Amartya, *Identity and Violence: The Illusion of Destiny*, New York: W.W. Norton & Company, Inc., 2006, p. 2.

[200] See THUROW, Lester C., *Fortune Favours the Bold: What We Must Do to Build a New and Lasting Global Prosperity*, New York: HarperBusiness, 2003, p. 31.

bold voyage of exploration they need to make." For too long, Rwanda has been a fearful society. A culture of terror gripped it since 1959. It is Kagame's pivotal role that has helped to eradicate such fearful culture and create, in its place, new conditions that support and catalyse a bold voyage of exploration so necessary in transforming the social and economic relations and attitudes in Rwanda.

Honourable Chancellor, this, I believe, is the environment that has supported and animated this University to become what it is today; a University at the forefront in building a new Rwandan social capital; a University that shapes a new Rwandan identity and ingrains a deep sense of trust and confidence in Rwandan society. This is the University that I am today profoundly proud and gratified to be closely associated through the degree conferred on me.

East African Universities and EAC Integration

My acceptance speech would be incomplete if I did not make reference to the East African Community and how East African Universities can help to promote deeper integration in the region. And I have every good reason to address this important subject at an occasion as this one having been, not only the Secretary General of the EAC but also a person closely associated with universities for several years. I have served as Deputy Chair of the Council of University of Dar es Salaam for 12 years and I am currently Chair of the Council of a new public University in Tanzania, The University of Dodoma.

Logically, I am passionate about the role and contribution our Universities can and should play in providing intellectual leadership both within countries and in the regional context. It was Tanzania's Founding President, Mwalimu Julius Nyerere who harped on this role when he spoke as the first Chancellor of the University of East Africa at the inauguration of the University of Zambia in July, 1966. Nyerere had aptly quizzed:

> Who is to keep us active in the struggle to convert nationalism to Pan Africanism if it is not the staffs and students of our universities? Who is it who will have the time and ability to think out the practical problems of achieving this goal of unification if it is not those who have an opportunity to think and learn without direct responsibility for day to day affairs? And cannot the universities themselves move in this direction?[201]

---

[201] See NYERERE, Julius K., "The Dilemma of a Pan Africanist," in NYERERE, Julius K., *Freedom and Socialism*, Nairobi and Dar es Salaam: Oxford University Press, 1968, at pp. 216-217.

What I deem as the large question is whether our universities in the EAC region are today well positioned and excited enough to play the role of promoting intellectual leadership on critical issues such as regional integration? As a former student of the University of East Africa, an institution of the East African Community that collapsed in 1977, I can honestly tell you that not only did the University of East Africa inculcate and ingrain in us a culture of what Nyerere described as "East Africanness" but it also became the hotbed and bedrock of an East African intellectual discourse.

Indeed, I can proudly state that some former students of the University of East Africa have become the bulwark of the ethos and thrust of EAC integration. On an auspicious occasion such as this, it is appropriate to recognize and celebrate some of these individuals: Yoweri Kaguta Museveni, Eriya Kategaya, Amanya Mushega, Amos Wako, Issa Shivji, Mahmood Mamdani, Jenerali Ulimwengu, Justices Harold Nsekela and Ben Odoki and, of course, yours truly here.[202] But there are many more in different walks of life in the region and outside. However, our region now greatly misses the presence and fervour of the University of East Africa.

Of course, for decades, the EAC prides itself of having the Inter-University Council of East Africa to coordinate the missions and activities of public and private universities in the EAC region. This is a unique institution not found anywhere else in the world. I think that this Council, which is presently under the Chairmanship of NUR's Rector, Professor Silas Lwakabamba, could, given higher spirited dynamism, rise to the challenge of infusing intellectual leadership in EAC integration.

The Challenge of Changing Mindsets of Dysfunctional Bureaucrats

As former EAC Secretary General, I can be honest in disclosing that the EAC suffers from acute zero sum attitudes anchored on growing nationalisms which are still rooted in EAC's past shortcomings and failures. One appreciates the fact that regional integration is largely a political project.

---

[202] All these former students and academics of University of East Africa have become serious opinion makers in the region: Yoweri Kaguta Museveni is the President of Uganda for the last 26 years; Eriya Kategaya is Uganda's First Deputy Prime Minister and Minister for East African Community Affairs; Amanya Mushega is former Secretary General of the East African Community; Amos Wako was Attorney General of Kenya for over 20 years; Issa Shivji is the holder of the prestigious Mwalimu Julius Nyerere Chair on Pan Africanism at the University of Dar es Salaam; Mahmood Mamdani is a Professor and Director of the Makerere Institute of Social Research at Makerere University, Kampala, Uganda, and the Herbert Lehman Professor of Government at Columbia University, New York; Jenerali Ulimwengu is a publisher and political commentator in Tanzania; Justices Harold Nsekela is President of the East African Court of Justice; Ben Odoki is the Chief Justice of Uganda; and Silas Lwakabamba is a Professor of Engineerin and the Rector of the National University of Rwanda.

Indeed, we are presently seized of what is happening in the Euro zone and how the European Union appears devastated by the impacts of national politics on its integration project.

However, what I see as the stumbling blocks in the EAC region, call them cogs, in the wheel of integration, is not political will, as it manifests itself in the EU, as much as a powerful, deep seated role of top bureaucrats of the partner states. It is simply incredible. I can assure you that in some of the EAC countries, including Rwanda, but probably worse in Tanzania, the top bureaucracy often leads the process of integration; a political process!

But this is the bureaucracy that was educated under the era of "fearful societies;" when EAC integration was deemed a zero sum game; when Kenya was viewed to be the dominant 'benefiter' of integration and all other partners as 'second fiddle' players. Thus, virtually every integration decision has had to be evaluated within a zero-sum framework and mental condition. The realities of globalization and of the trading relationships of the same EAC countries with other *non-EAC* trading partners such as South Africa, the United Arab Emirates, India, and China feature as less incongruent or destabilizing. Kenya is the problem trading partner, full stop! At best, it is a quibbling stance.

It is in the context of such an environment of hesitant and negative attitudes that the challenge for EAC Universities takes pre-eminence. Our Universities must take the lead to dramatically change and transform the source of thinking breeds such environment and human behaviour. Clearly, the EAC may not realize deeper integration and move into a political federation with such types of behaviour and mindsets in place.

Role of the Inter-University Council of East Africa

The Inter University Council of East Africa must lead an education revolution that creates a new breed of East Africans who would occupy vital governmental positions that determine the future of EAC integration.

Let me put this challenge in context. In his acceptance speech of an honorary doctorate degree from the African International University, Khartoum, Sudan in January, 2005, former South African President Thabo Mbeki, in reflecting on the role of the African University, surmised as follows:

> Undoubtedly, this world where there is absence of critical thinking, where many refuse to confront difficult questions would bring about a situation where the genius of the nation is stifled and the wisdom of the people is not harnessed to propel

society forward. In this situation, our project of regenerating the continent will fail.[203]

It is universities such as NUR that must lead in promoting such critical thinking away from what Harvard University Professor Howard Gardner describes in his book *Five Minds for the Future*[204] as thinking based on "inert knowledge"; a knowledge based on sheer accumulation of factual and subject matter knowledge devoid of mastery of important schools of thought, ability to integrate multidisciplinary ideas, capacity to clarify challenges and emerging trends and an acute awareness of human differences and diversity. The Inter-University Council of East Africa should lead in galvanizing and advancing such a regional mission and commitment.

Allow me to conclude by once again thanking the National University of Rwanda for this most memorable event and the honour bestowed on me which elevates my mental appetite, in the words of the English Poet, Alfred Lord Tennyson's Ulysses, not to "pause, to make an end; to rust unburnished, not to shine in use, as though to breathe were life."

---

[203] See www.thepresidency.gov.za.

[204] See GARDNER, Howard Gardner, *Five Minds for the Future*, Cambridge, MA.: Harvard Business School Press, 2007, p. 28-29.

PART 10

Local Government in Regional Integration

Part ten of this book attempts to locate the integration project within the grassroots context. One of the sensitive challenges facing the EAC has been how to get its role and impact felt at local levels in the region. Often times, the regional integration agenda has been a monopoly of central governments.

Yet, a great deal of economic activities and especially cross border trade takes place within the boundaries of local governments. Without local governments being mainstreamed in the decision making processes that relate to regional integration, a critical momentum may be lost and some measures of great import in moving the integration effort forward may falter. The following three chapters therefore examine how local government can become a partner in making regional integration succeed.

CHAPTER THIRTY SIX

Promoting Synergies with Local Communities[205]

It is a great honour for me to be associated with this auspicious and important Africities IV Summit. I convey to you warm wishes of solidarity and fraternity from the East African Community, the regional organisation that is spearheading the social, economic and political integration of East Africa.

As East Africans, we are proud that the beautiful city of Nairobi is hosting this Summit. This city, East Africa's largest, has the distinction of hosting the Headquarters of the leading global development agencies, United Nations Environment Programme (UNEP) and Habitat, important institutions in the global fight against poverty.

May I, at the outset, pay special tribute to His Excellency President Mwai Kibaki and the Government of Kenya for their resolute commitment to regional integration and global partnership in addressing the pressing issues of our time. Kenya's unflinching and steadfast role in East African integration and development is a beacon of hope for all East Africans.

The central theme of this Summit, namely *Building Coalitions for the Implementation of the Millennium Development Goals in African Local Governments,* resonates well with the East African Community's overarching goal and mission to uplift the standards of living of East Africans. Since its establishment, a decade ago, the East African Community has steadfastly laid the critical foundations for constructing a sustainable regional integration structure. Today, we have a functioning customs union in place and are in the process of moving towards implementing a common market. Our vision is clearly ambitious, and why should it not be in this age of globalisation with its underlying drivers of economies of scale, of speed, scope and skills? The ultimate goal of the Community is indeed to politically integrate the East African States at a supranational level.

However, the East African Community is seized of the reality that the success of its lofty project crucially hinges on the empowerment of the ordinary man and woman in East Africa's rural and urban settlements so that they can liberate themselves economically. Such empowerment revolves around how the people are engaged and involved in determining their future.

---

[205] Message on the occasion of the Africities IV Summit, Kenyatta International Conference Centre, Nairobi, Kenya, 18th September, 2006.

The ethos underlying building coalitions in fighting poverty centres on opening spaces for enabling maximum participation of the people. Yet, we all know of the extent of the participation deficit that engulfs us. Local communities are not sufficiently involved, and regional organizations are not sufficiently in tune with the development dynamics obtaining at grassroots levels.

This participation deficit should be urgently and decisively addressed, otherwise regional initiatives may be reduced to wish lists and declarations of good intentions having little bearing on tangible results. Therefore, strengthening local communities and local authorities would be an effective asset in addressing this deficit. It is clear that the raging storm of globalization can best be tempered by the sobering wave of localization.

The best illustration of how serious the participation deficit is in the East African Community is that, since the re-establishment of the Community over a decade ago, the organized contribution of the local authorities to the Community's discourse has been limited to two memoranda; one that was submitted during the negotiations of the Treaty for the Establishment of the East African Community in 1999 and, the other, during the exercise of collecting the views of the East African people by the Committee on Fast Tracking East African Federation in 2004.

We cannot, however, blame our Local Governments for this situation. For whereas EAC Sectoral Councils specific for Ministers responsible for various sectors of co-operation and integration have been constituted and meet regularly, no similar Council has been established for Ministers responsible for local government. Yet this is a key Ministry, one that is closest to the people and strategically positioned to mobilise the people, sensitise them and generally promote awareness on matters that underpin the success of regional integration.

It is gratifying though that the EAC is well seized of these shortcomings and is in the process of redressing them. Specifically, the measures under consideration for adoption include the institution of a Forum for Local Government Associations which will lead the process of building coalitions with the East African Community in deepening regional integration. The core members of this Forum will be the Association of local Government Authorities of Kenya (ALGAK), the Association of Local Authorities of Tanzania (ALAT) and the Uganda Local Governments Association (ULGA) as well as the umbrella East African Local Governments Association (EALGA). Together with the proposed Forum, the measures envisage the promotion of the EALGA to an institution of the EAC.

Moreover, the EAC is considering the establishment of a Sectoral Council of Local Government Ministers to address specific East Africa-wide policy issues and thereby put local government at the heart of EAC's programmatic plans in the prioritised areas of relevance. These sectors include energy, communications, environment, notably rural re-forestation programmes, habitat and settlements, upgrading of urban infrastructure, peace and security, revival and revitalization of extension services under the Agricultural and Rural Development Strategy, Lake Victoria Development Programme; and fight against HIV/AIDS, among other areas which are cross cutting with significant cross-border implications. In the specific case of the Lake Victoria Development Programme, there is already the Association of Lake Victoria Local Authorities as well as the Forum of Mayors of the cities around Lake Victoria. These grassroots organs are playing important roles in ensuring the success of objectives that underlie the development programmes on Lake Victoria and its Basin.

The regional integration project as a people centred goal cannot realise its vision and mission if it fails to mainstream local government in its tasks. Building an inclusive society heavily depends on the extent to which local authorities, rural and urban, are enabled to participate effectively in this project. This is a central and fundamental issue of our time and should be rigorously promoted in confronting the African development challenge. I therefore commend the Africities Summit for its focus on the enhancement of the role of local authorities in development. For our part, in the EAC, we have embarked on concrete measures to enthrone the role of local authorities and local communities in the integration and development effort. However ambitious these measures may seem or sound, it is our resolve and commitment to realise them. East Africa should be a much changed and different place by the year 2015 when the UN Millennium Development Goals come up for review.

CHAPTER THIRTY SEVEN

Role of Local Government in Integration[206]

I am very pleased to be associated with this auspicious and important Strategic Plan Workshop of the East African Local Government Association (EALGA). I would like, at the outset, to thank the members of the EALGA for the commitment they have consistently expressed to the East African regional integration process. This workshop with the theme, "Regional Co-operation for Sustainable Socio-Political Change and Local Economic Development" is a case in point and resonates well with the East African Community's overarching goal and mission to uplift the standards of living of East Africans.

Further, the EALGA Strategic Plan which is the main subject of this workshop sets out a clear way forward in building partnerships between governments so as to strengthen solidarity and cohesion among the people of East Africa in working towards the improvement of the quality and standards of life in our region.

Since its establishment, over a decade ago, the East African Community has laid the critical foundations for constructing a sustainable regional integration structure. Today, we have a functioning customs union in place and are in the process of moving towards implementing a common market. Our vision is clearly ambitious, and indeed the ultimate goal of the Community is to politically integrate the East African States at a supranational level.

However, the East African Community is seized of the reality that the success of its lofty project crucially hinges on the empowerment of the ordinary man and woman in East Africa's rural and urban settlements to liberate themselves economically. Such empowerment revolves around how the people are engaged and involved in determining their future. The ethos underlying building coalitions in fighting poverty centres on opening spaces for enabling maximum participation of the people. Yet, we all know of the extent of the participation deficit that engulfs us. Local communities are not sufficiently involved, and regional organizations are not sufficiently in tune with the development dynamics obtaining at grassroots levels.

---

[206] Address at the opening of the East African Local Government Association (EALGA) Strategic Plan Workshop, Impala Hotel, Arusha, Tanzania, 27th February, 2007.

The participation deficit should be urgently and decisively addressed, otherwise regional initiatives may be reduced to wish lists and declarations of good intentions that have no bearing on results. Strengthening local communities and local authorities would be an effective asset to addressing this deficit.

The best illustration of how serious the participation deficit is in the East African Community is that since the re-establishment of the Community, the organized contribution of the local authorities to the discourse about the Community has been limited to two memoranda, one that was submitted during the negotiations of the Treaty for the Establishment of the East African Community in 1999 and the other, during the exercise of collecting the views of the East African people by the Committee on Fast Tracking East African Federation in 2004.

But we cannot blame Local Governments for this situation. For whereas EAC Sectoral Councils specific for Ministers responsible for various sectors of co-operation and integration have been formed and meet regularly, no similar Council has been established for Ministers responsible for local government. Yet this is a key Ministry that is closest to the people and is critical to raising awareness, sensitization and mobilization of the people on matters such as regional integration.

The EAC is seized of these shortcomings and is in the process of redressing them. Specifically, the measures include the institution of a Forum for Local Government Associations - the Association of local Government Authorities of Kenya (ALGAK) the Association of Local Authorities of Tanzania (ALAT) and the Uganda Local Governments Association (ULGA) and now to include those of Rwanda and Burundi - along with the umbrella East African Local Government Association (EALGA) to engage and dialogue with the EAC on the role the local authorities can play in regional integration. Together with the proposed forum, the measures envisage the promotion of the EALGA to an institution of the EAC.

Importantly, the EAC is considering the establishment of a Sectoral Council of Local Government Ministers to address specific East Africa-wide policy issues and thereby put local government at the heart of EAC's programmatic plans in the prioritized areas of relevance, such as energy, communications, environment, peace and security; and specifically urban upgrading; rural re-forestation programmes, revival and revitalization of extension services under the Agricultural and Rural Development Strategy, Lake Victoria Development Programme; and fight against HIV/AIDS, among other areas which are cross cutting and have significant cross-border implications. In the case of the Lake Victoria Development Programme, there is already the Association of Lake Victoria Local Authorities as well as the forum of Mayors of the cities around Lake Victoria that are already playing important roles as institutions that are closest involved in ensuring the objectives that underlie the programmes on Lake Victoria and its basin.

The regional integration project as a people centred goal cannot realize its vision and mission if it fails to mainstream local government in its tasks. Building an inclusive society heavily depends on the extent to which local authorities, rural and urban, are enabled to participate effectively in this project. This is a central and fundamental issue of our time and should be rigorously promoted in confronting our development challenge. I therefore commend EALGA for the focus on the enhancement of local authorities' role in development. For our part in the EAC, we have embarked on the measures that enthrone the role of local authorities and local communities in the integration and development effort. However ambitious this might seem or sound, we believe, that given our resources and resolve, East Africa should be a much changed and different place by the year 2010 when the current (3rd) EAC Development Strategy comes up for review. I would appeal to you, the local authorities of our region, to play your part in promoting our partnership for the socio-economic transformation of East Africa.

CHAPTER THIRTY EIGHT

Local Governance in Regional Integration[207]

Introduction

I wish to thank the organisers of this Conference, the Research and Education for Democracy in Tanzania Programme (REDET), for giving me the honour to be with you this morning to share with you my personal insights about an extremely important subject, namely Democratic Transition in East Africa under the overarching theme: *Governance and Development at the Grassroots in the East African Region.*

This is the third Conference REDET is holding in Arusha, the headquarters of the East African Community, since its establishment in 1990. It clearly attests to the importance REDET attaches to this municipality which, since 1967, has become a historic centre not only of East African integration but also of peace building and legal adjudication of the worst crimes against humanity since the Nuremburg Trials. I need not adduce the other reasons of splendour and serenity; of peace and quiet which Arusha accords, second to none, for a serious intellectual conversation such as this one.

This is the second time REDET is inviting me to open its Conference. Last year, I was privileged to grace the opening of a REDET Conference held in Dar es Salaam, on a different but equally relevant subject to the East African region. Admittedly, it has always been a pleasure for me to accept your invitations for the simple reason that REDET always comes up with topical issues of serious implication to the dynamics and challenges of regional social, political and economic transformation. It thus follows that I should, at the outset, commend and applaud the REDET leadership, and especially its founder, my friend Professor Rwekaza Mukandala, but also the present REDET leadership for its solid intellectual work in sustaining a continuous political conversation, debate and grassroots-based research specifically on objectively assessing, annually, the state of political environment in Tanzania and how the people judge their political leadership.

REDET's Conferences are an important platform and vehicle for securing a broad-based multi-stakeholder engagement on important issues of the day; some of them, of course, having remained in a state of flux for decades without resulting in an acceptable conclusion or resolution. Importantly,

---

[207] Speech at the official opening of the 12th Conference of REDET on Democratic Transition in East Africa, Snow Crest Hotel, Arusha, Tanzania, 17th November, 2009.

these Conferences enable our intellectuals, policy makers and social activists from civil society (including the media and the business community) to exchange and share views and insights, not necessarily to construct a coalition of ideas, because, after all, a vibrantly viable society should and must celebrate diverse and contending ideas, but to engage on issues that have important bearing on promoting pluralism which is what fundamentally defines the stuff of democracy and governance.

The Local Governance Context

This Conference is taking place at an interesting time. The EAC is celebrating its 10th Anniversary this week. Much has been achieved by the EAC in the past 10 years. However, this is not the occasion to outline and debate this issue though some of the challenges that confront the EAC today are partly located in the thematic issues before this Conference. It should be recalled, in this context, that the Treaty establishing the EAC provides under Article 6 that the fundamental principles of the Community include, *inter alia*, good governance, adherence to the principles of democracy, the rule of law, accountability, transparency, social justice, equal opportunities, gender equality, as well as the recognition, promotion and protection of human and peoples' rights. Article 7 of the Treaty which deals with operational principles of the Community provides that the objectives of the Community shall include the principle of subsidiarity with emphasis on multi-level participation and the involvement of a wide range of stakeholders in the process of integration.

Indeed, Article 127 of the Treaty which provides for the creation of an enabling environment for the private sector and the civil society to take full advantage of the EAC, underscores, the need to promote a continuous dialogue with the private sector and civil society at the level of the Partner States and at that of the EAC with a view to ensuring that agreed decisions in all economic sectors are implemented. And if there is one critical challenge facing the EAC today, this has a lot to do with how to institute effective modalities to enable the civil society to contribute better to the development of the EAC. Good efforts have been made to realise this objective with respect to the business community and the EAC works very closely with the East African Business Council; there is also progress in forging a partnership with the media through the Annual EAC Media Summits.

But much more needs to be done. EAC Partner States, unfortunately, have not been positively inclined to allow institutions such as the East African Business Council and other civil society organisations to enjoy full institutional status in the EAC even where there is no financial obligation to the EAC. Yet such institutionalisation would have brought about the realisation of the objectives of Article 7 of the Treaty.

I strongly believe that any serious discussion about governance and development and especially about how grassroots or local governance impacts the nation-state in the context of the democratic transition from a preponderance of *national* politics to politics that embrace the grassroots space lies at the heart of the viability of the EAC political integration project. Indeed, I am of the firm view that the quest for an EAC political federation would be stopped in its tracks if it failed to give focus and impetus on viable systems of local governance. I realise, of course, that the subject of local governance is quite broad and has greater relevance to the national political paradigm than the regional in terms of a political federation. However, there are local governance dynamics at national levels which this Conference should seriously debate upon because of their close linkage to the fundamental quest for an EAC political federation.

National Political Dynamics

Consider the following dynamics at national levels: First what are the implications, for example, for EAC political federation of the ongoing struggle for governance space and legitimacy of the Baganda Kingdom in the national politics of Uganda, and indeed, of several Kingdoms in Uganda, including the recent one in Rwenzori which was supported by President Yoweri Museveni by creating an entente cordiale with a small and weak but destabilising tribal area on the Uganda border with the Democratic Republic of Congo? Can the EAC realise a viable political federation when, at national levels, we have ethnic-based princely states that challenge the national empires?

It must be recalled that it was the Baganda Kingdom's tenacity and princely ambitions in Uganda that undermined Mwalimu Julius Nyerere's quest for an East African federation after Tanganyika's independence. Has this situation changed? What does the current situation portend in terms of your deliberations about local governance in the context of a democratic governance system that fits the quest for East African federation?

Second, post 1997 elections violence in Kenya has heightened the Orange Democratic Movement (ODM) electoral plank of "*majimboism.*" Of course, this is not a new issue. It has featured in Kenyan politics from the on-set of independence. However, Kenya African National Union's (KANU) dominance in a *de facto* One Party State succeeded to deep freeze the matter. Now it is back on the political front burner and the new Constitution making enterprise appears not to avoid it. But as in the case of the tribal Kingdoms in Uganda and their quest for a federal Uganda, which incorporates them as constitutional governance entities, what does *majimboism* entail within the framework of an East African federation? One may not doubt Kenyan positive intention to devolve state power and governance to local or grassroots levels within the framework of propelling broad-based promotion and ownership of national development that is fair and equitable. What may be questioned is how *majimboism* fits with the vision and mission of an EAC political federation.

Third, is the state of play of the Tanzania Union. Whilst Zanzibar does not fit the typical local governance structure that falls within the broad themes of this Conference and of the *problematique* thereof, in the context of a unitary state, it still offers a challenging dimension to the whole question of the nature and viability of EAC federation. In sum, a profitable discussion on local governance in our region and its relationship to democratisation and development cannot be merely located at the national level, important as that may be, but at the regional level as well where there is a Treaty vision of an East African federation. This is the first part of my contribution to the theme of your Conference.

What Form of Local Governance is Relevant?

Your Conference places significant importance on the broad question of whether the democratic transition which most of our countries in the region have gone through in the past decade and a half has impacted the national grassroots. It is an important subject that requires dispassionate treatment. At its heart is the question whether local governance has manifested or embraced a broad based participatory system where the citizens enjoy the opportunity to determine the direction and the priorities of their development. Have we witnessed, in other words, a system that allows a hundred flowers to bloom at local levels with devolution of decision making authority or have we, instead, witnessed the de-concentration of central power to local levels? This central question about democratic governance and its relationship with development has in fact engaged all our countries in the region since independence.

The late Mwalimu Julius Nyerere was deeply occupied by this question which lay at the heart of his search for what kind or form of a political state Tanganyika was to be. In his booklet, *Democracy and the One Party State,*[208] Nyerere reflects a troubled mind about the role of political pluralism as a form of governance in the newly independent Tanganyika that was mired in deep poverty with no organised private sector worth a name, a country deeply divided along tribal and religious lines and economically stratified with a north and south divide in terms of regional resource endowments in wealth and education.

---

[208] See NYERERE, Julius K, "Democracy and the One Party State," in NYERERE, Julius K, *Freedom and Unity*, Nairobi and Dar es Salaam: Oxford University Press, 1966.

The adoption of a One Party State as a vanguard for promoting equitable development and human dignity unchallenged by political opposition was thus what democracy was all about to Nyerere. State governance had to take full responsibility for promoting economic development with distributive justice across the whole nation. Indeed, it became an inevitable policy thrust for Nyerere that Ujamaa and One Party democracy were to be effected together given their mutual reinforcement in a state governance system that sought to liberate the broad masses from the scourges of poverty, illiteracy and disease.

I am raising these historical issues to make a point that may fit the broad debate that confronts you in the next two days on local governance from several dimensions. Examining the various thematic topics of your Conference, one cannot avoid seeing the long standing debate about *devolution and de-concentration* in the context of local or grassroots governance. This is a debate that is not ideologically neutral. Mwalimu Nyerere, for example, strongly believed in de-concentration rather that in devolution of power to local levels of governance. His thesis, which drove the 1972 de-centralisation programme in Tanzania, and alluded to earlier, was primarily that in a poor country democratic freedom was an outcome of development and that only a powerful centralised state could provide such development. As such, political participation at local levels had to be exercised within the confines of the leadership of a techno-managerial bureaucracy supported by resources assigned from the Centre.

My friend Professor Issa Shivji has accused Nyerere of falling victim to the proposals of the US Consulting firm, McKinsey, for such a governance structure which, in his view, undermined the populist ethos of Nyerere's decentralisation programme of "power to the people." I reject Shivji's view because it fundamentally overlooks Nyerere's ideological thrust for a centralised political power and "Ujamaanisation" which constituted the key driving forces of the 1972 de-centralisation programme.[209] The McKinsey Consultants merely helped Nyerere in putting forward a professional organisational arrangement to fit his ideological political power objectives.

That said, it can be quite easy to differ with Nyerere's ideological thrust about governance and development from the standpoint of the devolution thesis and the central objective of political pluralism. The thrust of the

---

[209] On this programme see *inter alia*, MWAPACHU, Juma Volter, ""Operation Planned Villages in Rural Tanzania: A Revolutionary Strategy for Development," in COULSON, Andrew (ed.), *African Socialism in Practice: The Tanzanian Experience*, Nottingham: Spokesman, 1979, p. 114; SAMOFF, Joel, "The Bureaucracy and the Bourgeoisie: Decentralization and Class Structure in Tanzania," Volume 21 No. 1 *Comparative Studies in Society and History*, 1979, pp. 30-62; and PICARD, Louis A., "Socialism and the Field Administrator: Decentralization in Tanzania," Volume 12 No. 4 *Comparative Politics*, 1980, pp. 439-457.

opposing view is that de-concentration of power basically turns local communities into subjects of development rather than masters of their development. Professor Amartya Sen has been a powerful promoter of this argument. In his magisterial book, *Development as Freedom*,[210] the Nobel Laureate of Economics posits that "liberty of political participation" is a constituent part of development and that "viewing development in terms of expanding substantive freedoms directs attention to the ends that make development important." Put differently, governance that limits or undermines liberty of political participation is anti-development.

In a powerful rejection of Nyerere's thesis of de-concentration, Prof. Sen argues that the thrust of helping individuals to be participating citizen centres on the idea of the public being active participants of change rather than being passive and docile recipients of instructions or of dispensed assistance. Professor Shivji has also described Nyerere's de-concentration policy as "top-down state benevolence towards the peasant". In the context of today's challenges of climate change, of conflict over natural resources between peasants and pastoralists, of improving food security, there can be no doubt that active participation of citizens at local levels through grassroots governance is imperative, thus demanding that local governance should be based more on devolution than decentralisation of power.

This debate, focused on the opposing theses of devolution where there is substantial authority to make decisions at local levels independently of central government oversight and of de-concentration where there is redistribution of central resources to local levels on the sufferance of central government, lies at the heart of what needs to be done to promote more effective local or grassroots governance in the East African region. Admittedly, the ideological thrust of Nyerere that informed his system of local governance remains relevant particularly in the context of the neo-liberal economic agenda driven by the IMF, the World Bank and development partners such as the European Union. The reason being that these donor-driven economic policies emphasize fiscal centralisation whilst, promoting, at the same time, devolution of power for project implementation.

Making Local Governance Work

Yet, equally, there is strong research evidence to suggest that democracy functions well where it is rooted in local and participatory self governing institutions. What may be debatable is the character of such local self governing institutions in the context of the prevailing political economy as well as in the context of the capacity of local leadership. It is correct to argue, though, that local leadership capacity is achievable on the basis of

---

[210] See SEN, Amartya, *Development as Freedom*, Oxford: Oxford University Press, 1999.

empowerment, overtime, through fiscal decentralisation and skills formation. Indeed, one of the strong arguments for promoting local governance is to build a leadership corp from below which later brings to the national level the whole gamut of knowledge and experience of the local space. Of equal importance for intellectual discourse and application, is the question whether it is possible and how to balance the benefits of de-concentration with those of devolution.

Before I conclude, allow me to bring up the question of the role of women in governance at grassroots level. There is ample evidence to show that when women lack access to economic resources because of some ethnic or customary law or culture, development is impeded. It thus follows that an important element of local governance is the empowerment of women to own land and have access to capital. This is an area where the role of the business sector is key in transforming governance at grassroots levels.

The successful model of the Grameen Bank[211] in Bangladesh is one clear case of how women have been economically empowered to be key change agents in Bangladesh society – from family planning to protection of the environment. Put simply, in poor societies where women carry the brunt of development, governance structures that support the economic empowerment of women best ensures broad based development.

Your Conference has an important agenda for transforming the democratic space in our region. It is a broad and complex set of issues. In wishing you a robust and frank engagement, I wish to recall the wise sermon of the late Rajni Kothari, probably India's most revered social scientist. In his two volume book, *Politics of the People: In Search of a Humane India,*[212] he postulates: "Permanence is not a virtue in politics; success in playing the role assigned by history is." Your Conference has such role to play.

---

[211] The Grameen Bank is the brainchild of the Nobel Peace Prize winner Professor Muhammad Yunus, the former Head of the Rural Economics Programme at the University of Chittagong, in Bangladesh who launched an action research project to examine the possibility of designing a credit delivery system to provide banking services targeted at the rural poor. On this Bank see BORNSTEIN, David, *The Price of a Dream: The Story of the Grameen Bank and the Idea That Is,* London:Simon & Schuster, 1996; and DOWLA, Asif and Dipal Barua, *The Poor Always Pay Back: The Grameen II Story,* Hartford, CT: Kumarian Press, 2006. Professor Yunus himself has written extensively about his work and ideas. See for instance YUNUS, Muhammad, *Banker to the Poor: Micro-Lending and the Battle Against World Poverty,* New York: Public Affairs, 2003; YUNUS, Muhammad, *Creating a World Without Poverty: Social Business and the Future of Capitalism,* New York: Public Affairs, 2009; and YUNUS, Muhammad, Building Social Business: The New Kind of Capitalism that Serves Humanity's Most Pressing Needs, New York: Public Affairs, 2010.

[212] See KOTHARI, Rajni, *Politics and The People: In Search of a Humane India* 9Vol. II), New Delhi: Ajanta Publications, 1990, p. 264.

PART 11

Promoting Defence Co-operation

We are on the threshold of a new century where security will increasingly be interpreted as security of people, not just security of territory; security of individuals in their homes, in their jobs, in their streets, in their communities and in their environment; security through development, not through arms.

Mahbub Ul Haq[213]

In Part eleven of the book, a brief examination is made of the centrality of defence co-operation in EAC's integration. For a regional body that has a political federation as a goal, no instrument of national sovereign power is as sensitive as the control of defence forces. Precisely because of such sensitivity, it is critical as part of the gradual build up towards a political federation that mechanisms are put in place to forge some co-operation of the defence forces. In the EAC, this objective was recognized as early as 1998 that is even prior to the drafting of the Treaty establishing the EAC. That was the time when the old EAC member states had established a tentative co-operation framework.

---

[213] *Imperatives of Human Security*, Barbara Ward Lecture, Society for International Development World Conference, Mexico City, April, 1994.

CHAPTER THIRTY NINE

Towards a Mutual Defence Pact[214]

I am honoured to address this distinguished audience of Generals and Senior Officers of the Tanzania Peoples Defence Force (TPDF) at the end of my visit to the Defence Institutions in Tanzania. I would like to thank you for the warm welcome and hospitality which you accorded me and my delegation during a short and very brisk schedule that has been extremely rewarding.

My mission started here on Monday, with the courtesy calls on the Minister for Defence and National Service, Hon. Professor Juma Kapuya and the Chief of the Defence Forces, General George Waitara. This opened the doors to our visits to key military institutions, which have been identified and availed for sharing under the East African Community , in particular our visits to the Tanzania Automotive Technology Centre at Kibaha, the Mzinga Corporation in Morogoro and the National Service Corporation Sole industries here in Dar es Salaam.

It has been a really fantastic experience. We had useful exchange of views and perspectives with the leadership of the defence forces, both strategic and operational, on the role of the defence forces in the East African regional integration process. I would say that, more than we could have ever achieved through the formal structured reports that we receive or meetings in Arusha, we now have a better and clearer appreciation of the vision of the Tanzania defence forces and their operational strategies.

Our interlocutors during the visits have been very forthcoming on how they view the present state of defence co-operation in the East African Community and how best such co-operation can be elaborated, deepened and reinforced. On the whole, our mission has been well accomplished, way beyond its express purpose of a fact finding mission. To paraphrase a famous military chronicler, we came, we saw, and, well, we did not conquer … We have been overwhelmed.

I believe that this has been a good start for the programme of my visit to the military Institutions of the EAC Partner States which proceeds to Uganda next week, and thereafter to Kenya. It is our sincere hope that the same success that our mission has had here in Tanzania will be replicated in

---

[214] Address to Senior Officers of the Tanzania Peoples Defence Force, Defence Forces Headquarters, Dar es Salaam, Tanzania, 2nd March, 2007.

Uganda and Kenya; and that at the end of this exercise, I will be in a position to have a good report that feeds into the higher policy organs in strengthening defence co-operation in the East African Community.

We meet here today as the East African Community integration process gathers great momentum and, indeed, reaches a higher and critical stage. The encouraging progress of the East African Customs Union, the enlargement of the Community, with last November's admission of Rwanda and Burundi; the ongoing negotiations of the East African Common Market as well as the consultations on fast tracking East African Federation, underscore serious determination of the East African people and leadership to construct a powerful East African economic and political bloc.

The realization of a large regional economic bloc comprising of Kenya, Uganda, Tanzania, Rwanda and Burundi with a combined population of 120 million, land area of 1.85 million sq kilometres and a combined GDP of $ 40 billion, bears great strategic and geopolitical significance, imposing on the EAC Partner States enormous responsibility for regional defence and security.

Whereas the East African Community has an emphatic developmental mission, it is a generally acknowledged fact that peace and security are the prerequisites for social and economic development. With the rising threat of international terrorism and creeping instability in a multiplicity of hot spots across the globe, the issues of defence and security have assumed an even greater importance and significance in the agenda of nations and, indeed the agenda of the groupings of nations.

Experience around the world shows that socio-economic inadequacies and shortcomings have often been driven by the lack of basic peace and security of the people, in terms of lack of safety and lack of stability and order. Instability in Northern Uganda, for example, has had a huge cost in human life and economic destabilization. Equally in Burundi and, more tragically in Rwanda, given the 1994 genocide, serious economic crisis and social instability have been inflicted often spilling across the borders of the countries concerned.

East Africa's post-independence experience is replete with lessons underlining the virtual interface between peace and security and the pursuit of development. In this context, the EAC's defence and security policy is rooted in the empirical observation that, so long as the countries of the region are co-operating among themselves, in pursuit of human and economic development, they will have neither reason nor cause to resort to violent conflict among themselves.

The first East African Community would not have collapsed, as it did in 1977, had its peace and security structure not been put to severe test by the rise of a military dictatorship in Uganda. Uganda and Tanzania would not have gone to war in 1978 had the East African Community been in place.

It is against this dark background that, in reviving the East African Community in 1999, the Founding Fathers declared solemn commitment to good neighbourliness, good governance and peaceful resolution of conflicts as the cornerstones of sustainable regional integration and development. Thus prominently enshrined in the Treaty for the Establishment of the East African Community, under Article 5, are the fundamental principles of peace, security and good neighbourliness.

These principles are further elaborated under the EAC Treaty Articles 124 and 125 on the Co-operation in Regional Peace and Security. On the basis of these Treaty provisions, the EAC Partner States pursue a Memorandum of Understanding for Co-operation in Defence Matters within an elaborate programme of activities, largely of confidence building among the defence forces. These activities include exchange of visits and regular meetings of defence chiefs and other cadre of the defence forces; joint training; joint exercises and promotion of various joint sports and cultural activities and seminars; and mutual assistance in disaster management.

It is gratifying to note that the implementation of this Memorandum has been successful and exemplary in the EAC integration process. So far, three major joint military exercises have been held, namely the EX ONGOZA NJIA, held in Tanzania in February 2005 on peace support operations, the EX TREND MARKER, held in Kenya, in September 2005 on counter terrorism; and the EX HOT SPRINGS, held in Uganda in September 2006 on disaster management. Also, Kenya and Uganda have held joint manoeuvre exercises at bilateral levels in addressing the problem of cattle rustling in West Pokot and Karamojong.

These initial exercises, mainly command post exercises, are now set to move to a higher level of more elaborate field exercises and near real battle simulations involving larger numbers of forces personnel and military hardware. At another level, the defence co-operation has involved military training exchange programmes for Directing Staff and Students at Staff Colleges in Kimaka-Jinja, Karen-Nairobi and Monduli-Arusha as well as exchange of cadet training courses at Monduli.

Of equal importance in confidence building among our armed forces is the annual East African Military Sports and Cultural Week which have been held in Uganda in 2005 and Kenya in 2006. This event, which has been relatively low key in the past, will now be ratcheted up by giving it higher profile and more publicity starting with the next event that will be held in Zanzibar in May this year. The intention is not only to popularize the event but also to raise the sporting competitive levels thereby contributing to the highest standards within the East African region commensurate with international standards.

The experience of the EAC defence co-operation so far, offers clear prospects in reinforcing the foundations of the East African Community. There are discernible prospects for enhanced mutual trust and confidence and building solidarity among the States. We have collective and rational utilization of military resources; efficient utilization of training facilities and equipment; effective mobilization for peacekeeping and disaster management operation, including preservation of internal stability and enhancement of enforcement and management capability in dealing with spill-over effects of external conflicts such as influx of refugees and small and illicit arms trafficking.

Indeed, through defence co-operation, we envisage the channelling of substantial military personnel, equipment and other resources to humanitarian and civilian development efforts such as extension of humanitarian assistance, in the advent of adverse situations; involvement in the distribution of food, materials and medicines in emergencies and provision and maintenance of infrastructure. Military resources would also be applied to respond to emergencies and calamities of all kinds affecting the civilian society, protection of the environment and the adaptation and application of advanced military technology and skills to address civilian needs.

The EAC Memorandum of Understanding on Co-operation in Defence offers great scope and prospects for the consolidation of East African regional integration and development. It emphasizes that we need unity, peace, stability and strength to defend our common interests. When the people perceive that our defence forces are working together; carry out joint exercises and engage in other activities that project mutual trust and confidence, they inevitably garner higher levels of confidence in the East African Community project at both economic and political dimensions. Indeed, our common security future is best guaranteed by the moulding of an East African soldier and a unified territorial defence system.

In the context of the EAC Treaty, the quest of regional peace and security is holistic, taking into account the imperative to address the root causes of conflicts. Rivalry for resources and struggle for power are often the causes of conflicts. Therefore, through its broad range of areas of cooperation, EAC seeks to entrench systems of good governance in guaranteeing equal opportunities and equal participation of all sections of the population in the allocation and management of political and economic resources. Effective mechanisms are to be brought to bear on the redistribution of resources, both among and within the Partner States, in a manner that would reduce tensions and eliminate conflicts.

By the same token, the EAC is not oblivious to the international dimensions and dynamics in peace and security, particularly the existence of an elaborate and all-powerful alliance of the armaments industry, international arms merchants and governments that use or support arms trade which fuel regional and global conflicts. As a neighbour and contiguous area to a region that has been susceptible to blood diamond driven arms proliferation, the East African Community has to take a robust and vigilant stance in arresting and containing such destabilizing situations.

In the context of the foregoing, I would like to emphasize that the East African countries have a compelling and strategic mission in establishing wider areas of peace and security beyond the confines of their own borders. Our involvement in the Burundi and IGAD peace processes, involving Burundi, the Sudan and Somalia have thus been driven by noble intention as well as enlightened self interest. This also explains the EAC's leading contribution to the wider encompassing International Conference on the Great Lakes Process culminating in last December's signing of the Pact for Security, Stability and Development of the Great Lakes Region. It further explains the core reasons for the admission of Rwanda and Burundi into the East African Community.

In conclusion, I wish to point out that East Africa's pursuit of collective security and defence, as envisioned in the Treaty, is predicated on the development necessity that underpins the EAC integration process. H.E. President Jakaya Kikwete during his State visit to Uganda in November 2006 mooted the idea of an EAC defence pact. This idea whose time has come can be fertilized to give birth to a concrete collective defence and security pact. We have the need. We have the will and we have the means. So, let us work towards the realization of this noble objective.

With these remarks, I thank you for your attention and for your commitment and dedication to the protection of East Africa, its people and its cherished values.

CHAPTER FORTY

Concluding an EAC Defence Protocol[215]

Introduction

I have been charged with the responsibility of justifying why the East African Community should move towards much deeper integration in the critical area of defence cooperation. In my view, the rationale for this direction lies within the broader context of the stages in which we now find ourselves in within the overall framework of the pursuit of EAC's ultimate objective of a Political Federation. Since 2005, the EAC has taken bold steps in transforming our region into a powerful trading and economic bloc. The Customs Union which was established in January 2005 has seen enormous success to the point where effective January 2010 the trading regime in our region is now characterised by complete free movement of goods. In other words, intra regional trade of goods is now customs duty free. There are resolute moves on the way to ensure that this Customs Union becomes fully fledged through the introduction of a Single Customs Territory.

Equally, the EAC has now embarked on a higher stage of social and economic integration through the adoption of the Common Market Protocol in November last year. This Protocol is now in the process of ratification in all the Partner States and it is envisaged that effective 1st July this year this Protocol will be operationalised. With this Protocol the EAC will experience the opening up of a much larger economic space supported by a catalytic role of free movement of persons and labour. There is little doubt that through the free movement of services and capital, two important drivers of economic growth, our region should see not only greater intra-regional trade but also a greater sharing of experience in these motive factors of development.

It is also significant to observe that strides are being made towards the establishment of a Monetary Union. Whilst the time line of 2012 has been loosely set for the establishment of this Monetary Union, the EAC has found it wise to undertake an intensive and well considered Study on the practicality and viability of this Union in the context of the obtaining economic conditions especially in the areas of economic, fiscal and monetary policies in the Partner States. It may thus be possible that the time line may

---

[215] Statement at the Meeting to deliberate on Upgrading the EAC Memorandum of Understanding on Cooperation in Defence into a Protocol, Commonwealth Resort, Munyonyo, Kampala, Uganda, 22nd February, 2010.

be adjusted forward to fit an objective reality, notably the challenge to ensure that the Monetary Union is well supported by macroeconomic convergences in the region.

All these developments have taken and are taking place within a supporting framework on how best to ensure that there is in place both a physical as well as a social and soft infrastructure that is robust and reliable. In this context, the EAC has embarked on a number of projects and programmes geared at addressing a broad spectrum of infrastructural deficits in the knowledge that the trading and economic performance of our region critically hinges on these important factors of development.

The enlargement of the EAC through the integration of Rwanda and Burundi in the EAC family in July 2007 was a clear testament of the quest of the EAC to not only realise a larger trading and economic space with countries which enjoy traditional cultural and economic relationship with the founding countries of the EAC but also to ensure that our wider region that embraces the great lakes is brought within the objective of promoting peace and stability. Today Rwanda and Burundi are important players in the EAC Customs Union and will be significant contributors to the overall development of our region at all levels including that of sustaining peace and security.

The EAC has also recognised that as we pursue our ultimate quest of a Political Federation, the need to ensure that our region enjoys peace, security and stability, significant importance is placed on promoting defence cooperation. This is the reason why even prior to the signing of the Treaty establishing the East African Community in November 1999, the EAC Heads of State saw the importance of establishing a framework for defence cooperation through a Memorandum of Understanding which was signed on 30th April, 1998 when the EAC was a Tripartite Commission; and indeed the importance of defence cooperation became enshrined in the Treaty for the establishment of the East African Community. Articles 124 and 125 of the Treaty encapsulate this very clear objective.

The Contextual Rationale for a Protocol

I could speak for hours on where we have come from to where we wish to go in putting defence cooperation at the heart of the EAC integration agenda and notably, our ultimate goal of establishing a Political Federation. We know where we have come from – a colonial past which shows that our balkanisation under African chiefdoms made us weak and vulnerable to colonial manipulations. In spite of pockets of resistance and uprisings so well documented in our history of struggle against colonialism embracing the Mkwawa Hehe resistance against German colonialism;[216] to the Ngoni Maji Maji uprising also against German colonialism both of them in southern Tanzania;[217] the Mau Mau liberation struggle in Kenya[218] to Zanzibar's revolution against a British protected Sultanism in Zanzibar,[219]

---

[216] On Chief Mkwavinyika Munyigumba Mwamuyinga of the Hehe see REDMAYNE, Alison, "Mkwawa and the Hehe Wars," Volume 9 No. 3 *Journal of Modern African History*, 1968, pp. 409-436; ILIFFE, John: *A Modern History of Tanganyika*, Cambridge: Cambridge University Press, 1979; and REDMAYNE, Alison Hope, *The Wahehe People of Tanganyika*, Oxford: Oxford University Press, 1965.

[217] On Maji Maji uprising see *inter alia*, ILIFFE, John, "The Organization of the Maji Maji Rebellion," Volume 8 No. 3 *The Journal of African History*, 1967, pp. 495-512; GWASSA, Gilbert Clement Kamana,*The Outbreak and Development of the Maji Maji War 1905-1907*, Köln: Rüdiger Köppe Verlag, 2005; and ILIFFE, John, *Tanganyika Under German Rule 1905 – 1912*, Nairobi and Cambridge: East African Publishing House and Cambridge University Press, 1969.

[218] A lot has been written on Mau Mau war of liberation. See for instance HENDERSON, Ian and Philip Goodhart, *Manhunt in Kenya*, New York: Doubleday and Company, 1958; ANDERSON, David, *Histories of the Hanged: The Dirty War in Kenya and the End of Empire*, London: Weidenfeld and Nicolson, 2005; BERMAN, Bruce J., (1991). "Nationalism, Ethnicity, and Modernity: The Paradox of Mau Mau," Volume 25 No. 2 *Canadian Journal of African Studies*, 1991, pp. 181–206; BRANCH, Daniel, "The Enemy Within: Loyalists and the War Against Mau Mau in Kenya," Volume 48 No. 2 *The Journal of African History*, 2007, pp. 291–315; BRANCH, Daniel, *Defeating Mau Mau, Creating Kenya: Counterinsurgency, Civil War, and Decolonization*, New York, NY: Cambridge University Press, 2009; CLOUGH, Marshall S., *Mau Mau Memoirs: History, Memory and Politics*. Boulder: Lynne Rienner Publishers, 1998; CORFIELD, Frank, *The Origins and Growth of Mau Mau: an Historical Survey* - The Corfield Report, Nairobi: Government of Kenya, 1960; EDGERTON, Robert B., *Mau Mau: An African Crucible*. London: I.B.Tauris, 1990; ELKINS, Caroline, *Imperial Reckoning: The Untold Story of Britain's Gulag in Kenya*. USA: Henry Holt and Co., 2005; ELKINS, Caroline, *Britain's Gulag: The Brutal End of Empire in Kenya*. London: Pimlico, 2005; KANOGO, Tabitha, *Dedan Kimathi: A Biography*. Nairobi: East African Educational Publishers, 1992; KANOGO, Tabitha, *Squatters and the Roots of Mau Mau, 1905–63*. Nairobi: East African Educational Publishers, 1993; KARIUKI, Josiah Mwangi, *"Mau Mau" Detainee: The Account by a Kenya African of his Experiences in Detention Camps 1953–1960*. New York and London: Oxford University Press, 1975; LONSDALE, John, "Mau Mau and Nationhood: The Untold Story" In ATIENO-ODHIAMBO, Elisha Stephen and John Lonsdale, *Mau Mau and Nationhood*. Oxford: James Currey, 2003, pp. 46–75; MALOBA, Wunyabari O., *Mau Mau and Kenya: An Analysis of a Peasant Revolt*. Indiana: Indiana University Press, 1993; NEWSINGER, John, "Revolt and Repression in Kenya: The 'Mau Mau' Rebellion, 1952–1960," Volume 45 *Science and Society* 1981, pp. 159–185; NISSIMI, Hilda, "Mau Mau and the Decolonisation of Kenya" Volume 8 No. 3 *Journal of Military and Strategic Studies*, 2006, p. 131; and THROUP, David, *Economic and Social Origins of Mau Mau, 1945–53*. Oxford: James Currey, 1987. and HEWITT, Peter, *Kenya Cowboy: A Police Officer's Account of the Mau Mau Emergency*, Johannesburg: South Publishers, 2008.

[219] On the Zanzibar Revolution of 12th January, 1964 see DALY, Samuel, "Our Mother is Afro-Shirazi, Our Father is the Revolution," Senior Thesis, New York: Columbia University, 2009; INGRAMS, William H., *Zanzibar: Its History and Its People*, Abingdon: Routledge, 1967; LOFCHIE, Michaael F., "Was Okello's Revolution a Conspiracy?" Volume 33 *Transition* 1967, pp. 36–42; SPELLER, Ian, "An African Cuba? Britain and the Zanzibar Revolution, 1964," Volume 35 No. 2 *Journal of Imperial and Commonwealth History*, 2007, pp. 1–35; TRIPLETT, George W. (1971), "Zanzibar: The Politics of

our region has remained splintered and fractured defence-wise. Political independence has not in any way changed the character of this balkanisation. Indeed, the Idi Amin coup in Uganda in 1971[220] was one of the manifestations of our defence disunity.

The genocide in Rwanda in 1994[221] and a 15 year civil war in Burundi[222] are also post independence phenomenon manifesting the remnants of a colonial

---

Revolutionary Inequality," Volume 9 No. 4 *The Journal of Modern African Studies*, 1971, pp. 612–617; GLASSMAN, Jonathon (2011), *War of Words, War of Stones: Racial Thought and Violence in Colonial Zanzibar*, Bloomington: Indiana University Press, 2011; AL BARWANI, Ali Muhsin, *Conflicts and Harmony in Zanzibar – Memoirs*, Dubai, 2002; AYANG, Samuel G., *A History of Zanzibar: A Study in Constitutional Development 1934-1964*, Nairobi: Kenya Literature Bureau, 1970; BABU, Abdulrahman M., "The 1964 Revolution: Lumpen or Vanguard," in SHERIFF, Abdul and Ed Ferguson (eds.), *Zanzibar Under Colonial Rule*, London: James Curry, 1991; BAKARI, Mohamed Ali, *The Democratisation Process in Zanzibar: A Retarded Transition*, Hamburg: Institute of African Affairs, 2001; CLAYTON, A., *The Zanzibar Revolution and Its Aftermath*, London: C. Hurst & Co, 1976; JUMBE, Aboud, *The Partner-ship: Tanganyika Zanzibar Union - 30 Turbulent Years*, Dar es Salaam: Amana Publishers, 1994; LOFCHIE, Michael F., *Zanzibar: Background to the Revolution*, Princeton: Princeton University Press, 1965; MAPURI, Omar R., *Zanzibar - The 1964 Revolution: Achievements and Prospects*, Dar es Salaam: TEMA Publishers Company Ltd., 1996; MARTIN, Esmond Bradley, *Zanzibar: Tradition and Revolution*, London: Hamish Hamilton, 1978; OKELLO, John, *Revolution in Zanzibar*, Nairobi: East African Publishing House, 1967; PETTERSON, Don, *Revolution in Zanzibar: An America's Cold War Tale*, Boulder Colorado: Westview Press, 2002; and REY, L., "The Revolution in Zanzibar," No. 25 *New Left Review*, May-June, 1964, p. 29.

[220] On this see OCHIENG, Philip, "The Man who 'Gifted' Uganda to Amin," in ANGURIA, Omongole R. (ed.), *Apollo Milton Obote: What Others Say*, Kampala: Fountain Publishers, 2006, p. 159; SEFTEL, Adam (ed.), *Uganda: The Rise and Fall of Idi Amin*, Lanseria, South Africa: Bailey's African Photo Archives Production, 1994; and AVIRGAN, Tony and Martha Honey, *War in Uganda: The Legacy of Idi Amin*, Dar es Salaam: Tanzania Publishing House Ltd, 1982

[221] On the Genocide in Rwanda see AFRICAN RIGHTS, *Rwanda: Death, Despair and Defiance* (Revised Edition), London: African Rights, 1995; AFRICAN RIGHTS, *Rwanda: Not So Innocent – When Women Become Killers*, London: African Rights, 1995; BERRY, John A. and Carol Pott Berry (eds.), *Genocide in Rwanda: A Collective Memory*, Washington, D.C.: Howard University Press, 1999; DALLAIRE, Romeo (With Major Brent Beardsley), *Shake Hands with the Devil: The Failure of Humanity in Rwanda*, Toronto: Random House Canada Ltd., 2003; DESTEXHE, A., *Rwanda and Genocide in the Twentieth Century*, London and New Haven, Connecticut: Pluto Press, 1995; FORGES, Alison Des, *Leave None to Tell the Story: Genocide in Rwanda*, New York; Washington; London; Brussels and Paris: Human Rights Watch and International Federation of Human Rights, 1999; GOUREVITCH, Philip, *We Wish to Inform you that Tomorrow we Will be Killed With Our Families: Stories from Rwanda*, London: Picador, 1999; HUMAN RIGHTS WATCH/AFRICA, *Genocide in Rwanda* (Volume 6 No. 4), New York: Human Rights Watch, April/May, 1994; INTERNATIONAL PANEL OF EMINENT PERSONALITIES and ORGANISATION OF AFRICAN UNITY, *Rwanda: The Preventable Genocide*, Addis Ababa: Organisation of African Unity, 2000; MAMDANI, Mahmood, *When Victims Become Killers: Colonialism, Nativism, and the Genocide in Rwanda*, Kampala and Dar es Salaam: Fountain Publishers Ltd., and E & D Limited, 2001; MELVEN, L.R., *A People Betrayed*, London & New York, Zed Books, 2000; PRUNIER, Gerard, *The Rwanda Crisis: History of Genocide*, Kampala: Fountain Publishers Ltd., 2001;

divide and rule system of the 19th century. And whilst many of us would acclaim and applaud globalisation, this economic system if not well embraced and mustered, also has seeds of social stratification and even conflict.

Put differently, the struggle of African peoples to realise unity, peace, stability and development remains our central challenge; as Samora Machel had put it – *a luta continua* (the struggle continues).[223] The lesson of experience is that national sovereignty along the borders enacted by colonialism feeds on the structural weaknesses that I have postulated. It is our larger unity beyond these ex-colonial borders that constitutes a new basis for political and economic liberation for Africa and for our region.

In this overall context, defence cooperation of our Partner States in a way in which we begin a process of putting such cooperation at the heart of our quest for an ultimate Political Federation is logical and imperative. Citizens of East Africa need to live from the comfort that the ethos and spirit of integration is endorsed and supported by our defence forces. A sustainable

---

SEMUJANGA, Josias, *Origins of Rwanda Genocide*, New York: Humanity Books, 2003; CAPLAN, Gerald, "The Genocide Problem: 'Never Again' All Over Again," in MANJI, Firoze and Patrick Burnett (eds.), *African Voices on Development and Social Justice*, Dar es Salaam: Mkuki na Nyota Publishers, 2005, p. 74; DE WAAL, A. and R. Omaar, "The Genocide in Rwanda and the International Response," Volume 19 No. 591 *Current History*, 1995, p. 156; GORUS, Jan, "The State as an Instrument of Ethnicity: Ethnic Construction and Political Violence in Rwanda," in DOOM, Ruddy and Jan Gorus (eds.), *Politics of Identity and Economics of Conflict in the Great Lakes Region*, Brussels: VUB University Press, 2000, p. 175; GOYVAERTS, Didier, "The 'Dubious Discourse' on Rwanda: An Irreverent Essay", in GOYVAERTS, Didier (ed.), *Conflict and Ethnicity in Central Africa*, Tokyo: Institute for Study of Languages and Cultures of Asia and Africa, Tokyo University of Foreign Studies, 2000, p. 251; HEUSCH, L., "Rwanda: Responsibilities for Genocide," Volume 11 No. 4 *Anthropology Today*, 1995; JOSHI, Ravinder, "Genocide in Rwanda: The Root Causes," Volume 3 No. 1 *East African Journal of Peace & Human Rights*, 1997, p. 51; MAMDANI, Mahmood, "A Brief History of Genocide," Volume 01 *Kwani?*, Nairobi: Kwani Trust, 2003, p. 38; NEWBURY, David, "Understanding Genocide," Volume 41 No. 1 *African Studies Review*, p. 73; PLAUT, M., "Rwanda – Looking Beyond Slaughter," Volume 50 Nos. 8-9 *The World Today*, 1994; REYDAMS, L., "Universal Jurisdiction over Atrocities in Rwanda: Theory and Practice," Volume 2 *European Journal of Crime, Criminal Law and Criminal Justice*, 1996, p. 26; and REYNTJENS, F., "Rwanda Genocide and Beyond," Volume 9 No. 3 *Journal of Refugee Studies*, 1996, p. 240.

[222] On the problems in Burundi see BOWEN, Michael, *Passing by: The United States and genocide in Burundi*, New York: Carnegie Endowment for International Peace, 1973;LEMARCHAND, René, *Selective Genocide in Burundi*, London: Report – Minority Rights Group (Report No. 20), 1974; LEMARCHAND, René, *Burundi: Ethnic Conflict and Genocide,*(New York: Woodrow Wilson Center and Cambridge University Press, 1996; and NYANKANZI, Edward L., *Genocide: Rwanda and Burundi*, Rochester, Vermont: Schenkman Books, 1998.

[223] On Samora Machel see HEDGES, David, "Samora Machel: A Biography," Volume 19 No. 3 *Journal of Southern African Studies*, 1993, p. 547; CHRISTIE, Iain, *Machel of Mozambique*, Harare: Zimbabwe Publishing House, 1988; and MUNSLOW, Barry (ed.), *Samora Machel: An African Revolutionary*, London: Zed Books, 1985.

---

larger East African economic integration that is devoid of such deeper defence cooperation may not be sustainable. Defence cooperation is the pillar that holds together all the building blocs of EAC integration.

Current MOU and its Limitations

Though the EAC Secretariat prides itself of having Defence Liaison Officers of rank of Colonel and above from all the five Partner States, a structure that enables better coordination of defence cooperation, it is correct to state that the EAC MOU on Cooperation in Defence has probably outlived its purpose even when it has contributed significantly to confidence building and to the removal of mutual suspicion created after the collapse of the erstwhile EAC. In this area of confidence building we have seen over the last few years defence cooperation encompassing exchange of visits, training, joint military exercises and joint operations to combat challenges such as cattle rustling. Admittedly, the MOU includes joint operations in disaster management, search and rescue operations, provision of support to civil authorities and peace support operations. However, these activities are not clearly defined in terms of their operationalisation; neither are the mechanisms for peace support operations within the context of the United Nations and the African Union Charters given clarity particularly when it comes to mutual assistance in case of an invasion from outside the region.

In other words, the current MOU falls short of engendering deeper military cooperation. Nevertheless, it is important to recognise that, over time, the operationalisation of the MOU through funding by the EAC Partner States has demonstrated the capacity of the EAC to respond to crisis within the region though such capacity fell short when Kenya found itself in a state of instability after the 2007 General Elections. Yet the MOU has enabled the Partner States to share best practices on various forms of defence materials manufacturing, research and a secure communication system between the Defence Chiefs in the region.

Moving forward, it is imperative to view the limitations of this MOU in the context of the changing geo-political landscape of the East African region. The emergent phenomenon of piracy on the East African coast, the instabilities in Somalia and the Eastern DRC necessitate that defence cooperation in the EAC becomes more reinforced and expanded. Needless to state, global terrorism and narco-terrorism have not spared our region and these challenges demand that mutual defence assistance becomes entrenched in the EAC defence cooperation framework. Our region has not also been spared by insurgencies and other threats of territorial destabilisation. In sum, EAC needs to forge a defence cooperation system that can effectively deliver a more holistic, comprehensive, cost effective and results oriented defence cooperation.

Political Federation and Defence Cooperation

One may indeed boldly pose the question whether we can indeed move forward towards a Political Federation if our cooperation in defence continues to be on the basis of a simple Memorandum of Understanding that lacks a binding character. It is interesting to contrast the EAC situation today in so far as defence cooperation is concerned with what obtains in the Southern African Development Community (SADC). SADC does not have a vision of a Political Federation within its Treaty. Yet, it has a legally binding Protocol on politics, security and defence. Of course one can understand the rationale for SADC having such a legally binding framework given the historical background of apartheid South Africa and minority rule regimes in Zimbabwe, Mozambique, Angola and Namibia. That historical background of liberation has remained an important facet of SADC's work and supports why SADC has a mutual defence pact.

During this Forum we will have the benefit of presentations by two colleagues who have an intimate knowledge of the evolution of the security and defence architecture of SADC and how SADC has proceeded in putting security and defence at the forefront of its integration objectives. As such, I will not go into the intricacies of the SADC Protocol on politics, security and defence; neither will I cover the governance structure in the form of the Organ and the Troika of the Organ on politics, security and defence. What is important to state at this stage is that SADC offers us an excellent framework of a Protocol of the structure for the operationalisation and management of the Protocol as well as the framework of a mutual defence pact. We may thus not need to re-invent the wheel though it is important for the EAC to construct a defence cooperation system that befits its circumstances and peculiarities, the most important of which is EAC's commitment to a Political Federation.

Conclusion

Defence cooperation constitutes one of the most critical underpinnings of an EAC that is committed to establishing a Political Federation. As the process of political integration takes course, we will be failing in our duties if we do not ensure that defence cooperation becomes not only the pivot of integration but its key catalyst. I have always observed that when East African citizens in our cities, in our towns and in our villages see our five country Defence Forces working together, training together and socialising together through activities such as the annual military sports and cultural events, the belief in the possibility of a Political Federation becomes ingrained.

There could not be any further justification for the EAC to scale up defence cooperation from an MOU to a legally binding Protocol than this vision of Political Integration. No other Regional Economic Community in Africa shares this vision except from the continental AU vision perspective. As such, this Forum should endorse this critical direction in our integration. It is my hope that we will come out of this Forum with unreserved support for upgrading the current MOU into a Protocol along with other attendant institutional mechanisms to enable the Protocol to be operationalised and well managed.

PART **12**

The COMESA-EAC-SADC Tripartite Framework

The Context

It was alluded to in part one of this book that the multiplicity of RECs in Africa is viewed in some quarters as a dysfunction in the ambitious goal of moving Africa towards the African Economic Community. I pointed, out as one way to address such multiplicity, that COMESA, EAC and SADC had constituted themselves into a tripartite body with a clear mandate of not only constituting a grand free trade area and later a customs union but also to move towards a merger of the three RECs. With a membership of 26 countries, a population of 530 million people and a combined GDP of over US $ 640 million, the tripartite presents a unique and ambitious possibility for not only jump starting the AEC but also fast tracking its realization.

In the following part, I dwell on the background to the emergence of the tripartite and some of the work it is engaged in. Following the Second Summit of the Tripartite that took place in Johannesburg in June 2011, some momentum has been achieved in the roadmap towards the establishment of the grand free trade area. My hope is that zero sum issues and economic power interests of countries like South Africa and Egypt will not derail the much needed forward movement. What creates hope is that the negotiators of the grand FTA are seized of the need to incorporate variable geometry in the agreement so that parties prepared to move ahead on the basis of minimum conditions in rules of origin, for example, can do so.

CHAPTER FORTY ONE

Midwifing the Tripartite Framework[224]

It is an honour and pleasure for me to make a few remarks at this 6th Tripartite meeting of the Chief Executives of COMESA, EAC and SADC which is being held at his magnificent city of Maputo, a city not only rich in its history of trade and opportunity but also a symbol of the struggle for respect and dignity; a struggle that represents the effectiveness of collective action and reinforces the correctness of the adage that "in unity is strength". The origins of this Tripartite Forum are very much in line with the conviction that strength lies in unity and it is our hope that our sojourn in this historic city will help to draw inspiration for our Meeting to arrive a the most optimal outcome possible.

Our meeting takes place in the aftermath of some disturbing events in our region-from the post-election skirmishes in Kenya; the electoral fracas in Zimbabwe; and more recently the xenophobic attacks meted out to Africans of other nationalities living in South Africa. This all points to the need for us to rededicate ourselves to the full emancipation and unity of our people and to raise the bar in our commitments towards achieving what we have all agreed is the common destiny for the African people. It is on this basis that I hope that we can finalize the arrangements for hosting a Tripartite Summit of Heads of State of COMESA, EAC and SADC at the earliest. In this connection, we need to agree on, among other things, an appropriate theme for the Summit-whether it be an emphasis on market creation, or on development, or on the role of the Tripartite arrangement as a building bloc towards the African Economic Community.

You will recall that at our meeting held on 9th October, 2007 at Elephants Hill Zimbabwe we did underscore the need to deepen cooperation between the COMESA, EAC and SADC through a common Free Trading Arrangement for the region. We were convinced that this arrangement would not serve as a strategic intervention towards the creation of an African Economic Community but would also provide an effective interim measure for the enhancement of intra-regional trade and investments. To this end, we will only be too happy to contribute towards the development of a roadmap for the approval of the Tripartite Summit to guide the implementation of our cooperation.

---

[224] Remarks at the 6th Tripartite Meeting of Chief Executives of COMESA, EAC and SADC, Polana Serena Hotel, Maputo, Mozambique, 13th June, 2008.

On the agenda for the Summit is a proposal for economic and trade liberalization for our region. In this connection, it will be important to review our macro-economic frameworks on the basis of an agreed convergence criteria as well as different trade facilitation instruments to support this process. Likewise, it will be important to agree on a minimum programme for the facilitation of movement of persons for trade and tourism as well as the movement of capital for investment purposes. We are also of the view that we will need to address the issue of student visas and the harmonization of tuition fees charged in respect of students originating from the three REC's.

Infrastructure development is extremely critical to unlocking the potential of our region to develop and prosper. In this regard, we need to focus our efforts on promoting investments in road, railways and energy as well as ICT broadband interconnectivity. Other critical areas in this sector include the development of ports and harbours, inland waterways, the implementation of the Yamoussoukro decision as well as the harmonization of policy instruments, such as axle-load limits. It will equally be important to develop and mobilize funding mechanisms that will support private sector participation in this regard. More significantly, we will need to examine the viability of implementing the concept of "development corridors" to serve as the main vehicle for the implementation of regional project in this sector.

As I conclude, I would like to draw your attention to the overarching goal of regional integration which is poverty eradication. The livelihood of our people is indeed the cornerstone of our programmes and it is widely acknowledged that the achievement of the MDG's can best be realized through collective action in the form of regional integration. Fortunately, much has been achieved on this front, however I must hasten to add that there is an imminent catastrophe that may wipe away all that we have achieved so far, and that is the danger of climate change. This phenomenon is not only becoming a major preoccupation of the world in recent times but will cause major disruptions to our entire planning and development process including having a retrogressive effect on peace and security in the period ahead. I will therefore request that we begin to review our preparedness on this front and explore the possibility of joint programming in all sectors that may be impacted upon by this phenomenon.

Last but not least, I would like to convey our gratitude to the SADC Secretariat as well as the Government and people of this wonderful country for the warm hospitality and excellent facilities that have been put to the disposal of the EAC delegation since our arrival in Mozambique. I would also like to take this opportunity to thank the Secretariat of our Forum, namely the Regional Trade Facilitation Project, for the wonderful services that have gone a long way in ensuring the success of our Meeting.

CHAPTER FORTY TWO

Promoting the Tripartite Northern Transport Corridor[225]

May I, at the outset, join the previous speakers in thanking you, Honourable Minister, for gracing us, on behalf of H.E President Mwai Kibaki, with your presence. As immediate past Chair of the COMESA Summit, not to speak of his astute leadership as Kenya's President, President Mwai Kibaki has been a major influence on matters before this Conference.

Indeed the President's leadership within the COMESA-EAC-SADC tripartite framework has been unique and worthy of recognition. He has consistently reflected serious commitment to making infrastructure development a centre-piece of economic growth and the realization of Kenyan and regional competitiveness.

It requires no elaboration that the quality of infrastructure is what critically defines economic progress and the prosperity of the people. Yet, the development of infrastructure poses complex challenges because of its huge financial outlays. When viewed in the context of a regional perspective, it is quite clear that building, upgrading and modernizing infrastructure demands thinking outside the conventional geographical spaces which we are invariably boxed in. We often tend to forget that roads, railways and power transmission lines never stop at national border points. Where anyway would our inland waterways transportation on Lake Victoria and Lake Tanganyika stop? President Kibaki clearly understood and contextualized the meaning of these challenges when you powerfully intervened at the North-South Corridor Aid for Trade Pilot Project Conference in Lusaka in April this year.

In that eloquent intervention, as the then Chair of COMESA Summit, President Kibaki called for the quick replication of the North-South Corridor model to the Corridors in the East African Community region and beyond-the Northern Corridor which is the subject of our meeting here today, linking Mombasa, Kampala, Kigali, Bujumbura and Eastern DRC; the new Lamu-South Sudan-Ethiopia Corridor; and the Central Corridor linking Dar es Salaam with Kampala, Kigali and Bujumbura. President Yoweri Museveni who was in Lusaka as well, representing the current Chair of the EAC Summit, President Paul Kagame, was equally emphatic in supporting President Kibaki's call.

---

[225] Remarks at the Official Opening of the Northern Corridor Stakeholders Conference, White Sands Hotel, Mombasa, Kenya, 30th September, 2009.

As Secretary General of the East African Community and current Chair of the COMESA-EAC-SADC Tripartite Taskforce, which President Kibaki and his colleagues put in place in that historic Tripartite Summit held at Munyonyo, Kampala, Uganda in October last year, I wish to reaffirm the view that it is our ardent collective resolve and the robust marshalling of our collective resource, from within and without, that can enable us to successfully address the infrastructure challenges and other supply-side constraints, which currently shackle our economies from growing faster and becoming more competitive.

This Conference is being held specifically to leverage ideas and resolve as well as to mobilize the experiences of the best of our multi stakeholders, public and private, in our broader region in the direction of identifying what best needs to be done and how it is done in order to unshackle the chains that encumber and throttle the efficiency and effectiveness of this highly strategic Northern Corridor. I wish to thank the organizers of this Conference, a unique public-private partnership, for promoting this Conference.

It is quite clear that in order to leverage the efficiency and cost-effectiveness of the supply chain along this Corridor, we will have to move beyond incremental improvements. It is simply not enough, to open Mombasa Port for 24 hours: neither is it enough to reduce the number of weigh bridges and police road blocks between Mariakani and Busia or Malaba.

At another level, the introduction of One-Stop Border Posts along the Northern Corridor and the Central Corridor as well as the Arusha-Namanga-Athi River Corridor may surely help to reduce the costs of doing business especially if we will sort out bureaucratic and corruption practices at border posts and right along then Corridors. However, all these interventions, important as they are, could tantamount to tinkering at the margins of needed robust change in the infrastructure sector. At the heart of such effective change, of promoting real and sustainable low transaction business costs and bolstering higher levels of competitiveness are massive transformations of all our Corridors logistical and mindset character.

In this context, there is need to expand the berthing facilities and handling equipment at Mombasa Port, a process under execution, and up-grading and modernizing the road and railway networks linking Mombasa and the landlocked countries to the West. It is important also to recognize that these networks interface and link with other road and railway networks that feed into the Northern Corridor. These include the Moshi-Voi Railway Network and the Arusha-Namanga-Athi River Road now under modernization.

Under engineering feasibility studies are two new road networks linking Bagamoyo-Tanga-Horohoro-Mombasa-Malindi and Arusha-Moshi-Holili-Voi which also feed into the Northern Corridor. I am pleased to advise that, with the support of the African Development Bank, the EAC is also currently in the process of undertaking a full-scale Transport infrastructure Master Plan which incorporates Rwanda and Burundi. At the same time, with the support of DfID, USAID and JICA, the EAC is undertaking a Corridor Diagnostic Study covering the Northern and Central Corridors. This Study will complement a broader Corridor Master Plan within the framework of the COMESA-EAC-SADC Tripartite which ADB is supporting.

The aim of these studies, notwithstanding the "paralysis of analysis", will be to identity the challenges that exist in our regional Transport Corridors and propose Active Plans which will inform the level of resources required to be mobilized for upgrading and modernizing the requisite infrastructures. It is important to underscore, Guest of Honour, the need for the AfDB Group to work in close unison with other development partners I have mentioned as well as others. The Tripartite experience which we have acquired from the promotion and implementation of the North-South Corridor Aid for Trade Pilot Project, clearly shows that such partnership between development financial institutions and bilateral donors pays significant dividends both at the level of mobilization of resources and in providing support for implementation management.

I wish to assure you that COMESA, EAC and SADC continue to work very closely within the framework of the Tripartite Arrangement, an arrangement which is currently moving towards recommending the establishment of the Grand Free Trade Area cutting across the three Regional Economic Communities. We see this new synergy as being of critical importance in making our markets work better, improve trade flows and, generally, raise our levels of competitiveness. Working together in upgrading and modernizing the infrastructures in our various interlinked Corridors is what will drive these economic developments. We look upon President Kibaki, and his Tripartite colleagues, who lead us so admirably, for higher level political will, drive and commitment in this tripartite process that has attracted a great deal of attention and support at the levels of the African Union level, the International Financial Institutions, the European Union, the WTO and several bilateral development agencies, the key ones being represented here today. The prosperity, stability and competitiveness of our broader region crucially hinges on President Kibaki's brand of leadership.

CHAPTER FORTY THREE

A North-South Corridor Tripartite Project[226]

I am honoured and profoundly privileged as Chair of the COMESA-EAC-SADC Tripartite Task Force of Chief Executive Officers to thank your Excellencies, our dear Heads of State, for your distinguished presence at this event of historic importance to our region and to Africa.

This event marking the official Launch of the Chirundu One Stop Border Post, the first of its kind in Africa, is a lucid demonstration of the new dynamic in regional integration; a dynamic whose underlying ethos is the forward movement towards the realization of the African Economic Community.

Our region, sparked by the vision and resolve of our political leaders in COMESA, SADC and the East African Community, is path breaking in collapsing the artificial national borders created by colonialism and taking revolutionary strides towards unleashing a new economic integration momentum. A higher growth and sustainable trajectory and indeed the economic liberation of the people of our regional crucially hinges on this dynamic political leadership and on the measures being unfolded of which this One Stop Border Post is only a small manifestation.

The bigger resolve is what our leaders decided in October last year in Kampala, Uganda that COMESA-EAC and SADC proceed expeditiously to establish a Grand Free Trade Area followed by a Customs Union. Much headway has been realized on this front. Indeed as we meet here, all the Member States of our three Regional Communities are now reviewing concrete proposals which our Task Force led by the three CEOs have developed and tabled. Our plan is that our political leaders should by May next year pronounce themselves on the establishment of the Grand Free Trade Area.

Within the framework of the tripartite arrangements, there have been resolute efforts taken, even prior to the establishment of the Grand FTA, to address our region's transport and logistics deficits. This is in the realization that supply side constraints distort our region's costs of doing business and undermine our economic competitiveness. It is this realization that gave birth to the North-South Corridor Development Project within which the Chirundu

---

[226] Statement during the Official Launch of the Chirundu One-Stop Border Post, Chirundu, Zambia-Zimbabwe Border on 5th December, 2009.

One Stop Border Post is an inherent part. In April this year at Lusaka, the Tripartite Leadership supported by a number of close Development Partners, notably DFID, JICA, EU, World Bank, African Development Bank and Development Bank of Southern Africa, the North-South Corridor Project was able to attract US $ 1.2 billion in funding pledges. DBSA is raising an additional US $ 1.5 billion for the project.

Years of cross-border trade experience around the world and not just in Africa have shown that the costs of doing business are invariably distorted where the efficiency of supply chains, both in exports and imports, is thwarted by poor facilitation at border points. A recent study report of the World Bank points out that in fact only 25% of the supply chain high costs are attributable to poor physical infrastructure. 75% of the cost distortion is contributed by what are described as soft infrastructure deficits. These are principally people-driven and related to cumbersome customs procedures, bureaucratic behaviour and corruption.

It is these trade facilitation deficits that the One Stop Border Posts seek to address. And this Chirundu One-Stop Border Post is, in this vein, a milestone project. It is a model whose success will constitute a huge case for replication around our COMESA-EAC-SADC region and Africa generally. We have every confidence that this Chirundu Project will significantly reduce supply chain transaction costs, spur higher trade flows and boost the competitiveness of our industries and agriculture.

Let me offer a real example. Currently, it takes 2-3 days for a haulage truck to cross the Chirundu Border point. If you consider that Chirundu handles an average of 268 trucks per day, this translates to a traffic volume of 96,840 trucks per annum, as a minimum. From our calculation, it costs each truck USD140 per day in fixed costs and Drivers' time. Thus for 3 days, the cost per truck is US $ 420. This cost is saved by use of the Chirundu One Stop Border Posts because it is now estimated that each truck should not take more than 2 hours to cross and only 15 minutes for fast track pre-cleared traffic. In our estimation, the potential cost saving per annum is about USD 486 million which accrues to our economies and leverages competitiveness.

The advantages realized from the One Stop Border Post are not merely economic. They are also social and importantly so. Public health research in our broad region shows that there is close association between high incidences of HIV/AIDs transmission and delays in border crossings of haulage trucks. Chirundu and other planned One Stop Border Posts will contribute to a significant reduction in HIV/AIDs vulnerability in this important regional economic sector.

Allow me to conclude by thanking DFID and JICA for their financial and technical support to this Chirundu Project. DFID and JICA are working closely with the Tripartite to develop other Transport Corridors in the

COMESA-EAC-SADC region notably the Northern Corridor in Kenya and the Central Corridor in Tanzania. These corridors will further open up the economic spaces embracing Uganda, Rwanda, Burundi and Eastern DRC.

The Governments of Zimbabwe and Zambia have made a huge contribution to this Chirundu Project. The presence of Presidents Mugabe and Banda here today attests to their valued support of this One Stop Border Post Project. We hail this support and salute our comrade Presidents for their solidarity. Finally, I wish to extend special gratitude to Mr. Kingsley Chanda, the Manager and Coordinator of this One Stop Border Post Project. He has done a commendable job.

On behalf of the COMESA-EAC-SADC Tripartite Task Force, I have great honour to invite their Excellencies, President Robert Mugabe and President Rupiah Banda to address us and officially inaugurate the Chirundu One Stop Border Post.

PART 13

Partnership with Donors and International Agencies

Introduction

It is important to recognize that EAC's integration success has partly been enabled though the support of several Donor friends and collaborations with international institutions ranging from multilateral financial ones to United Nations Agencies. EAC prides itself of a highly successful aid co-ordination and harmonization system in Africa's regional economic communities. Its Partnership Fund is a model to be studied and replicated even at a time when donor fatigue seems bent to discredit the Paris Declaration of 2005 that laid the fundamental principles underlying aid harmonization.

In this part of the book, we offer few examples of the types of valuable relationship the EAC has been able to forge. In earlier parts of the book, more details have been given on the braid range of donor support the EAC has secured over the years in support of its integration projects and programmes.

CHAPTER FORTY FOUR

Partnership in Global Health Care[227]

On behalf of the East African Community, I am pleased to welcome you to the *Fifth European and Developing Countries Clinical Trials Partnership Forum*. Holding this important health care and research partnership forum in Arusha, the seat of the East African Community, is a great honour to East Africa. The timing of your Forum is also of historic importance to the East African Community. At the end of November this year, the EAC is celebrating its 10th Anniversary, marking ten years since the Treaty establishing the Community was signed, on 30th November, 1999.

Some of you will recall that this region has for almost half a century been at the forefront of promoting joint health research. The erstwhile East African Community that collapsed in 1977 was a global leader in promoting cutting edge scientific research in communicable and non-communicable diseases. The East African Medical Research Council (EAMRC), established in 1947, was a premier organisation in the world in the field of tropical medicine and health and its various centres in our region were globally recognised and respected in academia as Centres of Excellence, enabling many Doctor of Philosophy students to research and earn their degrees through research in these centres. I want to assure you today that one of my tasks, a lofty and challenging one at that, is to re-institute this past glory because national health research can never attain the level of capacity and excellence achieved collectively due to economies of scale, both financial and intellectual.

The EAC has lost on time since its tragic collapse in 1977. But time lost is both a cost as well as an opportunity; an opportunity to learn from history and to take advantage of becoming ever more in tune with current relevance and responding to new demands and challenges in a differently more unique and enabling environment. We can thus build on the past and turn it into a force for the present. I believe that the EAC treaty offers us the platform as well as the political will framework to get this new challenge moving. Indeed, the current EAC views the importance of putting effective health service delivery systems and research at the heart of regional cooperation. Article 117 and 118 of the Treaty establishing the EAC recognise this imperative. These treaty provisions put emphasis on joint action towards the prevention and control of communicable and non-communicable diseases including pandemics and epidemics; the promotion of management of health

---

[227] Address to the Fifth European and developing Countries Clinical Trials Partnership Forum, Ngurdoto Mountain Lodge, Arusha, Tanzania, 12th October, 2009.

delivery systems and their better planning; the harmonisation of health policies across the board; and the joint use of health research co-operation.

It is in this context that the EAC has moved forward to establish the East African Community Health Research Commission (EACHRC). We are presently awaiting the ratification by the Partner States of the protocol for the establishment of this Commission. This should not take much time longer. In the meantime, the EAC is in the process of rolling out massive collaborative effort among the East African countries in health research, exchange and utilization of research findings.

The approach to health delivery today is influenced by the rise of a highly discerning consumer of health services as, indeed, of other services. The challenge is not only to ensure the provision of health for all, but also to uphold the quality and efficacy of the heath services provided. There is a direct relationship between the focus on consumer demand and expectations for quality living and the demand for quality contribution by all to the sustenance of a healthy or growing economy and a healthy society. In his recent magisterial book, *Common Wealth: Economics for a Crowded Planet*,[228] Professor Jeffrey Sachs notes that the escape from poverty requires four basic types of investment. One of the types he outlines is health, including control of the main killers-infections, nutritional deficiencies, and unsafe childbirth-through the provision of preventative and curative health services.

In this region, we have had firsthand experience of the devastating impact of the HIV/AIDS and other pandemics which clearly points out to the close relationship between investment in the health sector and the quest for socio-economic transformation. Preventable communicable diseases which cause great social and economic havoc not only to the EAC region but the African continent as a whole could be solved with minimum cost and maximum benefit if only the right political commitment was applied. The challenge is to reduce and eventually eliminate the unnecessary burden of disease management, and allowing the release of scarce resources to productive ends.

A notable challenge is to invest more in the health sector as a basic requirement in the overall development effort. Taking into account the prevailing thrust towards public sector reform and privatization, it is critical to establish the appropriate role for the private sector in delivering health services.

Above all, the challenge of health provision calls for collaborative effort. Within sectors, across ideological divides and governance systems and within regions and the global community, the question and issues about

---

[228] See SACHS, Jeffrey, *Common Wealth: Economics for a Crowded Planet*, op. cit.

health know no boundaries. Health care provision demands systems and logistics that cut across national, regional and international boundaries and barriers; hence emphasizing the necessity for effective collective effort.

Some of these issues relate to the performance and management in the health sector. We need clear indicators for efficient and effective health delivery system. We need to establish benchmarks for assessing the performance of the health systems. And we need to establish adequate resource availability for health care in light of dwindling resource availability and mounting disease burden on our economies.

Indeed, there are competing demands of expenditure on, among others, education, poverty reduction, and defence programmes. The more, therefore, we need to put in place innovative and decisive interventions to shield health programmes demands from erosion or relegation of whatever kind or justification.

Health research, development and delivery, as we all know, are an extremely costly undertaking. Yet as implied in the Health for All clarion call, which has been universally embraced, access to effective health services cannot be reserved for only those nations or sections of the population that can afford it. Everybody must be taken care of, hence the imperative to involve global partnership in health development and provision.

In this regard, I would like to note with great appreciation that the current EAC health co-operation programme and strategy is buttressed and firmly rooted in both African continental and global, UN and other initiatives addressing the emerging global challenges, among them the focus on primary health, human reproductive health and fight against HIV/AIDS, Malaria, Tuberculosis and other health afflictions.

During the 59th Session of the World Health Organization (WHO) Regional Committee for Africa in Kigali in August 2009, the EAC reaffirmed its commitment to these same global initiatives, emphasizing the need to reverse the poor state of health systems in Africa, in particular, not only the need but the imperative of governments, regional and international agents to allocate adequate and sustainable financial resources to health research and development. This collective commitment should aim, above all to institute enforcement of legal and institutional framework with clear focus on the translation of the results of health research into relevant evidence-based national and regional policies and programmes.

It is on this appreciation that the EAC has prioritized health development under the 3rd EAC Development Strategy (2006 to 2010) and is implementing a comprehensive health sector development programme with the good support of the EAC Partner States as well as and tremendous goodwill and support by our development partners. Hence, the past five years have witnessed phenomenal revival of the health research and development in our region among which I would like to acknowledge the following ongoing projects and programmes:-

- The EAC Regional Integrated Multi-sectoral HIV and AIDS Strategic Plan:(2008-2012) whereby Sweden and Ireland have provided – USD $ 8,000,000.00;

- The EAC Regional Project on Cross-Border Human and Animal Disease Prevention and Control for which the Rockefeller Foundation has committed USD $ 500,000.00 over three years;

- The EAC Regional Project on Trade-Related Aspects of Intellectual Property Rights (WTO/TRIPS) and Pharmaceutical Production for which the Federal Government of Germany (BMZ) through the German Technical Cooperation Agency (GTZ) have contributed € 800,000.00 over three years (FY 2009 – 2011);

- The EAC Regional Strategic Plan on Sexual and Reproductive Health and Rights (SRH&R) 2008 – 2013 for which the International Planned Parenthood Federation (IPPF), the United Nations' Population Fund (UNFPA) and the European Commission are providing USD $ 3,000,000;

- The EAC Regional Health Policy Initiative (REACH) 2009-2014 programme under which the European Commission is providing Euros € 400,000.00 over five years;

- The EAC Regional Drug Regulation Harmonization and Pooled Bulk Procurement of Essential Medicines 2010 – 2014 under which the consortium of AU/NEPAD DRH , European Commission and the World Health Organization is providing USD $ 7,865,000.00;

- The EAC Regional Project on Prevention and Control of Human and Animal Trans-boundary Diseases In East Africa: 2008 to 2011 under which the European Commission and the United Nations Food and Agriculture Organization are providing € 3,000,000.00; and

- The EAC Project on *"Addressing Mobility-Induced Vulnerabilities and Gaps in Harmonized Responses to HIV and AIDS in the Lake Victoria Basin Region."* The project is coordinated by the Lake Victoria Basin Commission and is managed by the African Medical and Research Foundation under which the Royal Government of Sweden is providing USD $ 6,443,257.00 over three-years (2007 – 2010).

Also, within the overall EAC health development programme, major ongoing studies include:-

The EAC Situational and Feasibility Study on the Regional Pooled Bulk Procurement of Essential Medicines and Health Supplies in East Africa (2007) – EAC, WHO, JSI/Deliver (USA) and MSH (USA):

- Regional Comparative Study of the Provisions of the EAC Partner States' Patent Laws relevant for the Access to Generic Essential Medicines in East Africa (2008) - (EAC, GTZ, UNCTAD);

- Feasibility Study for the proposed Multinational East African Community Regional Health and Integrated Disease Surveillance and Response Project (2007-2008) – EAC, AfDB and WHO;

- EAC Regional Situational Analysis Study and Needs Assessment on Emergency Preparedness and Response to Avian Influenza (Bird Flu) in East Africa (2006) – EAC/GTZ; Regional East African Community Health (REACH)-Policy Initiative National Consultancy Studies on Health Policy Priority-Setting that can facilitate linking evidence to policy in the East African Community Partner States (2008) – EAC/WHO-AHPSR/IDRC; and

- EAC Regional Situational Analysis Study on Harmonization of Medicines Policies and Regulation in the East African Community Partner States (2009) – EAC/WHO.

The EAC is seized of the need to bring the various ongoing projects and programmes, in particular their research and development components into a coherent and centrifugal force for practical dissemination and application to the regional health challenges. In this regard, the annual East African Community Health and Scientific Conference has been instituted and held regularly, convened by the EAC Secretariat and hosted on a rotational basis in the EAC Partner States, since the 1st one that was held in Kampala, Uganda in 2007. An important adjunct of these Health Conferences is the medical exhibition which showcases and promotes the practical side of the health research content and we are now in the process of launching an East African Medical/Health Research and Development Journal which will further promote the collaborative effort.

With this appreciation of the place of health research and development in our regional and global contexts, I would like to conclude my remarks and thank you once again for holding this important Forum in our region. We look forward to your useful recommendations in promoting high quality health research and knowledge management practices in East Africa and Africa as a whole particularly in fighting HIV and AIDS, Tuberculosis and Malaria, among other priority diseases under the spirit of One World, One Partnership. I thank you for your attention and wish you great success.

CHAPTER FORTY FIVE

EAC-US Relations[229]

Following the recent decision by the Government of the United Republic of Tanzania to allow envoys accredited to Tanzania to also have accreditation to the East African Community, it is a singular pleasure for me to receive you, Your Excellency, at this historic occasion of the presentation of your credentials as the US Representative to the East African Community.

Whilst this system of accreditation of envoys to African institutions such as the African Union and the Regional Economic Communities has existed for several years, it is only now that it is being adopted in the EAC, thanks to the support of the Government of the United Republic of Tanzania. This system opens a new chapter in the development of relations between Governments, foreign as well as regional, and the East African Community. It offers new possibilities for the enhancement of development cooperation from a regional perspective.

The United States and the EAC enjoy a special relationship. It is a relationship founded on our mutual commitment to make regional integration the pivot and driver of faster and more robust social and economic development. Regional integration, after all, is an enabler, through shared benefits of larger markets and economies of scale, particularly in infrastructure development, in locking in peace and stability and spurring investments.

In the past few years, the US-EAC cooperation has grown with focus centring in areas such as infrastructure, civil aviation, trade and investments and defence. The US has assisted the EAC in regional aviation safety and security oversight leading to the establishment in April 2007 of the Civil Aviation Safety and Security Oversight Agency (CASSOA), the first regional body of its kind in Africa. CASSOA is now fully operational with headquarters in Entebbe Uganda.

In the context of civil aviation safety, the US Government has also assisted our region in the installation of state of the art baggage security scanners at the international airports of Jomo Kenyatta in Nairobi, Mwalimu Julius Nyerere in Dar es Salaam and Entebbe in Uganda. Expansion of this support is now being considered under the US Safe Skies for Africa Programme.

---

[229] Statement during occasion of receiving Letters of Accreditation from the Ambassador of the United States of America, at EAC Headquarters, Arusha, Tanzania, 19th March, 2010.

Under the same programme, senior staffs from our region have undergone high level on-the-job and programme training in aviation safety and security. The US government is also supporting the feasibility and design of the EAC Upper Flight Information Region and its system architecture as well as a follow-up Study on the sustainability of the Lower Airspace which will lead to the establishment of the Regional Control Centre.

It is our expectation that this broad support in the civil aviation area will allow our region, as a whole, to gain the US Federal Aviation Agency (FAA) Category 1 certification which will open up direct passenger air transport between the US and East Africa. Presently, Kenya and Tanzania are the only countries to have gained this certification. However, there are pending operational issues, mainly centred on threats of terrorism, which have delayed the commencement of direct flights. It is expected, that with the commencement of direct flights, the EAC region will experience higher levels of tourist visits from the United States.

All these activities, within the civil aviation field, are governed by an MoU which I signed on behalf of the EAC with the then Deputy Secretary of Transportation, retired Vice Admiral Thomas J. Barret in Kampala in April 2008.

In November 2008, the US Government invited the EAC Ministers of Infrastructure to visit the United States. The purpose of the mission was to explore areas of cooperation between the US and the EAC. During that mission, the US Government confirmed support for the feasibility study for the upgrading of the Dar es Salaam-Isaka Railway line to standard gauge and detailed design as well as the finalization of the administrative process for the Millennium Challenge Account (MCA) support to Tanzania. It is important to recognize that the MCA support to Tanzania has a strategic EAC linkage because one of the EAC road networks to benefit there from is the Bagamoyo-Pangani-Tanga-Holili-Mombasa-Malindi highway. It is our hope that the MCA will review its mandate so that it can cater directly for regional infrastructure projects as opposed to its current narrow focus on national projects.

On 16th July, 2008, the United States and the EAC signed a Trade and Investment Framework Agreement (TIFA) in Washington DC. The purpose of the Agreement is to strengthen US-EAC Trade and Investment relationships, expand and diversity bilateral trade and generally improve the business climate between the US and East African enterprises. The US-EAC TIFA has now been operationalised following the 1st Ministerial Council Meeting which took place in Kampala Uganda in February this year. That meeting examined US and EAC work with respect to the implementation of AGOA, as well as to issues related to market access, trade capacity building, the financial sector, agricultural trade and the business environment.

The meeting also had the opportunity to set priorities, identify objectives, outline current impediments and chart out the way forward for bolstering US-EAC relations under TIFA. It is important to point out that following the AGOA meeting that took place in Nairobi last year, a new momentum is now being seized in getting the EAC to backstop the engagement of the EAC Partner States in respect to AGOA issues.

Trade between the US and the EAC region in 2009 stood as follows:

- US exports to EAC – US $ 974 million; and
- EAC exports to US – US $ 384 million;

In other words, in 2009, the United States had a trade surplus of US $ 590 million. The challenge is for the EAC region to export more by exploiting the preferential access under AGOA as well as the opportunities under the TIFA. In this context, the EAC is exploring a number of avenues geared at improving the productivity of agriculture including value addition, and bolstering the capacities of small and medium enterprises in the region. In turn, the EAC is working closely with USAID-COMPETE whose thrust is to enhance economic growth and competitiveness and food security in our region.

Presently, the EAC and USAID and USAID-COMPETE are in the final stages of formulating a project plan for the EAC which seeks to enhance trade facilitation, access to markets, improve the regional competition law, harmonize export policies, develop an EAC Trade database and put in place an IT module for monitoring Non-Tariff Barriers and for dissemination of key policies affecting trade. We expect that this project will be initially funded by USAID during the US fiscal year October 2010 – September 2011. Let me also add that last year the EAC signed a 3 year Agreement with USAID to support the Lake Victoria Basin Commission on environmental management. This programme is operating well.

The US has had defence cooperation in our region dating several decades, particularly with Kenya. Happily, late last year, the US and the EAC were able to open a new chapter in defence cooperation through the field military training exercise code named, 'NATURAL FIRE,' in Kitgum, Northern Uganda. The Exercises involved troops from the US Africa Command (AFRICOM) and the Defence Forces from all the EAC Partner States. Presently, the EAC and AFRICOM are in the process of developing a framework of cooperation which the EAC Sectoral Council on Defence will be considering in June this year. Noteworthy, is that a team from AFRICOM was in Arusha last week to meet the EAC Defence Liaison Team to discuss and plan next Joint Military Exercises.

Related to defence cooperation is the piracy menace on the Indian Ocean that borders the EAC coastal Partner States. The EAC is deeply concerned about this piracy threat to its strategic trade routes. In this context, the EAC Partner States are collaborating with US Patrols in the western rim of the Indian Ocean. Our Ministers for Infrastructure have also directed the EAC to develop a Maritime Transport Policy as well as propose the establishment of a Maritime Patrol Unit and new maritime laws which should take into account maritime piracy in domestic and territorial waters and the legal measures needed to deal with it.

I have taken some time to reflect on current US-EAC relations, but I have done so deliberately because, as I said, this is a historic occasion; it is one which is beyond symbolism and grandeur. It is an occasion which I believe will trigger a new wave of deeper cooperation between the US Government and the East African Community. In fact, our hope is that the US Government will shortly be able to support the EAC Partnership Fund.

PART 14

EAC – Challenges, Some Milestones and the Way Forward

At the start of the Second EAC Decade, we need a new dynamism, greater resolve and boldness to look beyond the horizon. We need to ensure that the EAC is more strategically positioned for the world in 2020.

Jakaya Mrisho Kikwete[230]

President Jakaya Kikwete made an inspirational address as captioned in the extract above regarding how the EAC can boldly move forward and realize its great ambitions. In the chapter that follows which in my view stands out as probably the most important chapter in this book, I try to show that what will enable the EAC to indeed take giant steps forward hinges on how national politics play out on the integration front.

---

[230] Speech to the EAC Summit, Arusha, 3rd December, 2010.

CHAPTER FOURTY SIX

The EAC: Past, Present and Future[231]

Introduction

Without oversimplifying the challenge of regional integration, I believe it is powerful mindsets, cooked and baked in the kitchens and ovens of our societies that constitute the bedrock for realising the mission of regional integration. After all, regional integration, at heart, is an idea, a philosophy and, as the late Mwalimu Julius Nyerere argued in the case of socialism, that "socialism is an attitude of mind,"[232] so is regional integration. Thus East African societies have a special missionary responsibility to create the East African person who is deeply ingrained in the ethos, meaning and purpose of East African integration.

The Past and EAC's Lessons

At the outset let me state the evident, that the past is actually history. And in as much as we always learn from the past, and, indeed the past often provides an informed context for the future, I will only dwell briefly on East African Community's past; the details are for historians and political scientists. Suffice to state that the EAC, in its various historical forms, is the oldest regional economic organisation in the world. Its early form was inspired by a colonialist and imperialist purpose; that of a coordinated exploitation of East African resources by the British, especially from the end of the First World War period when Tanganyika, an ex-Germany colony, joined Kenya and Uganda as British administered territories.

The history of the East African Customs Union established in 1922, followed by the East African High Commission, established in 1948, and the East African Common Services Organisation (EACSO) constituted in 1961, before even Tanganyika became independent notwithstanding, are positive elements to celebrate in terms of the form, structure and operations of those colonial institutional arrangements. Quite clearly, the establishment of the erstwhile East African Community in 1967 drew significant and useful

---

[231] Contribution in First Magazine Special Publication of the *EAC 10 Years of Regional Integration*, 2010.

[232] See NYERERE, Julius K., "Ujamaa: The Basis of African Socialism," Dar es Salaam, April, 1962 (http://www.juliusnyerere.info/images/uploads/ujamaa_1962.pdf); and NYERERE, Julius K., *Ujamaa – Essays on Soci*alism, Dar es Salaam: Oxford University Press, 1973.

lessons as well as experiences from that colonial inspired regional organisation system. But as history would have it, the first broad experiment at regional integration in Africa failed with the collapse of the EAC in 1977. One needs to note though that the first form of regional integration in Africa was, in fact, the Southern African Customs Union (SACU) established in 1910. However, SACU constitutes a narrow form of integration. Indeed, as of 1967 when the EAC was being established, SACU did not qualify to be described as an African regional integration organisation because apartheid South Africa was at its heart and its other members were basically colonial states or surrogate African kingdoms.

At the time of its collapse, regional integration in East Africa had reached the highest level experienced in the world. The EAC was both a fully fledged Customs Union and a Common Market. It had robust shared economic institutions embracing railways and harbours, airline, civil aviation, inland waterways, road transport systems, post and telecommunication, power and lighting, customs and tax management, health and medical research, aviation training, pesticides research etc. Importantly, and until 1970, the EAC also had the University of East Africa with three constituent colleges at Makerere, Nairobi and Dar es Salaam and with a well clarified division of academic labour or discourse. At the same time, under the EAC umbrella, were the East African Court of Justice with final appellate jurisdiction for criminal and civil cases, an East African Legislative Assembly and a Secretariat headed by a Secretary General supported by a number of Ministers appointed by the then three Partner States with responsibility for various portfolios relevant to regional integration. Not even the current European Union has an institutional framework as elaborate and powerful in decision making as that of the EAC in the period up to April1977.

Lessons from the Past EAC

An objective assessment of the first EAC cannot avoid the fundamental question, namely: were the then three EAC Partner States well prepared for a bold and robust integration system of the type they had put in place in 1967 or was the adoption of that integration system driven more by a quick and loose acceptance of an inherited colonial legacy constituted in the East African Common Services Organisation? It is important to give this question a critical and objective examination bearing in mind that the proposal for an East African Political Federation which Nyerere had first touted in 1960 failed to garner support from Kenya and much less from Uganda where the politics of the Buganda Kingdom and of the other lesser kingdoms took sway. In other words, could it be that the establishment of the EAC in 1967 may not have enjoyed a strong political underpinning in the sense of its being sufficiently or widely people owned and driven?

In turn, because the top political East African leaders constituted the dominant decision makers in EAC affairs, could it be that the EAC then became vulnerable to the politics of nation-state power and differences in economic ideology at a time when the cold war was showing its ugly head in the newly independent countries of Africa? It would seem reasonable to conjecture that it was difficult to see how the EAC nation- states could sustain, for too long, the continued collective ownership of strategic social and economic services under the EAC framework that constituted the bedrock of national economic interest. At that stage, significant sovereignty had been ceded to the EAC over critical matters that ordinarily fell under the control of national agencies, such as taxation and revenue, trade policy and economic infrastructure development in the absence of a supporting solid political underpinning which could only be justified by a Political Federation.

The EAC at Present

The foregoing review constitutes what you can describe as the past in EAC's integration history. What is important is to determine the precise lessons that can be drawn from that history and contextualise it on the present and the future of EAC integration. In my view, there are at least six lessons that can be adduced from the past EAC history:

First, that regional integration is a highly complex and sensitive project. It needs to deepen and widen on the basis of a building bloc strategy; slowly, carefully but surely executed.

Second, the decision making process should be structured in such a way that there is respect for national interests and thus the importance of placing the role of the Partner States at the heart of the EAC decision making structure and process, allowing the principles of consensus and subsidiarity to rule whilst respecting the imperative of the big picture to inform the depth and speed of integration.

Third, that the Council of Ministers, instead of the Summit of Heads of State, takes the lead in the decision making process whilst assigning to the Summit the authority over politically sensitive decisions that are focused on matters such as the movement from one stage of integration to the next as well as on the enlargement of the organisation where allowing new members apply to accede to the Community.

Fourth, that the organisation should be people centred and market driven. This means that decisions regarding the deepening of integration should directly involve the people through a whole range of multi-stakeholder vehicles. Equally, as ideologies of the left and the right have retreated with greater focus being placed on what works best in the interest of the people's welfare and prosperity, the private sector should be more closely engaged in determining the direction of the organization and the pace thereof, always mindful of the centrality of win-win outcomes rather than zero-sum approaches to integration.

Fifth, the establishment of fully fledged EAC social and economic institutions that are jointly shared and owned by the Partner States should be more carefully established to ensure their efficacy, cost effectiveness and sustainability.

Sixth, since the ultimate goal of the EAC is a Political Federation, there is need to put in place the institutional framework that would support such ultimate objective. Thus, Organs such as the East African Legislative Assembly and the East African Court of Justice should be structured in such a manner and be given such responsibility that they are best able to support the realisation of the ultimate goal of a Political Federation.

It is the foregoing six principles that have underlined the form of the current legal structure and functioning of the EAC. Indeed, the Treaty establishing the EAC encapsulates them in clear terms. Of course, ten years after the signing of the Treaty, there are a number of weaknesses that feature in the Treaty. However, these weaknesses were in fact noted at the point of drafting the Treaty. They were nevertheless accommodated in the light of the lessons learnt from some of the underlying causes for the break-up of the earlier EAC. Thus, for example, the decision making process based on consensus does, in fact, pose a number of challenges to the EAC because when one Partner State is not able to attend a statutory meeting, quorum is undermined.

As a result of such weakness, the EAC has had to move largely on the basis of the application of the breaks rather than of the accelerator, to use a motor industry expression. But it is a system that has been politically correct. Pleasingly, notwithstanding this seemingly decision making gridlock, informed observers outside the EAC view the achievements made by the EAC, so far, as exemplary. During the US-Africa AGOA Forum held in Washington DC on 3rd August, 2010, the US Secretary of State Hilary Clinton had this to say about the East African Community:

> We can see the benefits of greater regional integration in the progress and potential of the East African Community which brings together 127 million people of Kenya, Tanzania, Uganda, Rwanda and Burundi and their combined GDP of US $ 73 billion. In 2005, these nations launched a Customs Union and last month they declared a Common Market. The East African Community eliminated or reduced tariffs on goods traded within the Community, made it easier for workers and companies to do business in any of their countries and created institutions to implement policies uniformly across the region. And look at the results already: trade between East African

Community nations has increased by nearly 50% since the Customs Union was established.

Investment and foreign trade has followed. Between 2008 and 2009 trade between the East African Community and America rose by more than 13%. Now, there is certainly more work to be done, but the United States believes in the potential of regional integration like the East African Community and we are committed to supporting it. We signed a Trade and Investment Framework Agreement with the Community in 2008 and this spring we became the first nation to accredit an Ambassador to the Community. And later this year we will launch a new technical assistance programme. We are working together with the EAC nations on improving aviation security and infrastructure development, addressing piracy in the West Indian Ocean and ensuring that the benefits of economic integration are translated into broad-based prosperity for the people. Because, ultimately, success must be measured in the results people see in their daily lives. Sub-Saharan Africa has some 14 Regional Trade or Cooperation Agreements, many of them overlapping and not all as successful as the East African Community.

Celebrating EAC's Present Successes

You can thus understand and appreciate that there is much to celebrate for in what the EAC has achieved in the past ten years of its existence. The EAC is the only other Customs Union in Africa after the Southern African Customs Union (SACU). Indeed, whilst SACU is more than 100 years old, its leadership visited the EAC in 2009 to learn from the EAC within the confines of the Customs Union and, more broadly, on how a regional integration institution is best run. Yet it is important to recognise that the negotiations towards the establishment of the Customs Union took almost four years because there was strict adherence to the principle enshrined in the Treaty that the EAC integration process must be people-centred thus necessitating a broad participatory approach to the adoption of integration programmes. And whilst the EAC Customs Union continues to face a number of challenges to become more effective, challenges such as non-tariff barriers, (NTBs), represented by inefficient border posts, too many road blocks, too many transit road weigh bridges, long clearances at ports, corruption and poor roads and railways infrastructure, intra-EAC trade has grown by as much as 50% between January 2005 and currently. Of course, this regional trade performance represents a mere 12% of EAC trade with the rest of the world.

What is clear though is that this share of EAC trade to the rest of the world could be as high as 30% were the NTBs removed and the physical infrastructure improved. Contrast this position with that in SACU. There the share of intra-SACU trade to the rest of the world averages about 85% in the case of countries such as Namibia, Swaziland, Botswana and Lesotho. This status is largely attributed to the centrality of the large South African economy in that trade relationship regime. The reality is that there is no good reason why the EAC region cannot equally realise a higher share of intra-regional trade. The solution lies in giving greater attention to scaling up industrialisation especially with respect to adding value to agricultural commodities. In this regard, the EAC is presently finalising an industrialisation policy and strategy which should help in shaping a new direction towards growing the intra-regional market and trade.

Moreover, the EAC has become the first African regional economic community to establish a Common Market, effective 1st July this year. The only other Common Markets in the world are the European Union and the Caribbean Economic Community. EAC's achievement is thus of no small measure. The EAC region will, in the next five years, steadily open up to the free movement of persons, labour, capital and services. It is a process that will lead to the region becoming a fully fledged economic community with massive benefits in higher economic growth, jobs creation and improvement in per capita incomes. Evidently, there will be challenges on the way. But then, who says that regional integration outside a political integration structure is easy?

A French politician, Paul-Henri Spaak remarked in June 1961:

> Those who, in trying to meet the economic challenges set out by the Treaty of Rome (the treaty that established the European Union) neglected the political dimension have failed. As long as (those) challenges will be addressed exclusively in an economic perspective, disregarding their political angle, we will run-I am afraid-into repeated failures.[233]

What is important to note, however, is that the EAC Common Market Protocol took 18 months to negotiate, and a host of multi-stakeholders-government and the private sector as well as professional organisations-were involved in the negotiation process. Indeed, some of the Annexes to the Protocol are yet to be finalised. But precisely because of the highly participatory process that has taken place in arriving at complex decisions

---

[233] He is quoted with approval as an inspirational figure to regional integration in Europe in MONTI, Mario, *A New Strategy for the Single Market – At the Service of Europe's Economy and Society: Report to the President of the European Commission José Manuel Barroso*, op. cit. at p. 1.

and programmes, there is plausible certainty that the challenges in implementing the Common Market would be smoothly confronted and resolved.

18 years after the establishment of the Single Market, the European Union continues to face a number of challenges in getting its Single Market to operate fully and effectively. In the case of the EAC, the movement towards attaining a fully fledged Common Market is supported by appropriate institutions and programmes already in place. For example, through the Inter University Council for East Africa (IUCEA), which is an EAC institution and the only one of its kind in an African regional integration organisation, there are ongoing measures to harmonise educational systems, curricula and academic qualifications in the EAC region much along the Bologna Process in the European Union.

Indeed, there are unfolding attempts at enabling the IUCEA to be authorized to issue single accreditation for tertiary education institutions that seek to open institutions of higher learning on a regional-wide basis with campuses in some or all of the EAC Partner States. The work of the IUCEA should support one of the goals of the Common Market, namely the free movement of labour in the region. In the area of trade in services, notably, air transport, the EAC has a specialised civil aviation institution in the Civil Aviation Safety and Security Oversight Agency (CASSOA), also the only one of its kind in Africa. This Agency is spearheading the promotion of air safety and security oversight, including the development of harmonised civil aviation systems and regulations and the establishment of a free skies regime in line with the Yamoussoukro Decision which seeks to liberalise Africa's airspace in order to lower the costs of air transport in Africa. The EAC is also working closely with the East African Social Security Association which binds all the states' Social Security Organisations to develop a Social Security Benefits Scheme that would inspire free movement of labour in the region.

Equally, there are concrete developments in getting the East African Stock Exchanges and Securities Exchange operators to forge a policy and legal framework that would allow the establishment of an East African Stock Exchange. It is envisaged that the evolution of a regional platform where companies shall be able to raise non-debt capital through IPOs from East African citizens shall support endeavours in funding regional economic activities, notably in infrastructure development.

And since 2000, the EAC has been working closely with the East African Business Council (EABC), the voice of the private sector in East Africa, in ensuring that private sector interests and concerns are captured, enshrined and promoted in EAC's programmes and projects. Thus, in partnership with the EABC, the EAC has been able to mainstream an Annual EAC

Investment Conference since 2008 and an Annual EAC Media Conference since 2007. The Investment Conferences have succeeded in putting the EAC region in the regional and global investment and tourism map. The Media Conferences, on the other hand, have catapulted greater interest by the media in covering EAC integration affairs.

Deepening EAC Integration

Following the establishment of the Common Market, the EAC is now placing serious emphasis on the next stage of its integration, namely the establishment of the Monetary Union. Admittedly, this is a more complex stage of integration. Only the European Union has been able to achieve it. Many of us would, however, be aware of the challenges that confront the EU Monetary Union. Indeed, because of its complexity and the lessons that are emerging from the European Union, the EAC is tackling this next stage of integration with serious care and caution. That said, the EAC Central Bank Governors are seriously committed to proposing realistic measures to be undertaken as well as a roadmap towards the realisation of the Monetary Union and a common currency objective. A clearer picture of this process should be ready by the end of 2010.

The Infrastructure Challenge

As all these integration processes move forward, the EAC is well seized of the fact that what critically drives economic integration is the existence of robust, reliable and cost effective infrastructure. There is little doubt that the current state of EAC's physical infrastructure- roads, railways, ports and harbours and energy- erodes the region's competitiveness and its attractiveness to serious local and foreign investment. As noted earlier, the size of the regional market could be much higher and more vibrant had these infrastructures been equally vibrant. For these reasons, the EAC has a number of plans and programmes for addressing infrastructure challenges. It already has in place well developed Master Plans for railways, roads and energy, all of them from a regional perspective. The critical challenge, however, is how to mobilise the requisite resources needed to implement these projects. For example, the modernisation of the East African Railways System alone requires about US $ 20 billion.

Experience shows that dominant reliance on resources from multinational financial institutions such as the World Bank, the African Development Bank and the Japan Bank for International Development, amongst other financial institutions, is not the most appropriate choice largely because funding is always inadequate and takes a long time to materialise. In this context, the EAC is searching for alternative sources for raising capital. On the one hand, the EAC is in the process of establishing a Development Fund to be financed by the Partner States from their budgets as well as by Donors. On the other hand, the EAC is discussing with the Partner States on the possibility of raising risk capital through infrastructure bonds, to be floated regionally and globally. Such bonds could be national; but they could also take the form of regional bonds and using financial vehicles such as the East African Development Bank supported by state guarantees issued by the national central banks. The challenge involved here is for the member states to have internationally acceptable credit risk grades.

EAC Future Prospects

A key feature of the EAC in the future lies in the quest for a Political Federation. It is clear that Mwalimu Julius Nyerere was right when he said in June, 1960 when addressing the Second Conference of Independent African States on East African Federation that delaying the East African Federation could undermine its realisation in the future because, after complete independence, it would be difficult to surrender "sovereignty and all the prestige and symbols of such sovereignty." However, even with these challenges looming large, the EAC remains committed to the ideal of a Political Federation. In the past two years, efforts have been taken to consult the citizens of East Africa on this lofty goal. Results from the consultation processes indicate that 80% of the citizens of East Africa, on average, support the idea of a Political Federation.

However, many of the citizens have concerns regarding the pace towards such Federation and on the basic nature of the Federation itself. The EAC Summit of Heads of State in November 2009 decided to constitute a Team of Experts drawn from all the five Partner States to delve deeper into the views and concerns of the East African citizens on the Political Federation and submit practical proposals on the way forward. This team has been meeting since February this year and its recommendations will be tabled at the Summit of Heads of State in early December 2010.

Conclusion

Ten years after the establishment of the EAC, there is much that has been achieved to offer hope for deeper and wider integration. Confidence of the people on integration has been regenerated. The entry of the terrestrial television has given birth to East African music and soap operas that have helped to shape an East African identity and galvanise the youth around regional themes of solidarity and common pursuits of prosperity. There is little doubt that the EAC integration project has reached its watershed. It can thus only move forward. As Brutus philosophises in *Julius Caesar*:

There is a tide in the affairs of men.

Which, taken at the flood, leads on to fortune;

Omitted, all the voyage of their life,

Is bound in shallows and in miseries.

On such a full sea are we now afloat,

And we must take the current when it serves,

Or lose our ventures.

The EAC is presently afloat at a full sea. It is committed to taking the current; it cannot afford to lose the ventures it has realised. Its future holds for greater ambitions and achievements.

CHAPTER FORTY SEVEN

EAC: Key Milestones - 2006-2011[234]

African countries have adopted numerous regional co-operation and integration arrangements, many of which are purely ornamental. The roles of bigger markets in stimulating technological innovation, fostering economies of scale arising from infrastructure investments, and the diffusion of technical skills into the wider economy are some of the key gains Africa hopes to derive from economic integration.

Calestous Juma[235]

Introduction

Let me begin by wishing you all a happy and productive new year 2011. I hope the festive season went well and that you were able to relax with your families and returning fresh to face yet another year of hard work. There is so much more for the EAC to realise and 2011 will be yet another year when all of us will be called upon to give the best for the interest of our integration.

This is my last New Year Address. As you all know, my term of office ends on 24th April. As such, I may not have another opportune stage than this to bid you farewell and to share with you some of my insights regarding the state of the EAC. Allow me, therefore, to wish you the best for the future as you continue in the years ahead to build this important institution, working towards the lofty goal of integrating not only our economies but our people as well – socially and politically.

I want to thank all of you for the journey we have walked together since I took over as Secretary General on 25th April, 2006. Five years is indeed a short time as we now realise. The past near five years have been eventful and, together, we have worked closely and tirelessly in moving the process of integration forward. I do not believe in self congratulation; other people should judge us from an objective standpoint for the work we have done. Yet I believe we can look back to these past five years and identify a number of important milestones realised, successes made and the challenges that continue to confront us.

---

[234] New Year Message to EAC Staff, Tausi Hall, Arusha International Conference Centre 20th January, 2011.

[235] JUMA, Calestous, *The New Harvest-Agricultural Innovation in Africa*, Oxford: Oxford *University Press*, 2011.

Human Resources Development

You will recall that when I came to the EAC, our total staff complement was 41 Professional Staff and 49 General Staff. Our salaries and perks were quite low. Since January 2007, you will recall new salaries and perks were approved providing a more motivational terms and conditions of service. For example, there was almost a doubling of the basic salary across the board, from the Executive to the Professional to the General Staff. Today, we have a staff force of 96 Professionals and 79 General Staff which excludes staff at the Lake Victoria Basin Commission (LVBC) which is 25 Professional Staff and 16 General Staff. It is important also to note that at the EAC Secretariat we also now have 29 project staff.

I realise, however, that some positions within the EAC are yet to be accorded justice insofar as salaries and perks are concerned commensurate with the status and responsibilities of their positions. I have in mind, for example, the status of the position of the Counsel to the Community, a position which is recognised in the Treaty establishing the EAC. I have for some time now argued the case for this post to be elevated to an Executive level and the Sectoral Council on Legal and Judicial Affairs has fully supported this proposal. I hope that justice will be done soon.

Financial Resources Development

On another plane, you will recall that EAC had serious budget challenges when I joined. Of course, there was significant reliance on budget contributions from the Partner States which was a brilliant idea considering the goal of self reliance and ownership of the integration process. However, as we know, there have been serious challenges to get the 3rd EAC Development Strategy, 2006-2010 well implemented by relying overly on budget contributions from the Partner States. The total EAC Budget for the Financial Year 2005/2006 was USD 18,936,092 of which the contribution of the Partner States was US $ 10,476,257 and the contribution of the development partners was US $ 8,459,235. There is a huge contrast between that financial position and the current one. In the current Financial Year 2010/2011, the total budget of the EAC is USD 78,568,833 of which the Partner States contribution is US $ 30,821,989 and the contribution of the development partners is US $ 47, 746, 844. Thanks to our collective ingenuity, we have been able to secure greater support from the friends of the EAC through a Partnership Fund we established in 2007.

I take this opportunity to recognise the diligence and excellent quality of resource mobilisation work of Dr. James Njagu for the achievements we have made in this area of resource mobilisation; but I also wish to thank the friends of the EAC who have come to believe in us and believe in the serious and productive work we are doing as so vividly expressed by the level of support they now extend to the EAC. Of course, the evident picture that emerges is that the EAC is too heavily reliant on development assistance for supporting its programmes and projects. Whilst this is not a sustainable position, it reflects the reality that obtains in most of the EAC Partner States. We mirror the realities of our owners.

For quite some time now the EAC Secretariat has been pursuing the idea of finding more sustainable means of financing the EAC budget. Since 2005 proposals have been tabled in this particular respect with insignificant results. Lately, this matter has been re-visited at the Council level where various options for raising finance from the Partner States to meet EAC's budget requirements have been proposed. Unfortunately, the usual decision that Partner States need more time to examine and review the proposed options has delayed the adoption of a firm decision. In parallel, over the last two years serious effort has been made to put in place a development fund which is intended to, on the one hand, help to ameliorate loss of revenue by Partner States where these arise for whatever reason in implementing EAC's programmes and, on the other, to provide support funding for implementing EAC's development projects. A draft protocol for the establishment of this fund has been finalised and a decision is now being awaited from the Council of Ministers.

Internal Financial Controls

It is important to note that we probably could have mobilised even more resources had we also improved our internal financial controls and audit management. One area of major weakness in the EAC in the last few years has been in this area of financial controls and internal audit. This is an area which has also suffered significantly in terms of capacity. For this reason, the EAC has been unable to secure a contribution agreement with the European Commission and we continue to be served insofar as the management and disbursement of EU funding under the 9th and 10th European Development Funds (EDF) through COMESA. But thanks to the support over the last one year, firstly from DFID and latterly from Trade Mark East Africa (TMEA), the EAC Secretariat is now on course in putting in place better systems of financial controls, internal audit, procurement, risk management and even human resource management system. This capacity development support which includes the revamping of staffing in all these areas, including improvement in the computer based control systems will enable us to secure our own contribution agreement with the European Commission in the next Financial Year.

Institutional Development

Another issue that we recognised from the onset of my taking up the post of SG was that there was urgent need to transform the EAC organisation structure to respond adequately to the strategy and tasks of the EAC. Crowning over three years of consultations and seeking solutions, during the last one year, significant work has been ongoing to further review the EAC organisation structure and its manning levels from a longer term and strategic perspective. The institutional review report is now ready and will be tabled at the next Council of Ministers meeting for decision. I should add that both the East African Legislative Assembly and the East African Court of Justice have also benefited from the overall organisation change processes that started early in 2007.

At the level of the institutions, some work has also been ongoing to give proper legal structure to the IUCEA, the LVBC and CASSOA. The Bill for the IUCEA was passed and there is now a proper reporting relationship between this Council and the EAC organs. Unfortunately, the Bills in respect of CASSOA and LVBC have met with some difficulty at the level of the EALA but there is light at the end of the tunnel. Also, some of the proposed institutions are yet to be put in place regrettably because the politics of equitable sharing of benefits have cropped up with too much sensitivity. As such the hosting of these institutions has proven to be a stumbling block though I have every trust that we shall overcome these bottlenecks during this calendar year.

Admission of Rwanda and Burundi

One of the historic moments of my term of office was the negotiations for the accession of Rwanda and Burundi into the EAC. Looking back, those negotiations were quite hard. Indeed, some of us were even accused of circumventing due processes by not following the establishing rigorous evaluation criteria. Happily, Rwanda and Burundi joined and today the EAC is a more vibrant institution as a result. However, with any form of enlargement, even of our own families, challenges invariably present themselves. Some of these challenges continue to face us even three years after the accession of Rwanda and Burundi.

We all know the continuing saga about the roadmap on integrating Rwanda and Burundi into the EAC, the equitable sharing of benefits, the issues relating to employment quotas etc. I am glad to observe that finally the process is underway to further reorganise the structure of the Secretariat to leverage our efficiencies but also to allow Rwanda and Burundi take up some senior positions to earn visibility but also to begin a process of giving weight to geographical distribution of positions in the EAC. We have to face these challenges boldly and work towards ensuring that all the Partner States, old and new, feel adequately recognised as equal members of our organisation.

Collaboration with EABC

I have earlier alluded to our collaboration with the East African Business Council. If there is one area of success which we must celebrate, it is our relationship with the EABC. If you recall, it took me just about a month after joining the EAC to address an important EABC Conference at Ngurdoto where I defined the kind of relationship I wanted the EAC to develop with the EABC and the private sector generally in East Africa. The record is there to see. From the Annual EAC Media Summits, the Annual EAC Investment Conferences, the constant dialogues and interfaces between the EABC Executive Council with the Summit, to several other joint programmes in areas such as NTBs, counterfeits and piracy, illicit trade, HIV and AIDs etc. The EAC has been able to translate the Treaty vision of an EAC that is market driven into tangible results. This is not to say that our relationship has reached the final station. The road to that destination remains potholed. Much remains to be done in our region to lower the cost of doing business, effectively integrate small and medium enterprises into the regional economy and transform the overall regional economy to be competitive with itself and with the rest of the world. In my next life "after April this year" I hope to rejoin the ranks of the East African Business Community to continue this worthy partnership with the EAC in addressing these remaining challenges.

Programme Delivery

In response to EAC's enlarged mandate and the need to forge sector specialisation in promoting the EAC Development Strategy 2006-2010, we have succeeded to propose the establishment of specialised institutions in the areas of Health, Science and Technology, Kiswahili and Culture and Sports, including the EAC Civil Aviation Safety and Security Oversight Agency (CASSOA) which came into being in 2007.

CASSOA

Considerable work has so far been done to get CASSOA moving and come up with important results in the areas of safety and security oversight in the field of civil aviation. CASSOA has managed to undertake the revision and harmonisation of the Civil Aviation Safety Regulations covering aircraft airworthiness, flight operations and personnel licensing. Indeed, the EAC is the first region in Africa and the developing world to undertake this work. CASSOA has also harmonised the airport security and air navigation regulations which will enhance civil aviation safety, security and traffic facilitation.

The EAC is therefore making positive progress with regard to the liberalisation of air transport under the framework of the Yamoussoukro decision. The EAC Council of Ministers has already directed all the Partner States to remove capacity and frequency restrictions in their bilateral air transport agreements. This decision has allowed multiple designations of air operators. The decision has also resulted in capacity expansion on many EAC regional routes with some city pairs having more than ten frequencies per day by multiple operators. This expansion provides greater consumer choice in the region, promotes competition and removal of air fare distortions. A major study on the unification of the EAC upper flight information region was completed last year and the Council of Ministers has adopted the Report. A Study on the sustainability of the lower air space is awaiting funding. I wish to take this opportunity to applaud Mr. Maugo for his leadership of CASSOA.

IUCEA

With regard to the Inter-University Council for East Africa (UCEA), a lot of progress has been made in the quest for harmonization of curricular and enhancement (quality assurance) of education in East Africa. Allow me also to take this opportunity to recognise the excellent work undertaken by Prof. Chacha Nyaigotti Chacha at the IUCEA. Prof. Chacha has completed his term of office and is now back to his former University at Egerton. We wish him well knowing that we shall always resort to his expertise and experience in supporting the IUCEA in the years ahead.

LVBC

During the past few years we have also seen the Lake Victoria Basin Commission (LVBC) take up its own independent location and management in Kisumu. I want to use this opportunity to applaud the leadership of Dr. Tom Okurut and his colleagues in growing the LVBC to a position of stature recognised internationally. LVBC has received increasing support of development partners, the World Bank the AfDB and Habitat to support a number of projects covering water and sanitation, trans-boundary ecosystems, HIV and AIDs and other programmes. All this support is explained by the status which the LVBC has reached and the manner in which the institution has been managed. Through the RV *Jumuiya*, the Research Vessel the EAC owns, LVBC has been undertaking commendable work in preparing new navigation maps for the Lake Victoria as well as structuring an effective search and rescue communication system in collaboration with Airtel and Erikson.

Through the initiative of the LVBC, a Lake Victoria Transport Act has been enacted which provides the necessary legal and regulatory framework supportive of investments on the Lake and its basin. Early in December last year, the LVBC organised the 1st Investment Conference in Mwanza which was well attended with successful outcomes. The Conference was able to showcase a number of investment opportunities that exist in areas such as passenger shipping, cargo transport, tourism, water sports etc but equally the Investment Conference was able to outline opportunities that exist for philanthropic organisations to participate in search and rescue operations.

Customs Union

We have made similarly spectacular achievements at the broader programmatic levels of the major pillars and stages of the integration process. Thus, during the past 5 years we have seen the Customs Union take greater shape with greater confidence emerging within the business sector. The result has been a phenomenal rise in intra-EAC trade – of as much as 50%. Cross-border investments have taken wings and Kenya is today a top investor in the other EAC countries. Those who exclaim about this dominant Kenyan position forget that in most regions of the world a regional champion constitutes the critical factor in catalysing the development of the rest of the region.

Japan was such champion in Asia, propelling the rise of the Asian tigers in the 1980s and 1990s. China is now taking over the lead as regional champion of Asia. Brazil occupies a similar role in South America. Germany has always been the motive power of the EU economy. Thus when President Nelson Mandela, upon assuming the South African presidency in 1994, stated that South Africa had to move away from a regime where 'beggar thy neighbour' was the dominant environment to a regime that fostered an environment of prospering South Africa's neighbouring countries. Equitable and balanced development in the EAC region will crucially emanate from Kenya playing an even deeper investment role and catalyse investments and growth in the other Partner States as well. I believe that following the signing of the double taxation avoidance agreement this past December our region will see greater impetus in cross border investments as well as in the flow of foreign direct investment.

The success of the Customs Union however, has to be tampered by some serious challenges that diminish its vital force. NTBs continue to distort the cost of trade logistics and erode the competitiveness of our goods and services. There are moves to establish One Stop Border Posts as one possible solution to curtailing NTBs. But this intervention would have to be supported by a number of other measures which continue to elude us which include drastically reducing the number of weighbridges, policy roadblocks as well as transforming the mindsets of our border customs officials who still tend to think nationally rather than regionally.

Delaying to take resolute action in these areas would mock the very purpose of a Customs Union. Indeed, the continuation of the sensitivity list of raw materials undermines the functioning of the Customs Union and distorts the free play of the market in the Customs Union. It is important that these sensitivity lists are totally eliminated by end of June this year. We should also work towards the finalisation of the Sanitary and Phyto-Sanitary issues which also hamper the growth of trade in agricultural commodities and products.

Curbing Illicit Trade

Intra-EAC's trade presently represents only 11% of EAC total trade with the rest of the world. It is clear that we are yet to develop a worthwhile internal market in the region. All the challenges that I have made reference to have an impact on this low level of trade amongst us. However, a big contributing factor is the state of illicit trade in our region. The incentives necessary to spur higher levels of industrialisation in the region are currently undermined by the high level of counterfeit and pirated goods that enter the Customs Union territory. This menace has to be eradicated as soon as possible if there is any serious attempt to make industrialisation an important driver of bolstering a bigger internal market.

The EAC is about to finalise an industrialisation strategy which will define the industry location as well as the priorities which will induce investments. However, the success of such industrialisation strategy crucially hinges on how quickly the menace of counterfeits and piracy is addressed. The EAC is about to finalise a regional law as part solution to this menace. It is hoped that the EAC Anti-Counterfeits and Piracy Bill will be tabled before the EALA in the 1st half of this year. On the whole, in order to make the Customs Union more effective, it is important that a single Customs Territory be established as considerations are further determined in putting in place an East African Customs Authority. The last Summit of the EAC Heads of State was seized of this particular development and decided to spend more time in deciding on it when they next meet in April this year.

Common Market

In July last year, the EAC became the first Regional Economic Community (REC) in Africa to move into a Common Market. This is a huge milestone for the EAC. However, as I had stated at the time of the launch of the Common Market, this higher level of integration is more of a marathon run rather than a short distance dash. After 19 years since the establishment of a single market, the European Union is still struggling to realise the full potential of that market. I believe though, that our task will be simpler. Having said this, there are a number of critical legal and regulatory systems that would have to be reviewed, changed or reformed at the level of the Partner States to enable the Common Market regime to function. All the Partner States have committed to undertaking these reforms by 2015. There are some of us who would have wished that the time frame for achieving full Common Market Protocol compliance be shorter. I know that often running whilst others walk is a lofty ideal; but we cannot be like ostriches and be oblivious of the realities and the politics that always go with reforms that are too fast paced.

What is pleasing is that some countries are already moving faster than others in putting in place measures that allow the Common Market provisions to begin to operate. This process has the advantage of showcasing results that may help to allay fears about speed that could be more psychological than real. At the EAC level, there will be need to determine in the next few months what kind of supra interventions of a policy and legal form that would need to be taken to steer the implementation of the Common Market Protocol. For example, it should be possible for a regional law that harmonises social security provisions to be enacted. Such a law would catalyse the free movement of labour.

Another example would be the harmonisation of the educational systems particularly at the tertiary level and such harmonisation could also take a legal form. Of course, there are some amongst us who are more revolutionary who harp on the idea that the EAC could enact an omnibus law to guide, manage and control the overall process of implementing the Common Market protocol, almost in a similar fashion as had been done in the case of the Customs Union. This is a debatable proposal and knowing the sensitivities surrounding the implementation of the Common Market Protocol, the views of the Partner States may be different. In my view, comparing the implementation of the Common Market Protocol and the Customs Union is like comparing oranges and apples.

The Common Market is a complex array of multi-sectoral issues with myriad policies, laws and regulations, unlike in the case of the Customs Union. There is also the fundamental challenge of having a supra law that responds to varying time frames for implementing the Protocol as determined by the Partner States. At the end of the day I believe that the realisation of the Common Market Protocol crucially hinges on a resolute political will; a clear and focused acceptance of the basic goals of the Common Market and of the costs and benefits that may accrue, over time, to each EAC Partner State.

Negotiating as a Block

Following the EAC Summit decision in 2002 that the EAC should negotiate regional and multilateral issues as a bloc, a state of flux had intervened delaying the implementation of that decision. However, thanks to our consistent efforts, supported by EALA's Private Members' Bill on Trade Negotiations, we have been able to galvanise unity of Partner States to negotiate the Economic Partnership Agreements with the EU as a bloc. And in as much as these EPA negotiations have been complex and slow moving, our collective approach has not been dampened and the negotiations are now poised to take a new momentum.

It is important to note though that the role of the EAC Secretariat in these negotiations is one of facilitation and backstopping. The EAC is not a "State Party" to the Cotonou Agreement. As such, it is not a negotiator. It is the EAC Partner States in their individual legal capacities that negotiate. It is important to clarify this point because any funds that the EAC receives from development partners in support of EPA negotiations is to enable the Partner States to ease their financial burdens in what is a long and complex negotiating process. The funds could actually go directly to the Partner States. However, that would mean that the whole idea of EAC being seen to negotiate as a bloc would be frustrated. It is important therefore, that whilst we all seek to promote the lofty idea that our Partner states be more self reliant when it comes to setting aside funds for negotiations with third parties, to assure that our independence is not in any way prejudiced or jeopardised, we also note that our goal of fronting an EAC identity and image as a galvanising force of the partner states is not hampered.

In the same context of EAC negotiating as a bloc, we have been able to conclude a Trade and Investment Framework Agreement with the United States of America. Though we are yet to fully operationalise this Agreement in terms of seeing tangible results, the opportunities for mutual gains from the Agreement exist; they only wait to be exploited. Indeed, within the TIFA, the EAC Partner States are now working in unison under the EAC umbrella to negotiate trade terms under AGOA.

Monetary Union

May I also observe that in the past five years and specifically in the past two years we have made significant progress in laying the basic foundations for a monetary union. The basic architecture is ready and we are now set during this first quarter to commence Partner States' negotiations of the Monetary Union Protocol. This is a major step forward. Along with these negotiations, EAC is working closely with the World Bank in promoting financial markets infrastructure in the region. The World Bank has committed over USD 60 million in the next eight years to support this work. In a similar context our East African Stock Exchanges Association is also making headway towards the establishment of an East African Stock Exchange which will be a regional platform to raise capital through IPOs on an East African wide basis.

Regional Infrastructure

It is often claimed that the ultimate success of the Customs Union and Common Market hinges on the state of the physical infrastructure – roads, railways, energy, maritime and airport transport, ICT etc. In the past five years, the EAC has done more in developing master plans which define our collective quest for improving the regional physical infrastructure. But recently some effort has now taken place to move from master plan to project implementation. The flagship of this positive outcome is the Arusha-Namanga-Athi River road as well as the power interconnection at Namanga. There are a number of other road projects which are now under implementation at the level of completion of engineering studies and funds mobilisation for construction. These roads include the Arusha-Moshi-Holili-Taveta-Voi Road and the Bagamoyo-Tanga-Mombasa-Malindi Highway.

There is also serious development on the railways front particularly the extension of the Tanzania Central Railway from Isaka to Kigali and Bujumbura. The African

Development Bank has indicated willingness to support the establishment of the East African Railways Project Implementation Unit which will be a precursor to the establishment of a Railways Regulatory Authority at the EAC Secretariat. The five EAC Partner States and the EAC Secretariat are on course towards the development of national and regional public-private partnership frameworks which will lay the legal and regulatory framework that will drive private sector participation in the development of infrastructure in the region.

Studies relating to the East African Transport Development Strategy and a Road Development Programme covering the period up to 2018 are on course for completion. The final report of this study will actually be considered by the EAC Regional Transport Task Force in Kigali in the next one week. These Studies will now inform a strategic approach to construction and modernisation of road networks that provide regional interconnectivity. In turn, a Study on EAC Transport facilitation strategy covering areas like axle load control, transit facilitation and implementation of transport facilitation agreements in the region has commenced. Overall, the estimated cost of all these roads infrastructure development in the region in the next 10 years is in excel of USD 25 billion. In the area of broadband technology, infrastructure network, a project to interconnect the five EAC Partner States via a high capacity fibre optic link progress has been made in securing the support of the AfDB. The estimated development cost of the infrastructure component is USD30 million.

The EAC is now working closely with COMESA and SADC under the tripartite framework to promote a vibrant transport corridor model of infrastructure development and trade facilitation. In November last year, a Conference was held in Nairobi involving the three Tripartite RECs plus IGAD to identify the priority corridors and define their resource needs. Later this year, an Aid for Trade Investment Conference will be held to mobilise resources for developing the identified transport corridors and One Stop Border Posts. The Tripartite is working closely with Trade Mark Southern Africa and Trade Mark East Africa, with full backing of DFID-UK in staging this investment conference.

In mid December last year, I led a team of CEOs of EAC, COMESA and SADC to London for discussions with Rt. Hon. Andrew Mitchell, the UK Secretary of State for International Development within this particular context. The British Government is committed to supporting the Tripartite and will mobilise other development partners including the World Bank, AfDB and JICA to render support to the Tripartite Corridor Transport development. However, as you all know, the COMESA-EAC-SADC Tripartite is working towards the establishment of a Grand Free Trade Area. A lot of work has been done in this area to set the stage for a Tripartite Summit which is planned for March this year where hopefully, the respective Heads of State from these three RECs will pronounce themselves on the way forward towards the establishment of the FTA.

I mentioned that the ultimate success of the Customs Union and Common Market hinges on the state of physical infrastructure. But there is also the side of the soft infrastructure. In this area the EAC sees a great deal of importance in the harmonisation of the legal and regulatory regimes that closely interface with the various free movements under the Customs Union and Common Market. We have in mind, for example, the approximation of commercial laws and much has been done in the past two years in this area. The EAC is currently working closely with the Investment Advisory Services of the World Bank Group in formulating an EAC Investment Climate programme focused on improving regulatory quality and harmonisation of the investment climate. This is a four year programme and it will commence this year.

Energy Sector

I cannot overemphasize the great effort that has been placed on the establishment of adequate and reliable energy supply for the region. As part of building a harmonised policy framework involving a number of critical areas, we have institutionalised conferences such as the Petroleum Conferences organised once every two years to forge common positions on how to develop the energy sector and realise shared benefits there from. Oil and natural gas will prove to be the critical drivers of energy generation in our region in the next five years.

The EAC Power Master Plan recognises this potential and how it can be exploited to bolster industrialisation, the green revolution and cheaper transport. The oil pipeline projects from Kenya to Uganda and onward to Rwanda and Burundi are ongoing. So is the study for a natural gas pipeline from Mtwara to Mombasa. The integration process of the East African Power Master Plan and the broader Eastern Africa Power Pool (which incorporates Ethiopia and Sudan) is ongoing. And so is the integration of our East African Power Pool with the Southern Africa Power Pool. The COMESA-EAC-SADC Tripartite is the new vehicle for integrating all these power pools.

Social Sectors

Apart from the emphasis on economic development and growth, we have paid attention to the social and human development dimensions. Activities of co-operation in social security, solidarity and development were undertaken under the EAC Forum for Ministers responsible for Social Development. These activities are being pursued in the management of cross-cutting social concerns in health co-operation, gender and community development; education, science and technology, culture and sports development; and environmental and natural resources management towards the realization of the Millennium Development Goals (MDGs).

On the health front, particularly, the EAC has seen real growth in promoting a regional health policy framework. The establishment of the East African Health Research Commission in the next one year will provide a fillip to this trend. The health Directorate at the Secretariat has grown from one person in 2006 to 7 Professional Staff. We are now opening focal points in all the Partner States that are health project focused. Since 2006 the EAC holds an Annual Health Scientific Conference that brings together leading East African and Foreign Health Sector Scientists around well selected health themes. These conferences have contributed to a healthy exchange of scientific theory and practice that positively impacts policy formulation and improved health delivery.

We have also held a successful Conference on Persons with Disabilities early last year. This year we will determine how to proceed with the enactment of a regional law on persons with disabilities. Plans are also underway to organise the first EAC Conference on Women. Hon. Valerie Nyirahabineza of EALA is helping in developing a concept which will inform the organisation of this conference. The Conference will seek to address the challenges women in the EAC face in terms of giving their voice to regional integration issues as well as in participating in the regional economy.

Other areas include migration issues which are inevitable as the regional economy becomes more integrated; refugees and internally displaced persons, again an inevitable phenomenon much as we may not wish it but recent events in our region show that we cannot be oblivious of its reality; gender mainstreaming in all EAC programmes, which is a Treaty requirement of which we have only recently began to develop a policy on natural resources development and management, including the topical climate change. In this area of climate change there is a clear thrust and following the recent Summit on Food Security and Climate Change, a policy on mitigation and adaptation is being finalised along with supporting measures. But so is the area of Food Security which the last Summit addressed leading to the adoption of an EAC Food Security Policy and Plan which will be finalised during the first quarter of this year. In the area of tourism, the EAC in the past five years has promoted an integrated identity, promoting East Africa as a single tourism destination at key international tourism fairs in Berlin and London. This work will continue and will be extended to Asia. Work towards the adoption of a single tourist visa is also ongoing.

Cooperation in Political Matters

Some clear development has also taken place in putting shape to the goal of Political Federation. The Wako Report on Fast Tracking the EAC Political Federation opened a new momentum in this area leading to the national consultative processes which bore meaningful positions and proposals on the federation idea. Even the new Partner States of Rwanda and Burundi have been quick to participate in the consultative process. We now know that the majority of East Africans favour the Political Federation. The question that remains is the determination of the form of the Federation and whence the Federation could be constituted.

A Report of the team of experts appointed in February 2010 has finalised its Report based on these large questions and the Summit will later in the year consider the Report upon receiving concrete recommendations from the Council of Ministers. What is pleasing to note is that as the momentum on the Political Federation question takes shape, the EAC has finally adopted its anthem this past December and I am sure you will agree with me that this anthem will become an important symbol of our unity and a key strategic factor in our quest towards a Political Federation.

I have always argued that one important facet of the process towards the EAC Political Federation is deepening cooperation in the defence sector. Defence is an important pillar and benchmark in the construction of a political federation. During the past three years we have seen deepening cooperation amongst our defence forces, in joint military exercises and operations. Indeed, we have now reached an advance stage in upgrading the MoU on Defence Cooperation to a legally binding Protocol. This Protocol should be ready for signature by April this year. In this similar regard, we should applaud increasing cooperation in the areas of peace and security involving all the Security Agencies – defence, police and intelligence. The Peace and Security Protocol is also set to be signed by April this year.

In addition, another important constituent part of the process towards the EAC Political Federation, relates to the development of improved and harmonised governance structures and systems embracing a wide array of constitutional issues such as rule of law, human rights, anti-corruption, elections observation and monitoring etc. Of course we still face the challenge of fully mobilising the East African Civil Society to play a role in the overall process of regional integration as well as Political Federation. An initial process has been undertaken in mobilising the youth through a Special Summit which was held in Arusha in 2008.

I am pleased to state that the EAC collective relations with the rest of Africa and the world are now reinforced by the Protocol on Foreign Policy Coordination which was signed on 3rd December last year. EAC now has a new identity; it will forge relations with other countries and institutions within a more collective decision making framework. Negotiating as a bloc has received a shot in the arm from this Protocol. In this context, the recent flurry of accreditations of various foreign missions based in Tanzania to the EAC is symptomatic of the realisation by foreign countries that the EAC is a dynamic regional organisation worth working with within a regional perspective.

Of course, this system of accreditation to African RECs is not new. Actually the EAC is one of the last of such organisations to have these types of accreditation which, historically, are more symbolic than effectual. Thus ECOWAS, COMESA and SADC, not to speak of the AU itself, have, for years, had diplomatic accreditations from both African and non-African missions. The difference with the EAC is that we are far more advanced than other RECs in Africa by having a Protocol on Foreign Policy Coordination which makes diplomatic accreditation to the EAC less symbolic and probably more practical and meaningful.

Information and Communications

From the time I joined the EAC I placed the highest emphasis on strengthening the information, education and communication function. I believe that we have tried our best in the past few years to promote EAC's visibility in the public domain. The East African Media Summits which we started in collaboration with the East African Business Councils in 2007 have helped to build bridges of knowledge and information between us and the leading media institutions in East Africa. The emergence of the East African Newspaper, Uganda's East African Business Week and cross-border TV Stations and programmes like EATV have helped to shape and promote a culture and identity of East African-ness. Powerful East African-wide FM radio stations like the Mwanza based Radio Free Africa and small ones like Kisumu based Jaluo FM (which reaches over 3 million East Africans on the Lake Victoria Basin) broadcast East African news in both English and Kiswahili but also in the tribal vernacular.

The EAC Secretariat itself has made serious efforts to promote information about EAC's activities and programmes. The EAC web portal has several websites covering a broad range of EAC's programmes and plans is one of the best among the RECs in Africa. In an effort to improve our information and communications, we have finalised an EAC Communications Policy and Strategy which the Council of Ministers will consider for adoption during this quarter of this year. This policy and strategy will better define our approach to information sharing and more clearly identify our target groups and their information needs. This year we will also work towards establishing Radio *Afrika Mashariki*.

Tenth Anniversary Celebrations

The celebrations marking the EAC 10th Anniversary marked a high point of EAC marketing and publicity of its mission and vision. The Celebrations were characterized by the enthusiastic response and participation of East Africans, of all walks of life, throughout the Partner States. The events, including the 1st EAC Symposium that was held in Arusha in November 2009 had great impact on raising positive awareness of the EAC and helped to demonstrate the benefits and achievements of regional integration. I would like to thank Magaga Alot for the high level of commitment and passion with which he discharged the role that was entrusted to him as co-ordinator of the Celebrations.

Finance and Administration

• Monitoring and evaluation

We continue to work towards realising several other measurable programmes. These include monitoring and evaluation; as you will recall one of the structural weaknesses that the EAC faced for a number of years was the lack of an effective monitoring and evaluation system. It is only in the last three years that we have been able to introduce the system with only one person directly responsible for the function. I think all of us will agree that in-spite of the low capacity in this function, Julius Birungi has done an outstanding job in building a solid M&E foundation and today we can claim that the EAC Secretariat is able to produce good and timely monthly, quarterly and annual reports. I wish also to thank Philip Wambugu for working closely with Julius in the attainment of the quality output that is coming out of the M&E Division. Other areas include labour where we are in the process of undertaking an East African Labour Market survey that can help shape policies on human resources development that fits the challenges of our regional economy as well as globalisation.

• Statistics

The EAC continues to face serious challenges on the statistic front. Since the establishment of the Department of Statistics four years ago, this function has faced serious shortage of staff, frequent staff turnover and lack of supporting IT infrastructure that links the Secretariat with the National Bureaux of Statistics in the

Partner States. As a result, the EAC remains weak in terms of producing timely and correct statistical data on trade, investments and other key economic indicators. As a REC, we must move quickly to having this kind of data and on a timely basis.

EAC Headquarters

In case you think that I forgot one of my happiest legacies in the EAC is the construction of the EAC Headquarters. It required a bit of effort to convince our friends, the German Government, to agree to increase their funding support for this headquarters from the original figure of Euro 8 million to Euros 14 million a cost escalation attributed to EAC's enlargement following Rwanda and Burundi joining the EAC. Construction is going on well and warm compliments are due to our colleague Phil Kleruu, the EAC Senior Estates Officer for a job well done. Do not forget to invite me to the official opening of the building and show me the room where I would have sat.

Inter-Organ Relations

I believe that we can also applaud the relationship that the EAC Secretariat has been able to develop with other organs and with the EAC institutions. It has not been an easy exercise. Often, the Kigali spirit has not resulted in a less acrimonious relationship. But who would say that as human organisations it is easy to completely eradicate sentiments that often underlie the very nature of institutional responsibilities. I believe though that there now exists a better framework for assuring harmonious relationships. In the case of the EAC institutions, I believe that we have succeeded in giving adequate elbow room to the institutions to operate autonomously. There is also greater realisation that along with the Secretariat, these institutions have a collective role to play and cannot operate in a pigeonhole type of fashion. It is pleasing to note that in recent times the Lake Victoria Fisheries Organisation and the East African Development Bank have increasingly seen themselves as part and parcel of the EAC and playing more visible roles in EAC affairs.

Finally, in thanking our Partner States for what is a necessary, even if at times, difficult relationship, I wish to point out the decision making challenge that EAC faces. Moving forward, the decision making structure of the EAC will have to be reformed. I have said this many times, including tabling the matter before the EAC Summit at its Kigali meeting in June 2008. Based on the stance of the Summit, significant work has been done in the last two and a half years to review the provisions of the Treaty that relate to consensus decision making as well as to the regulations that relate to quorum for statutory meetings.

The Sectoral Council on Legal and Judicial Affairs supported by our Team of Expert from the Partner States and the excellent backstopping work of the Office of the Counsel to the Community has responded well to this task. Yet it has been a frustrating exercise in two ways: first the Sectoral Council has often been unable to meet for various reasons. These delays have resulted in this exercise not being completed in good time. Secondly, there is a paradoxical perception in some of the EAC Partner States that this exercise of reforming the decision making structure is intended to shift the authority of the EAC from the Partner States to the Secretariat whose ambition is to become a Commission in the same form as the European Commission, as if the idea of a Commission is, in itself, an anathema.

In turn, there is a feeling that watering down the consensus principle may jeopardize the interests of the new EAC entrants. Overall, my view is that there is a bit of trying to jump the gun in all these perceptions and apprehensions. It is important in moving the process of treaty reform forward that we delineate decisions that have underlying *political ramifications* from those that are primarily of an *administrative character*. What would make the Secretariat more efficient and effective in the delivery of its mandate pursuant to Article 71 of the Treaty is greater decision making authority on those functions. Presently, the Council of Ministers is too involved in "kitchen work". I recall, during the one Party system days in Tanzania, the late Mwalimu Nyerere used to caution the ruling Party, *Chama Cha Mapinduzi* (CCM), not to "enter into the kitchen", a place where the government should be afforded maximum space to cook the food. The Party's role was limited to determining whether the food put on the table was uncooked or did not contain the right ingredients as to make it palatable.

Let me add, for posterity, that my personal interpretation of Article 71 of the Treaty is that the Secretariat has total authority to exercise the listed functions without interference or involvement of the Senior Officials, the Coordination Committee or the Council of Ministers. The role of the Council, as defined under Article 14 of the Treaty is limited to policy matters. The only administrative responsibility granted to the Council is limited to making staff rules and regulations and financial rules and regulations of the Community – Article 14(3) (g). This particular administrative responsibility has been vested in the Council largely because it relates to matters that have policy ramifications, largely that centre on the budget.

At this stage of EAC's maturity, it is important that on matters such as these which seem to slow down the decision making process in the EAC should be given legal clarification if not well understood and appreciated. The Council is empowered under Article 14(4) to seek an advisory opinion from the East African Court of Justice. It may further be added that the Council at any rate has the power to issue directives to the Secretariat under Article 14(3) (d) and those directives may relate to how the Secretariat is performing its administrative functions as provided for under Article 71.

It has been my wish during these past five years that I would preside over the reform of the EAC decision making structure. I believe that the reform process is now in high gear and it is my hope that in the near future this reform will bear the required fruits. It can only be for the good of the EAC and the beneficiaries of our integration process. On a related matter, I hope that the video conferencing facility which TMEA is helping us to install to link the Secretariat with all the Ministries of EAC Affairs will equally support the much needed and more cost effective channel of communication that should add value to information sharing and quick decision making. Of course, the challenge of the reform or amendment of the Treaty extends beyond issues related to empowering greater efficiency in the EAC Secretariat.

The Sectoral Council on Legal and Judicial Affairs is already seized of a number of areas in the Treaty that need to be adapted to fit the current situation in the integration process. For example, there is the important question related to the extended jurisdiction of the EACJ. The adoption of the Common Market Protocol will increasingly pose a number of legal issues which could not appropriately be dealt with under municipal jurisdiction. To this extent, the urgency to review the Treaty in an extensive way is imperative. In the same context, it will be necessary to also revisit some of the laws which have been enacted by the EALA in the light of changed circumstances. Take the case of the Competition Law which does not encompass many of the areas related to trade in services as well as capital movements and the role of financial markets and institutions.

The EAC will start implementing the 4th Five year EAC Development Strategy in July 2011. It will be important for all of you to be well acquainted with this new development strategy. A Special Retreat for relevant Ministers and Permanent Secretaries will be organised in March this year centred on creating a deep appreciation of what this Development Strategy encompasses. It will also be important for the usual EAC Staff Retreat which I hope can be organised by May this year to also focus on the 4th EAC Development Strategy.

Uganda is going into General Elections next month. I want to take this opportunity, on your behalf, to wish the leadership and the people of Uganda free, fair and peaceful elections.

As you all know the Heads of State decided at their last Summit to hold a Special Summit on 19th April this year with an already fixed Agenda. One item on that Agenda will be the swearing in of the new Secretary General. The media in recent weeks has featured a number of stories as well as cartoons on the SG's succession. It is important that we, as public servants, avoid, in absolute terms, to partake or to be seen to partake in any discussion relating to this matter which falls within the exclusive purview of the EAC Summit of Heads of State.

There is also going to be considerable work to be done to prepare for the other items on the Agenda of this Summit, including the Single Customs Territory issue and the Report of the Team of Experts on the Political Federation. I call upon all those responsible for these items to ensure that we undertake proper preparation because the items are of a complex and sensitive nature.

Let me end by once again wishing you a happy and prosperous New Year, a year which I believe will mark the achievement of higher levels of integration as we see the operationalisation of the Common Market Protocol and as the process towards the establishment of the Monetary Union plays out.

Conclusion

I regret to bore you with a long statement. As I said earlier, I may not have a similar opportunity to express my inner feelings about the journey we have travelled together these near five years. There has been fun, excitement and frustrations during this journey but there has always been the hope that in our collective work the EAC will be a stronger institution and justify the purpose for which it has been established. I thank you all for your comradeship sometimes under difficult situations.

I know that some of you have sometimes forgotten your oath to the EAC, not to behave as nationals of your own countries and thus filtering out information. Today I want to beseech you all to avoid such temptations because they can undermine and destroy this institution. On the first day of my being sworn in, President Kikwete was very emphatic in saying to me: "You are not the Secretary General for Tanzania; you are Secretary General of the East African Community". If we all adhere to this important rule of professional behaviour in an inter-governmental organisation as ours, we will be able to work in unison and achieve more for this organisation.

As noted above, a meeting for the Ministers and Permanent Secretaries responsible for EAC affairs had to be organized to discuss the underlying features of the 4th EAC Development Strategy. In the following chapter the context of that meeting is outlined and fundamental questions are posed about the direction the EAC was going to take to deepen its integration.

CHAPTER FORTY EIGHT

Impact of National Politics on Integration[236]

Introduction

Regional integration is essentially a political process; in the sense that what drives integration is mainly rooted in nation-state power over economic and political interests.[237] It follows, therefore, that national political support for integration is central to the successful realization of integration objectives. Understanding the dynamics of such support is important in determining the viability and prospects of any regional integration project. Indeed, in the specific case of the East African Community (EAC), the capacity to understand and appreciate the dynamics of national politics as they relate to regional integration may crucially feed into a more objective formulation of mutually acceptable strategies that fit and respond to the realities of national politics and thereby bolster greater political support for integration.

In this chapter, we examine the place, role and impact of national politics on EAC integration, from its different and multidimensional character and proposing plausible measures and interventions that could foster greater political support of the EAC partner states for deeper integration. We further examine how national politics have played out in the European Union (EU) integration as a model for critical analysis of the EAC perspective.

Theoretical Synthesis on National Politics and Regional Integration

The question of national politics and regional integration has occupied academic discourse for the past forty years. It has centred on two, apparently conflicting theories of regional integration, the neofunctionalist theory (or supranationality) and inter-governmentalism.[238] Neofunctionalists advance

---

[236] Paper delivered at the EAC Dialogue on Political Integration, Kampala, Uganda, 17-18 November, 2011.

[237] See BUJRA, Abdalla, 2003: Political Aspects of Regional Integration, Presentation to TRID Meeting of Regional Economic Communities, Addis Ababa. http://www.bujra.com/documents/Political%20Aspects%20of%20Regional%20Integration October%2030-2003.pdf. See also RUPPEL, Oliver C., "Regional Economic Communities and Human Rights in East and Southern Africa," in DIESCHO, Anton Bosl (ed.), *Human Rights in Africa: Legal Perspectives on their Protection and Promotion*, Windhoek: Konrad Adenauer Stiftung and Macmillan Education Namibia, 2009, p. 375.

[238] See HOOGHE, E.A.E.B. and G.W. Marks, "The Neofunctionalists were (Almost) Right: Politicization and European Integration," in CROUCH, C. and W. Streeck (eds.), *The*

the view that politicization, which refers to increasing the contentiousness of decision-making in the process of regional integration, determines the speed, direction and intensity of integration. Thus regional integration has to be understood "as a broadly-based political process" that involves multi-stakeholders (supranational actors) and not simply national governments.[239]

Inter-governmentalism, on the other hand, conceives regional integration as an outcome of bargaining among the national states; institutional decision-making is thus primarily premised and predicated on the role of state actors. In the EAC context, inter-governmentalists conceptualise regional politics as inherently part and parcel of inter-state cooperation sustained by a regional legal regime in the form of the treaty establishing the EAC.

Notwithstanding the contrasting theories outlined above, it is possible to view regional integration from a dynamic dimension that incorporates both supranationality and inter-governmentalism and to consider the impact of national politics on regional integration from both dimensions, de-linked and inter-connectedly. As will be examined and argued in this paper, it would be overly simplistic to characterise regional integration in Africa, generally, and in the EAC specifically as either "inter-governmental" (much as there is more of it in the integration processes) or "supranational."

We accept the thesis advanced by Sweet and Sandholtz that there is "a continuum that stretches between two ideal-typical modes of governance: the intergovernmental and the supranational."[240] The two authors point out that the key players in intergovernmental politics "are the national executives of the member states, who bargain with each other to produce common policies. Bargaining is shaped by the relative powers of the member states, but also by state preferences, which emerge from the pulling and hauling among domestic groups. These preferences are then given agency, as negotiating positions, by national executives... such as the Council of Ministers."[241]

The role of the European Commission or, for that matter, of the EAC secretariat, in this vein, becomes one of enhancing efficiency of interstate bargaining. In turn, at the level of supranational politics, the governance structure rests on a centralized intergovernmental system which exercises jurisdiction over specific policy issues and "capable of constraining the behaviour of all actors, including the member states" (Sweet, ibid: 303). It is, in a way, a form of federal politics.

Diversity of Democracy: Corporatism, Social Order and Political Conflict, Cheltenham: Edward Elgar Publishing Ltd., 2006, pp. 2005-222 at pp. 205-206.

[239] Ibid, at p. 215.

[240] SWEET, Alec Stone and Wayne Sandholtz, "European Integration and Supranational Governance," Volume 4 No. 3 *Journal of European Public Policy,* September, 1997, pp. 297-317 at p. 302.

[241] Ibid., at p. 303.

The question of national politics and regional integration in the EAC should, in the context of the foregoing, be thus examined within the framework of the intergovernmenalist governance system, on the one hand and, on the other hand, the dynamic movement of the governance system and process from integovernmentalism to supranationalism where supranational institutions such as the Secretariat, the East African Legislative Assembly, and the East African Court of Justice would be deemed to exhibit significant autonomy in defining and pursuing a politically relevant agenda.

This movement cannot be simply viewed as conjecture. As the EAC consolidates the Customs Union, with the adoption of the Single Customs Territory and the establishment of a Regional Customs Administration Management Agency (areas considered to fall under significant national politics since they invoke issues of sovereignty, trust and confidence on supranationality) and the implementation of the Common Market takes a vibrant momentum, the need for regional standards, rules, regulations, dispute settlement mechanisms and centralised coordination will be heightened and, resultantly, make supranationality increasingly inevitable.

In other words, the impact of national politics on deeper EAC integration is equally a matter of a continuum; a logical transition from one lower level of integration governance to a higher and more intricate one. As Sweet and Sandholtz have argued, "Governmental actors clearly have their own interests, which may include maximizing their autonomy and control over resources... Governments can also attempt to slow integration or push it in directions favourable to their perceived interests, but they do not drive the process or fully control it. In a fundamental sense, governments are reactive, constantly adjusting to the integration that is going on all around them."[242]

National Politics and Regional Integration in the European Union

The European Union (EU) is, in the current era, the most relevant model to examine in determining the nexus between national politics and regional integration and the impacts thereof. The failure of the EU to reach a political consensus over the Constitutional Treaty in 2005 provides a powerful testament on the impact of national politics on regional integration. It also exemplifies the disjuncture between the authority of the State and the will of the people. The decision by the EU governments that the Constitutional Treaty should not end with the agreements of the governments but should also go through a ratification process that allows the people, either through their elected representatives (Parliament) or directly to have the last word, evidences the centrality of national politics in determining regional integration. Indeed, the earlier proposal that the treaty be approved in a

---

[242] Ibid, at p. 306.

European-wide referendum was turned down precisely because national sovereignty positions would have been dominantly influential.[243]

The rejection of the Treaty in referendums in France and the Netherlands was clearly driven by the state of national politics. In France, the then President, Jacques Chirac, used the referendum "as an instrument of executive politics to gain the domestic advantage"[244] whilst the general French citizenry was more concerned about the social and economic situation and saw the European Constitutional Treaty as another deflection by the political elite from addressing the perceived erosion of the welfare state. With respect to the Netherlands, the rejection of the Treaty by the Dutch was founded more on the dissatisfaction with the Euro in the national economy.

It is well worth to have in mind the fate of the European Constitutional Treaty as the EAC ponders its quest for a political federation which will necessarily involve the development of a federal constitution, and, going by the recent experiences in Kenya and Zanzibar where referendums were used to determine people's choices, and most likely the application of referenda as well in the process of constitution ratification. The clear lesson to be drawn is that the European situation attested to "a wide discrepancy between the legal and political culture of the European elites and that of the general public."[245]

Evidently, the political elite romanticized the idea of supranationality whilst the political allegiance of the general public is traditionally centred on the nation state. As Professor Tuori has surmised, "the general public does not want the EU to supersede their nation state. Seen against the background of their nation state constitutional culture, that is exactly what the EU's constitutional project in their eyes threatened to do. It has not been an easy task for the European elites to detach constitution (European) from its nation state connotations."[246] The will of the people in the EAC will have to be sanctified.

I need not go into details about the broader issues of EU's challenges in securing unanimity over its various integration projects. Suffice it to state that national politics of EU member states have also had a significant positive impact on the determination of a number of integration projects.

---

[243] KRAL, David, "The Constitution is Dead: Long Lives the Treaty of Nice?" Volume 5 No. 3 *Romanian Journal of European Affairs*, 2005, p. 45.

[244] MAZZUCELLI, Colette, "The French Rejection of the European Constitutional Treaty: Two-Level Games Perspective," in LAURSEN, Finn (Ed.), *The Rise and Fall of the EU's Constitutional Treaty*, Leiden: Nijhoff, 2008, p. 177.

[245] TUORI, Kaarlo, "The Failure of the EU's Constitutional Project," Volume 3 *No Foundations: Journal of Extreme Legal Positivism*, 2007, pp. 37-48 at p. 37.

[246] Ibid, at p. 47.

Several examples could be cited. One is the Schengen Agreement whose treaty was signed in June 1985 and the Convention implementing the agreement signed in 1990. What the Schengen Agreement has done is to create a borderless zone covering 25 EU and non-EU countries. The United Kingdom and the Republic of Ireland did not sign the Agreement (exercising their right of 'opting out' which was incorporated in the Schengen Agreement) largely because of their domestic immigration sensitivities.

Another example is the European Economic and Monetary Union (EMU) which was initiated by the Maastricht Treaties of 1991. Those treaties encapsulated the rights of the minority in the form of an opt-out clause. On 1st January, 1999, 11 of the then 15 EU members (except Denmark, Greece, Sweden and the UK) joined the Euro. Interestingly, all the 15 members (except Greece) had fulfilled the Maastricht convergence criteria.[247] However, In Britain, the Conservative Party under Prime Minister John Major had a large faction of Euro-sceptics. In a postal ballot exercise in 1990, 84.4% of the members of the Conservative Party rejected the Euro. John Major himself made a statement to the effect that the British government used the Maastricht negotiations to "reassert the authority of national governments ... It is for nations to build Europe, not for Europe to attempt to supersede nations."[248]

Even the more EU-positive New Labour under Tony Blair had misgivings as represented by the statement: "Any decision about Britain joining the single currency must be determined by a hard-headed assessment of Britain's economic interests."[249] Clearly, national politics in Britain impacted the decision of the British government (both Conservatives and Labour) not to join the Euro.

However, everything considered, negative reactions to deeper EU integration have been rather few in spite of the challenges of economic recession and growing neo-nationalist and ultra-nationalist sentiments. Indeed, the full ratification of the Lisbon Treaty by all EU member states by December 2009 attests to a new, more realist, post 2005 pan-European identity politics which has been so well evidenced in the face of the hugely destabilising Greek and now Italian fiscal crisis. In many respects, the Lisbon Treaty incorporates key provisions of the rejected European Constitutional Treaty; but the environment has significantly changed and the approach to treaty ratification has also taken a more subtle approach, away from the dominance of

---

[247] Greece later joined the Euro and it is now in deep crisis – almost at the verge of leaving the arrangement.

[248] MAJOR, John, "Raise Your Eyes, There is a Land Beyond," *The Economist*, 25th September - 1st October, 1993, p. 27.

[249] RISSE, Thomas, *et al*, "To Euro or Not to Euro? EMU and Identity Politics in the European Union," Volume 5 No. 2 *European Journal of International Relations*, 1999, pp. 147-187 at p. 160.

referenda. Time and real-life lessons can be useful healers of misconceptions and misdirected sentiments; a useful lesson to East African integration especially on the political federation question.

Yet, it is important to return to the question about the overall negative national politics that feature in some EU member states about integration. In many respects, it fuels the discourse, so much heightened by the Greek fiscal crisis and the measures being taken not only to bail out Greece but also to put in place a European Financial Stability Facility initially worth € 1 trillion fund (later to leverage other funds) for bailing out other fragile EU economies. The Fund is also intended to capitalize banks that become vulnerable to huge debts that arise from defaults by national governments. The abiding question emerging is whether deeper integration of the monetary union should not, in fact, involve a political union, to assure its sustainability.

These are important questions. On the one hand, there is the view that integration projects like a monetary union are highly susceptible to intense pressures in a political system that has been created more for "a low-level regulatory style of politics" thus necessitating to approach monetary policy "in an apolitical manner."[250] On the other hand, there is a view that there is insignificant evidence to support the view that the EMU would spur a political union and that, if anything, the Euro and political integration reflect signs of decoupling.[251]

What is important to underscore is that the Greek sovereign debt crisis flows from total violation of prudential management of public finances within the parameters of the EU Growth and Stability Pact and monetary policies set out by the European Central Bank. The violations arose out of national politics of a socialist government that appeased a large and ballooning public sector whose wages doubled in the past ten years. The country had over borrowed and the country's competitiveness had eroded. Clearly, there is a price to be paid when national politics override an agreed regional integration compact and the Greek crisis is a model of it.

To sum up this critical examination of the EU experience and the question of the impact of national politics on regional integration, it may be concluded that the EU integration project, over certain strategic aspects, has been influenced by the state of national politics. Indeed, as Professor Fraser Cameron has put it, "there is little public appetite for 'more Europe', and

---

[250] SMITH, Ed, "Will EMU Lead to Political Union?" Bulletin No. 2 *Centre for European Reform,* October, 1998.

[251] HODSON, Dermot, "EMU and Political Union: What, If Anything, Have we Learnt From the Euro's First Decade?" Volume 16 No. 4 *Journal of European Public Policy,* 2009, pp. 508 - 526.

national politicians seem increasingly reluctant to make a case for a strong EU."[252]

Cameron has gone further to postulate that "while not always politically expedient, national governments would be wise to put the long-term goal of cooperation above more immediate domestic priorities. More importantly, if integration is to succeed, governments and publics should believe that it is in their vital national interest. Without such commitment, regional groupings will crumble at the first bump in the long road to integration."[253] This is the environment that is increasingly fuelling ideas promoted by Angela Merkel and Nicolas Sarkozy around forging a new treaty that would bind Eurozone countries more tightly over fiscal and budget matters.

However, from the *Economist's* Charlemagne's Notebook titled, *The Euro Crisis: One Problem, Two Visions (Part II)*,[254] one discerns serious fault lines even between Merkel and Sarkozy on the methodologies to be used in reforming the monetary union. In a speech which would attract a typically Tanzanian mindset on how to approach deeper integration in the EAC, Sarkozy has argued:

> Europe without politics, Europe on automatic pilot that blindly applies rules of competition and free trade, is a Europe that cannot confront crises - A more democratic Europe is one where responsible politicians decide … The foundation of Europe is not the march towards more supranationalism … The crisis (sovereign debt) has pushed heads of state and government to assume growing responsibilities because, in the end, only they have the democratic legitimacy to be able to decide. Thus European integration will pass through intergovernmentalism because Europe must make strategic choices, political choices …[255]

Mrs Merkel, in contrast, is more disposed towards strengthening supranationality through greater reliance on European institutions and would like the new treaty to bind all EU member states and not just those in the Eurozone.[256] Clearly, the British Conservatives will oppose such a move. However, such a move is bound to rock the collation with the liberal democrats who are highly pro-European.

---

[252] CAMERON, Fraser, *The European Union as a Model for Regional Integration* (Working Paper) New York: Council on Foreign Relations, 2010, pp. 1-6 at p. 4.

[253] Ibid, at p. 5.

[254] See *The Economist*, 2nd December, 2011.

[255] Ibid.

[256] Ibid.

The large question is how the EAC would learn from these EU experiences, with their flip-flops, on the impact of national politics on integration? Does the EAC have its own unique environment upon which national politics could take a different form and content on deeper regional integration? Are there any African specific and relevant examples that could be drawn upon over this question? In the following section we examine the contextual background to the question of national politics in EAC's integration.

The Birth of National Politics in the EAC Integration

A proper examination of the impact of national politics on EAC integration is crucially predicated on the history of the EAC in the post independence period. As the European experience has shown, the history of the EAC is equally bound in a similar discourse on the relationship between a political union and deeper economic and monetary integration. It was Tanzania's Founding President, Mwalimu Julius K. Nyerere who, in June 1960, proposed at the second Conference of Independent African States that 1961 be *"East Africa's Year of Independence in Unity,"* arguing that "the feeling of unity which now exists could, however, be whittled away if each country got its independence separately and becomes open to the temptations of nationhood and the intrigues of those who find their strength in the weakness of small nations."[257]

Nyerere was more apt in his address to members of the East African Central Legislative Assembly in August 1965 when he referred to the challenges of unanimity in decision-making within the framework of regional cooperation:

> Each of our three governments is answerable to the people of its own country. Each of them is beset with the urgent needs of one part of the total East African area.[258]

In reference to the potential collapse of the East African Common Services Organization under which the three original East African Community states belonged within a Common Market and Monetary Union, Nyerere regretted that the "lack of organic unity" in the form of an East African Federation, by 1964, forced Tanzania "to seek actively for an equalization of the advantages and disadvantages of the common market."[259]

Nyerere was making specific reference to market-size asymmetries in East Africa which had heightened perceptions in Tanzania that Kenya

---

[257] See NYERERE, Julius K., "East African Federation," in NYERERE, Julius K., *Freedom in Unity*, Nairobi and Dar es Salaam: Oxford University Press, 1966 at p. 85 and 98 respectively.

[258] See NYERERE, Julius K., "Problems of East African Cooperation," op. cit. at p. 63.

[259] Ibid. at p. 66.

monopolized the economic benefits of integration.[260] Nyerere's arguments fit into the neorealist argument about the concerns and fears of partners over disproportionate gains that arise from a regional cooperation framework.[261]

It could thus be argued that Nyerere in fact laid down, not only the basic framework to analyse the relationship between national politics and regional integration but also for determining the impact of national politics on integration. Indeed, the principal cause of the collapse of the erstwhile EAC in April 1967 could be summed up as a serious clash between national politics and the ideals of regional integration. As Goldstein and Ndung'u have posited, "political differences widened in the ten years from the creation (of the erstwhile EAC) to the collapse of the EAC and the political will to overcome difficulties disappeared." At the same time "differing political orientations all too clearly led to a divergence in economic management."[262]

Put in context, with the failure to establish the East African political federation, the political unity that could have democratized and legitimised regional integration in the EAC disappeared and, in its wake, national politics took command in determining the form, depth and pace of regional integration. The collapse of the erstwhile EAC further weakened the regional integration legitimacy, reinforcing the centrality of intergovernmentalism because of its dominant nation state focus as a locus of representation and decision making, and diminishing the role of supranationalism.

The EAC Treaty and the Dynamics of National Politics

It is in the context of the foregoing historical development of East African Cooperation, its rise and its fall that the Treaty establishing the EAC, adopted in November 1999 entrenched several clauses that put national politics at the heart of EAC integration. It is important to note, though, that some of the treaty provisions, particularly those that fall under Articles 6 defining the fundamental principles and 7 enshrining the operational principles of the EAC, 50 on the election of Members of the East African Legislative Assembly, 27 on the limited jurisdiction of the East African

---

[260] See MWASE, Ngila R.L., *The East African Community: A Study of Regional Disintegration*, Economic Research Bureau (Paper No. 77.10), University of Dar es Salaam, 1979, p. 6; and MBOGORO, Damas A.D., *The Common Market Concept and Economic Development: Tanzania's Experience*, Economic Research Bureau (Paper No. 77.8), University of Dar es Salaam, 1978, p. 20-21.

[261] GOMEZ-MERA, Laura, "Domestic Constraints on Regional Cooperation: Explaining Trade Conflict in MERCOSUR," Volume 16 No. 5 *Review of International Political Economy*, 2009, pp. 746-777.

[262] GOLDSTEIN, Andrea and Njuguna S. Ndung'u, *Regional Integration Experience in the Eastern African Region*, Paris: OECD Development Centre (Working Paper No. 171), March, 2001, p. 12.

Court of Justice and 49(2)(b) on powers of the East African Legislative Assembly in approving the EAC budget, have imposed some elements of supranationality as we shall later explain.

These provisions should be celebrated to the extent that they are allowed to function. However, as we shall note later in this paper, in the specific case of Article 50, the *Anyang' Nyong'o* ruling prompted a different reaction that led to the erosion of the sanctity of the Treaty.

Be that as it may, let us first of all examine how the EAC Treaty itself has placed national politics in command of the EAC's decision making process; national politics being used herein as national sovereignty. Without going into an elaborate discussion, the following treaty clauses can be cited as paramount examples around which there has been great sensitivity in the determination of the content and pace of integration projects:-

• *Equitable distribution of benefits* accruing or derived from the operations of the EAC (Article 6(e) of the treaty). This fundamental principle has aroused strong sentiments from the new EAC members, namely Rwanda and Burundi who, upon acceding to the EAC, strived to quickly benefit from new employment opportunities, and through a Council of Minister's decision, froze fresh recruitments until a positive decision was taken. Along with the intervention from day one that Rwanda and Burundi had to equally be offered a post each of Deputy Secretary General as it was in the case with the old partner states, it is clear that national politics was at play in securing these equitable benefits. There was the expected rallying point at national levels as to what immediate benefits Rwanda and Burundi would marshal through joining the EAC; call them "quick wins". The large question that should openly be debated is how to strike a delicate balance between the objective of equity in employment and merit. A regional organisation like the EAC has a crucial role to play in managing the integration process. It is a role that demands a great deal of intellectual capital, experience and diplomatic tact. Without such competences the integration project could risk underachievement.

The question of equitable sharing of benefits raises another dimension where the principle of equity is more easily realised much as it also raises political overtones of nationalism. For example, at the end of October 2011, the EAC Council of Ministers, after an almost two years of indecision because of national interests being placed above equity determinants, had to give in to consistent pressure from Rwanda and Burundi to locate the EAC Science and Technology Commission in Kigali and the EAC Health Research Commission in Bujumbura. Whilst it is the Treaty that won from these developments, it has to be admitted that national politics played a signal role in that success.

- *The principle of subsidiarity* (Article 7(1)(d)) with emphasis on multi-level participation and the involvement of a wide range of stakeholders in the process of integration. This operational principle of the Treaty aims at fostering a democratic decision making process the builds legitimacy and better consideration of national realities. However it is a principle that has evoked, over the years of EAC's integration, a great deal of heat, fears, and concerns around national economic interests. The EAC Customs Union Protocol, for example, took more than three years of negotiations largely because national politics unleashed the application of the subsidiarity principle which saw a number of national stakeholders, especially from the business or private sector, taking strong zero-sum positions on issues such as the number of tariff bands for the Common External Tariff (CET), applicable percentages, list of sensitive products to be exempted from the CET, and general opposition to harmonization of consumer taxes.

Similar intense roles were exhibited in the negotiations of the Common Market Protocol. Indeed, there was a period in the negotiations of this protocol when national politics relating to issues like 0wnership of land and the use of identity cards for cross border travel being incorporated in the protocol almost undermined approval of the protocol. National politics, particularly espoused by Tanzania, had to be accommodated for that higher level of integration to be realized. As it is, the Schedules for implementation of the Common Market Protocol are largely informed and underpinned by national preferences as to timeframes making the full realisation of the Common Market more of a mirage.

It is interesting to note, for example, that even prior to the entry of the Common Market, Kenya, Uganda and Rwanda had liberalised their capital accounts to enable their citizens and institutions such as mutual and social security funds to buy shares in listed companies and bonds in the EAC partner states. Tanzania and Burundi refrained to take a similar action. In the case of Tanzania, national politics revolving around capital flight and money laundering issues informed monetary policy in that regard.

At the end of October, 2011, the Bank of Tanzania announced that it has opened up the capital account only within the framework of the EAC Common Market. The news has been warmly received even though it is not clear whether the opening up is immediate or, as has featured in the East African Newspaper, the Bank of Tanzania will "set the timeline to remove all obstacles in the next two years." The statement would, in that case, not add value to what already features in the Schedules for the implementation of the Common Market Protocol.

The main argument against the principle of subsidiarity is that it could at times weaken a government's political commitment to the integration project. In the case of the EAC Customs Union, which had taken too long for its protocol to be concluded, the national political leaders (the Heads of State) had to choose to give greater priority to the regional strategic partnership over national considerations by short-circuiting the slow ministerial decision making process and fast tracking the adoption of the protocol. Striking a balance between national sovereignty and the regional purpose could thus be the stuff of rational national politics in a new era of regional and global interdependence.

- ***The principle of variable geometry*** (Article 7(1)(e)) which allows for progression in cooperation among groups within the EAC for wider integration schemes in various fields and at different speeds. Nyerere had in fact floated the idea of variable geometry when he met the three East African leaders who had been appointed as a working party to draft an East African Federation Constitution, on 10th May, 1964 in Dar es Salaam. During that meeting Nyerere stated, "It is better that two countries should federate now if three cannot."[263] The EAC Treaty has incorporated this clause of variable geometry along with that on asymmetry (Article 7(1)(h)), to cite Henry Kibet Mutai "primarily to allay the fears of Tanzania and Uganda, which feared that, given their relatively lower levels of development, their economies ran the risk of being swamped by Kenyan goods if they were obliged to liberalize at the same rate. These principles have since proved to be central to the strategy being undertaken by partner states."[264]

In other words, the application of the principles of variable geometry and asymmetry is located primarily at national levels and informed by national politics. It would be recalled that at the height of the consultative process on fast-tracking the East African political federation, strong sentiments were expressed from Tanzania that the country's position on the issue should not frustrate the ambition of other partner states ready and willing to federate as long as the door was left open to her to join later. Is this practical? Going by the experience of the European Union, variable geometry works on matters of trade and monetary affairs. It failed on political integration much as the Lisbon treaty which has been ratified by all EU member states incorporates elements of political integration, such as the role of co-decision making between the EU Parliament and the Council and on the role of a High Representative on Foreign Affairs.

- ***The domestication of EAC law*** by way of Partner States undertaking to make the necessary legal instruments to confer precedence of EAC

---

[263] See NYERERE, Julius K., "Desire for a Federation of East Africa," in NYERERE, Julius K., *Freedom and Unity*, op. cit., at p. 297.

[264] MUTAI, Henry Kibet, "Regional Trade Integration Strategies under SADC and the EAC: A Comparative Analysis, Volume 1 *SADC Law Journal*, 2011, pp. 81-97 at p. 83.

organs, institutions, and laws over similar national ones pursuant to Article 8(4). It remains somewhat innocuous what the term "undertake" under Article 8(5) actually entails. For example, does it impose a legal obligation? This fuzziness has partly been responsible for significant acts of omission on the part of some partner states in domesticating EAC laws. Again it could be concluded that where national politics support domestication, Article 8(5) is enforced and, where national politics are not supportive of domestication, then a state of drift predominates. For example, in respect of domesticating the EAC Common Market Protocol, to date it is only Kenya that has taken serious steps to draft an omnibus statute, The Miscellaneous Amendment Bill 2011 which seeks to amend several laws that pertain to or impinge on the Common Market Protocol. Other EAC partner states are only at the infant stage of identifying the pieces of legislation that demand amendment. Clearly, delays in this process of domestication will impede and hamper the fast-paced realization of the common market objectives.

- *The ratification of Protocols* pursuant to Article 151(3) of the EAC Treaty. This is yet another area where national politics play a deterministic role. Even where protocols have been approved by the Summit of Heads of State, their ratification has never been a smooth exercise except where the Heads of State themselves have taken it upon themselves to ensure that the ratification process is well time-lined. Thus, the EAC Protocol on the Environment and Natural Resources which was approved in 2006 is yet to be fully ratified and as such it remains unoperational. The Protocol on Foreign Policy Coordination which was approved on 3rd December 2010 is also yet to be ratified by all the partner states. And there are a number of other Protocols approved in 2007, including those for establishing the Science and Technology, the Health Research and Kiswahili Commissions which are yet to be ratified by all the original three partner states. Paradoxically, Tanzania which has been allowed to host the EAC Kiswahili Commission, based on its application, is yet to ratify the protocol for the Commission's establishment!

In sum, one can conjecture that national politics still determines the pace in which protocols are ratified. One challenge that confronts the ratification of protocols is of course where the ratification process requires the involvement of National Assemblies (or Parliament) as opposed to a mere Cabinet decision then the full force of national politics becomes unleashed, opening up a broader debate about the costs and benefits of the protocols at the national levels. In this context, there is a view, largely propagated by the

East African Legislative Assembly that the EAC should move away from protocols and adopt, instead, the system of Parliamentary Bills.

This proposal is partly driven by the cumbersomeness in securing ratifications of protocols and partly by the view that once laws are passed by the EAC legislature they automatically become part of municipal laws by virtue of the Treaty. Unfortunately, this thinking whilst valid on the face of it, overlooks the nature of national politics. Bills will still have to be moved by the Council of Ministers where national politics take command. Moreover, Bills have still to be assented by all the EAC Heads of State, another area strongly influenced by national politics. This said, where bills are proposed by the Council of Ministers, the route of passing laws through the EAC legislative process may be more efficient that that of negotiating protocols and going through the laborious channel of ratifications. In this regard, the decision taken, for example, to move the EAC Development Fund away from the protocol route to that of legislation, an idea that was proposed by the Sectoral Council on Legal and Judicial Affairs, is apt and should be pursued more frequently.

The Challenges of EAC Decision Making Process

Apart from the foregoing examples which manifest the primacy of national politics in EAC integration, one may wish to note that in general, the EAC Treaty places most areas of cooperation, which fall between Chapters Eleven and Twenty Seven, under the influence, engagement and decision of and by the Partner States. And to ensure that decisions are arrived at with the involvement of all the Partner States, the Treaty, under Articles 12(3) and 15(4), provides that the decisions of the Summit of Heads of State and of the Council of Ministers, respectively, *shall* be by consensus. The short history of EAC integration is replete with delayed decisions and even failure to decide on critical issues particularly at the level of the Council of Ministers because of overriding national politics which are given force of law through the consensus rule. Examples include: the draft protocol on Immunities and Privileges; adoption of a new and equitable system of financing the EAC's budget; determination of the Seat of the East African Court of Justice pursuant to Article 47 of the Treaty; the Single Customs Territory; the Single Tourist Visa; draft protocol on establishing the East African Tourism and Wildlife Management Coordinating Agency and draft protocol for the establishment of a Development Fund.

The intransigence of the Partner States in as many as eight years to-date to allow a different funding system for the EAC budget to be adopted instead of relying on the ruling fixed contribution which is not equitable, and be based, for example, on a small percentage of each country's VAT receipts earned from intra-regional trade, could only be explained by the enduring culture of partner states wanting to retain direct control over EAC's mandate and working. This failure or lack of resolute interest to adopt more effective and fair systems of budget contributions, which includes the highly delayed decision to set up a Development Fund that could assist the EAC to finance some of its priority infrastructure projects, are clear manifestations of the continuing tension between maintenance of a strict inter-governmentalism and the ceding of some sovereignty to the EAC Secretariat.

This situation is in stark contrast to the one that obtains in the European Union where the budget of the Commission is fixed on the basis of a percentage of a member county's GNP enabling the institution to even set aside special structural and development funds to support equitable development for member states.

What is disconcerting is that even at the level of the Summit of Heads of State, national politics have, in few instances, taken an overriding position in determining the depth of regional integration. Thus, though Article 87 of EAC Treaty provides for financing of projects jointly in each others' territory especially those that promote integration and includes joint mobilization of foreign capital for financing such projects, this type of cooperation has not been forthcoming. Indeed, at a Special Retreat of EAC Heads of State held in Kigali at the end of June 2008, the EAC Secretariat, with the support of the Council of Ministers, had put up a proposal to operationalise Article 87 by enabling the EAC Secretariat to exercise authority in mobilising finance for regional infrastructure projects.

The idea was not positively received by some of the Heads of State who felt that the locus for infrastructure development should remain at national levels even when the Heads of State were positively inclined to helping the EAC Secretariat reach out to foreign sources to secure project finance. However, unless these funds are only in the form of grants, they cannot be secured by the EAC because regional projects are "regional" only in name; not in terms of execution. The Partner States are still the legal borrowers of funds and the executing agencies.

In this overall context, it remains unclear whether the application of the principle of variable geometry under Article 7(1)(e) also requires consensus. This is an important point to the extent that some Partner States could wish to proceed outside the consensus prescription. The Advisory Opinion delivered by the East African Court of Justice on 24 April 2009 on this question merely held that "consensus is simply a decision making mechanism while variable geometry is a strategy of implementation". It would appear that the Court's opinion is that there is consistency between the principle of variable geometry and the rule of consensus decision making though their application happens at different stages within a common process.

To the extent that the Court ruled that consensus did not equate with unanimity, it opened up the application of variable geometry to a non-consensus requirement. Indeed, in the view of Professor James Gathii, the definition of variable geometry adopted by the court:

> is consistent with accommodating laggard partner states. In essence, variable geometry gets a very positive spin; it is a policy of allowing forward movement without compelling unwilling countries to do so.[265]

In the Maastricht Treaties, this principle of variable geometry has been incorporated through the "opt-out" clause. Indeed in a recent Charlemagne in the *Economist*,[266] it has been argued that "the creation of a more flexible EU of variable geometry should ease many of the existing tensions (in reference to the crisis of the Euro over the sovereign debt crisis) further need no longer be imposed on those who do not want it (that is the Euro)." Going forward, especially over the negotiations for the monetary union and the subsequent consideration of the political federation, the EAC may well be advised to incorporate an "opt-out" clause in its protocols and thus building variable geometry into the legal framework of the monetary union protocol.

The Role of the East African Court of Justice (EACJ)

In the important area of the role of the EACJ in regional integration, the centrality of intergovernmentalism and the supremacy of national politics in integration features prominently. The jurisdiction of the EACJ is highly limited, vested with only a mandate over the interpretation and application of the EAC Treaty (Article 27(1)). Whilst there have been efforts in the past five years to extend the Court's jurisdiction through a protocol, in line with Article 27(2) of the Treaty, support of the partner states for the Protocol has been weak in the least largely because national politics view the extended jurisdiction of the Court as tantamount to opening up of the floodgates of references and cases particularly those related to alleged human rights violations.

Interestingly, the EACJ, however, has found itself exercising jurisdiction in references that in fact have a human rights dimension. For example, in the *Katabazi Case* the EACJ ruled that while it would not:

> assume jurisdiction to adjudicate on human rights disputes, it will not abdicate from exercising its jurisdiction of

---

[265] GATHII, James Thuo, *African Regional Trade Agreements as Legal Regimes*, New York: Cambridge University Press, 2011, p. 57.

[266] See *The Economist*, 2011.

interpretation under Article 27(1) merely because the reference includes allegations of human rights violation.[267]

It is a very fine line that the court struck in terms of drawing a distinction over the jurisdictional issue. The SADC Tribunal, in contrast, was bolder on a similar matter. In the case of *Mike Campbell (Pvt.) Limited and 78 Others v. Republic of Zimbabwe*[268] the Tribunal held that it had jurisdiction to hear the case which had involved the confiscation of lands belonging to Zimbabwe white farmers under a land reform programme. The Court ruled that its jurisdiction was based on the fact that SADC member states are bound by the Treaty to uphold the principles of human rights, democracy, and the rule of law and that in the petition before it was quite clear that the Zimbabwe Government had violated those binding principles by denying the applicants access to the Zimbabwe courts and engaging in racial discrimination through the land confiscation action.

The Court indeed ruled that the 78 white farmers had the right to keep their farms. Following the ruling, Zimbabwe withdrew its recognition of the Tribunal and rejected the ruling. Of course the Zimbabwe action was reproached by several members of SADC. The reaction damaged the sanctity of the SADC Treaty and the integration objective.

More broadly, and of particular regret insofar as the role of the EACJ in EAC integration is concerned is the subjection of commercial disputes that arise from regional trade and investment transactions falling under the Customs Union and the Common Market Protocols, which constitute regional law by virtue of being integral parts of the EAC Treaty (Article 151(4)), to municipal legal regimes. Thus, in the EACJ in the *Modern Holdings (EA Limited) Case* in which the claimant sought an award of damages for loss of business occasioned by the respondent's failure to clear perishable goods at the port of Mombasa following the Kenya post-election violence, the EACJ ruled that it had no jurisdiction to entertain the reference because the Kenya Ports Authority was not one of the respondent's envisaged under Article 30 of the EAC Treaty.[269] Article 30 limits references to the Court to decisions, directives, regulations or actions of a Partner State or an institution of the EAC of which the Kenya Ports Authority was neither.

---

[267] See *James Katabazi and 21 Others v. Secretary General of the East African Community and the Attorney General of the Republic of Uganda,* East African Court of Justice at Arusha, Reference No. 1 of 2007.

[268] See *In the Matter between Mike Campbell (Pvt) Ltd. and 78 Others v. The Republic of Zimbabwe,* In the Southern African Development Community (SADC) Tribunal, Windhoek, Namibia, SADC (T) Case No. 2/2007.

[269] See *Modern Holdings (EA) Limited v. Kenya Ports Authority,* East African Court of Justice at Arusha, Reference No. 1 of 2008.

Under municipal legal regimes, however, courts in each partner state would have to interpret and apply the provisions of the protocols and other regional laws in isolation from each other and thereby, invariably so, undermining the legal assumptions upon which the Customs Union and the Common Market are surely based. In contrast, in the case of the EU, the European Court of Justice, in the case of *Costa v. ENEL*,[270] ruled that EU law has primacy over national law where national law is in conflict with EU law. That principle was well manifested in the 1978 case of *Cassis de Dijon*,[271] where the European Court ruled that a product – in that case, a French liqueur – approved for sale in one country must be accepted by other EU member states.

The ruling ushered in the principle of automatic mutual recognition of standards as a cornerstone of the single market. Thus, in spite of the fact that countries like Britain have come to regard the European Court "as an unguarded back door through which national sovereignty is being carted away,"[272] the case law cited clearly lays down the emergence of supranationality in the European Union that ensures the vitality and vibrancy of the single market. In the case of the EAC, the EU case law would pose the pertinent question whether the Customs Union and the Common Market Protocols can be fully unleashed without commercial disputes that arise from their applications being allowed to feature as part of the original and appellate jurisdiction of the East African Court of Justice.

Jurisdictional questions notwithstanding, it is important to also point out that a huge lacuna in the EAC Treaty remains in the area of enforcement of EACJ rulings. For example, in the *Katabazi Case*, the Court made reference to Article 29(1) of the Treaty which imposes on the EAC Secretary General powers which "are so encompassing and are pertinent to the advancement of the spirit of the re-institution" of the EAC. It remains fuzzy what the court meant by "re-institution of the community". Was it in reference to the re-establishment of the EAC after its collapse in 1977? Hypothetical as it may seem, it would be interesting to find out what the court would ultimately do were the Secretary General to fail in his interventions under Article 29 (1) and (2) within the set four months to secure submission of observations from a Partner State which is deemed to have infringed a provision of the Treaty?

The Treaty provides under Article 29(3) that where a Partner State fails to respond suitably to the Secretary General's enquiry, the Secretary General is required to table the failure before the Council of Ministers and, upon a directive of the Council, can refer the matter to the EACJ. There are two

---

[270] See *Flaminio Costa v. ENEL* [1964] ECR 585 (6/64).

[271] See *Rewe-Zentral AG v. Bundesmonopolverwaltung für Branntwein* (The Cassis de Dijon), ECJ Case Number 120/1978.

[272] See "European Court of Justice: Biased Referee?" – *The Economist,* 19th May, 1997.

issues here: first, the Partner State accused of infringement of the Treaty can block any action in the Council of Ministers by applying the doctrine of consensus. Secondly, the Treaty is silent as to what the EACJ can or may do where the matter goes back to it. In sum, Article 29 of the Treaty is one of those provisions which clearly reflect the general weakness of the Treaty and how the primacy of national sovereignty features in the Treaty with respect to EAC integration.

One would have thought that empowering the Secretary General to directly seek an Advisory Opinion of the EACJ would provide an outlet or a cure to some of these decision making blockages or lacunas. Unfortunately, and again largely because of the primacy of national politics and sovereignty issues in the Treaty provisions, the Secretary General has no authority under Article 36 of the Treaty to seek such opinion from the Court.

The Role of East African Legislative Assembly (EALA)

Another interesting feature of the impact of national politics on regional integration is the application of Article 50 of the EAC Treaty on the election of members of the EALA. On the face of it, the election process could be taken to be benign. However, as experience of the Kenyan electoral process in 2006 showed, there are strong underlying political forces and interests involved in the EALA elections. Following the Kenyan election process, a reference was made to the EACJ challenging that process as having violated Article 50 of the Treaty.

In the now famous *Peter Anyang' Nyong'o Case*, the EACJ granted an interim injunction restraining the Secretary General of the EAC and the Clerk of EALA from recognizing nine persons from Kenya as duly elected members of EALA or permitting them to participate in any function of the EALA until the final determination of the Reference.[273] That case clearly reflected that there exists strong national politics in the whole process of obtaining country representatives to the EAC legislative system.

Indeed, following the ruling of the Court, Kenya appealed to the other Partner States to have the Treaty amended with particular reference to Article 30 which enshrines the rights of legal and natural persons to refer to the EACJ for determination the legality of any Act, regulation, directive, decision or action of a Partner State or an institution of the Community on grounds that such Act, regulation, directive, decision or action is unlawful or an infringement of the provisions of the Treaty. Two new provisions were added under Article 30 primarily to ensure that the court does not exercise

---

[273] See *Prof. Peter Anyang' Nyong'o and 10 Others v. Attorney General of Kenya and Others*, Application No. 1 of 2006.

jurisdiction where "an Act, regulation, directive, decision or action has been reserved under this Treaty to an institution of a Partner State."

This amendment should be examined in the context of the more elaborate change done to Article 27(1) where the Court's jurisdiction over the interpretation and application of the Treaty is now subject to a proviso to the effect that "the court's jurisdiction ... shall not include the application of any such interpretation to jurisdiction conferred by the Treaty on organs of Partner States." In sum, following the *Anyang' Nyong'o Case*, national politics have found it in their interest to limit the court's jurisdiction even further.

In this overall perspective about the relationship between national politics and the quest for supranationality, it could be observed that the EALA itself has also become a hotbed of politics. There are a number of instances that reflect this development, attempts as it were, of using the regional legislative arm to confront deemed deficits in national politics. One example is the unilateral passage of a Private Member's Bill in September 2011 titled, The East African Elections Bill 2011 that seeks to harmonize East African electoral systems and processes. The Bill failed to secure the support of the EAC Council of Ministers and would, going by previous practise, fail to secure assent of the EAC Heads of State. Another relevant example is the intransigence on the part of EALA over what should be the ideal management and organizational system for running the Lake Victoria Basin Commission (LVBC) regard being had to what is already determined in the Protocol establishing the Commission.

The Council of Ministers had tabled a Bill before EALA so as to properly incorporate the LVBC away from reliance on the Protocol, the intention being to clarify the Commission's relationships with the Organs of the EAC under the Treaty and extend its mandates. For almost two years the EALA sought to include in the Bill new organizational and management systems that contradicted the fundamental principles underlined in the Protocol and which would have markedly reduced the role of the Partner States in the management and direction of the LVBC. Put differently, EALA was attempting to transform the LVBC from being an intergovernmental institution into a supranational one. The Council of Ministers of course rejected those proposals and finally opted to withdraw the Bill altogether from the legislature.

These two legislative cases, amongst others, present examples of a direct clash between national politics that operate within the ambit and spirit of intergovernmentalism and the politics of supranationality as exhibited by an activist regional legislative assembly. Undoubtedly, if such clashes take root they may, in good time, damage both the spirit and the pace of regional integration.

National Politics and Political Integration

After this exhaustive examination of the EAC Treaty provisions that feature national politics and the workings of the EACJ and the EALA in relation to the interface and clash between intergovernmentalism and supranationality, we can now turn to yet another subject that evokes a great deal of sensitivity in EAC's integration. This relates to the relationship and impacts between national politics and the quest for political integration or, for that matter, for the political federation. This is not a subject that is unique or peculiar to the EAC as Peter Hilpold has observed: "by adopting a purely economic perspective one risks ignoring one of the most important motives for regional integration: the political one."[274]

In other words, an economic perspective lacking a political driver risks setbacks. In the EU, such political perspective is increasingly viewed as central in not only locking in the gains of integration but also in advancing deeper integration. The attempts at adopting a Constitution Treaty in 2005 were intended to provide this political perspective to integration. 'Federalist' countries like Germany and Belgium believed that the Constitution was a logical pathway on the long road to building a one, integrated Europe.

In fact, because of the enduring lack of a robust political driver in EU integration, there are genuine fears about regression in realising the full potential and benefits, for example, of the Single Market. This picture features well in the European Commission President Jose Manuel Barroso's letter to Professor Mario Monti appointing him as EU Consultant to examine the functioning of the EU Single Market. In that letter, President Barroso refers to the strong temptation by EU member states "to roll back the Single Market and seek refuge in forms of economic nationalism" and urged a "renewed political determination" to reinvigorate the Single market.[275]

In the EAC context, on the other hand, the impact of national politics on regional integration is well orchestrated in the region's final stage of integration, which is the quest of a political federation in line with Article 5(2) of the Treaty.

The place of national politics in the idea of political federation has a long historical context which we have earlier alluded to from the thinking of the late Mwalimu Julius K. Nyerere. It also features prominently in the Wako Report on Fast-tracking of the EAC Political Federation. In that report, the following main national concerns of a political character were outlined as

---

[274] HILPOLD, Peter, "Regional Integration According to Article XXIV GATT: Between Law and Politics," op. cit. at p. 222.

[275] See MONTI, Mario, *A New Strategy for the Single Market – At the Service of Europe's Economy and Society: Report to the President of the European Commission José Manuel Barroso*, op. cit.

requiring attention in the quest to establish a political federation in East Africa:-

- The challenge of disparities in development that needed a step-by-step integration to allow the partner states to expand competitive capacity in social and economic sectors;
- Loss of sovereignty requiring clarification of the relationship between nation states and the federal state;
- Erosion of revenue at national level given the revenue needs of a federal government;
- Loss of markets because political integration would entail the establishment of a single economic space; and
- Loss of land which would have to be shared by a new East African citizenry.

The interesting feature about these national concerns from the Wako Report is that they similarly existed in 1960 when Nyerere proposed a federation of East Africa. The difference, as Nyerere feared, is that the entrenchment and consolidation of the sovereign nation state has basically now come to haunt the very spirit and ethos of political integration. Take the case of the border dispute between Uganda and Kenya over the ownership of the Migingo rock island on Lake Victoria that flared up in February 2009. Surely, for two countries that are passionately committed to an East African federation, the dispute and the fiery conflictual political statements that surrounded it, did little to lend support for a federation. In this vein, it could not come as a surprise that the EAC consultative process on fast-tracking the East African federation which was undertaken over the period October 2006 and mid-2009, covering all the five EAC partner states, a number of political concerns should have emerged with adverse impact on a consensus decision to proceed with an early political federation.

Those concerns, by and large, reinforced once again the national politics that had featured in the Wako process. They continue to centre on: loss of national sovereignty, disparities in the culture and best practices of constitutionalism, governance systems, anti-corruption, respect for human rights, history of civil strife and ethnic tensions, the leapfrogging of laid-down stages of integration as set out in the EAC Treaty, stages which constitute important building blocks for moving to a political federation, circumspection about the political ambitions of some national leaders on federation leadership, lack of a proper system to have equitable sharing of benefits of integration in an environment where there is lack of economic asymmetry, divergences in quality of education, etc.

In the specific case of Tanzania, the question of the status of the Tanzanian Union in a future East African political federation continues to raise much disquiet. Zanzibaris appear to hold a firm opinion that the United Republic of Tanzania would need to resolve this particular question as an inherent component of the broad consideration of the federation. Zanzibaris seem to fear that were Tanzania to join the East African Federation as a Union, then Zanzibar would lose its status, being called upon to play second fiddle, as it were, in matters of its own interest within the federation. One of the emerging questions in relation to the federation idea is whether the Tanzanian Union could be sacrificed on the altar of the East African Federation or would Tanzania regard its Union as a more developed form of political integration to a federation and thus seek to retain it even if it means not joining the federation? Alternatively, could Zanzibar join the federation in its own right, but what would such 'right' mean in the context of the Tanzania Union in which sovereignty currently lies?

Equally, the politics of the Buganda Kingdom which partly frustrated the realization of the East African federation in 1963 continue to dominate the thinking, isolated as it maybe, in Uganda, with respect to the form the East African federation would take.

All the foregoing concerns as well as political paradigms seem, unfortunately, to fuel or even galvanise some form of a loose political consensus against the political federation and particularly so in Tanzania though it may be pertinent to also ask whether a solution could be found from the application of the principle of variable geometry as Nyerere had conjectured in 1960, that is allowing those East African states ready to federate to do so whilst allowing others to join when it best suits them.

In sum, the tragedy about all the foregoing concerns is that EAC integration has so far failed to propel a broad political movement at national levels supportive of political integration. Yes, as Professor Abdalla Bujra has noted, integration is a political process. Unfortunately, however, the political process has largely involved political leaders in government and their bureaucracy executives. Ideally and practically, the process should involve the broad political system as well as the civil society.

Increasingly, and particularly with the new momentum on how the EAC could steadily move towards a political federation, a large question has indeed emerged as to how many political parties in the EAC region do actually incorporate EAC integration in their political agenda or even in their election manifestos. This is an interesting question when one considers how the EAC could exercise supranationality over national politics that appear to violate Article 3(3) of the Treaty that sets out the principles that underlie admission of a country into EAC membership.

It would be recalled that in the period preceding the Burundi general elections in 2010, several political parties pronounced a boycott of the elections. Evidently, the boycott was contrary to Article 3(3)(b) of the EAC Treaty which requires "adherence to universally acceptable principles of good governance, democracy, rule of law, observance of human rights, and social justice." Through the EAC framework, the Ministers of Foreign Affairs of the four partner states other than Burundi went to Bujumbura and unequivocally called upon the boycotting political parties to stop the boycott, failure of which sanctions and travel embargoes would be imposed upon the political leaders of those parties.

The EAC action bore positive results and established a precedent of supranationality in addressing what had earlier been regarded as an exclusive national political question requiring a national solution. The flipside of this development is the importance that should be attached to the integration of political parties in the whole regional integration agenda, including giving them a better understanding of the governance best practices that underlie membership in the EAC and the ambition of political federation.

This point probably reinforces Professor Mwesiga Baregu's view that the position and role of political parties in the integration movement crucially hinges on the nature of the imperatives that drive integration. From his perspective, where the imperatives that support deeper integration are seen to be more a matter of "necessity than choice," the greater the likelihood that political parties would be enthused to actively participate in integration.[276] However, Baregu's point could be interrogated in the sense that it could be begging the question why political parties should not in the first place be the strategic drivers of the imperatives for integration. Why should a particular political agency, probably the one in power, be the determinant of the so-called imperatives?

Recent efforts undertaken by the EAC Secretariat in involving political parties from all the Partner States in the integration process, with crucial support from Trade Mark East Africa and other donors, is a welcome intervention in building a critical mass of thinking, understanding, and appreciation for integrating regional integration issues within national politics. The meetings of political parties from the EAC region have helped to shape a regional agenda on integration and has helped to forge a bridge of similar thinking across different political parties. This process will take an important dimension when the EAC considers transforming its Legislative Assembly into a directly elected one.

---

[276] BAREGU, Mwesiga and Bashiru Ally, *Participation of Political Parties in the East African Integration Process*, East African Community Occasional Papers, Issue No. 1, March, 2009, p. 76.

On a broader scale, one could plausibly question whether the whole debate around the impact of national politics on regional integration is well thought-out when in fact national politics are not always, *necessarily*, politics that are national? In other words, how often do we not witness politics that represent minority thinking and interests either of those in political authority, their benefactors, or of neo-nationalists who have little appreciation of and for the objective realities of a new global and regional economic environment become the <u>principal</u> determinants of national policies?

Another dimension that one could consider is the huge lacuna that exists in the whole constitutional reform process taking place in East Africa relative to the quest for the East African political federation. During the constitutional reform process in Kenya, one never got the feeling that the East African Federation was seriously given a mental space in that process. Indeed, the new Kenyan Constitution is silent on a future East African federation. In Tanzania, on the other hand, ongoing debates about the planned new Constitution have so far not made any reference to the idea of an East African Federation.

In this overall situation, the EAC Secretariat should be complimented for establishing, for example, a regional forum of the Chief Justices of EAC Partner States, a move and a platform that could trigger requisite sensitivity and focus over some of the critical constitutional issues raised and emerging. It was interesting to read, for example, a powerful statement of the Chief Justice of Uganda, Honourable Benjamin Odoki, made at the Forum of Chief Justices in Kampala in October 2011 calling for the urgent revamping of the East African Court of Justice and the adoption of the Protocol on the extended jurisdiction of that court. Such interventions by respected jurists in East Africa would go a long way in catalysing a new spirit for deeper integration founded on and driven by law.

What is of further interest is the emergence of thinking among constitutional jurists in East Africa, notably Professor Palamagamba Kabudi of the University of Dar es Salaam and Dr Adams Oloo of the University of Nairobi that for the EAC to proceed, constitutionally, to a Monetary Union and the Political Federation, it will have to negotiate a new Treaty.[277] Their argument is based on the ground that the Treaty, in its present form, ends with the Common Market. Evidently, Article 2 of the EAC Treaty which provides for the establishment of the Community (defined as the East African Community under Article 1) stipulates, under Article 2(2), the establishment of the Customs Union and the Common Market "as transitional stages to and integral parts of the Community." That establishment provision omits any mention of the Monetary Union and the Political Federation. These are covered under Article 5(2) as "objectives of

---

[277] See *The Monitor* (Uganda), 5th February, 2012.

the Community". Indeed, it could further be argued that the treaty is silent on the modalities for the establishment of the Monetary Union and the Political Federation of the type set out for the Customs Union and the Common Market under Articles 75(7) and 76(4) respectively.

I do, however, differ with Professor Kabudi's views in particular which I critique below. Dr Oloo's points of law, in contrast, rest more on whether the new Kenyan Constitution is in consonance or at variance with the EAC Treaty. This position needs to be examined in detail to determine its adequacy for the EAC Treaty to be amended or re-negotiated. In my view, as regards the establishment of the Monetary Union, the EAC Treaty under Chapter Fourteen and Articles 82-86 outlines in clear terms the measures to be undertaken to forge monetary and financial cooperation. Article 82 (1) (a) specifically states that the partner states shall "cooperate in monetary and financial matters and maintain the convertibility of their currencies as a basis for the establishment of a Monetary Union." Thus, whilst there is no specific Treaty provision for the negotiation of a Monetary Union, the Treaty clearly recognizes what ought to be done to move towards such union.

Moreover, the Treaty has an omnibus clause on enabling protocols for the realization of diverse areas of cooperation in the EAC. Article 151(1) provides that "the partner states shall conclude such protocols as may be necessary in each area of cooperation which shall spell out the objectives and scope of and institutional mechanism for cooperation and integration." Article 151(4) moreover stipulates that the Annexes and protocols shall form an integral part of the EAC Treaty. In sum, I do not agree that the establishment of the Monetary Union requires the partner states to renegotiate the treaty.

The same arguments above hold for the establishment of the Political Federation. Article 123(1) of the Treaty provides that in order to promote the achievement of objectives of the Community as set out under Article 5 of the Treaty particularly with respect to the eventual establishment of a Political Federation of the Partner States, the Partner States shall establish common foreign and security policies. One of the objectives of such policies is stated to be the enhancement of the eventual establishment of a Political Federation (Article 123(3) (f)). Moreover, Article 123(6) provides that the Summit of Heads of State shall initiate a process towards the establishment of a Political Federation of the Partner States by directing the Council of Ministers to undertake the process. In the light of Articles 151(1) and 151(4), I fail to agree with Professor Kabudi on the necessity for the EAC Treaty to be re-negotiated in order to move the EAC into the Monetary Union and the Political Federation stages of EAC's integration. These issues can, however, be tested through legal process. Jurists like Kabudi can petition the East African Court of Justice under Article 30 of the EAC Treaty for determination of whether the Monetary Union and the Political Federation necessitate the EAC Treaty being re-negotiated. EAC Partner States can do the same under Article 28(2) of the Treaty. An advisory opinion of the EACJ can also be petitioned, either by the Summit, the Council of Ministers or a Partner State regarding any question of law arising from the treaty.

Another important strategic move in addressing some of the national concerns which often translate themselves into zero-sum sentiments that frustrate deeper integration is to formulate measures that begin to correct economic imbalances and spur asymmetries. The EU has some elaborate measures through structural funds of different forms and purpose. In this vein, it is important that an EAC Development Fund is quickly put in place to finance regional projects such as the Regional Industrialisation Strategy, the Lake Victoria and Lake Tanganyika Investment Programmes; harmonisation of education systems, learning from the Bologna Process in the EU; the EAC integration into the COMESA-EAC-SADC Tripartite Grand Free Trade Area; joint development of Infrastructure Corridors; implementation of One Stop Border Posts; promoting energy interconnections; air traffic liberalisation as part of the Yamoussoukro Decision requirement; harmonisation and approximation of laws, etc. It is the effective implementation of such concrete programmes of development that will help to show tangibility of integration and thereby catalyse greater confidence of the people on integration.

In this context, it may be noted that part of the challenge for the EAC to implement a regional development programme is the existing lack of harmonization of the development visions of the EAC Partner States. Surely, there cannot be a viable quest for a concrete regional development programme when the development visions of EAC countries differ in thrust, priorities, and time spans, and when, moreover, almost all of the visions lack a focus on regional integration. It is difficult to conjecture though how some form of harmonisation of the development visions could be worked out at a time when the national economies exhibit varying resource bases, poverty levels and challenges in the social sectors. It would have been easier to address such variances through what Nyerere described as "organic unity"; in effect, through a political federation.

In the absence of organic unity, the EAC countries need to give greater attention to achieving macro-economic policy convergence and monetary integration; improve physical infrastructure as well as interconnections across borders for roads, railways, inland transport waterways, energy and communications; promote regional co-operation in addressing food security, agricultural productivity and climate change; jointly develop, manage and protect transboundary water resources as well their catchment areas. Finally, EAC Partner States have to work closely together in promoting and sustaining peace and security whose demands go to the root of strict adherence and respect of the fundamental and operational principles set out in Articles 6 and 7 of the Treaty establishing the EAC.

Creating a People-Centred EAC

It is all these questions and perspectives that bring to the fore the point earlier raised in this chapter whether regional integration indeed constitutes a "broadly based political process" where multi-stakeholders, and not simply national governments, play a leading role in determining national politics and their implications on regional interests. The EAC Treaty envisaged such a political process partly through the establishment of the East African Legislative Assembly under Article 50 much as this institution falls within the ambit of the nation-state. In fact, a key question relating to the people-centredness of the EAC could very well be whether the EALA, indeed, provides legitimation of people centredness?

Korwa Adar has posed some interesting questions in this regard. He notes that election of EALA representatives and the process of elections itself raises several short- term and long- term issues and ramifications with respect to EAC integration: "First, direct elections---through the application of the principle of universal adult suffrage should be inscribed in the Treaty as the central modus operandi in the region". Second, Korwa points out that the practice of nominating candidates by political parties "is at the core of the exclusion of East Africans."[278]

Interestingly, the Uganda Democratic Party has challenged this very process in the EACJ, arguing that the process is discriminatory against small political parties to the extent that it denies them adequate representation in the EALA. However, whatever the ruling of the court maybe, the core issue, in my view, is not how to increase representation of political party nominees, as much as whether the EALA, in its present form, is truly representative of the people of East Africa as opposed to being an amalgam of national politics within the National Assembly system?

The Treaty, moreover, provides for the political process through Article 127(4) under which it calls for a forum to be used for consultations between the private sector, civil society organizations, other interest groups, and other appropriate institutions of the EAC both on national issues that impinge on regional integration as well as on the EAC integration itself.

---

[278] See ADAR, Korwa G., "Federalism and East African Community Integration Process: The Role of the East African Legislative Assembly," a paper prepared for presentation at CIGI/GARNET conference on Mapping Integration and Regionalism in a Global World: the EU and Regional Governance outside EU, Bordeaux, France between 17th and 20th September, 2008.

At the private sector level, there has been notable progress in building a powerful nexus between the EAC and East African business community through the East African Business Council. Indeed, through the annual investment promotion conferences and the media summits, with the support of active national business oriented public and private institutions and associations, the EAC integration process has been able to enjoy the crystallisation of supranational thinking and policy making especially in injecting a private sector focus to integration.

Thus making the EAC private sector driven as per Article 7(i)(a) of the EAC Treaty has been given a shot in the arm through the role of the East African Business Council at the EAC level. To some extent, the East African Law Society has also contributed in important ways in forging a regional ethos around issues of human rights and the rule of law as well as in supporting the role of the East African Court of Justice.

However, in the broader civil society context attempts have been made to promote the establishment of an East African Civil Society Organizations' Forum (EACSOF) only since 2005. This forum has now held a number of dialogue workshops under different themes but focused on regional integration. Early this year, the EACSOF was properly constituted with a fulltime secretariat and a Chief Executive Officer.[279] Trade Mark East Africa has extended financial support to the institution so as to give it the necessary capacity to become effective in regional advocacy and coordination. EACSOF will work towards becoming the regional voice in influencing integration policy making at the EAC level.

A word of caution to the EACSOF is that in spite of describing itself as an umbrella organization of all non-governmental organizations and civil society organizations in East Africa, it will still have to work hard to create powerful national structures and networks to be able to succeed in influencing national politics, the current main locus of policymaking for regional integration. The East African Business Council has often, in its fourteen years history, suffered from a legitimacy deficit at national levels because of behaving and acting in an overly supranational manner.

Overall, a major weakness of the EAC Treaty is its failure to create the conditions for enabling a people centredness integration to take place. The EAC remains predominantly a "community" of trade and economic relationships; not one of peoples. A review of all Treaty Articles that have some reference to a role of the "people", such as Articles 104 (ease border crossing for citizens; forging of social partnerships between the governments, employers and employees) 121 (on role of women in socio-economic development) 122 (role of women in business) and 127 (promoting an enabling environment and providing a platform for the

---

[279] See: http://www.eacsof.net

participation of and consultations with civil society) there is a clear omission in the Treaty of the people being staged as an important pillar in the EAC integration. In ECOWAS, in contrast, there is free movement of people in spite of a highly diverse cultural environment compared to that in the EAC and which has bolstered a "West Africanness" to emerge.

It would be recalled that when launching the University of East Africa in June 1963, Mwalimu Julius Nyerere had made reference to the importance to build a sense and culture of "East Africanness" as a bulwark for the realisation of an East African political entity. The EAC is far from the realisation or even for the construction of this culture. Clearly, it is East African identity formation that will spur political integration and provide the much needed fillip as well to all the trade and economic integration projects.

Conclusion

Going forward, EAC integration will be beset by a number of trends which could upstage greater role of national politics. A leading trend will be the changing dynamics of mass democracy that has played a significant role in Africa's 50 years of independence. The recent Arab Spring and the entrenchment of multi-party democracy in an era of rising impact of social media in the social milieu, show that mass politics are giving sway to emerging de-massification of politics and even to a re-definition of the fundamentals of democracy itself. The futurist, Alvin Toffler, cautioned back in 1990 that a "mosaic democracy" manifested in "rising localism, resistance to globalisation, ecological activism, and heightened ethnic and racial consciousness" was fast replacing mass politics and, in its wake, will rise a new order of power which he describes as "power shift."[280]

Another trend is the growing national inequalities fuelled by neo-liberal economic policies and the intensifying impact of globalization. The youth bulge phenomenon will particularly heighten the growing problem of joblessness catapulting zero-sum politics, ultra-nationalism and even social terrorism. The threat of social tension and resulting destabilisation of peace and security is thus real in the current economic environment. This threat is well articulated by Professor Nouriel Roubini:

> Any economic model that does not properly address inequality will eventually face a crisis of legitimacy. Unless the relative economic roles of the market and the state are rebalanced, the protests of 2011 will become more severe, with social and

---

[280] TOFFLER, Alvin, *Powershift; Knowledge, Wealth and Violence at the Edge of the 21ˢᵗ Century*, New York: Bantam Books, 1991, pp. 244-245.

political instability eventually harming long-term economic growth and welfare.[281]

The threat of inequality is exacerbated by the tension around issues of grand corruption and exploitation of national resources without perceived equitable advantage accruing to the producing economies.

The adverse impact of climate change, which is wreaking havoc on food security and putting greater pressure on rural poverty in the EAC region, largely due to constant drought, is equally fostering an upsurge in economic nationalisms which is the antithesis of a culture of regionalism. For example, this year has seen serious national actions being taken to stop cross-border movements of food, particularly sugar. In Tanzania, the actions have even involved the use of armed forces. What this situation brings out is that the fertility of regional integration crucially hinges on the vibrancy of national economies. Unity in poverty seems unrealistic and farfetched.

In as much as the service sector in the EAC region is becoming the most important sector in generation of tax revenues, the role of manufacturing remains crucial in creating the jobs needed for the millions of youth coming out of schools and universities. However, manufacturing jobs are increasingly under threat because of the growing role of India and China in the goods sector. The EAC region is becoming a huge market of all kinds of simple manufactures from Asia. The influx of such goods can be explained partly by the region's weak industrial competitiveness due to low-level technology and innovation uptake; but it is also part of a vivid violation of intellectual property rules and laws. The region is presently inundated by counterfeits and pirated products. This is a problem requiring a regional approach and solution because it could, as it seems likely, undermine industrialisation and thus the critical jobs creation endeavour.

All these national insights help to garner a better understanding of the EAC regional dynamics and how a more viable regional integration agenda could be forged. An important realization in this exercise is to see national politics not as a drag on regional integration but as an essential ingredient.[282] Equally important in the new pluralistic environment, is how to secure the deep involvement of the political parties whom Professors Hooghe and Marks describe as "the primary aggregators of political interests" at national levels in regional integration issues.[283] Essentially, the EAC region has to catalyse an effective balance and trade off between creating a system of governance in policy making which is supranational and intergovernmental.

---

[281] ROUBINI, Nouriel, "The Instability of Inequality," *Project Syndicate*, 13th October, 2011, p. 1.

[282] See HOOGHE, E.A.E.B. and G.W. Marks, "The Neofunctionalists were (Almost) Right: Politicization and European Integration," op. cit.

[283] Ibid., at p. 209

The EAC Institutional Review Report which was, in principle, adopted by the Council of Ministers' meeting held in Zanzibar, at the end of October 2011, heralds a move towards making the EAC Secretariat a more effective executive organ than presently. This is historic as it marks the beginning of a positive realisation that the EAC will be as strong as its constituent parts will endorse.

In drawing judgment or in making a critical evaluation of the impact of national politics on EAC integration, let us recall, in conclusion, the wise words of the late Mwalimu Julius Nyerere:

> The fact that problems exist is in itself an achievement, for it is a sign of life. There is nothing which is worth doing which does not cause problems in the doing of it; there is nothing achieved which does not give rise to new problems as it creates a new situation. East African cooperation is alive; its problems are those of action, achievement, and advance.[284]

My hope is that political will and resolve will take a bolder dimension and become the important catalyst and driver for the realisation of deeper integration.

---

[284] See NYERERE, Julius K., East African Cooperation is Alive," in NYERERE, Julius K., *Freedom and Development*, op. cit. at pp. 241-242.

CHAPTER FORTY NINE

Where Next for the EAC?[285]

I wish to join the Chairperson of the Council of Ministers to welcome you to the Rock City - Mwanza, a place of nostalgic meaning to me as I was born here and spent my effervescent early childhood here. I know for certain that you will love Mwanza for its geography, ambience, night life and excellent food.

This is a Retreat; it is not a formal statutory EAC Meeting. You meet here at leisure. Therefore, be casual, informal and as relaxed as possible whilst transacting what is a highly important business. The purpose of this Retreat is to afford you the opportunity to reflect on a number of critical issues that relate to EAC's integration.

The first purpose is to have a clearer understanding of where the EAC has reached after a decade of integration. There are a number of successes as the presentation will show; but there are also challenges that have impacted the content and speed of integration. These challenges are inevitable because our kind of integration is a political process. In this vein, some activities could not be undertaken even when they formed part of the 2nd and 3rd EAC Development Strategies from 2001 – 2006 and 2006 – 2010. It is important to dwell on these challenges in order to determine lessons of experience – lessons that cut across issues of clarity of objectives, of priorities, of resources – financial, human, and systems and their adequacies.

There are also fundamental issues about the clarity of roles and their delineation among the Partner States, the Council of Ministers and the Secretariat with respect to decision making. Equally, the roles of the Legislative (EALA), the Court (EACJ) and the EAC Institutions as key players in the integration effort have often been in a state of flux, searching for greater meaning and engagement. The extent of their roles and relationships within the whole integration system and process require greater clarity.

Secondly, you are here to determine the visionary question about where you want to see the EAC, say in 2020. During the last Summit, President Jakaya Mrisho Kikwete reflected on the next EAC Decade and proposed a number of perspectives some of which are embraced in this morning's presentation.

---

[285] Statement at the Retreat for Ministers and Permanent Secretaries responsible for EAC Affairs, Mwanza, Tanzania, 8th March, 2011.

This ten year perspective is important if you are to better set out the integration priorities for the next five years under the framework of the 4th EAC Development Strategy (2011 – 2016), some of the priorities are work in progress in the sense that they emanate from the 3rd EAC Development Strategy. The presentation will clarify these pending priorities.

In a nutshell, however, the priorities primarily cover the consolidation of the customs union, the operationisation of the common market, finalizing the negotiations and the setting up of the monetary union, laying firm foundations for the political federation, extending the jurisdiction of the EACJ, leveraging the authority of EALA, implementing the EAC Institutional Development Programme through ceding of some powers from the partner states to the EAC Secretariat, and generally building the capacities of EAC institutions. At the heart of these priorities is the need to boost EAC's funding capabilities both for recurrent and development needs; to see a major shift from current over reliance on donor funding to self funding through the resources of the partner states. The establishment of the development fund is one way in which the EAC can develop in-built mechanisms for achieving financial self reliance.

.Other priorities inevitably emanate from the next stages of integration deepening and widening and they constitute part of EAC's goals encapsulated in the Treaty. Overall, you will need to be guided by Mwalimu Nyerere's mantra from the early 1970's that "To plan is to choose". A strategic plan must focus on priorities that are SMART.

Third, you cannot avoid reflecting on the forces that are reshaping the regional and global economy and how these impact EAC integration. It is clear that there is ongoing shift in regional and global political and economic activity with the intensification of emerging markets and the clear shift in the direction of African trade from the preponderant traditional European markets to Asia; the growth of urbanisation in Africa; the emergence of an African consumer middle class; the educated youth bulge and its grave implications on jobs; the role of multinational and transnational companies in the EAC region's economic performance and competitiveness; the region's overall and worrisome competitiveness indices as reflected in the Annual Global Competitiveness Reports of the World Economic Forum as well as in the World Bank Annual Doing Business Reports; the entry of free flow of information via *Facebook,* Twitter and other social media driven by a mobile telephone revolution in the EAC region and the consequent implications for democratization, peace and stability. All these forces, along with climate change, have to be examined in depth in order to contextualize them in EAC's development paradigm, direction and the plausibility and viability of proposed development strategies.

Fourth, I believe that you do appreciate the fact that a good development strategy cannot achieve results if it is not supported by a good organizational structure, systems and processes. Organisational gurus have always stated that structure follows strategy. This approach is easier said than done especially when you deal with a complex and dynamic ecosystem such as the EAC. If you thus fail to appreciate and recognize the strategic need to develop EAC's organizational capabilities that help the institution to thrive in the face of new demands, the Development Strategy is bound to falter. Organisational design work is thus inevitably hard and time consuming and it usually involves difficult institutional politics and even personality issues. We have witnessed these difficulties in the exercise involving the EAC Institutional Review in the past one year.

By remaking the EAC Organisation in order to mobilize the mind power of the workforce, catalyse the use of talents, knowledge, relationships and skills, the EAC can best realize the goals set out in the Development Strategy. As one management expert has recently put it, "Strategic – minded Executives may not be able to control the weather, but they can design a ship and equip it with a crew that can navigate the ocean under all weather conditions".

Tomorrow, there will be a presentation on the EAC Institutional Review Report. That Report forms an intimate part of the exercise before you today. Organisational review and design is nothing short of developing and implementing a corporate or institutional strategy. There are always evident issues about costs and benefits in new organizational designs and proposals. In the EAC case, you could not be oblivious of the reality that integration is fundamentally a political process with enormous political costs. This is why Kwame Nkrumah's vision of African unity was underlined by the thesis "Seek ye first the political kingdom and the rest will follow". In making such a radical proposal Nkrumah knew well that the language of costs and benefits of African integration would always emerge and frustrate the lofty goal of continental unity and thus sought to nip it in the bind.

The EAC political leadership has to champion the political cause of integration and absorb the costs of its realisation. Half way measures would only delay the fruits of deeper integration. Thus, as you undertake this important conversation about where next the EAC should go, you will, at the same time, think deeply about the institutional capability required to enable the EAC realize its next level of deeper integration. One of the critical components of this institutional capability centres on the question of the decision making structure in the EAC, clarifying in a bold way the division of the roles of the Council of Ministers under Article 14 of the Treaty and of the Secretariat under Article 71. Such clarity, from a deep interpretation of the Treaty, will also help to better determine the relationship between the Partner States and the EAC Secretariat with significant cost savings on EAC's operations.

Of course, there are a number of other important areas for consideration under the Institutional Review in terms of forging capacities and capabilities. They include the proposals to enhance the representation of EALA and transforming the legislature into a full time one in the same way that National Assemblies and Parliaments are. This transformation would correspond to the strategic direction of the EAC towards the political federation.

In similar vein, the East African Court of Justice has to be transformed from a temporary Court to a permanent one. After all, if the SADC Tribunal and the African Court of People's and Human Rights are permanent even when they have so far been less busy than our Court, what could justify its ad hoc character. Moreover, as the EAC Common Market entrenches, the EACJ will find itself dealing with several commercial disputes even without the so-called extended jurisdiction. Many of such disputes are bound to feature as part of the interpretation provisions of the Common Market Protocol and its Annexes which form on integral part of the Treaty.

The EAC is at a critical juncture in its integration. There are huge expectations in East African Society being awaited for: a larger internal market to emerge, beyond the current 11% intra-EAC trade share to total trade, small and medium enterprises becoming the principal drivers of growth of regional markets and job creation, regional infrastructure development taking major leaps forward; power interconnectivity to address some of the serious deficits such as those currently faced by Tanzania; promotion of industrialisation with a regional perspective; establishment of border markets; unleashing of a vibrant and robust regional capital markets; deeper regionalization of higher education supported by a regional system of accreditation and quality assurance; promotion of private and public-private partnership investments in teacher training for primary and secondary schools in order to uplift the quality of basic education in the EAC region and generally forging a much closer collaboration between governments, universities and business in promoting Research & Development and technology innovations especially in the fields of agriculture, food security and value added manufacturing.

Allow me to reiterate once again that you meet here primarily to brainstorm as well as to storm the brains, both important mind exercises, and help to shape and fine-tune the strategic direction EAC should embark upon. It is an exercise worthy of your love for the EAC and of your resolute commitment to its future success.

PART 15

Conclusion

In the concluding part of this book, there is not much more to add to what I believe is a reasonably extensive treatment of EAC's integration from broad perspectives. I have thus decided to make my farewell address as I relinquished the post of Secretary General in front of the EAC Heads of State, the conclusion to the book.

CHAPTER FIFTY

Farewell: Much Achieved; Much Abides[286]

What another historic day in my life when, in welcoming you, dear Excellencies and this distinguished audience, to this Extraordinary EAC Summit, I should also be bidding you farewell. Welcomes are easier to pronounce; farewells, on the other hand, are always filled with emotions; of tears of joy but also of sadness. But as the English Poet and Novelist George Eliot surmised, "only in the agony of parting do we look into the depth of love."

Five years ago, you gave me the distinguished honour and the rare opportunity to serve my fellow East Africans. Today, I want to thank you, from the bottom of my heart, for what has been an unforgettable journey for me; a journey of exploration, of adventure, of learning and of experience. Today, I wish to pay special recognition and gratitude to President Jakaya Mrisho Kikwete for his trust and confidence in me.

In April 2006, he had the opportunity of nominating a candidate for the Secretary General position from thousands of able and competent Tanzanians. He chose me. I will remain ever grateful for the opportunity I have had. History will of course judge me for my achievements and for my shortcomings. Yet I believe that the past five years have been momentous for the East African Community. Thanks to the astute political leadership, will and commitment of you, our Heads of State, our community has achieved much, though much abides.

Today, the EAC prides itself as being not only a well functioning Customs Union in Africa along with the Southern African Customs Union, but is also the only African Regional Economic Community that is constructing a well-structured Common Market.

The accession of Rwanda and Burundi into the EAC has widened and deepened the scope of our regional integration, our peace, stability and development. All in all, and in the words of Tennyson's Ulysses, the EAC is today blessed with one equal temper of heroic hearts that is strong in will, to strive, to seek, to find and not to yield over its ambitions to become a monetary union and a politically federated East Africa. In other words, the EAC is on course and determined to seek a newer world for itself.

---

[286] Farewell Statement at the 9th EAC Extraordinary Summit of Heads of State, Dar es Salaam, Tanzania, 19th April, 2011.

Today, I also wish to pay tribute to an institution that is imbued with a rare organisational culture; a culture strong in shared objectives and a focused pursuit of its goals. The EAC is a unique institution; its democratic systems of governance are truly reflective of its abiding commitment to a Political Federation. The close interplay of the various forces of EAC integration involving Partner States, the Council of Ministers, the East African Legislative Assembly, the Court of Justice, the Secretariat, the autonomous institutions and the private sector, sometimes in a jig-saw fashion, but always informed by the overarching powerful vision – to build a prosperous, competitive, secure, stable and politically united East Africa – is the bedrock of unity of purpose.

I wish to thank all the Ministers, the Permanent Secretaries and senior government officials for their close cooperation and support. I wish to thank the Rt. Hon. Abdirahim Abdi, the Speaker of the East African Legislative Assembly for his friendship, counsel and understanding, sometimes under difficult conditions. I also wish to thank the Judge President of the East African Court of Justice, Honourable Harold Nsekela, my friend and primary school classmate since 1956, whose role and insight have contributed significantly to transforming the East African Court of Justice.

The Heads of EAC Institutions-the Lake Victoria Commission, the Inter-University Council of East Africa, the Civil Aviation Safety and Security Oversight Agency, the Lake Victoria Fisheries Organisation and the East African Development Bank; they have all been close partners in our collective effort at the EAC Secretariat to make a difference in our integration efforts. I wish to pay special tribute to Dr. Tom Okurut, the Executive Director of the Lake Victoria Basin Commission (LVBC) whose term of office is ending on 30th April this year. Dr Okurut has provided sterling leadership at the LVBC. He leaves behind a landmark contribution.

To my colleagues, the Deputy Secretaries General, the Director General (Customs and Trade), the Directors, Senior Staff and all the EAC workers, I say to them, you have been my blood and sinews in an unforgettable journey. Continue the good work. I want to specifically thank Mr. Aloyse Mutabingwa, the outgoing Deputy Secretary General from Rwanda. His role in the Common Market negotiations, in setting the stage for the monetary union negotiations and leading the conclusion of an important agreement with the World Bank on the integration of financial markets in the EAC all attest to an excellent professional leadership. I wish him well in his future roles.

Around Africa and the world, these past five years have exposed me to a wide spectrum of new relationships and new insights. In this hall today, I wish to recognise two individuals who have worked closely with me to forge a unique partnership in African integration but who have also instilled in me insights and lessons of exposure in regional integration. They honoured me over the last three years to lead this partnership as their Chair.

I am making reference to Mr. Sindiso Ngwenya, Secretary General of COMESA and Dr. Tomaz Salomao, Executive Secretary of SADC; I salute you dear brothers. The COMESA-EAC-SADC Tripartite is a living epitome of all that is good about our hopes for an economically integrated Africa. I pray for the Tripartite's success.

In this hall, there are also several development partners and friends from the diplomatic community with whom I have worked closely with. They were all quick to share the EAC vision with me. Above all, they were quick to believe in the leadership of the EAC Secretariat and become its true partners in supporting many of EAC's strategic plans and projects. The German Government's support for the EAC Headquarters, which will be ready for occupation later this year, stands out as a testament of true friendship and cooperation. I thank them all and call upon them to scale up support to the EAC.

Today, a new Secretary General will be sworn in to lead the East African Community. I have known Dr. Richard Sezibera for a few years now, more as a friend than as a senior public and lately political figure in Rwanda. Richard and I are closely involved in the Society for International Development of which I am its global Vice President. President Paul Kagame could not nominate a better person for this high office. Richard has the youth, the temperament, the intellect, the diplomatic etiquette, a world view and excellent interpersonal skills to move the EAC to greater heights. It is a pleasure and joy for me to hand over to Dr. Sezibera. And I wish him well.

I wish to thank my wife Rose for enduring a very difficult five years. It is an inevitable sacrifice that comes with the kind of role I have had to play.

It is great to have known you all and to have worked with you to build our East Africa.

Long live the East African Community,

Long live African Unity.

SELECTED REFERENCES

I. Books and Monographs

ALUOKA, Otieno *et al*, *Old Vision – New Plans: Stakeholders' Opinion on the Revival of the East African Community*, Nairobi: Konrad Adenauer Stiftung, 2001.

BALDONI, Emiliana, *The Free Movement of Persons in the European Union: A Legal-historical Overview*, (State of the Art Report PIONEUR Working Paper No. 2), Centro Interuniversitario di Sociologia Politica (CIUSPO) – Università di Firenze – Italy, July, 2003.

BAREGU, Mwesiga and Bashiru Ally, *Participation of Political Parties in the East African Integration Process*, East African Community Occasional Papers, Issue No. 1, March, 2009.

BOK, Derek, *Universities in the Marketplace: The Commercialization of Higher Education*, Princeton, New Jersey: Princeton University Press, 2003.

CHACHAGE, Chambi and Annar Cassam (eds.), *Africa's Liberation: The Legacy of Nyerere*, Oxford and Kampala: Pambazuka Press and Fountain Press, 2010.

DIHEL, Nora *et al.*, *Reform and Regional Integration of Professional Services in East Africa: Time for Action* (Report No. 57672-AFR), Washington, D.C.: Poverty Reduction and Economic Management Unit 2 of the International Bank for Reconstruction and Development, October, 2010.

DRAPER, Peter, *Rethinking the (European) Foundations of Sub-Saharan African Regional Economic Integration: A Political Economy Essay*, Working Paper No. 293, Paris: OECD Development Centre, September, 2010.

DRUCKER, Peter F., 1989: *The New Realities: in Government and Politics, in Economics and Business, in Society and World View*, New York: Harper & Row. 1989.

EVANS, Mary, *Killing Thinking: The Death of the Universities*, London and New York: Continuum International Publishing Group, 2004.

FERGUSON, Niall, *Civilization: The West and the Rest*, New York and London: Penguin Group, 2011.

GARDNER, Howard Gardner, *Five Minds for the Future*, Cambridge, MA.: Harvard Business School Press, 2007.

GASTORN, Kennedy *et al* (eds.), *Processes of Legal Integration in the East African Community*, Dar es Salaam: Dar es Salaam University Press, 2011.

GATHII, James Thuo, *African Regional Trade Agreements as Legal Regimes*, New York: Cambridge University Press, 2011.

GIBB, Richard, *Rationalisation or Redundancy? Making Eastern and Southern African's Regional Trade Units Relevant*, Brenthurst Discussion Paper No. 3, Johannesburg: Brenthurst Foundation, 2006.

GILLSON, Ian, *et al., Harnessing Regional Integration for Trade and Growth in Southern Africa*, Washington, D.C.: International Bank for Reconstruction and Development, March, 2011.

GOLDSTEIN, Andrea and Njuguna S. Ndung'u, *Regional Integration Experience in the Eastern African Region*, Paris: OECD Development Centre (Working Paper No. 171), March, 2001.

HARBESON, John Willis and Donald S. Rothchild (Eds.), *Africa in the World Politics: The African State System in Flux*, Boulder, Colorado and Oxford: Westview Press, 2000.

HOEKMAN, Bernard and Aaditya Mattoo, *Services Trade and Growth* (Policy Research Working Paper 4461) Washington, D.C.: The World Bank Development Research Group, January, 2008.

JENSEN, Michael F. and John C. Keyser, *Non-Tariff Measures on Good Trade in the East African Community*, Washington, D.C.: The World Bank, 2008.

JJUUKO, Frederick W. and Godfrey Muriuki (eds.), *Federation Within Federation: The Tanzania Union Experience and the East African Integration Process: A Report of the Kituo Cha Katiba Fact-finding Mission to Tanzania*, Kampala: Fountain Publishers, 2010.

JUMA, Calestous, *The New Harvest: Agricultural Innovation in Africa*, New York: Oxford University Press, 2011.

KAAHWA, W.T.K., *East African Community: EAC Treaty and Challenges to the Community*, Arusha: East African Community Secretariat and German Agency for Technical Co-operation – GTZ, 2003.

KAPTEYN, P.J.G. and VerLoren van Themaat, P., *Introduction to the Law of the European Communities*, London: Graham & Trotman, 1998.

KENNEDY, Paul M., *Preparing for the Twenty-First Century*, New York: Vintage Books, 1994.

KINZER, Stephen, *A Thousand Hills: Rwanda's Rebirth and the Man Who Dreamed It,* Hoboken, New Jersey: John Wiley & Sons, Inc., 2008.

KOTHARI, Rajni, *Politics of the People: In Search of a Humane India,* Far Hills, New Jersey: New Horizons, 1989.

LIUNDI, Christopher C., *Quotable Quotes of Mwalimu Julius K. Nyerere: Collected from Speeches & Writings,* Dar es Salaam: Mkuki na Nyota Publishers, 2012.

MAMDANI, Mahmood, *Scholars in the Marketplace: The Dilemmas of Neo-Liberal Reform at Makerere University,* African Books Collective, Oxford, 2007.

MBOGORO, Damas K., *Global Trading Arrangements and their Relevance to Tanzania Economic Development: Challenges and Prospects,* Dar es Salaam: Friedrich Ebert Stiftung, 1996.

MBOGORO, Damas K., *The Common Market Concept and Economic Development: Tanzania's Experience,* Economic Research Bureau (Paper No. 77.8), University of Dar es Salaam, 1978.

MEREDITH, Martin, *The Fate of Africa: from the Hopes of Freedom to the Heart of Despair,* New York: Public Affairs, 2005.

MOHIDDIN, Ahmed (ed.), *Deepening Regional Integration of the East African Community,* Addis Ababa: Development Policy Management Forum (DPMF), 2005.

MONTI, Mario, *A New Strategy for the Single Market – At the Service of Europe's Economy and Society: Report to the President of the European Commission José Manuel Barroso,* 9th May, 2010.

MVUNGI, Sengondo E.A. (ed.), *The Draft Treaty for the Establishment of the East African Community,* Dar es Salaam: Dar es Salaam University Press, 2002.

MWAPACHU, Juma V., *Confronting New Realities: Reflections on Tanzania's Radical Transformation,* Dar es Salaam: E&D Limited, 2005.

MWASE, Ngila R.L., *The East African Community: A Study of Regional Disintegration,* Economic Research Bureau (Paper No. 77.10), University of Dar es Salaam, 1979.

NJAU, Adrian, *23rd EAC Council Meeting Concluded Partner States Agree on Key Issues,* Arusha: East African Community, September, 2009.

NYERERE, Julius K., *Freedom and A New World Economic Order: A Selection from Speeches 1974 – 1999,* Dar es Salaam: Oxford University Press (T) Ltd, 2011.

NYERERE, Julius K., *Freedom and Liberation: A Selection from Speeches 1974 – 1999*, Dar es Salaam: Oxford University Press (T) Ltd, 2011.

NYERERE, Julius K., *Freedom, Non-Alignment and South-South Cooperation: A Selection from Speeches 1974 – 1999*, Dar es Salaam: Oxford University Press (T) Ltd, 2011.

OHMAE, Kenichi, *The Next Global Stage-Challenges and Opportunities in Our Borderless World,* Upper Saddle River, New Jersey: Wharton School Publishing, 2005.

PAARLBERG, Robert, *Starved for Science: How Biotechnology is Being Kept out of Africa,* Cambridge, Massachusetts, Harvard University Press, 2008.

PETER, Chris Maina and Fritz Kopsieker (eds*.), Political Succession in East Africa: In Search for a Limited Leadership*, Kampala and Nairobi: Kituo cha Katiba and Friedrich Ebert Stiftung, 2006.

SACHS, Jeffrey, *Common Wealth: Economics for a Crowded Planet*, New York, The Penguin Press, 2008.

SCHWAB, Klaus (Ed.), *The Global Competitiveness Report 2010 – 2011*, Geneva: World Economic Forum, 2011.

SCHWAB, Klaus (Ed.), *The Global Competitiveness Report 2011 – 2012*, Geneva: World Economic Forum, 2011.

SEN, Amartya, *Development as Freedom*, Oxford: Oxford University Press, 1999.

SEN, Amartya, *Identity and Violence: The Illusion of Destiny*, New York: W.W. Norton & Company, Inc., 2006.

SOCIETY FOR INTERNATIONAL DEVELOPMENT, *East African Integration: Dynamics of Equity in Trade, Education, Media and Labour*, Nairobi: SID, 2011.

THUROW, Lester C., *Creating Wealth: The New Rules for Individuals, Companies and Countries in a Knowledge-Based Economy*, Boston and London: Nicholas Brealey Publishing, 1999.

THUROW, Lester C., *Fortune Favours the Bold: What We Must Do to Build a New and Lasting Global Prosperity*, New York: HarperBusiness, 2003.

TOFFLER, Alvin, *Powershift; Knowledge, Wealth and Violence at the Edge of the 21st Century*, New York: Bantam Books, 1991.

WAGH, Smita Wagh, Andrew Lovegrove, and John Kashangaki, *Scaling-up Regional Financial Integration in the EAC* (Africa Trade Policy Notes - Note #22), Washington, D.C.: International Bank for Reconstruction and Development, July, 2011.

WOLF, Alison, *Does Education Matter? Myths about Education and Economic Growth*, London: Penguin Group, 2002.

YABARA, Masafumi, *Capital Market Integration: Progress Ahead of the East African Community Monetary Union* (Working Paper – WP/12/18), Washington, D.C.: International Monetary Fund, January, 2012.

YAHYA-OTHMAN, Saida (ed.), *Politics, Governance and Co-operation in East Africa*, Dar es Salaam: Research and Education for Democracy in Tanzania – REDET and Mkuki na Nyota Publishers, 2002.

YUMKELLA, Kandeh K.; Patrick M. Kormawa; Torben M. Roepstorff; and Anthony M. Hawkins (eds.), *Agribusiness for Africa's Prosperity*, Vienna: UNIDO, 2011.

II. Articles in Journals and Chapters in Books

COLLIER, Paul, "Building an African Infrastructure," Volume 48 No. 4 *Finance & Development*, December, 2011.

COLLIER, Paul, "The Politics of Hunger: How Illusion and Greed Fan the Food Crisis," Volume 87, No. 6 *Foreign Affairs*, November-December, 2008.

DOBBS, Richard; Jeremy Oppenheim; and Fraser Thompson, "Mobilizing for a Resource Revolution," *McKinsey Quarterly*, January, 2012.

GOMEZ-MERA, Laura, "Domestic Constraints on Regional Cooperation: Explaining Trade Conflict in MERCOSUR," Volume 16 No. 5 *Review of International Political Economy*, 2009, pp. 746-777.

HILPOLD, Peter, "Regional Integration According to Article XXIV GATT: Between Law and Politics," Volume 7 *Max Planck Yearbook of United Nations Law*, 2003, p. 219-260.

HODSON, Dermot, "EMU and Political Union: What, If Anything, Have we Learnt From the Euro's First Decade?" Volume 16 No. 4 *Journal of European Public Policy*, 2009, pp. 508 - 526.

HOOGHE, E.A.E.B. and G.W. Marks, "The Neofunctionalists were (Almost) Right: Politicization and European Integration," in CROUCH, C. and W. Streeck Eds.), *The Diversity of Democracy: Corporatism, Social Order and Political Conflict,* Cheltenham: Edward Elgar Publishing Ltd., 2006, pp. 2005-222.

KRAL, David, "The Constitution is Dead: Long Lives the Treaty of Nice?" Volume 5 No. 3 *Romanian Journal of European Affairs*, 2005, p. 45.

MAZZUCELLI, Colette, "The French Rejection of the European Constitutional Treaty: Two-Level Games Perspective," in

LAURSEN, Finn (Ed.), *The Rise and Fall of the EU's Constitutional Treaty*, Leiden: Nijhoff, 2008, p. 177.

MSAMBICHAKA, L.A. et al, "Economic Co-operation in East Africa," in MBELLE, Ammon et al (eds.), *The Nyerere Legacy and Economic Policy Making in Tanzania*, Dar es Salaam: Dar es Salaam University Press, 2002, p. 248.

MUNCHAU, Wolfgang, "Original Sin: the Seeds of the Euro Crisis are as Old as Euro Itself," *Foreign Policy*, 7th April, 2011.

MUTAI, Henry Kibet, "Regional Trade Integration Strategies under SADC and the EAC: A Comparative Analysis, Volume 1 *SADC Law Journal*, 2011, pp. 81-97.

NYAMNJOH, Francis B., "Intellectual and Social Responsibility in Scholarship: Lessons from Professor Issa Shivji," Issue 343 *Pambazuka News*, February, 2008.

NYERERE, Julius K, "Democracy and the One Party State," in NYERERE, Julius K, *Freedom and Unity*, Nairobi and Dar es Salaam: Oxford University Press, 1966.

NYERERE, Julius K, "The Link Between the Economy, the Society and the University," Volume 3, No. 5-7 *Change Magazine*, 1995, pp. 46-51.

NYERERE, Julius K, "The Role of Universities," in NYERERE, Julius K. *Freedom and Socialism*, Nairobi and Dar es Salaam: Oxford University Press, 1968, pp. 179-186.

NYERERE, Julius K., "Desire for a Federation of East Africa," in NYERERE, Julius K., *Freedom and Unity*, Nairobi and Dar es Salaam: Oxford University Press, 1966, p. 295-297.

NYERERE, Julius K., "East African Co-operation is Alive," in NYERERE, Julius K., *Freedom and Development*, Nairobi and Dar es Salaam: Oxford University Press, 1973, pp. 240-242.

NYERERE, Julius K., "Problems of East African Co-operation," in NYERERE, Julius K., *Freedom and Socialism*, Oxford University Press, 1968, pp. 60-70.

NYERERE, Julius K., "The Dilemma of the Pan Africanist," in NYERERE, Julius K., *Freedom and Socialism*, Nairobi and Dar es Salaam: Oxford University Press, 1968, pp. 207-217.

NYERERE, Julius K., "Unity Must be Worked For," in NYERERE, Julius K., *Freedom and Development*, Nairobi and Dar es Salaam: Oxford University Press, 1973, p. 14-22.

PUCHALA, Donald, J., "Institutionalism, Intergovernmentalism and European Integration: A Review Article," Volume 37 No. 2 *Journal of Common Market Studies*, June 1999, pp. 317-331.

RISSE, Thomas, *et al*, "To Euro or Not to Euro? EMU and Identity Politics in the European Union," Volume 5 No. 2 *European Journal of International Relations*, 1999, pp. 147-187.

ROUBINI, Nouriel, "The Instability of Inequality," *Project Syndicate*, 13th October, 2011, p. 1.

SHIVJI, Issa G., "Pan-Africanism or Imperialism?" Published in Issa G. Shivji, *Where is Uhuru? Reflections on the Struggle for Democracy in Africa*, Dar es Salaam: E&D Vision Publishing, 2009.

SMITH, Ed, "Will EMU Lead to Political Union?" Bulletin No. 2 *Centre for European Reform*, October, 1998.

SWEET, Alec Stone and Wayne Sandholtz, "European Integration and Supranational Governance," Volume 4 No. 3 *Journal of European Public Policy*, September, 1997, pp. 297-317.

TUORI, Kaarlo, "The Failure of the EU's Constitutional Project," Volume 3 *No Foundations: Journal of Extreme Legal Positivism*, 2007, pp. 37-48.

III. Reports

AFRICAN DEVELOPMENT BANK, *African Economic Outlook 2010*, Tunis: AfDB, 2010.

AFRICAN DEVELOPMENT BANK, *African Economic Outlook Report 2008,* Tunis: AfDB, 2008.

AFRICAN DEVELOPMENT BANK, *African Economic Outlook, 2011, Tunis: African Development Bank, 2011.*

AFRICAN DEVELOPMENT BANK, *High-level Panel Issues Report on Prospects for African Development Bank*, Tunis: ADB, 2008.

EAST AFRICAN COMMUNITY, *Report of the Committee on Fast Tracking East African Federation,* Arusha: EAC Secretariat, 2004.

ECONOMIC COMMISSION FOR AFRICA AND AFRICAN UNION, *Economic Report on Africa 2011: Governing Development in Africa – The Role of the State in Economic Transformation*, Addis Ababa, Ethiopia: United Nations Economic Commission for Africa, 2011.

INTERNATIONAL MONETARY FUND, *Regional Economic Outlook: Sub-Saharan Africa – Recovery and New Risks,* Washington, D.C.: IMF, 2011.

SOCIETY FOR INTERNATIONAL DEVELOPMENT, *East African Integration: Dynamics of Equity in Trade, Education and Media*, SID, Nairobi, 2011.

SOCIETY FOR INTERNATIONAL DEVELOPMENT, *State of East Africa Report 2012: Deepening Integration, Intensifying Challenges*, Nairobi: SID, 2012.

UNITED NATIONS INDUSTRIAL DEVELOPMENT ORGANIZATION, *UNIDO-Partner for Prosperity Report 2010*, Vienna: UNIDO, 2010.

UWEZO EAST AFRICA, *Are Our Children Learning? Numeracy and Literacy across East Africa*, Nairobi and Dar es Salaam: UWEZO East Africa and Twaweza East Africa, July, 2011

WORLD BANK, *East African Community-Reshaping the Geography of East Africa: From Regional to Global Integration,* Washington, DC: International Bank for Reconstruction and Development (IBRD), 2012.

WORLD BANK, *Global Economic Prospects 2008: Technology Diffusion in the Developing World*, Washington, DC, International Bank for Reconstruction and Development (IBRD), 2008.

WORLD BANK, *Harnessing Regional Integration for Trade and Growth in Southern Africa*, Washington, D.C.: International Bank for Reconstruction and Development (IBRD), March, 2011

WORLD BANK, *Non-Tariff Measures on Good Trade in the East African Community: Synthesis Report* (Report No. 45708-AFR), Washington, D.C.: International Bank for Reconstruction and Development (IBRD), October, 2008.

WORLD BANK, *The World Bank Logistics Performance Index 2010 and Transformational Logistics*, Washington, D.C.: International Bank for Reconstruction and Development (IBRD), 2010.

INDEX

405

Food security, 25
Foreign Direct Investment (FDI), 2, 14, 18, 48, 166, 232
Federal Aviation Agency (FAA), 322
Free Trade Areas (FTAs) 31, 46-47, 233, 312, 380

Gapco, 230
Gardner, Howard (Professor), 204, 277
GDP
     See East African Community GDP
Generalized Scheme of Preferences (GSP), 16
Global Express Association, 44
Good Governance Protocol, 126-7
Grameen Bank (Bangladesh), 291
G77 Conference, 41
G8 Summit, 13

Heritage Insurance, 230
Hilpold, Peter, 374
Hirschman, Albert O. 200
HIV/ AIDS, 20, 150, 193, 281, 283, 313, 317-20
Hooghe, E. A. E. B. (Professor), 384
Human resources development, 337

Industries, 233, 238
     See also Trade
IGAD Peace processes, 297
Illicit trade, 342
     See Also Counterfeit Products
India, 2, 15, 41, 94, 230, 238, 241
Information and Communication Technology, 17-18, 26, 180-1, 193
Institute of Development Management (IDM), 258
Inter-University Council of East Africa (IUCEA),
     35, 51, 73, 98, 149-52, 206, 259-60, 268, 270-1,
     276-7, 332, 338, 340
International Business Machines (IBM), 44
International Civil Aviation Organization (ICAO), 17, 153
International Labour Organization (ILO), 13
International Monetary Fund (IMF), 10, 18, 50, 290
Investment Promotion, 217-220, 229-31
Investment Promotion Agencies, 219
IPP Media (Tanzania), 217, 230, 248

Jabbo-Obbo, Henry (Mr) 159
JICA, 44-45, 118, 123, 313
Jinja General Staff Retreat, 196
Juba (Southern Sudan), 45
Jubilee Holdings, 89
Jubilee Insurance, 89

Juma, Calestous, 336

Kaahwa, Wilbert (Hon), 159
Kabudi Palamagamba (Professor), 378-9
Kagame, Paul (President), 38-39, 309
Kalema, William (Dr.), 241
Kampala International University, 86
Kapuya, Juma (Professor), 293

Karume, Abeid Amani (Former President - Zanzibar), 134
Katabazi, James, 59
Kategaya, Eriya, 275
Kenya African National Union (KANU), 287
Kenya Airways, 34, 85, 88, 230
Kenya Bureau of Standards, 241
Kenya Commercial Bank (KCB), 34, 85, 89, 136, 230
Kenya Electricity Power Generation Company (Ken Gen),
        215, 225
Kenya Nation Group, 85, 247
Kenya's Regional groupings, 128, 287-8
        Used for Majimboism
Kennedy, Paul (Professor), 21, 92
Kibaki, Mwai (President-Kenya), 162, 195, 229, 279, 309, 311
Kigali Stock Exchange, 89
Kilimo Kwanza, 235
Kikwete, Jakaya Mrisho (President - Tanzania), 109, 187, 220,
        325, 352, 386, 391
Kituo Cha Katiba, 202
        Used for Centre for Constitutional Development
Kothari, Rajni (Social scientist), 291
Lafarge, 136, 230
Lagos Plan of Action, 29
Lake Tanganyika, 218
Lake Victoria Basin Commission (LVBC), 34, 51,
        45, 149-50, 206, 242-44, 337, 340-1, 373
Lake Victoria Development Programme, 193, 218, 281
Lake Victoria Fisheries Organization (LVFO), 36, 51,
        150, 152-3, 207, 350
Lake Victoria Maritime Communications and Safety Project, 244
Lancaster, Carol (Professor), 15
Leon Sullivan Business Summit, 220
Local government, 278-91
        Regional integration, 285-90
        Role of, 282-4
        Synergies, 279-81
Lwakabamba, Silas, 275

Maastricht Treaty, 104, 369
MA Consulting, 68

Madhvani, 34, 230
Maersk Line, 230
Majimboism,
        U*se* Kenya's Regional groupings
Makerere University, 259
Malaba (Border post), 44, 83, 227
Mamdani, Mahmood (Professor), 128, 259, 266, 275
Mandela, Nelson (Former President-SA), 341
Maputo Development Corridor, 11
Marks, G. W. (Professor), 384
Martin, Paul (Former Canadian Prime Minister), 24
Mazrui, Ali (Professor), 263
Mbeki, Thabo (Former President- SA), 276
Media (role in EAC), 245-51
Meredith, Martin, 12-13
Migingo Island, 126, 375
Millenium Development Goals (MDGs), 13, 20, 281
Minimum Integration Programme (MIP), 2-3
MM Integrated Steel Mills, 64
Moi, Daniel Arap (Former President-Kenya), 130, 132
Monetary Union, 34-35, 51, 110, 109-112, 344, 378-9
        Used for East African Community - Monetary Union
Monitor Newspaper Group (Uganda), 85
Monitoring and Evaluation, 349
Monterrey Consensus of 2000, 13
Monti, Mario (Professor), 76, 96, 374
Moshi (Tanzania), 85
Moyale (Kenya-Ethiopia Border), 45
Mozambique, 5
Mselle, Conrad (Ambassador), 183-4
Msuya, Cleopa David (Former PM-Tanzania), 239
Mugabe, Robert (President-Zimbabwe), 314
Mukandala, Rwekaza (Professor), 285
Mukwano Group of Companies, 34, 230
Mutabingwa, Aloyce (Deputy Secretary-EAC), 392
Mutai, Henry Kibet, 365
Museveni, Yoweri (President - Uganda), 61, 92, 110, 133,
        162, 184, 195, 263, 275, 287, 309
Mushega, Amanya (Hon), 176, 275
Muthaura, Francis (Ambassador), 176
Mwananchi Communications (Tanzania), 85
Mwapachu, Rose, 393

Nabudere, Dan Wadada (Professor), 123-4
Nairobi Stock Exchange, 89
Nakumatt, 85, 136, 230, 237
Namanga (Border Post), 44, 227
Nanyuki Conferences, 186-9, 191-2
Nation Media Group, 89

National Assemblies, 146, 366

National University of Rwanda, 272
National Social Security Fund (NSSF), 97
National Resistance Movement (NRM), 131
Ndulu, Benno (Bank Governor), 109, 112
Nelson Mandela African Institute of Science and Technology, 18
New Partnership for African Development (NEPAD), 11,
        17, 118, 216
Ngwenya, Sindiso (Secretary General-COMESA), 393
Njagu, James (Dr.), 337
Nkrumah, Kwame (Former President – Ghana), 164, 388
Non Tariff Barriers (NTBs), 83-4, 214, 323, 330-1
Non Tariff Measures (NTMs), 83
North Atlantic Free Trade Area (NAFTA), 8
Northern Transport Corridor, 45, 309-11
North-South Corridor Tripartite Project, 312-14
Norway, 244
Nsekela, Harold (President- EACJ), 141-2, 275, 392
Nyaigotti-Chacha, Chacha, 268, 340
Nyerere Centre for Peace Research, 207
Nyerere, Julius (Former President - Tanzania), 41, 61, 92-3,
        104, 111, 124, 133-4, 136, 164, 168, 199, 220, 261-2,
        288-90, 326, 351, 361-2, 375-6, 383, 385
Nyirahabineza, Valerie (Hon.), 346
Nyong'o Anyang' Peter, 372-3

Odoki, Benjamin (CJ-Uganda), 275, 378
Official Development Assistance (ODA), 2, 123
Okri, Ben (Poet), 272
Okurut, Tom (Dr.), 242, 392
Oloo, Adams (Dr.), 378
One-Stop Border Posts (OSBPs), 44-45, 69, 84, 234, 310, 312
Orange Democratic Movement (ODM), 287
Organization for Economic Cooperation and Development
        (OECD), 2, 13, 17
Organization of African Union (OAU),

Paarlberg, Robert (Professor), 270
Pan African Common Market, 29
Pan African Movement, 8, 29
Pan African Parliament, 10
Pan Africanism, 24
Parastatal Pensions Fund (PPF), 97
Paris Declaration on Aid Harmonization, 37-8, 174, 315
Paris Declaration Principles, 123
Peace and Security Protocol, 126

Political federation, 121-31
　　　　Leadership (role of), 132-3
Precision Air, 85, 230
Public Private Partnerships (PPPs), 45, 219

Ramos, Maria (Chairperson - ABSA), 232
REDET, 285-6
Regional Economic Communities (RECs), 2-4, 22-24, 28, 33, 77
　　　　Used for African Regional Economic Communities
Regional projects, 117-20
Reich, Robert (Professor), 22-23
Research Partnership, 268-71
Results Oriented Management (ROM), 196
Rodney, Walter, 263
Rogoff, Kenneth (Professor), 116
Rotary District Conference, 7
Roubin, Nouriel (Professor), 383
Rwanda, 15, 31, 37, 45, 49-50, 63, 80, 85-6,
　　　　89-90, 99, 115, 127, 144, 155, 200
　　　　Admission of, 157-62, 339, 363
　　　　Genocide, 301
Rwanda Investment and Export Promotion Agency (RIEPA), 229
Rwegasira, Delphin (Economist), 25

Sachs, Jeffrey (Professor), 8, 13, 24, 269, 317
SADC, 4-6, 11, 36, 47, 81, 144, 192, 233-4, 3,04-11, 348
　　　　See Also ECOWAS, ECA, EAC
Salomao, Tomaz (Executive Secretary-SADC) , 393
Sameer Group of Companies (Kenya), 34, 85, 136, 230
Sandholtz, Wayne, 355
Schengen Agreement, 358
Secretariat
　　　　Use East African Community Secretariat
Secretary General
　　　　Use EAC Secretary General
Sen, Amartya (Nobel Economics Laureate), 273, 290
Serena Group/Hotels (Kenya), 85, 136, 230
Serengeti Breweries, 85-6
Sezibera, Richard (Secretary General-EAC), 393
Shellys Pharmaceuticals, 34, 194
Shivji, Issa (Professor), 124, 259, 266, 275, 289
SIDA, 145-6, 270
Single Customs territory (SCT), 68
Society for International Development (SID), 182
Somalia, 297, 303
Sopa Hotels and Lodges, 230
Soto, Hernando de, 20
South Africa, 2-3, 5-6, 14, 16, 41, 78
South African Breweries, 230

www.ingramcontent.com/pod-product-compliance
Lightning Source LLC
Chambersburg PA
CBHW050448270326

41927CB00009B/1659